WALTER E. BILLIET, Ed. S., a graduate of Wayne State University, Detroit, Michigan, is the author of numerous auto repair books. Billiet is certified as an Automobile Technician by the National Institute for Automotive Service Excellence. He was formerly Director of Technical Education for the New Jersey Department of Education and has taught automotive courses in high school, community college, and industry.

AUTOMOTIVE ELECTRONIC & ELECTRICAL SYSTEMS

A Beginner's Troubleshooting and Repair Manual

Walter E. Billiet

Prentice-Hall, Inc., Englewood Cliffs, New Jersey 07632

Library of Congress Cataloging in Publication Data

Billiet, Walter E.
Automotive electronic & electrical systems.

"A Spectrum Book."—T.p. verso.
Includes index.
1. Automobiles—Electric equipment. 2. Automobiles—Electronic equipment. 3. Automobiles—Electric equipment—Maintenance and repair. 4. Automobiles—Electronic equipment—Maintenance and repair. I. Title. II. Title: Automotive electronic and electrical systems.
TL272.B543 1985 629.2'54'0288 85–561
ISBN 0–13–054255–5
ISBN 0–13–054248–2 (pbk.)

Cover design: Hal Siegel
Production coordination/interior layout: Fred Dahl
Buyer: Frank Grieco

This book is available at a special discount when ordered in bulk quantities. Contact Prentice-Hall, Inc., General Publishing Division, Special Sales, Englewood Cliffs, N. J. 07632.

A SPECTRUM BOOK

10 9 8 7 6 5 4 3 2 1

Printed in the United States of America

Prentice-Hall International (UK) Limited, LONDON
Prentice-Hall of Australia Pty. Limited, SYDNEY
Prentice-Hall Canada Inc., TORONTO
Prentice-Hall Hispanoamericana, S.A., MEXICO
Prentice-Hall of India Private Limited, NEW DELHI
Prentice-Hall of Japan, Inc., TOKYO
Prentice-Hall of Southeast Asia Pte. Ltd., SINGAPORE
Whitehall Books Limited, WELLINGTON, NEW ZEALAND
Editora Prentice-Hall do Brasil Ltda., RIO DE JANEIRO

ISBN 0-13-054255-5

ISBN 0-13-054248-2 {PBK.}

Contents

5

Starting System, 62

6

Charging System, 74

7

Ignition System, 89

8

Emission Control Systems, 113

9

Computer Control Systems, 133

Preface

The federal restrictions placed on automobile emissions plus the need to conserve fuel have brought about a number of changes in automobile engine design. This is particularly true in the case of the ignition system and the emission system. Much has been done to bring about more complete burning of the air/fuel mixture.

If an engine were operated at a fixed load and speed, the air/fuel mixture, spark intensity, and ignition timing could be designed to give maximum economy with a minimum of exhaust emissions. However, to serve its intended purpose the automobile engine must produce variable amounts of power to fit all types of load and speed conditions.

Until recent years the ignition system used a distributor that employed a movable set of contact points to interrupt the current flow through the primary section of the ignition coil. This resulted in the secondary section of the ignition coil producing a high-voltage spark. A centrifugal mechanical advance unit and a vacuum-operated, advance-retard timing were incorporated into the distributor as part of the ignition system.

At the present time most engines are equipped with an electronic ignition system. This system uses a magnetic pulse triggered, transistor controlled inductive discharge ignition arrangement eliminating the need for movable contact points. In addition, most manufacturers are equipping engines with on-board computers to reduce exhaust emissions and make for better performance and economy.

The computer is programmed to better coordinate the different components according to changing operational modes. Numerous sensors are used to feed information about operating conditions to the computer (microprocessor). The computer, in turn, sends signals out to the different components, which causes them to adjust to a more efficient operating mode. An on-board computer may also be used on some installations as a means of providing operational information about fuel consumption, distance to a predetermined destination, elapsed time, and the like.

An important feature built into most of the computer systems is the self-diagnostic feature. When troubles develop in the system, a warning light may display. Activating the self-diagnostic system will result in pinpointing the area where trouble exists.

In order to troubleshoot a system you need to have an understanding of the operation of the system. For this reason operating principles are covered for each component along with its interrelationship to other components.

With the incorporation of the electronic ignition system, equipping the vehicle with a diagnostic connector, and using an on-board computer, emissions have been reduced. The need for service has been reduced as well as, in many cases, simplified. The period of time and mileage between recommended maintenance operations has been extended considerably in recent years.

When trouble does occur, it is for the most part related to the basic operating components of the ignition and fuel system. In most cases the procedure used to troubleshoot and tune up an engine before the adoption of the computer will clear up operational problems without disturbing the computer system.

Understanding the functions and relationship of the various components should provide the know-how needed to perform the different troubleshooting and repair operations.

I wish to acknowledge the camera work done by C. Crawford Brewer that is used throughout the book.

Walter E. Billiet

1 Introduction to Troubleshooting and Repair

Purpose of This Book

This book presents material that should enable the reader to understand the function and operation of the various electrical and electronic components to the extent that malfunctions can be located and repairs made to correct the problem.

With federal regulations mandating greater fuel economy and lower engine emissions, the various manufacturers have incorporated considerable sophisticated electrical equipment as well as the use of additional electronically controlled components. At times it is difficult to differentiate terminology when discussing electrical and electronic components because of their complete interrelationship. A unit using transistors and/or diodes is generally labeled as an electronic device. Regardless, in the servicing process you are dealing with circuits, electrical flow, and electrical values.

To reduce engine emissions a greater compatibility of the air-fuel mixture, operating temperature, and variations in the timing of the spark have been incorporated to bring about a more complete burning of the air-fuel mixture. This is accomplished by the use of various electrical and electronic devices such as transistors, diodes, and sensors. The results are a cleaner burning engine with better performance under varying load, speed, and temperature conditions.

Figure 1-1 is a schematic drawing illustrating the various components that help to control engine emissions.

When you understand the purpose and function of a unit, it is generally an easy matter to determine if it is operating properly. Usually only simple tests have to be made to determine if a unit is functioning in the correct manner.

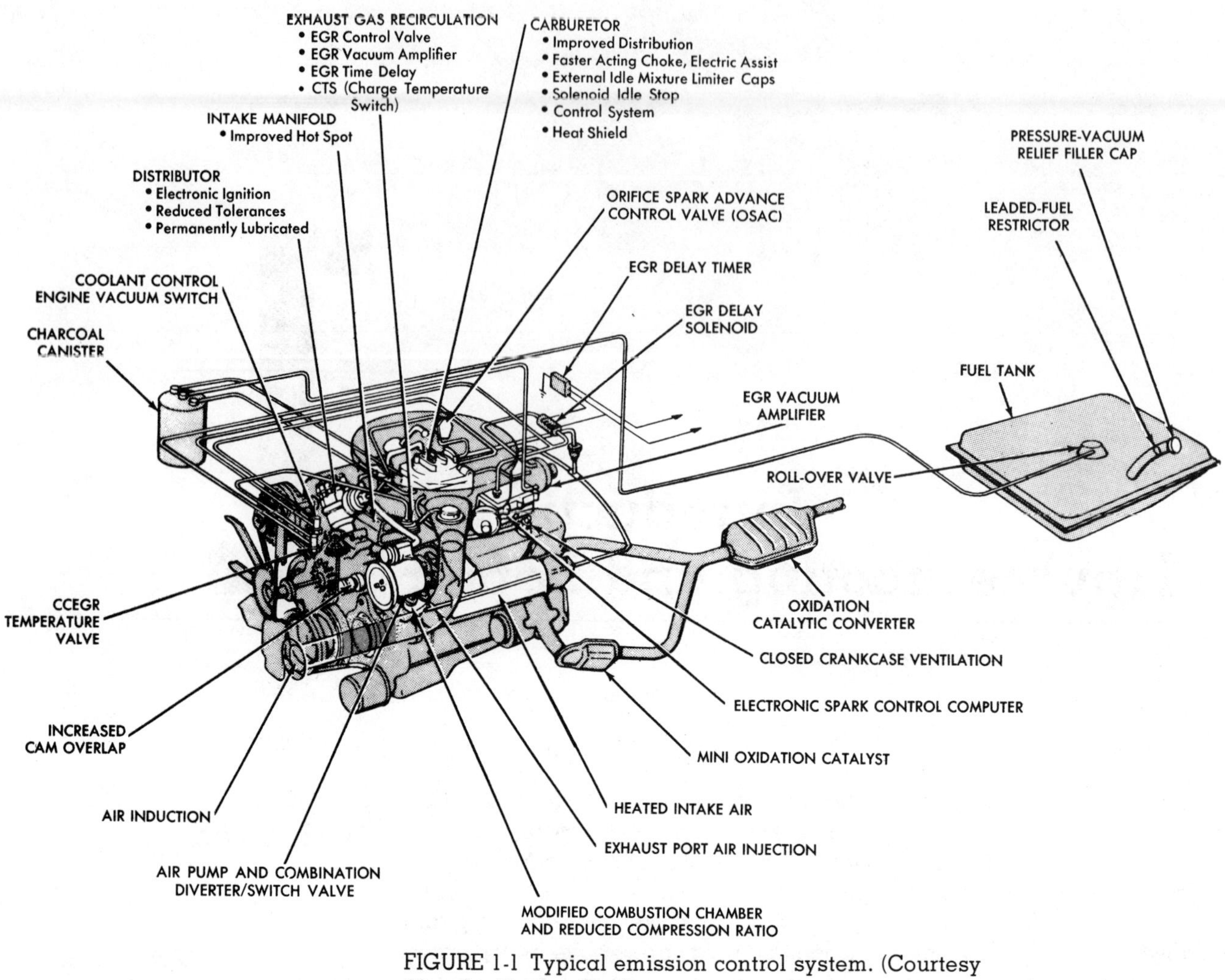

FIGURE 1-1 Typical emission control system. (Courtesy Chrysler Corporation)

Tools and Equipment

To completely diagnose and analyze the entire electrical, ignition, engine, and emission systems and make the necessary adjustments for efficient operation, rather sophisticated equipment is needed that may include an infrared exhaust analyzer, an oscilloscope, an ammeter-voltmeter with a variable resistance, an ohmmeter, a diode tester as well as a battery-starter tester, a tachometer, vacuum gauge, compression gauge, and a timing light. Many vehicles are equipped with an electrical diagnostic connector to which a special analyzer can be connected. It then becomes simply a matter of pressing a series of buttons to locate malfunctions. Each make of automobile will require a special analyzer for the particular vehicle.

Some vehicles use an on-board computer (the so-called black box) as the control system for an electronic fuel injection system. Another vehicle uses a computer system to bring about modular cylinder displacement. A particular type of computer unit may also be used as the control of an electronic type of catalytic converter. Sensors and solenoids are usually used in conjunction with the computer. These are highly complex components and normally cannot be repaired in the field. It is usually a matter of exchanging the entire unit when trouble is present. Regardless of the complexity of the specific component, understanding the function of the component and knowing how to check the various circuits are generally all that are needed to pinpoint the source of trouble.

Ordinary hand tools plus a test lamp which can be made from a 12-volt bulb and socket and a universal type ammeter, voltmeter and ohmmeter will permit you to check current flow and current values in diagnosing electrical and electronic problems. A timing light and a tachometer are necessary to make ignition and carburetor adjustments. A compression gauge and vacuum gauge are also necessary to determine internal engine conditions. The vacuum gauge is valuable in checking units in the emission system. For the most part these are relatively inexpensive pieces of equipment but are invaluable for the person wanting to make an evaluation and perform service and maintenance operations on an automobile.

The various automobile test equipment manufacturers have different combinations of units in the different testers. Most of the commercial test units consist of a tachometer, dwell meter, vacuum gauge, combustion tester, cylinder leakage tester, voltmeter, condenser tester, coil tester and an oscilloscope. A combustion analyzer is available as is an infrared exhaust analyzer. They also market individual testers as well as various combinations of test units. Figure 1-2 is an exhaust analyzer that may be used to verify air/fuel mixture, detect faulty feedback system components, carburetor defects, catalytic converter problems and driveability complaints.

FIGURE 1-2 Multiple gas analyzer. (Courtesy Sun Electric Corporation)

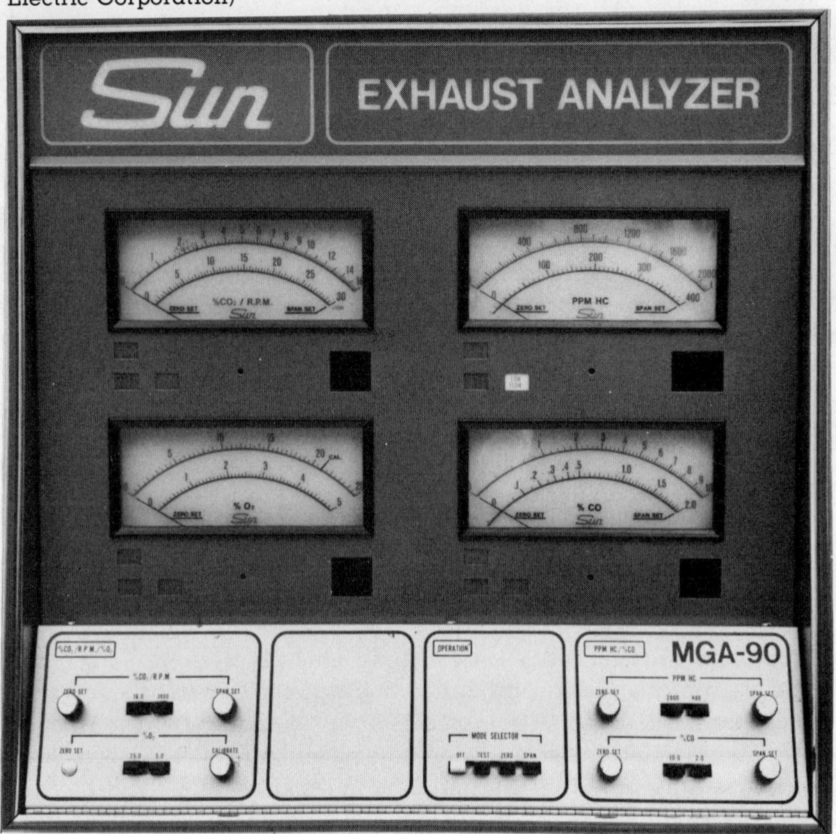

An ohmmeter is a valuable instrument for checking external computer circuits. An ohmmeter is also used to check the module of the electronic distributor. The general use of the various pieces of test equipment will be covered as each unit is discussed.

Carefully studying the book should remove the mystery of the various electrical and electronic units that are part of the modern automobile. From there on it becomes simply a matter of testing, adjusting, and repairing.

Troubleshooting

Specifically, the book deals with troubleshooting and repair of the automobile electrical and electronic systems. It must be remembered that the electrical and electronic components are a part of the entire power plant. Power plant operation can be separated into three major divisions: compression, ignition and carburetion. If problems occur in one section or component the overall efficiency of the automobile is usually affected. These three divisions, for troubleshooting purposes, can be classified as engine, electrical systems, and the fuel system.

In the engine troubleshooting category, engine compression must be within manufacturer's specifications in order for the engine to function properly. Compression is affected by the sealing ability of the piston rings, valves, and gaskets.

The fuel system includes the carburetor, fuel pump, air cleaner, charcoal cannister, filters, fuel lines and tank. Some engines use a fuel injector system in place of a carburetor.

Although the emphasis of this book is on the electrical and electronic systems the other two categories cannot be ignored. If problems occur in either or both it generally affects the total overall operation of the power plant; therefore the problems must be identified to obtain maximum operating efficiency. All phases of the power plant must be operating at as near maximum efficiency as possible.

While troubleshooting and repair of the engine and fuel system is not covered in this book, a brief procedure for checking the two systems is included. When the problem has been identified a decision can be made relative to what must be done to eliminate the problem.

Locating the problem is of major importance and is usually done by a systematic diagnosis or troubleshooting procedure. Troubleshooting is the discovery and correction of the problem. It is generally accomplished by analysis and diagnosis. In reality, it is a series of simple operations, each step leading toward the desired result. You want to eliminate as quickly as possible all units or systems not involved from further consideration and definitely establish the trouble as being in a particular unit or system.

Compression Test

A compression test is made to determine if the piston rings are sealing, if the valves are seating properly, and whether or not the cylinder head gasket is leaking. A compression variation of 25 percent or more between the different cylinders indicates a leakage; some components are not sealing properly. Normal compression readings will be from approximately 100 psi to 175 psi. Always check the manufacturer's

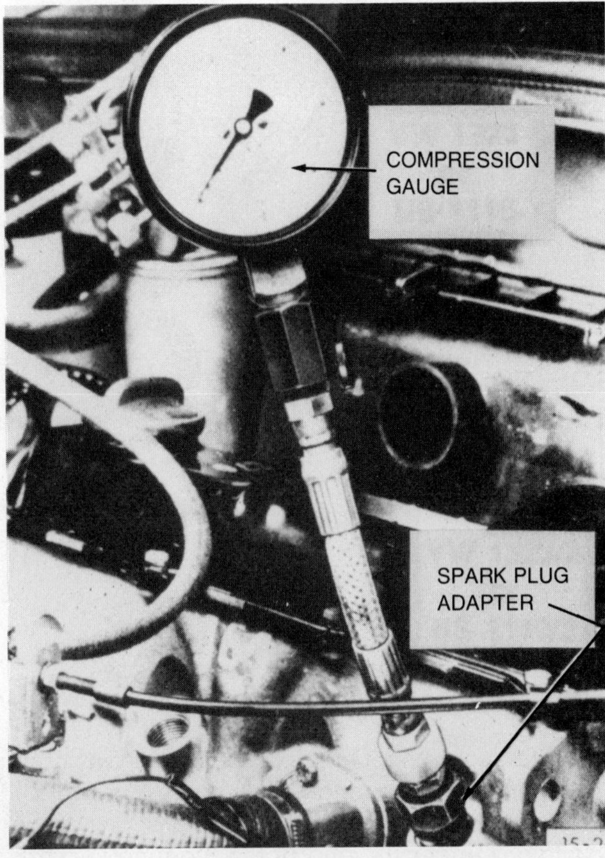

FIGURE 1-3 Checking compression. (Courtesy Volkswagen of America)

specifications for the particular make and model of vehicle. The engine will not run smoothly or perform properly if the compression of each cylinder is not within specifications.

To make a compression test the engine should be at normal operating temperature. Clean the spark plug recesses with compressed air or wipe with a cloth to remove all foreign matter so dirt will not get into the engine when the plugs are removed. Remove all of the spark plugs. Block the throttle valve wide open. Insert the compression gauge in the spark plug hole. Crank the engine about 6 to 10 revolutions. Record the reading. If one or two cylinders have a low reading, squirt about a tablespoon of oil on top of the piston in each cylinder. Recheck the compression. If the compression improves considerably on the low cylinders, it indicates that the piston rings are leaking. If there is little improvement, the valves are sticking or not seating properly. If two adjacent cylinders are low and oil does not improve the reading, the problem could be a cylinder head gasket leak between the cylinders. Minimum compression must be at least 75 percent of the highest cylinder. Figure 1-3 shows a compression gauge that screws into the spark plug hole. Others may have a tapered rubber tip which must be held in the spark plug hole.

Check Fuel System

If problems are suspected in the fuel system which result in the engine not starting and there is fuel in the tank, remove the air cleaner and pump the accelerator. If fuel is reaching the carburetor and the accelerator pump is operating, fuel should squirt out into the air horn.

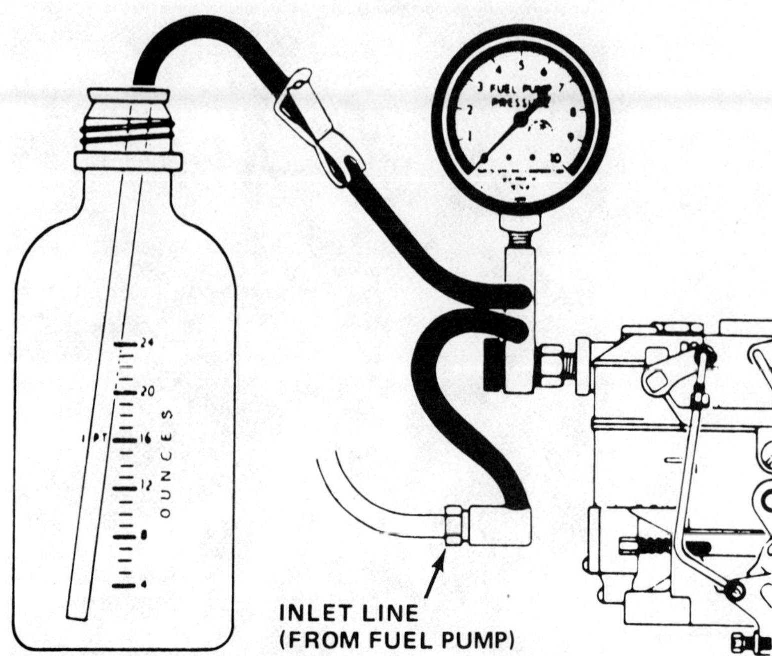

FIGURE 1-4 Fuel pump pressure test. (Courtesy American Motors Corporation)

To determine if fuel is reaching the carburetor disconnect the fuel line from the carburetor inlet. Be sure to hold the carburetor fitting while unscrewing the fuel line fitting so as not to twist the line. Place a container under the end of the fuel line to catch the fuel. Crank the engine. If there is a good flow of fuel from the line the fuel system is satisfactory to the carburetor. A normal fuel pump should deliver approximately one pint of fuel in thirty seconds. If not enough fuel is being delivered trouble exists in the fuel filters, fuel pump or fuel lines.

Normally the carburetor requires little in the way of service. Choke action can be observed after removing the air cleaner. The choke valve must operate freely without binding when the throttle valve is partly open. The choke must be fully open when the engine is running at normal operating temperature. The choke must completely close when the engine is cold, not running and the throttle is partly open.

Some indications of faulty fuel system operation are as follows:

1. If the engine starts but fails to keep running, the fuel system could be at fault.
2. A strong odor of gasoline in the engine compartment and/or gasoline around the carburetor indicates carburetor troubles.
3. Black exhaust smoke indicates too rich an air/fuel mixture.
4. Lack of response on acceleration and/or loss of speed may indicate that the engine is starved for fuel.

These are some of the more common indicators of malfunctions in the fuel system. Figure 1-4 shows how a fuel pump pressure gauge is installed between the inlet fuel line and carburetor for measuring fuel pump pressure.

Engine Vacuum

A properly functioning engine is a good vacuum pump. One of its functions is to create a vacuum in the intake manifold. A vacuum gauge connected to the intake manifold will give an accurate reading of engine vacuum. There are different vacuum outlets on the intake manifold which are used for emission control units. A vacuum gauge can usually be attached to one of these openings. A vacuum hose routing diagram is generally shown on the specification sticker in the engine compartment. This should give you an idea as to where a vacuum gauge hose connection can be made to the intake manifold.

An engine in good operating condition should have a steady vacuum reading of from 19 to 21 inches at idle speed and a reading of approximately 8 to 10 inches at a uniform 50 mph. Various readings on the gauge will indicate different engine conditions, as follows:

1. A slow fluctuation of the gauge needle shows a need to adjust the carburetor idle mixture.
2. A steady low reading indicates a vacuum leak.
3. A constant drop in reading indicates a leaking valve.
4. An intermittent fluctuating motion indicates a sticking valve.
5. A consistent low reading can also indicate late timing.

Figure 1-5 shows a vacuum source (hose) at the carburetor which can be disconnected and attached to a vacuum gauge to measure intake manifold vacuum.

FIGURE 1-5 Vacuum gauge and vacuum hose. (Courtesy Chrysler Corporation)

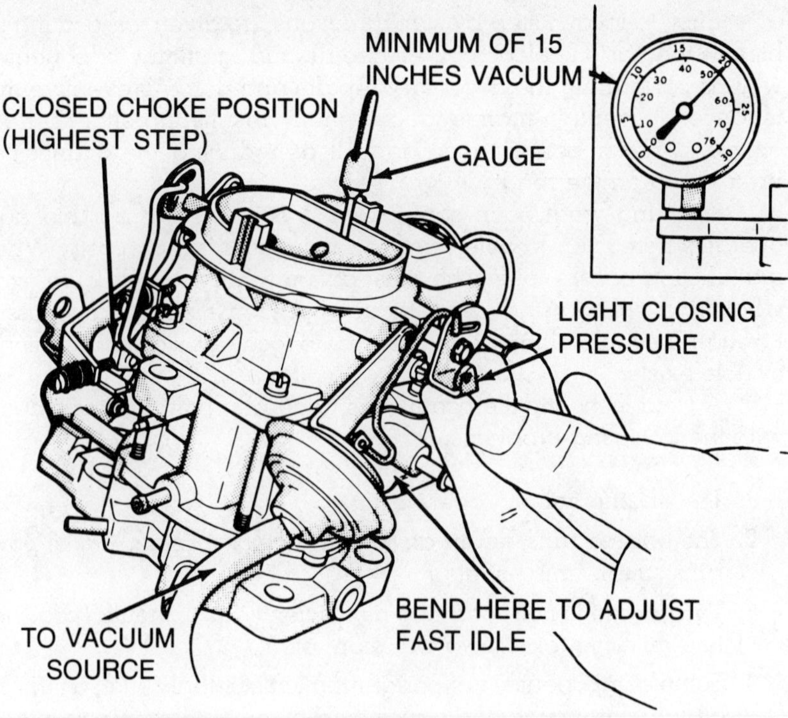

Cylinder Balance

An engine cylinder power balance check can be used to determine if each cylinder is producing equal power. Unequal power may be the result of problems with the rings, valves, fuel system, intake manifold or head gasket leaks. A tachometer is needed to make this test. A tachometer, when hooked to the distributor, indicates RPMs. With the engine at normal operating temperature, set the engine speed between idle and 1,000 RPMs. Remove a spark plug wire from the spark plug and ground it to the engine block. Do not pull on the wire to remove it from the plug; twist the boot that covers the plug while pulling on the boot. Start the engine and let idle. Record the RPM reading. Reconnect the wire and repeat the operation for the other cylinders. Compare the readings for each cylinder. All readings should be relatively uniform. One or more cylinders with RPM readings that differ from the rest indicates problems in the particular cylinder.

When it has been established that the problems are not in the engine or fuel system, a systematic check can then be made of the electrical and electronic system and the necessary service operations performed.

Electrical and Ignition System

The electrical and ignition systems are interrelated. It is difficult to separate one from the other when troubleshooting and servicing. The same applies to the electrical and electronic components. For this reason the various components are discussed as complete units regardless of whether they are considered to be a part of the ignition system, electrical system, and whether or not they involve electronic components.

Easy-to-follow, step-by-step directions are given for locating troubles in the various electrical, electronic and ignition components, as well as performing the necessary repairs and doing preventive maintenance. Preventive maintenance usually results in better fuel economy and better performance as well as reducing the chances of a breakdown on the road.

Knowing what each component is supposed to do and how it operates helps you to determine if it is functioning properly. When a malfunction occurs, often the most difficult thing is to decide exactly what is wrong. By using a systematic approach it is generally possible, through a simple elimination process, to locate the area in which the trouble exists.

A troubleshooting procedure is generally helpful when dealing with the following problems:

1. The engine will not operate
2. The engine runs but in an unsatisfactory manner (lacks power, runs rough, misses, etc.)
3. The engine is not operating as efficiently as it should (poor gasoline mileage, excessive emission, etc.)
4. Some component is not performing satisfactorily such as the generator, starting motor, lighting system, emission components, etc.

5. While not classified as a troubleshooting procedure, certain maintenance operations should be performed periodically in order to maintain efficient operation such as cleaning, adjusting or replacing spark plugs, generator drive belts, etc.

To become more familiar with basic electricity—why it acts as it does and how it can be controlled and measured—the following chapter discusses the fundamentals of automotive electricity. It provides an introduction to the operation of the basic components which make up the electrical and electronic systems.

The electron theory (electron movement is electrical flow) is covered in two sections; the first part explains the basis for electrical flow and how magnetism is involved in many of the electrical components; the second part provides additional information relative to the electron theory as it applies to semiconductors which are the foundation for most electronic components. Although it may be possible to perform many of the troubleshooting operations without a detailed understanding of the fundamental theory, it is much easier when you have a knowledge of why certain units must operate in a particular manner. When new problems occur, you will be much better equipped to handle them without guessing when you understand the principles of operation.

Following the chapter on fundamentals is a chapter on electrical and electronic systems in general. The chapter provides general information relative to circuitry, what makes up the various circuits, the components which are included in the different systems, and the interrelationship of the different units. The basic principles of troubleshooting, testing and test equipment are discussed.

The remaining chapters cover in detail the individual components which go to make up the different systems. The purpose of the system and how the different components function will be presented at the beginning of the chapter. The information will not be directed to a specific make or model of vehicle; rather, it will be broad enough to cover the subject in such a manner that it can be applied to the particular component regardless of minor construction differences.

Fundamentals of Automotive Electricity

The electrical/electronic system used in an automobile is interrelated to most of the components of the vehicle. Engine performance—gasoline mileage along with satisfactory emission control—is for the most part dependent upon the satisfactory performance of the electrical and ignition system.

In order to effectively locate and correct problems which may occur in the various automotive electrical and electronic components it is essential that you have some understanding of the fundamentals of the generation and flow of electricity as well as the role of magnetism in the electrical/electronic system.

Electricity is a form of energy. It cannot be seen or handled such as a liquid or solid substance. It does, however, have certain characteristics which enable you to control and measure the flow, measure the pressure available, and check the resistance to flow.

A knowledge of the basic fundamental principles of electricity should enable you to better understand the operation of electrical devices and be of considerable aid in diagnosing, troubleshooting, testing and working with the various electrical/electronic components found in the automobile. If you understand how a unit operates, it simplifies the troubleshooting and repair operation. It should be remembered that electricity, electronics, and magnetism are all closely related. One cannot be considered without the other. Understanding what must take place in order for a unit to function eliminates much of the "guess work" when diagnosing problems. A great deal of troubleshooting is simply being able to trace and measure the flow of electricity.

It is also important to have some knowledge of electron flow and action in order to troubleshoot electronic circuits involving the use of transistors, capacitors, various diodes and resistors. These are components which are included in the electronic ignition system, AC charging system, computer-controlled emission system, fuel injection system, as well as any on-board computers.

The majority of malfunctions occurring in the automobile are related to the electrical and ignition system. With mandated emission controls and better fuel economy, more sophisticated equipment is being used to regulate engine timing as it relates to temperature, air-fuel mixture, and exhaust emissions. This control is brought about through the use of engine vacuum, sensors, electrical units, various transistors, resistors, and diodes.

The use of on-board computers is becoming more commonplace with each new model. Electricity and electronics play an important role in computerized equipment. Computers may be used to regulate air-fuel mixtures for cleaner burning, to regulate air-fuel supply on engines equipped with fuel injection, to provide for temperature sensitivity for clean burning, and on a few engines, to control the number of cylinders to be operating in accordance with the load requirements. Some engines are equipped with a diagnostic outlet into which can be connected a computerized analyzer to give a read-out relative to the operation of the different components.

While most of this equipment is specifically tailored to a particular make and model of automobile and may require specialized test equipment, in most instances test equipment such as an ammeter, voltmeter, ohmmeter, and a test lamp will suffice to isolate the problem, provided you know what the unit is supposed to do and can properly test the circuitry. In most instances the complex modules and control units must be replaced as complete assemblies if they are malfunctioning.

The purpose of this chapter is to familiarize you with the fundamentals of electricity and electronics. These fundamentals will apply throughout the book.

Electron Theory

To better visualize and understand the characteristics of electricity it is essential to accept the electron theory that electrical flow in a circuit is the movement of electrons along a conductor. The electron theory also establishes polarity, both negative and positive.

Although the following paragraphs dealing with the electron theory may seem to be highly theoretical in nature and perhaps somewhat complex and irrelevant at the present time, it does account for the way electricity reacts and can be utilized. In the area of electronics, particularly in the case of diodes and transistors, accepting this theory will justify why the transistor and diode are such important parts of the various systems.

As more and more electronic devices are being used it is very helpful in troubleshooting to have some understanding as to why certain conditions must exist and how the different components function. You may wish to skip over these particular paragraphs and then refer back to them when you feel there is a need for a better understanding of the theoretical aspects.

Everything around us such as automobiles, chairs, tables, boats, books, etc., all occupy space and have weight. These objects are called matter. All matter is made up of molecules. The molecules, in

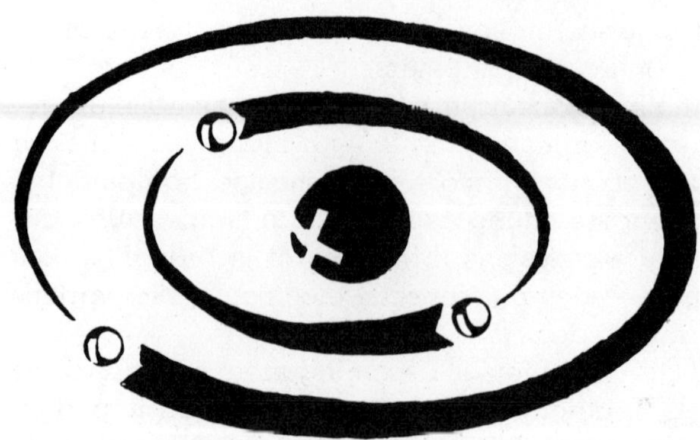

FIGURE 2-1 Electrons revolving around the nucleus.

turn, are composed of atoms. Atoms are made up of electrons, protons, and neutrons. The protons and neutrons are in a group in the center of the atom and form the nucleus, while the electrons are in circles or orbits revolving around the nucleus. This arrangement is often compared to the way in which the planets orbit around the sun. Figure 2-1 illustrates how the electrons (negative charges) revolve in a circle or path around the nucleus, which is composed of neutrons (neutral) and protons (positive charge).

Each individual atom has a specific name, such as lead, iron, oxygen, copper, gold, silver, etc. The atom, when it is not combined with anything (pure) is known as an element. When one type of atom (element) is combined with another type (element) the resulting mixture is a molecule. There are approximately 100 different known elements.

The protons within the atom have an attraction for the electrons. This is what holds the electron in a particular orbit.

All atoms must have at least one electron and one proton.

All atoms are electrical in nature. The electrons are said to have a negative electrical charge while the protons have a positive electrical charge. Neutrons have no electrical charge, they are neutral and along with the protons form the nucleus of the atom. Each electron is balanced with a proton.

Unlike electrical charges attract each other; like charges repel each other in an attempt to balance. Positive attracts negative and vice versa. One electron tends to repel another electron. Because of the attraction of positive to negative the electrons tend to stay in orbit around the nucleus.

The electrons revolve in a definite ring or circle around the positive charge (nucleus). The first ring around the nucleus can carry only two electrons; the second ring a maximum of eight. Each successive ring will only hold a fixed number of electrons.

FIGURE 2-2 Hydrogen atom.

The number of electrons in an atom determines what the element is and the number of rings around the nucleus. Carbon has six electrons and six protons, while an atom of germanium has 32 of each, and uranium contains 92 of each. Figure 2-2 illustrates the simplest form of atom (hydrogen). One electron orbits the nucleus which has one proton.

In theory, electricity is the flow of electrons in a conductor. The flow can be compared to the flow of water—it takes the path of least resistance. A moving stream of electrons constitutes an electric current. Normally the atom has an equal number of electrons and protons. The positive charge equals the negative and the atom is thus balanced and neutral. No flow of electrons take place. This balance must be upset to create a flow of electricity. Figure 2-3 illustrates an oxygen atom. The outer ring has six electrons. The inner ring is completely filled with two electrons. The nucleus has eight protons.

According to the makeup of the atom it may be that the outer ring of the atom will have only one, two or three atoms after the other rings have been filled. Since only a few electrons make up the outermost ring, the ring is not completely filled. So the ring is not as closely attached to the nucleus as electrons making up the inner rings, and the atom will not be as stable as the atom having the outer ring completely filled. These electrons have a tendency to leave the atom to which they belong and join another. Such electrons are referred to as free electrons. Materials composed of atoms with incomplete outer rings are called conductors because electrons can easily pass from atom to atom. Common materials which are good conductors include copper, aluminum, zinc, and silver. Materials having complete outer rings have electrons that are held strongly to the nucleus. These atoms are stable and therefore poor conductors. Materials having these characteristics are called insulators. Good insulating materials include rubber, neoprene, glass, and paper.

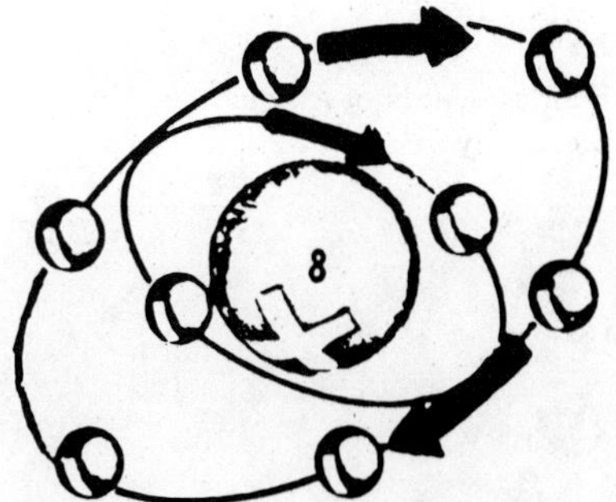

FIGURE 2-3 Oxygen atom.

Sources of Electricity in the Automobile

It takes an electrical device such as a battery or generator to bring about electron movement in a conductor. Under certain circumstances heat will cause electrons to move in a conductor. Electricity (movement of electrons) can be created chemically (battery), mechanically (generator-induction coil), heat (sensor), and friction (static electricity).

In the automobile the battery and generator are the sources of electricity. When the engine is not running the battery is the single source of electric power. After the engine has been started, the generator and battery operate together to supply the electrical needs of the automobile. In addition, the generator keeps the battery charged. The application of the electron theory to the use of electronic components in the automobile will be covered at the beginning of the section on "Electronics in the Automobile."

Electrical Flow

Just as water seeks its own level, the electron is attracted to whatever point that will tend to restore the natural electrical balance (equal number of electrons and protons). Conductors provide the path along which the electrons move. Electrons will travel from a point where they are concentrated to a point where they are less concentrated. In other words, they flow from a point of high concentration (more negative charge) to a point of lower charge. The end of the path, which is the source of the high negative charge, is called the negative terminal. The point to which the current flows is called the positive terminal. Current will flow between these two points if there is a charge differential and a path (conductor) present.

While it is of no importance to servicing the automobile electrical circuit, there is a conflict between the scientific treatment of electron flow and dealing with the actual automotive electrical circuits. Scientifically, the electron flow in a circuit is from negative to positive. The automotive circuitry is established on the basis of current flow from positive to negative. Regardless, electricity is the flow of electrons (negative charges). The electrical term positive does not refer to the proton. Positive is a term that identifies a lower electron charge. Negative is the location of a larger number of electrons.

Electrical Potential

An electric charge has potential energy. Water flows from high places downward because of its potential energy. This is due to gravity. The potential energy of water is determined by measuring differences in height, with the lower level being taken as zero. The higher the water above the low point the more potential energy.

In the case of electrical potential (voltage) it is the amount of force required to move electrons in a circuit causing a current flow. Potential difference is the difference in electrical pressure (voltage) between two points. It resembles the pressure differential of liquids.

If a source of water is connected to a pipe and a pump is used, a pressure differential will exist between the ends of the pipe. This forces the liquid to flow. The rate of flow depends on the amount of pressure exerted by the pump. The flow of water stops when the pressure difference is gone. More pressure causes more water to flow.

Similarly, free electrons in a conductor, will move from areas of concentration to areas of fewer electrons. Just as water in a high tank will flow to a lower tank until both tanks reach the same level, electrons in a circuit will flow from the negative terminal to the positive terminal until the potential of the two points is equal. The flow continues until the potential difference between the two points no longer exists as long as there is a path (circuit). Batteries and generators are the sources of potential energy in the automobile. Heat is also used in some cases to create an electron movement.

Basic Electrical Terms

Electrical flow, unlike water, cannot be seen. However, to make practical use of electricity, you must be able to determine the amount available, the amount needed, and the amount lost, and to control the flow. Units of measurement have been established and meters are used to make accurate measurements.

Electrical potential or pressure is measured in VOLTS. A volt is defined as the amount of pressure required to force one ampere of current through a resistance of one ohm. A voltmeter is used to measure voltage.

The rate of current (electrical) flow is measured in AMPERES (usually called amps). This is the quantity of electrons passing through a given point in one second. An instrument called an ammeter is used to measure the flow or volume.

All materials, whether conductors or insulators, offer some resistance to the flow of electricity. The resistance is measured in terms of OHMS. One ohm is equal to the resistance offered by a conductor in which one volt produces one ampere of current flow.

OHM'S LAW

The flow of electricity is directly proportional to the voltage and is inversely proportional to the resistance. The relationship between voltage, current and resistance can be summarized as follows: The current flowing in any circuit is equal to the voltage divided by the resistance of the circuit. If I (intensity) represents the amount of current in amperes, E (electro-motive force) the pressure in volts and R the resistance in ohms the relationship can be expressed mathematically as

$$I = \frac{E}{R},\ E = I \times R,\ R = \frac{E}{I}$$

This is known as Ohm's Law and applies only to direct current (DC).

In a circuit, trouble often is due to changes in the resistance of the circuit. Higher than normal resistance may be caused by frayed wires, burned, pitted or worn contacts, and dirty or loose connections. Lower than normal resistance often indicates "shorted" wires in the circuit. A circuit is shorted when resistance is lowered to the point that it causes an abnormally large amount of current to flow.

Magnetism

It would be impossible to discuss electricity without considering magnetism. Magnetism is used in starting motors, starting motor switches, generators, ignition coils, relays, and various other electrical components.

Magnetism is an invisible force which attracts certain metals and has several characteristics which are utilized in the development of electrical components.

Magnets may be found in two forms: a magnet made from iron or certain other metals sometimes called a natural or permanent magnet, or an electromagnet. Of importance is that magnets can be used to produce electricity and electricity can produce magnetism.

A permanent magnet can be made by stroking a hardened steel bar with a permanent magnet. This is not always too satisfactory. The best way is to place a coil of wire through which current is flowing (an electromagnet) around the steel bar. Permanent magnets are usually in the form of a horse shoe or a straight bar. The compass needle is an example of a bar magnet.

A temporary magnet can be made by using a soft iron bar in the same manner. As soon as the bar is moved away from the permanent magnet or the electricity is disconnected from the electromagnet, the soft iron bar will lose its magnetism.

Magnets have two poles, a north pole and a south pole. The poles are always at the outer ends of the magnet. This is where the strength is concentrated. It can easily be seen by sprinkling iron filings on a stiff piece of paper and placing a magnet under the paper. This will show the strength of the magnet, as well as how lines of force are present.

Unlike poles of a magnet attract each other while like poles repel. The stronger the magnet the greater the force will be. Also, the force of attraction or repulsion diminishes with distance.

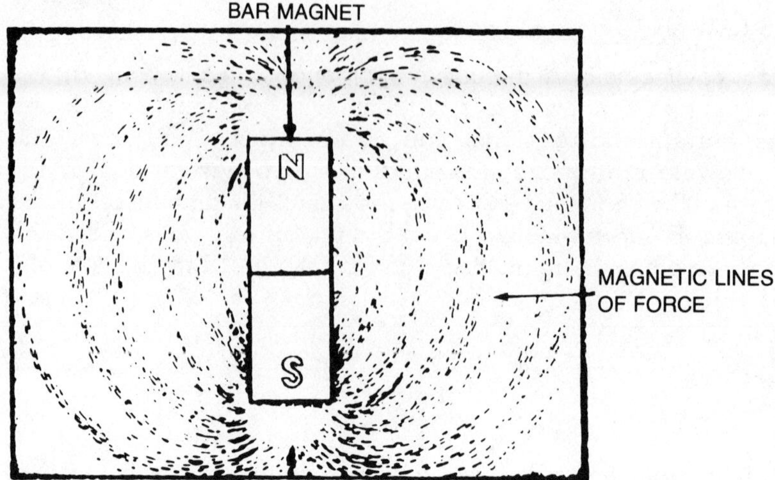

FIGURE 2-4 Pattern of magnetic lines of force.

The space around a magnet in which the magnetic force is exerted is called the magnetic field. This field is made up of lines of force which travel from the north pole to the south pole outside the magnet and from the south to the north pole within the magnet. The lines of force can be seen by placing a sheet of paper over a magnet and sprinkling iron filings on the paper. The iron filings arrange themselves in a pattern which follows the lines of force exerted by the magnet. The greater the number of lines of force per unit area the greater is the magnetic strength. Figure 2-4 shows the formation of iron filings around a bar magnet. This illustrates the pattern of the magnetic lines of force.

Electromagnetism

The flow of electricity through a wire creates magnetism around the wire. This is known as electromagnetism. The strength of the magnetic field varies with the amount of electricity flowing in the wire. Also the magnetic effect is increased if the wire is wrapped so as to form a coil (solenoid) and is increased more when wrapped around an iron core. The more turns of wire and/or the greater the current flow the more lines of force. Electromagnets are magnetized by the flow of current and demagnetized when the current flow stops.

Summarizing, the strength of an electromagnet is determined by the intensity of the magnetic field around it which in turn is controlled by the amount of amperes flowing and the number of turns of wire in the coil. The maximum strength of the coil is reached when the wires are carrying as much current as possible without heating. When this condition is reached the coil is said to be saturated. Figure 2-5 illustrates the magnetic lines of force which are created when electricity flows through a wire.

As previously discussed, when electricity flows through a conductor (wire) a magnetic field is produced around the conductor. The reverse is also true in that electricity is generated (induced) when a conductor is moved within a magnetic field. Mechanical energy can thus be transformed into electrical energy. This is called electromagnet

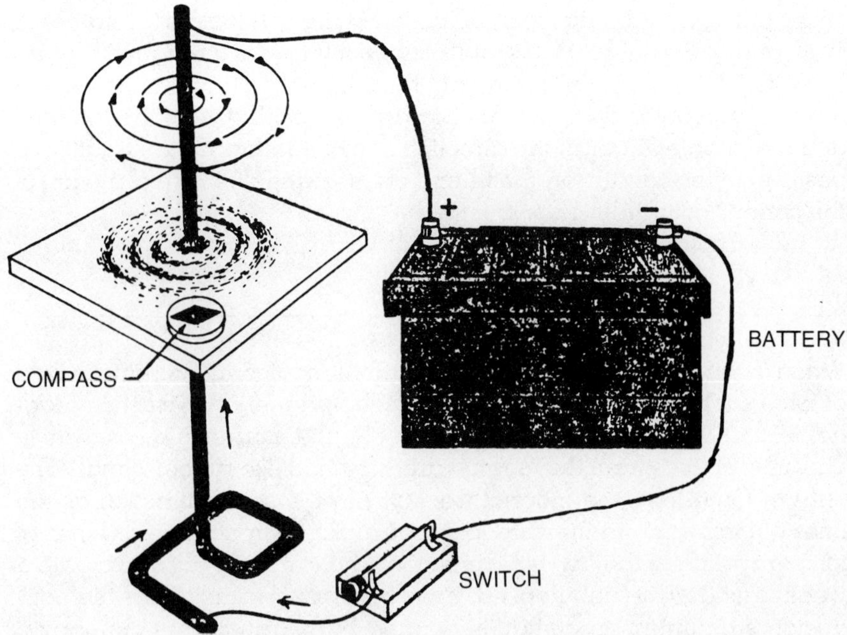

FIGURE 2-5 Magnetic lines of force created around a wire.

ic induction. The result of the motive force causing the current flow is known as an induced electromagnetic current. The amount of induced electromotive force (electricity) in the conductor depends on the number of lines of force (strength of the magnet), the number of conductors cutting the magnetic lines of force, and the speed at which they are cut.

The basic theory for producing an electric current in this manner (by self-induction) states that whenever magnetic lines of force are cut at right angles with a conductor, an electric current is induced in the conductor. The more lines of force that are present, the more conductors that cut the lines of force, and the faster the lines of force are cut, the more electricity will be induced. Figure 2-6 illustrates how electricity can be created by cutting magnetic lines of force with a conductor. There must be movement in order to produce electricity.

The direction of current flow, magnetic field, and wire motion can be established by what is known as the right-hand rule for motors. This

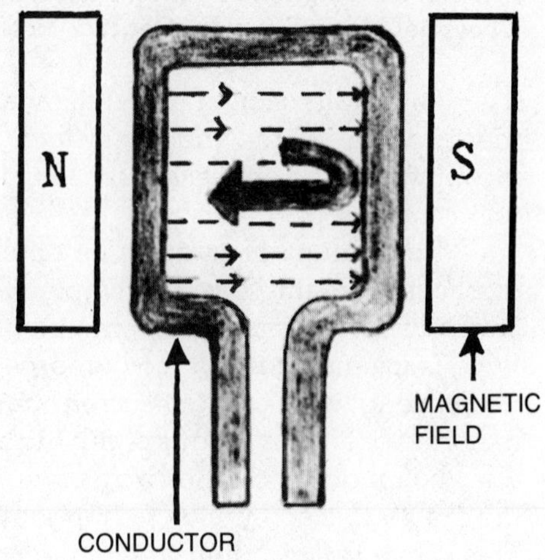

FIGURE 2-6 Principle of self-induction.

states that to find the direction of motion of the conductors (armature of a motor as an example) the thumb and first finger of the right hand are extended at right angles to one another. If the first finger is pointed in the direction of the lines of force (toward the south pole of the magnet) and the middle finger in the direction of current flow (from negative to positive) in the conductor, the thumb points to the direction of motion of the conductor in relation to the field.

Using Magnetic Lines of Force to Produce Movement

When a conductor (wire) carrying current is located in a magnetic field of force such as that created by an electromagnet or horseshoe magnet, distortion of the lines of force between the magnetic poles results. The lines of force from the magnet are stretched like rubber bands. The lines of force from the magnet traveling in the same direction as the lines of force around the wire join and make a stronger field. Lines of force traveling in the opposite direction tend to cancel out and create a weaker field. This unbalanced force can result in motion if the conductor is mounted on a shaft supported by bearings so it can move. Figure 2-7 shows how an armature is rotated by the concentration of magnetic lines of force on one side of the conductor and lack of magnetic lines on the other side.

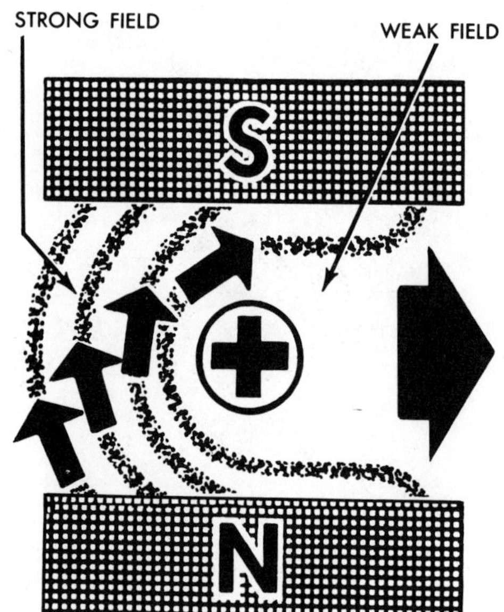

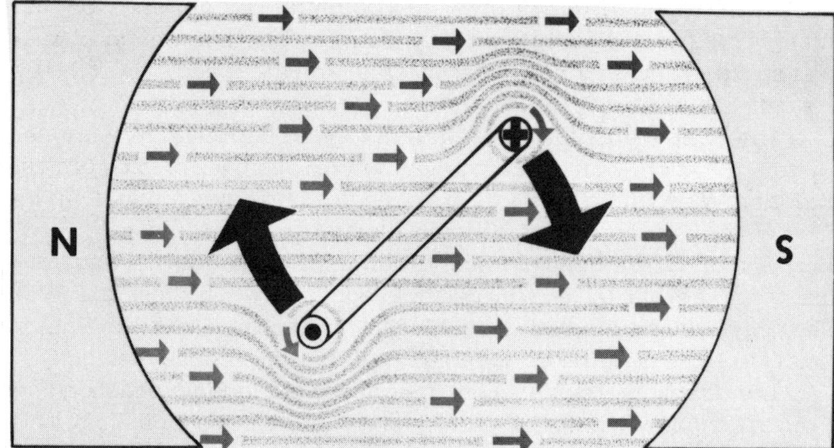

FIGURE 2-7 Magnetic field rotational effect. (Courtesy Chevrolet Motor Division, General Motors Corp.)

As the direction of current flow through the conductor determines the direction of the magnetic lines of force around the conductor, movement in the opposite direction is obtained when the current direction is reversed.

The design of many electrical units is nothing more than an application of this basic principle. This turning action is used in the construction of meter movements. The same principle of magnetic force is used in starting motors, except that electromagnetic fields are used along with a high current capacity. In the case of a starting motor, to get a continuous revolving action when the conductor (armature) has moved to a halfway point between the pole shoes (poles of the magnet), a commutator changes the direction of the flow of current. This keeps the armature revolving smoothly in one direction.

Using Magnetic Lines of Force to Produce Electricity —Self-Induction

The principle of electromagnetic induction plays an important part in the automotive electrical and ignition system. The basic rule of electromagnetic induction states that whenever a conductor is moved through a magnetic field at right angles, a voltage is induced in the conductor, and current will flow when an external circuit is complete. This also applies when the conductors are stationary and the magnet moves. The same condition exists when both the magnet and conductors remain stationary, but the magnetic lines of force move due to the current flow to the electromagnet being turned on and off by an external device.

The right-hand rule applies in determining the direction of current flow. The lines of force between the magnetic poles are stretched like rubber bands. As the conductor is moved through the magnetic field, the lines of force tend to wrap around the conductor. The right-hand rule for straight conductors is used to determine the direction of lines of force created by the current flow. Reversing this rule, the direction of the lines of force around a moving conductor may be used as a right-hand rule to determine the direction in which voltage will be inducted in a conductor.

When a conductor is forced through a magnetic field in a clockwise direction the lines of force are cut or wrapped around the conductor on the leading side. This induces a voltage in the conductor which would cause the current to flow away from the observer. Reversing the movement of the conductor (to the left), the lines of force building up on the leading side would induce voltage in the opposite direction, which would cause the current to flow toward the observer.

By turning coils of wire (conductors) through a magnetic field or turning a magnetic field across stationary conductors, a voltage is produced. When there is a continuous rotation of the conductors or of the magnets it enables a generator to supply a steady flow of electric power. This is the principle upon which the automobile generator operates. All electricity produced in this manner is alternating in nature.

As direct current (DC) is needed to charge a battery, if the automobile is equipped with a DC generator a commutator is used on the armature to convert the alternating (AC) current to DC. When an AC generator (alternator) is used, diodes are employed to convert the electricity to direct current before it goes to the battery.

A third method of producing voltage by electromagnetic induction does not use moving parts. The ignition coil operates on this principle to produce a high voltage current at the spark plugs. A primary winding and a secondary winding are wound on the same core. A magnetic field created by current from the battery flowing into the primary winding also surrounds the secondary coil. Voltage is induced in the secondary coil windings when there is a change in the magnetic field. As current from the battery flows in the primary winding the magnetic field cuts through all of the primary windings. The direction of the lines of force is such as to create a voltage opposed to the battery voltage. This is known as a counter-voltage. As the magnetic lines of force expand they also engulf the secondary windings. When the current flow in the primary windings is interrupted, the contracting lines of force cut all turns of wire in both the primary and secondary windings. The voltage induced in each turn (coil) of wire is propor-

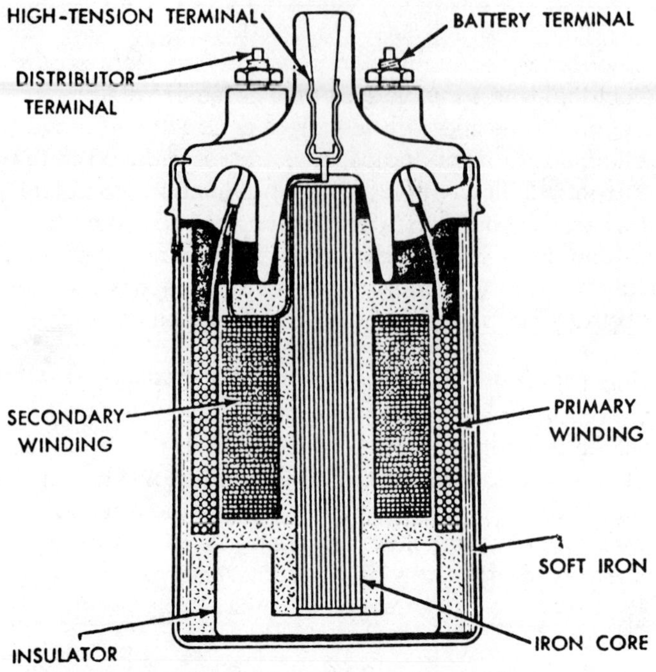

FIGURE 2-8 Cutaway view of an ignition coil.

tional to the number of turns in each winding. With over 200 turns of wire on the primary winding of an automobile ignition coil, it is possible to develop nearly 250 volts. Since the secondary coil has over 100 times more turns, it is possible to induce more than 25,000 volts. Figure 2-8 is a drawing of a cutaway ignition coil illustrating the internal construction.

The flow of current into the coil windings from a battery is interrupted by ignition contact points on older model vehicles, or movement of the pole piece in the transistor-controlled distributor.

Conductors

To control and utilize electron flow, a definite path must be established. The path is generally established by using a copper wire, copper being a good conductor.

A good electrical conductor is a material having the ability to carry an electrical current with little resistance. The most common conductor used in the automobile is copper wire. Carbon-impregnated thread is used as the conducting material in the high tension cables from the distributor cap to the coil and spark plugs. This is to reduce radio interference.

The resistance to the movement of electrons in a wire increases with length and high temperatures. It decreases with an increase in the cross-section area (size) of the conductor. The longer the wire or the smaller the diameter, the greater the resistance. When the temperature of the wire rises the resistance also increases. Good conductors have less resistance than insulators. Insulators have very high resistance.

In the automobile, different components will use different size wire. The battery cables which connect to the starting system have to be large because of the high amperage which is carried when cranking the engine. Small wires are used for lighting and other purposes.

When a path for electricity exists, a circuit is formed. A circuit is like a circle—electrons follow the circuit. The electrons are not used up; they just move from place to place in the circuit.

Resistors

A resistor is an electrical device used in a circuit that presents a specific resistance to the flow of current. The resistor may be a metallic wire or of carbon composition. It dissipates electricity in the form of heat. Resistors may be used to control the intensity of the instrument lights, current flow to the ignition coil, and circuits of the windshield wipers and rear window defogger.

The amount of resistance is measured in ohms. When current passes through a resistor a voltage drop occurs across the resistor. The voltage drop in the circuit is established by the capacity of the resistor. The resistor is connected into the circuit in series.

Capacitor

A capacitor, sometimes called a condenser, is a device for holding or storing an electric charge. The capacitor is made up of layers of tinfoil which are insulated from each other by layers of insulating material such as waxed paper. The tinfoil and waxed paper are rolled into a cylinder. One sheet or plate of foil is connected to the metal container (ground). The other sheet of foil is connected to a terminal wire which extends outside the container. Electricity cannot pass through the capacitor as there is no direct connection between the plates. Electric current will flow into the capacitor, where it will remain. When the flow stops, the capacitor will discharge back into the circuit. The capacitor is used to prevent ignition point arcing in the ignition system having contact points. A capacitor may be used to absorb current surges.

Switches and Relays

Basic control of electrical circuits is provided by switches and relays. A switch is a device used for opening, closing or changing the connections in an electrical circuit. A switch simply completes a circuit. The switch is connected in series in the circuit.

A relay is also a type of switch. It is an electromagnetic device using low current flow to open or close high current circuits or to interrupt an electrical current flow. The relay is generally operated by means of a switch. A coil is energized which magnetically closes or opens a set of contacts to operate an electrical unit. The starting motor switch is an example of a relay. A small amount of current flows through the start side of the ignition switch. This energizes a solenoid, an electromagnet with a movable core, which in turn connects the heavy battery cable to another heavy cable connected to the starting motor. Relays are designed as normally open or normally closed. This refers to the position of the contacts when the relay is off.

Electrical Circuits

There must be a complete circuit made up of wires or other conductors before current can flow. If the wires are disconnected or broken the current stops flowing. When the circuit is incomplete, not a complete path for the current to flow, it is said to be an open circuit. Short circuits are short-cuts within the circuit. A short circuit occurs in the circuit before the current reaches the load. Because the circuit is short there is little resistance and the current flow will be high. High current flow results in high temperature which can burn the insulation on the wire and/or burn out whatever electrical component is included in the circuit. In order to prevent damage from short circuits, fuses, circuit breakers, and/or fusible links are used. A fuse and fusible link are pieces of metal which conduct electricity but melt at fairly low temperatures. A circuit breaker is designed to protect the system by opening the circuit if the load becomes too great. The advantage of the circuit breaker is that it can be reused. The circuit breaker is primarily a set of contact points mounted on a bimetal strip which will distort under the heat created by a short circuit and open the contact points thus breaking the circuit. Figure 2-9 shows the location of a circuit breaker in the fuse panel.

There are three types of electrical circuits: the series circuit, the parallel circuit, and the series-parallel circuit. A series circuit is one in which electrical devices are connected one after the other so that the same current will flow through each in succession. A circuit is in series when the current is the same at every point in the circuit, the resistance is equal to the sum of the individual resistances, and the voltage across the circuit is equal to the sum of the voltages across the separate resistances.

FIGURE 2-9 Circuit breaker located in a fuse panel.
(Courtesy Chevrolet Motor Division, General Motors Corp.)

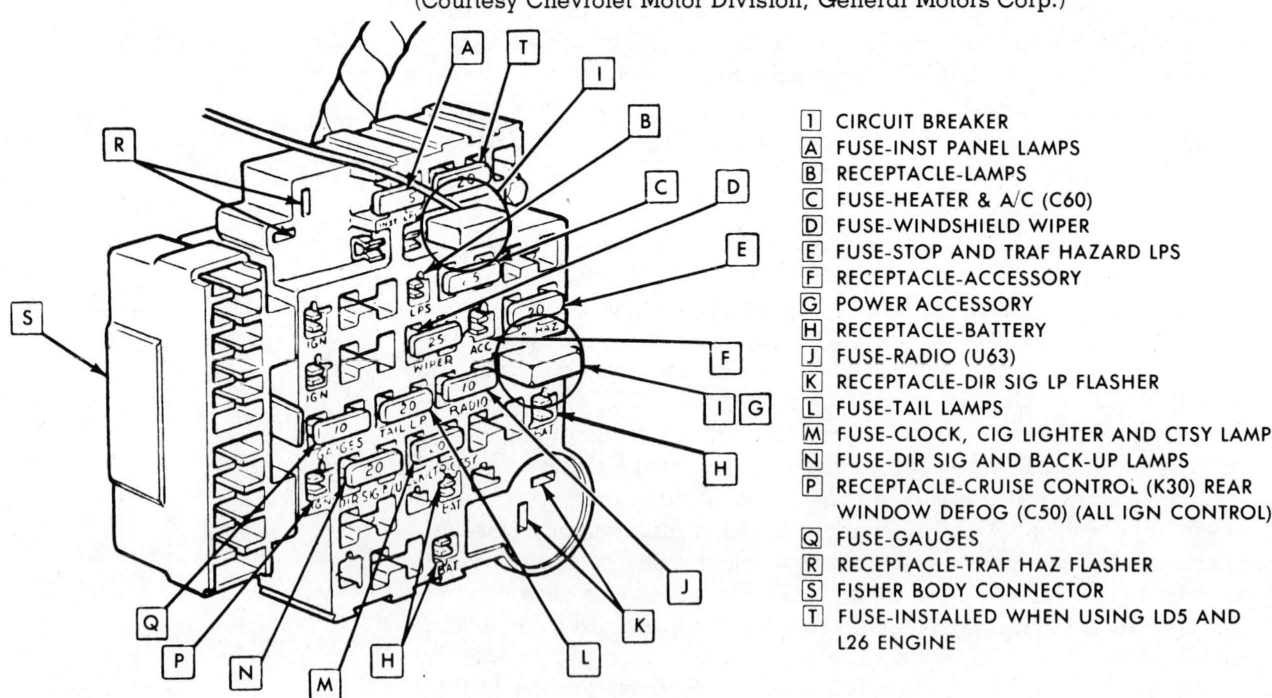

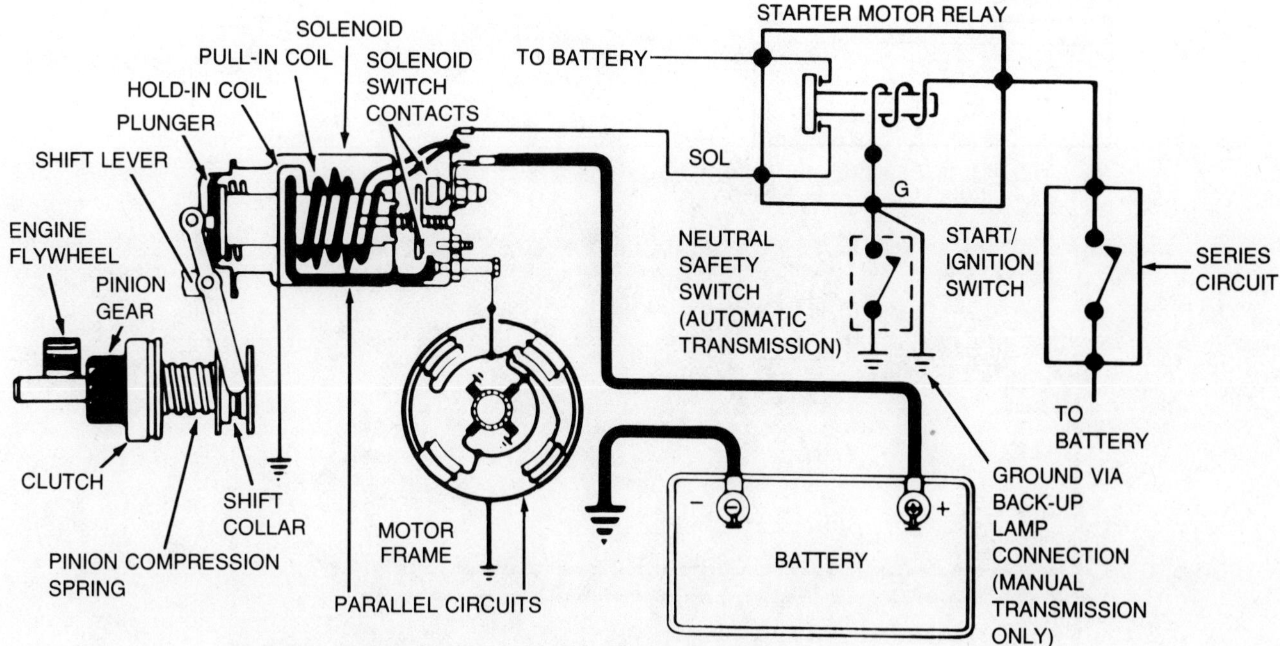

FIGURE 2-10 Series-parallel circuits in a starting motor circuit. (Courtesy American Motors Corp.)

A parallel circuit is one in which several electrical loads are connected to the main circuit so that the current flowing from the source is divided among them and returns to the source through a common return line. In a parallel circuit the voltage across the circuit is the same as the voltage across each branch. The current flow in the circuit is the sum of the individual branch currents. The reciprocal of the total resistance of the circuit is equal to the sum of the reciprocals of the branch resistances.

A series-parallel circuit is a combination of both series and parallel connections in a single circuit. Figure 2-10 shows a series-parallel circuit. The starting motor and solenoid are in parallel with the battery. The ignition switch is in series between the starter motor relay and battery.

In most cases the various switches used throughout the automobile are connected in series in the circuit. The parallel type circuit is most generally used in the automobile. In an automobile wiring system the metal parts of the vehicle act the same as a wire supplying the path which completes the circuit. That is why it is important that all electrical units be grounded. The term ground is used to refer to the path the electricity follows in completing the circuit. By using metal parts of the automobile to carry electricity, only one wire is needed between the electrical unit and the battery. All wires which carry current must be insulated to prevent the electricity from short circuiting, completing the circuit before reaching the unit it is to operate.

To enable you to trace the various circuits used in the automobile, the wires usually are color coded. A wiring diagram for a particular model of vehicle will be found in the shop manual for the car. Figure 2-11 shows a typical headlamp wiring diagram. A wiring diagram of the specific vehicle being serviced is extremely helpful when it is necessary to trace a circuit.

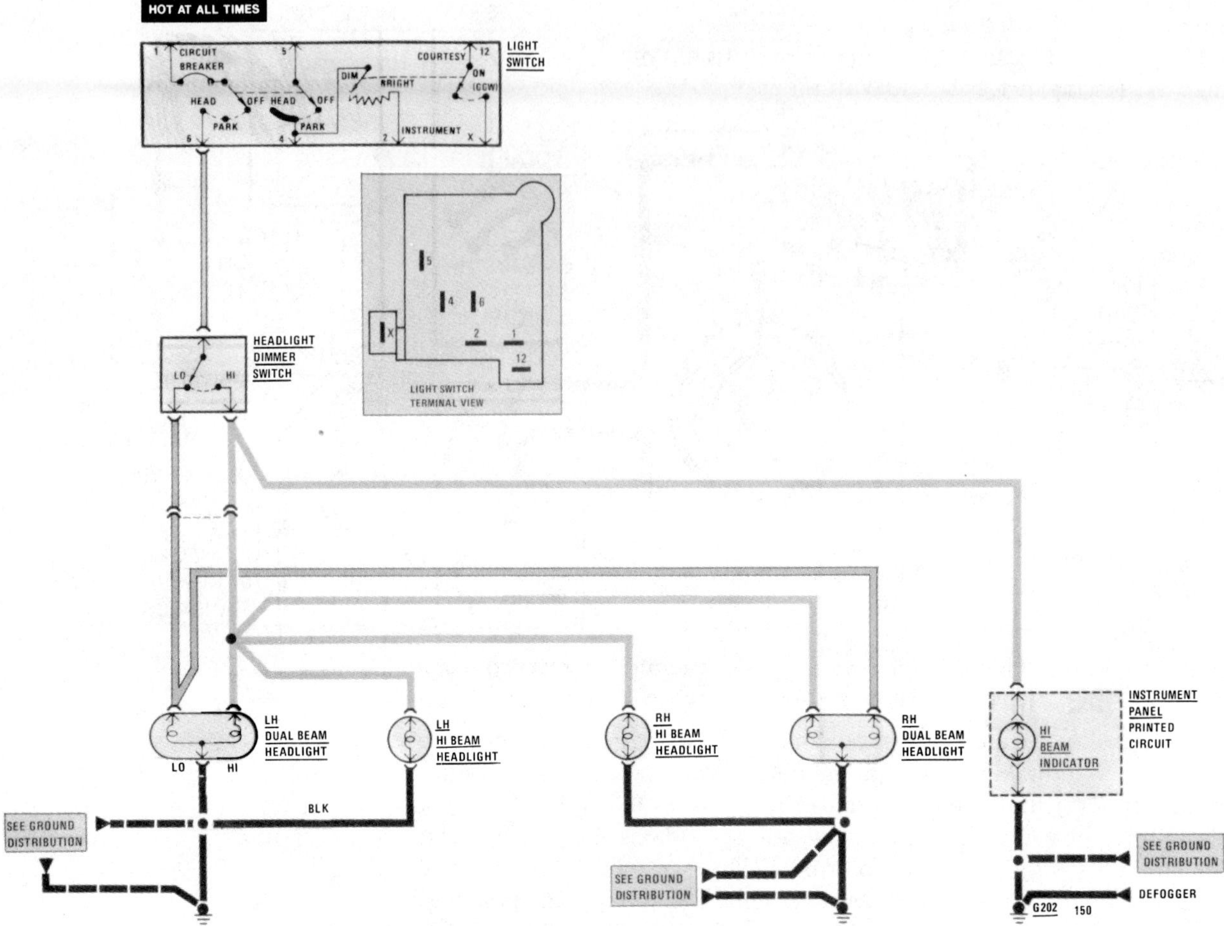

FIGURE 2-11 Headlamp wiring circuit. (Courtesy Chevrolet Motor Division, General Motors Corp.)

To save space as well as the expense of copper wires, printed circuits are used in place of wires on certain installations. This is particularly true for the instrument panel, as well as the radio and other accessories on most vehicles. A printed circuit is a panel on which conductor strips are located. The conductor strips carry a current load the same as a wire. Terminals are used to which wires may be connected. The printed circuit cannot be repaired and should a circuit be damaged the entire panel is replaced. Care must be exercised when working around the panel so as not to cause damage.

Electrical Measurement

As with the flow of water, it is important to be able to measure the pressure and flow of electricity. Pressure is important because it causes the current to move. Flow is important because it is the amount of current flowing that determines the amount of work that can be done.

Voltage

VOLTAGE is the term for the pressure that causes the current to flow through the conductor. The pressure in a water system is measured by a gauge that registers in pounds per square inch. Pressure, sometimes called potential or electromotive force (EMF), in an electrical system is measured by an instrument called a voltmeter. Volt is the electrical term for pressure. A 12-volt battery and/or generator provides the pressure needed to operate the automobile's electrical and ignition system.

Ampere

To measure the flow of either water or electricity, measure the amount that passes through a pipe or, in the case of electricity, a wire in a given time. Water is measured in gallons per minute. Electrical flow is measured in amperes. When a current of two amperes is flowing through a wire, it means that a specific amount of electricity is moving through the wire every second. Amperage is registered by an instrument called an AMMETER.

Resistance

The OHM is the unit of measurement that indicates the amount of resistance to the flow of current. The amount of current (AMPERAGE) that can flow through a wire depends upon the pressure (VOLTAGE) moving the electrons and the resistance of the wire. The greater the resistance the less current there will be at the unit to which the wire is connected. Ohms can be measured directly with an ohmmeter.

Large wires have less resistance than small wires because the larger wire provides more space in which the current can flow. If too much current is forced through a small wire the high resistance will create heat which may burn the wire. As an example, a starting motor needs a large amount of current in order to turn over a cold engine; therefore large cables with low resistance are used in the starter circuit to carry the high amperage without overheating. This is the same as with water flow—a large pipe can carry more water than a small pipe. The ignition system, lighting system and other accessories need only a small amount of current, therefore smaller wires can be used for these units.

Corrosion on a terminal creates a high resistance. It acts as interference to impede the flow of electricity. Loose connections, corrosion, and dirt on wire terminals cut down on the amperage so much that the starting motor, lights, and other accessories may not operate properly. Frayed or broken wires will also cause high resistance.

For a circuit to function properly there must be a balance between voltage, amperage and resistance. If one factor changes at least one of the others must change and in many cases both factors will change.

Meters

Measuring electrical flow by meters is an important part of diagnosing and servicing the automobile electrical system. The most necessary electrical test equipment is the ammeter, voltmeter and ohmmeter.

The basic construction of an ammeter and voltmeter is the same. Magnetic lines of force cause the meter indicator to move on the same principle as an electric motor. The difference between an ammeter and a voltmeter is the way in which they are hooked into the circuit. A shunt is used in conjunction with an ammeter to carry the electrical load.

An AMMETER is always connected in series in the circuit; thus the circuit must be broken in order to use an ammeter. Current must flow in order to get a reading. The major portion of current flow goes through the shunt rather than the meter movement. The shunt is a conductor bridging across (parallel to) the meter winding. This establishes an auxiliary path for the current to flow. As the shunt has less resistance than the meter, most of the electricity will flow through the shunt. The flow through the meter and shunt is proportional to the flow in the circuit.

BAT. VOLTS
AMPS
Snap-on
FUNCTION
AMMETER ZERO
FIGURE 2-12 Volt-ampere meter. (Courtesy Snap-On Tools Corporation)

A VOLTMETER is connected across the circuit. One lead, on most automobiles the negative, is connected to ground. The other lead is connected to the positive terminal of the circuit to be tested. The voltmeter has a resistance unit in series with the meter coil. The resistance creates an opposing force to the flow of electricity so only a small amount will flow through the meter. The flow through the meter will be proportional to the amount of electrical flow in the entire circuit. Figure 2-12 pictures an inductive volt-amp meter. Three leads are used, two battery leads and an inductive ammeter lead which clamps on a wire for an ampere reading. One knob is for meter selection, the other for zero set.

To check for dirty or loose connections and terminals, a voltage drop test is invaluable. A low-range, expanded-scale voltmeter of 0 to 1 volt is used. One lead is placed on one side of the terminal, the other lead on the opposite side. There must be current flowing in the circuit.

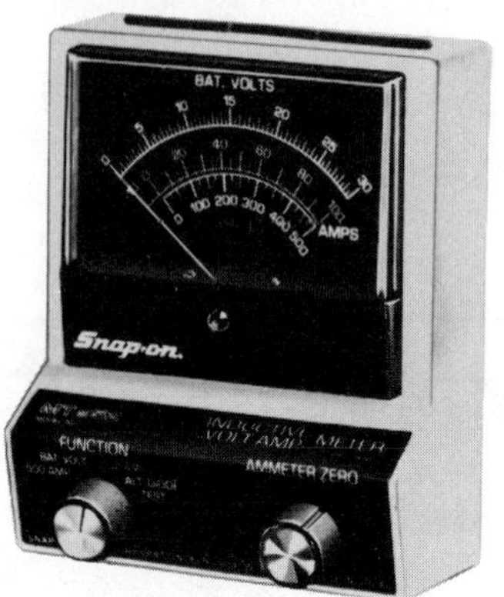

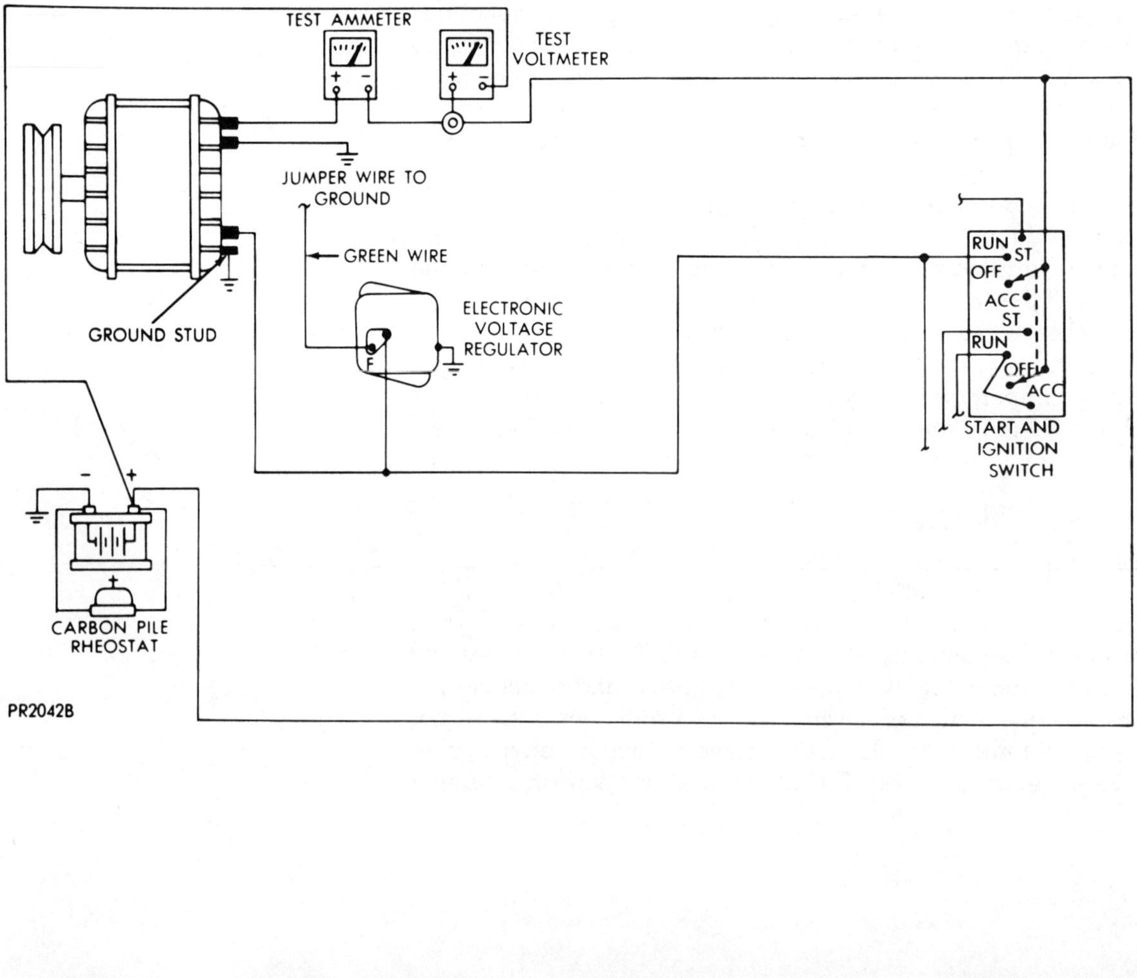

TEST AMMETER
TEST VOLTMETER
JUMPER WIRE TO GROUND
GREEN WIRE
GROUND STUD
ELECTRONIC VOLTAGE REGULATOR
F
RUN
ST
OFF
ACC
ST
RUN
OFF
ACC
START AND IGNITION SWITCH
CARBON PILE RHEOSTAT
PR2042B
FIGURE 2-13 Circuit resistance. (Courtesy Chrysler Corporation)

Except for battery post terminals, a reading of more than 0.01 volt indicates resistance. A voltage drop of no more than 0.02 volt is acceptable at the battery terminals. This is a convenient way to check for dirty or loose connections. Figure 2-13 shows an ammeter and voltmeter hooked into a charging circuit. The voltmeter in this particular hook-up will show the total resistance between the generator output terminal and the battery. With seven connections the voltage drop should not exceed 0.7 volt.

An OHMMETER is used to measure the resistance in a circuit. It is also used for continuity tests. The ohmmeter can measure the resistance in such units as coils, wires, resistors, switches, transistors, diodes, and many other items. It is indispensable when checking out the units in a computer circuit. Resistance is generally checked against specifications. It can be used for continuity tests in place of a test lamp. The scale of the ohmmeter is graduated to read in ohms. There is usually a selector switch to permit the use of a wide range of readings, generally from 0.2 to 500,000 ohms. The meter requires a source of power which is usually a small flashlight battery. A zero adjustment permits adjusting the meter for accuracy should there be a variation in battery voltage.

Selecting the proper range on the ohmmeter can be a problem. Checking specifications will help to determine what range to use. A midscale reading is considered to be the most accurate. It is important that the component being tested with an ohmmeter be disconnected from the operating circuit. The meter can be damaged if power from a circuit is applied to the meter. Resistance is a critical factor in electronic components. Figure 2-14 pictures a typical ohmmeter which is used to check circuit resistance and continuity. This meter uses a range selector knob, a zero set knob, one lead with an alligator clip and another lead with a probe.

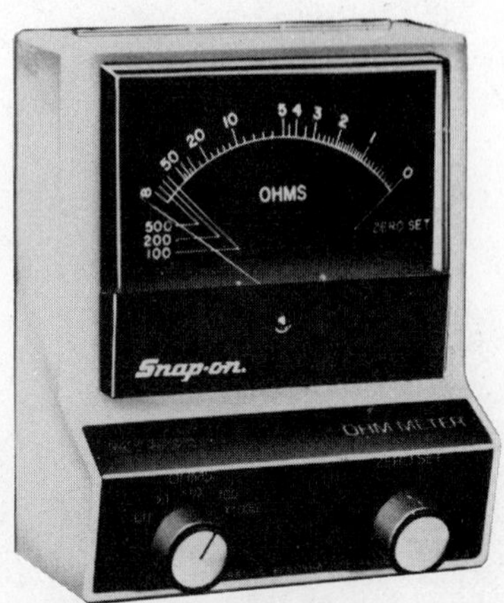

FIGURE 2-14 Ohmmeter. (Courtesy Snap-On Tools Corporation)

Types of Meters for Test Purposes

Meters are available in many different forms. The simplest is the individual meter. The range is important. The voltmeter used for testing the battery and charging system should have a range from 0 to 18 volts. For voltage drop tests and cell testing a 0 to 3 volt range graduated in tenths is essential. An ammeter should have a 0 to 100 range for generator and circuit testing while an ammeter with a 0 to 500 ampere capacity is essential for starter circuits and battery loads.

Many ohmmeters will have four ranges that permit measurements from 0 to 20,000 ohms. Other types may use a high, low or medium scale selection while still another type uses a single scale with a switch indicating the size of the multiplier such as 1, 100, or 1,000. A zero adjustment is provided to calibrate the meter for variations in battery voltages.

Most automotive circuits will have a constant or near constant resistance for each circuit. Manufacturer's specifications are usually available for the electrical circuits used. These should be checked to find what the normal resistance should be. When checking with an ammeter, a higher than normal amperage reading will indicate a lower than normal resistance assuming the current supplied by the battery is constant. The reverse is true if the amperage reading is lower than normal; the resistance in the circuit is higher than normal.

A voltmeter installed parallel to any part of the circuit through which current is flowing can be used to determine the voltage within that part of the circuit. Any difference is referred to as voltage drop.

When current is being used in excess of the source's ability to supply it, the voltage at the source becomes less. When the starting motor is operating the battery voltage drops below open circuit voltage. The differences in voltage drop in the various parts of the circuit indicate differences in resistance. Trouble in electrical components can usually be found by comparing the voltage readings against manufacturer's specifications.

Most automobile service establishments will use a volt-ampere tester, which in addition to having a multi-scale ammeter and voltmeter, will have a variable load resistance unit for battery testing and a generator field control for generator testing. This unit will have an expanded scale voltmeter for voltage drop tests.

For general electrical testing a multi-tester is available. While not as accurate as the more sophisticated testers, this unit is reasonably inexpensive and can perform many tests on the automobile. The multi-tester sometimes called a VAO meter for voltage, amperage, and ohms consists of a multi-scale voltmeter, ammeter and ohmmeter. For general electrical testing this type meter will work reasonably well.

Electronics in the Automobile

The use of electronics in the automobile involves the use of semiconductors. Following is a discussion of the theory behind the operation of semiconductors. Although you can do a good job of locating troubles without understanding the theory, knowing what is taking place within the component makes the job much simpler.

Semiconductors

In order to have some insight into the operating theory of electronics as it is applied to automobiles, it is well to remember it is the number of electrons in the outer ring of the atom which is of significance to the development of semiconductors. The commonly used semiconductors in the automotive electrical and ignition system are the diode and transistor. A semiconductor is an electrical device which acts as an insulator or non-conductor under certain conditions and as a conductor under other conditions.

The basic atom used to develop a semiconductor contains four electrons in the outer ring. This material is neither a good conductor nor a good insulator. Silicon and germanium are widely used materials for semiconductors. Both elements have four electrons in their outer rings. Atoms (elements) of this type, when combined with certain selected other elements can be used to develop a material which is negative in nature or positive in nature, depending upon the material which is added. A negative material will have an excess of electrons. A positive material will have a deficiency of electrons. The "P" positive material and the "N" negative material form the basis for semiconductors.

In production of "N" material when silicon is used, a number of silicon atoms are combined in a crystalline form. The result is called covalent bonding. This means the outer ring of one silicon atom is combined with the outer ring of another silicon atom so the atoms share the electrons in the outer ring. When this happens, each atom has a complete outer ring with eight electrons. The ring is complete and the material is stable and a good nonconductor. Figure 2-15 illustrates covalent bonding. The outer ring of one atom is combined with the outer ring of the other atom. With this combination of atoms a stable material is created which is a good insulator (nonconductor).

FIGURE 2-15 Covalent bonding.

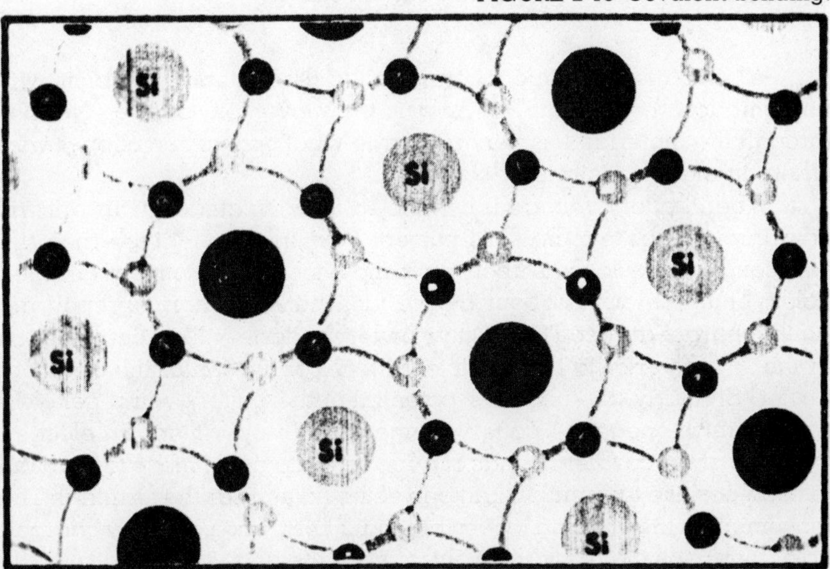

When certain other materials are added to the silicon in a controlled amount the material is said to be "doped" and the new material is no longer a good insulator. When phosphorous is combined with silicon, covalent bonding occurs. But as the phosphorous atom has five electrons in its outer ring, when bonding takes place one electron is left over. This electron is called a "free electron" and can move through the material easily. Any material having an extra electron is called negative or "N" type material.

When the silicon or germanium atom is "doped" with an element (atom) such as indium or boron, which have only three electrons in their outer rings, a different reaction will occur. When boron is added to silicon, covalent bonding occurs around the nucleus but there is a deficiency of one electron for complete bonding. The resultant void is called a "hole." The electron is known as a negative charge of electricity, but the "hole" is considered a positive charge of electricity. Materials of this type are called "P" or positive type material. To understand semiconductor operation it is necessary to look upon the hole as a positive current carrier in the same way that the electron is a negative current carrier. The hole can effectively move from atom to atom, the same as the electron. Figure 2-16 illustrates covalent bonding with an atom having three electrons. This results in a deficiency of one electron for complete bonding. The lack of one atom results in a void "hole." This hole can easily move from atom to atom resulting in a good conductor.

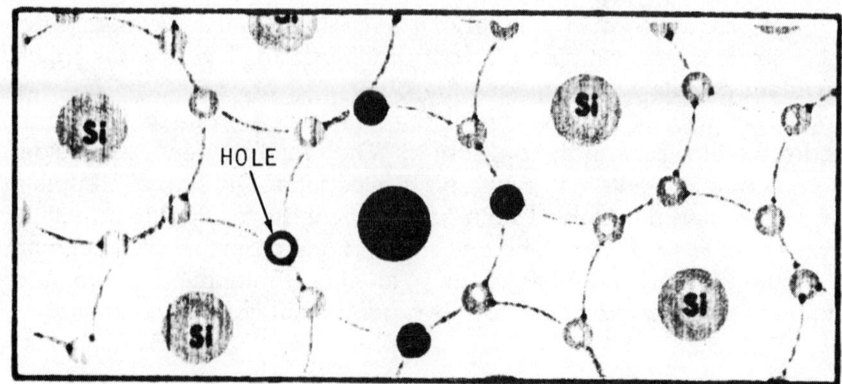

FIGURE 2-16 A "hole" as a positive current carrier.

When battery voltage is connected to "N" material, electricity will flow through the circuit. This flow is the movement of free electrons through the material. It is very similar to what occurs in a copper wire when an electrical circuit is complete.

When battery voltage is connected to "P" material a current will flow through the circuit. This current flow in the "P" type material semiconductor is looked upon as a movement of positively charged holes. This is brought about by the fact that like charges repel and unlike charges attract. The positive battery voltage will attract electrons in the "P" material to the positive battery connection of the semiconductor. Similarly, the negative potential of the battery will repel electrons from the negative battery connection. In operation, an electron from one of the covalent bonds of a "doped" atom will move toward the left and positive terminal, filling one of the holes near the terminal. The movement of the electron leaves behind a hole. The positively charged hole, then, has moved to the right, toward the negative terminal of the battery. Another atom will then move to fill this hole creating another hole nearer the negative terminal. This process is continuous, with the hole moving to the right until it is in the vicinity of the negative con-

FIGURE 2-17 Holes and electrons near junction.

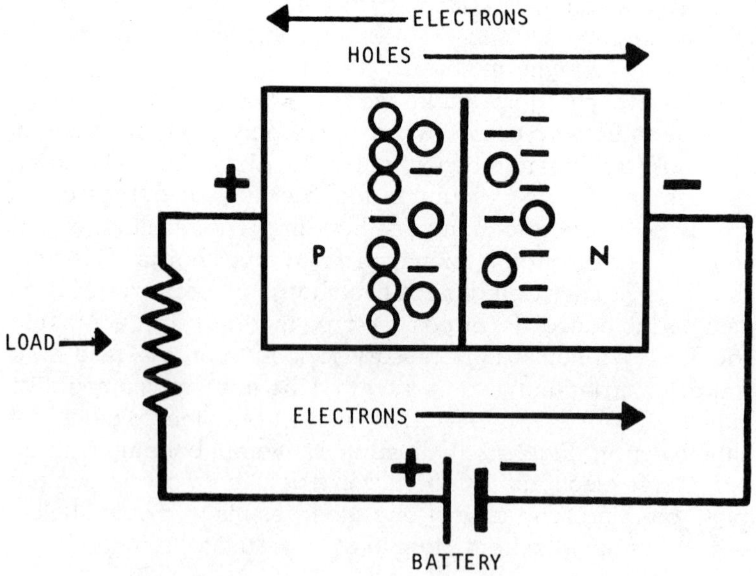

ELECTRONS
HOLES
P
N
LOAD
ELECTRONS
BATTERY

nection at the semiconductor. At this time the hole is filled by an electron which leaves the negative wire connected to the semiconductor and the positive wire removes an electron from the semiconductor. The process is then repeated.

The continuous movement of holes from the positive terminal to the negative terminal can be looked upon as current flow in "P" type material and occurs when battery voltage causes the electrons to shift around in the covalent bonds. The hole movement occurs only within the semiconductor while electrons flow through the entire circuit. Figure 2-17 illustrates hole movement from positive to negative. This occurs only when there is a complete circuit.

Diodes

Diodes which are used in most automotive electronic components such as the AC generator, ignition system control module and computer system, utilize semiconductors. A diode is an electronic device that allows current to pass through in one direction only. Basically it operates as a one-way switch. A diode is made up of a wafer of "P" type material and a wafer of "N" type material which are fused to one another.

Utilizing the theory just discussed, for electrons to move into the "P" material, there must be holes present in the "P" material near the junction into which the electrons can move. The diode, when connected into a circuit, will allow current to flow if the voltage across the diode causes electrons and holes to congregate at the junction area. The diode will not allow current to flow if the voltage across the diode causes the junction area to be void of electrons and holes. This can be made to happen because the characteristics of electricity are such that unlike charges attract which means that negative and positive charges have an attraction for one another.

When "N" and "P" material is formed an attraction exists between the electrons and holes. The electrons will drift across the junction area and fill the holes in the "P" material in a limited fashion. As the electrons drift toward the junction area they leave behind charged particles called positive ions. An ion is an atom having an excess or a deficiency of electrons. These positive ions exert an attractive force on the remaining free electrons and prevent additional electrons from crossing the junction. In a like manner, the holes leave behind negative ions which exert an attractive force on the remaining holes to prevent them from crossing the junction. The result is a stabilized condition with a deficiency of electrons and holes in the junction area.

As unlike charges attract and like charges repel, when the negative terminal of a battery is connected to the "N" connection of the diode the negative battery voltage will repel the electrons in the "N" material and the positive battery voltage will repel the holes in the "P" material. With sufficient voltage, electrons will move from the negative terminal of the battery across the junction to the positive battery connection, which constitutes a current flow. Also, the positive holes, in effect, move through the "P" material and through the junction area.

As the electrons move from the "N" material to the "P" material the battery will inject electrons into the "N" material and attract electrons from the "P" material to maintain a given rate of electron move-

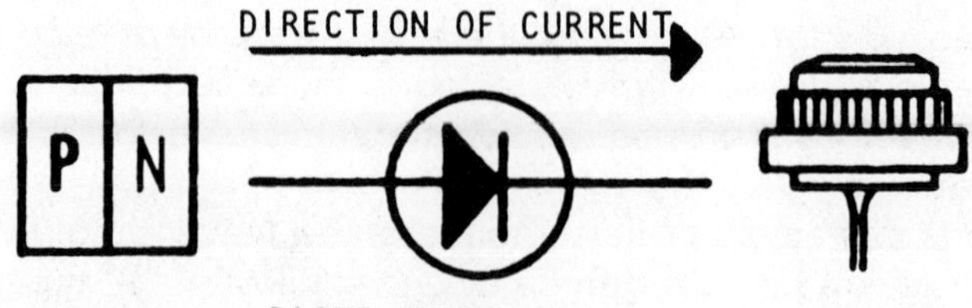

FIGURE 2-18 Diode symbol.

ment. This electron movement within the circuit constitutes an electrical current flow. It must be remembered that in order for this to take place there must be a source to create a concentration of electrons and holes near the junction. The source in the automobile electrical system is the battery. Figure 2-18 shows the symbols for a diode. The purpose of a diode is to permit electrical flow in one direction and prevent flow in the opposite direction (one way switch).

The circuit arrangement with the battery negative terminal connected to the "N" type material and the positive battery terminal connected to the "P" type material is known as a forward bias connection. The repelling action of the battery voltage causes the electrons and holes to congregate at the junction area in considerable amounts. This is needed for current to flow through the diode.

When the battery connections are reversed, negative battery terminal connected to the "P" material, and the positive battery terminal connected to the "N" material, the electrons and holes drift away from the junction. When the junction is void of electrons and holes there can be no current flow as this makes for a very high resistance. Basically, the diode allows current to flow when the electrons and holes congregate at the junction. The diode will not allow current to flow if the polarity of the voltage across the diode causes the junction area to be void of electrons.

The diode is used in an AC generator to convert the alternating current to direct current to charge the battery. Current moving in one direction flows out of the alternator. Current moving in the opposite direction is stopped by the diode (one-way switch). They also are used in transistorized control units.

Zener Diode

For certain applications it is necessary to block the reverse flow of current only up to a specific voltage. Specially designed type diode called a zener diode is used to block out the reverse flow of current up to a certain voltage. When the voltage reaches a predetermined potential the diode begins to conduct the reverse current. This type of diode is used to control specific circuits.

Transistors

The diode is a semiconductor that will allow current to flow through in one direction. The transistor is another type of semiconductor which is made up of two diodes "back to back," sharing a common base material. The transistor is used in circuits to control current flow. It will allow current to flow under certain conditions and prevent the flow under other conditions.

The same material is used in a transistor that is used in a diode. A diode consists of "P" and "N" material. When a second section of "P" material is formed on a PN junction a transistor is created. To better understand the operation of a transistor the "P" material on the left is called the emitter, the "N" material in the center is the base and the "P" material on the right is called the collector. This arrangement results in what is known as a PNP transistor. It is also possible to form an NPN transistor by using two areas of "N" material and one of "P" material. The PNP transistor is the type generally used in the automobile. Figure 2-19 is an enlarged drawing of a transistor which illustrates the relationship between the emitter, base and collector.

The most commonly used elements in transistors are germanium doped with indium to form "P" material and germanium doped with antimony to form "N" material. Transistors are constructed so as to have a very thin base material. A metallic ring is attached to the base at the outer circumference with provisions for an electrical connection. A very thin base material provides for a very short distance between the emitter and collector. This accounts for the operating characteristics of the transistor. Current can easily flow between the emitter and collector when turned on. Figure 2-20 is an illustration of a transistor in a circuit. It can serve as a switch without any moving parts.

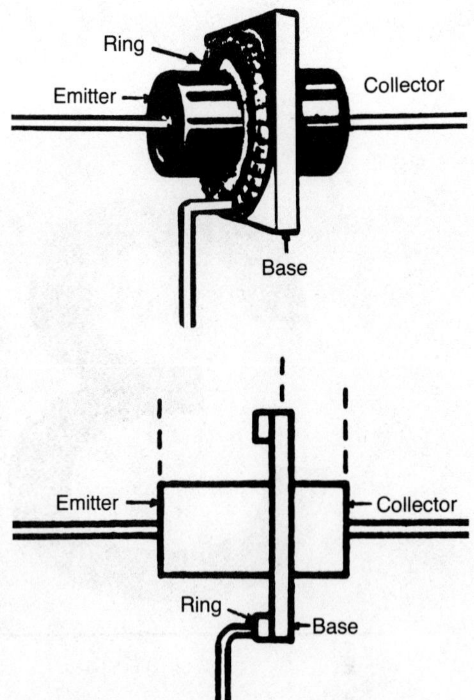

FIGURE 2-19 Drawing of transistor parts.

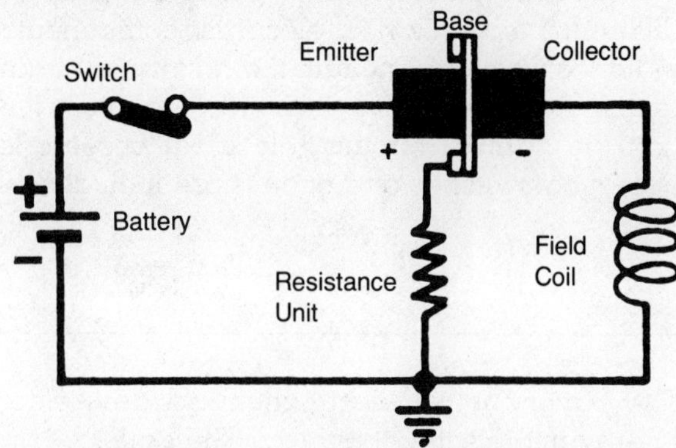

FIGURE 2-20 Drawing of a transistor in a circuit.

One characteristic of the transistor that is important to the automotive ignition system is that when a small amount of electric current is applied to the base material and emitter a large amount of current can flow through the emitter and collector. This current flow can be turned on or off by reversing the voltage bias (polarity) across the emitter-base. The transistor can be made to operate like a relay, turning on or off the current flow like a switch but without any moving parts.

The transistor operates on the hole movement theory, the same as the diode. The current flow in the transistor is considered to be a movement of holes through the "P" material to the "N" material. This movement of holes is looked upon as current flow.

The transistor is used in the control module of the electronic distributor. It acts as a switch to charge and discharge the ignition coil. Transistors are also used extensively in all computers.

3 Electrical, Electronic, and Ignition Components in General

This chapter presents, in a general manner, the relationship of the different major electrical-electronic components in the automobile. The major components include the battery, charging system, starting system, ignition system, and the electrical-electronic control units. In addition the lighting circuits, electrical accessories, and the necessary operating switches and circuits are included.

Battery

The battery is an electrochemical device for converting chemical energy into electrical energy. The battery, by chemical reaction, furnishes electricity when the engine is not operating. When the engine is operating the generator will recharge the battery and supply the electricity needed by the engine and accessories. When insufficient electricity is produced by the generator the excess requirements are supplied by the battery. The battery also provides power to operate the starting motor and other units when the generator is not charging. The battery is considered to be the heart of the electrical and ignition system. Figure 3-1 shows a typical sealed battery with side terminals and a built-in hydrometer.

Battery maintenance is dependent upon the charging system. A generator regulator is used to control generator output according to the needs of the battery and electrical system. The regulator (limiter) prevents the battery from becoming overcharged and protects both the battery and generator. The battery is included in all of the electrical circuits.

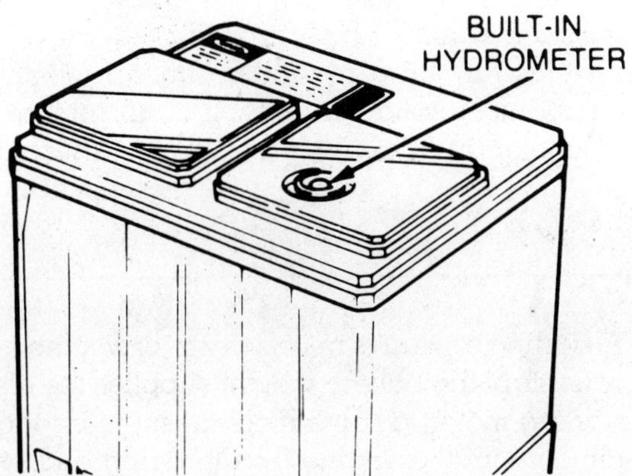

FIGURE 3-1 Typical sealed battery. (Courtesy Chevrolet Motor Division, General Motors Corp.)

Charging System

The charging circuit includes the generator, battery, regulator, charge indicator or ammeter, and the necessary wiring. The regulator limits the production of electricity according to the electrical needs of the vehicle. Figure 3-2 is a drawing of a typical charging system which uses an integral type of voltage limiter.

All generators produce alternating current, but the battery can only be charged with direct current. The older generators, prior to the early 1960's used a commutator as part of the armature to convert alternating current (AC) to direct current (DC). All present generators, sometimes called alternators, use diodes to convert the alternating current to direct current before it leaves the generator.

The generator regulator on older model vehicles depended upon electro-magnetism to open and close contact points to cut in and out

FIGURE 3-2 Charging system. (Courtesy Chevrolet Motor Division, General Motors Corp.)

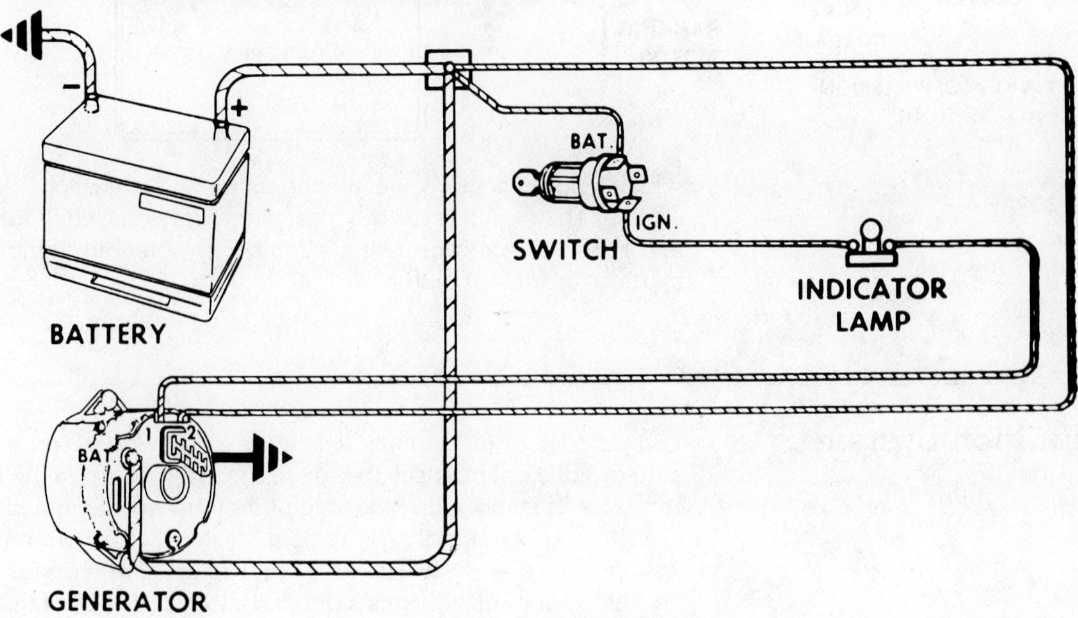

resistance units which limited the rate of charge. Present charging systems rely on a regulator (limiter) which consists of transistors, diodes, and resistance units. It is an integral part of the generator. A voltmeter and ammeter are used to check generator output.

Starting System

A starting system is necessary to crank the engine. The starting system consists of the battery which supplies the electric power to operate the starting motor, a drive mechanism to engage the starting motor drive pinion with the engine flywheel ring gear when cranking, a solenoid

FIGURE 3-3 Complete starting (cranking) circuit. (Courtesy Chevrolet Motor Division, General Motors Corp.)

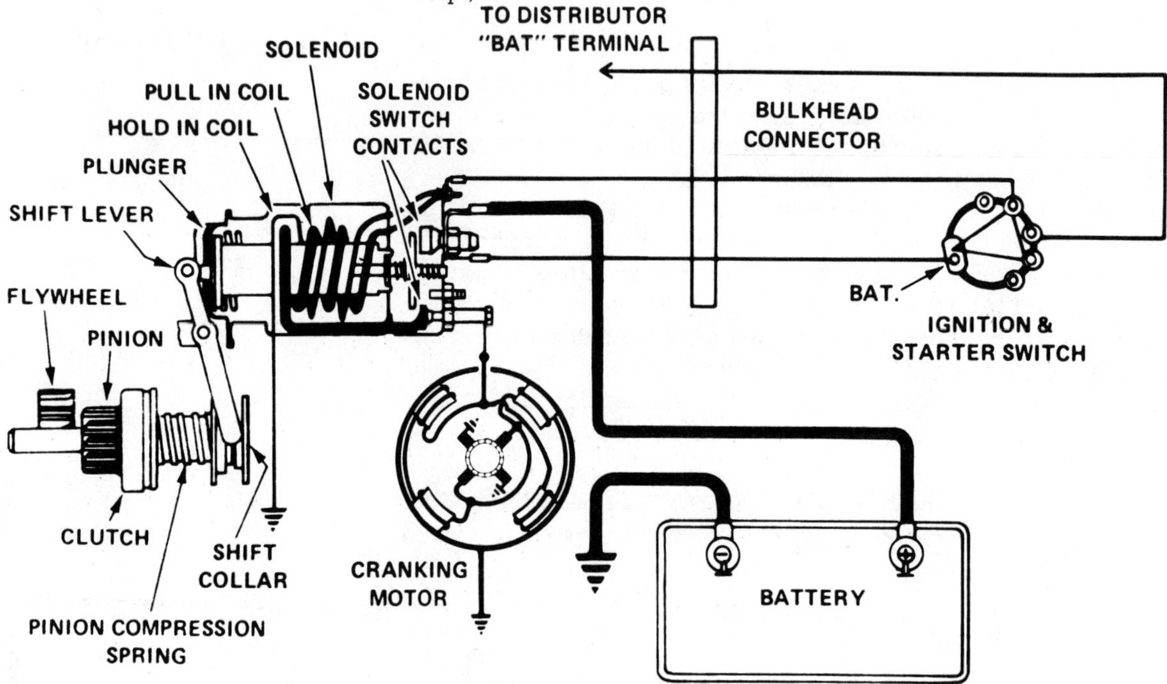

which engages the drive mechanism, and a switch to activate the system. The switch is usually part of the ignition switch unit. Figure 3-3 is a schematic of a cranking circuit. The solenoid is mounted on the starting (cranking) motor.

Ignition System

The purpose of the ignition system is to provide a spark at the spark plug of sufficient intensity to fire the air/fuel mixture at the right time for complete burning. The older type ignition system, sometimes referred to as the conventional type ignition system which was used until the late 1960s and early 1970s, has been replaced with a high energy type ignition system using transistors and diodes instead of ignition contact breaker points.

The so-called conventional ignition system is divided into two circuits, a primary (low voltage) circuit and a secondary (high voltage) circuit.

The primary circuit operates at battery voltage (12 volts) and is made up of the following:

Battery
Ignition switch
Primary windings in ignition coil
Breaker (Contact) points
Resistance wire or Resistor
Capacitor (Condenser)

The secondary (high voltage) circuit is made up of the following:

Secondary windings of ignition coil
Spark plugs
Rotor
Distributor cap
High tension wires

The high energy ignition system, sometimes called the electronic ignition system or dura spark ignition is a transistor controlled ignition system. The primary circuit (low voltage) is made up of the following units:

Battery
Ignition switch
Pick-up coil
Electronic control module
Magnetic pole piece
Primary winding of the ignition coil

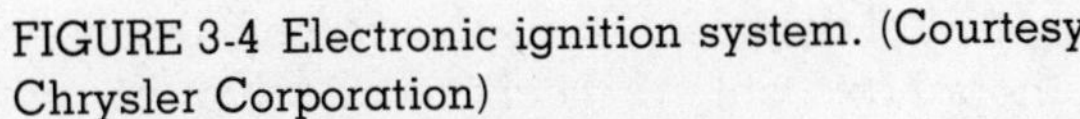
FIGURE 3-4 Electronic ignition system. (Courtesy Chrysler Corporation)

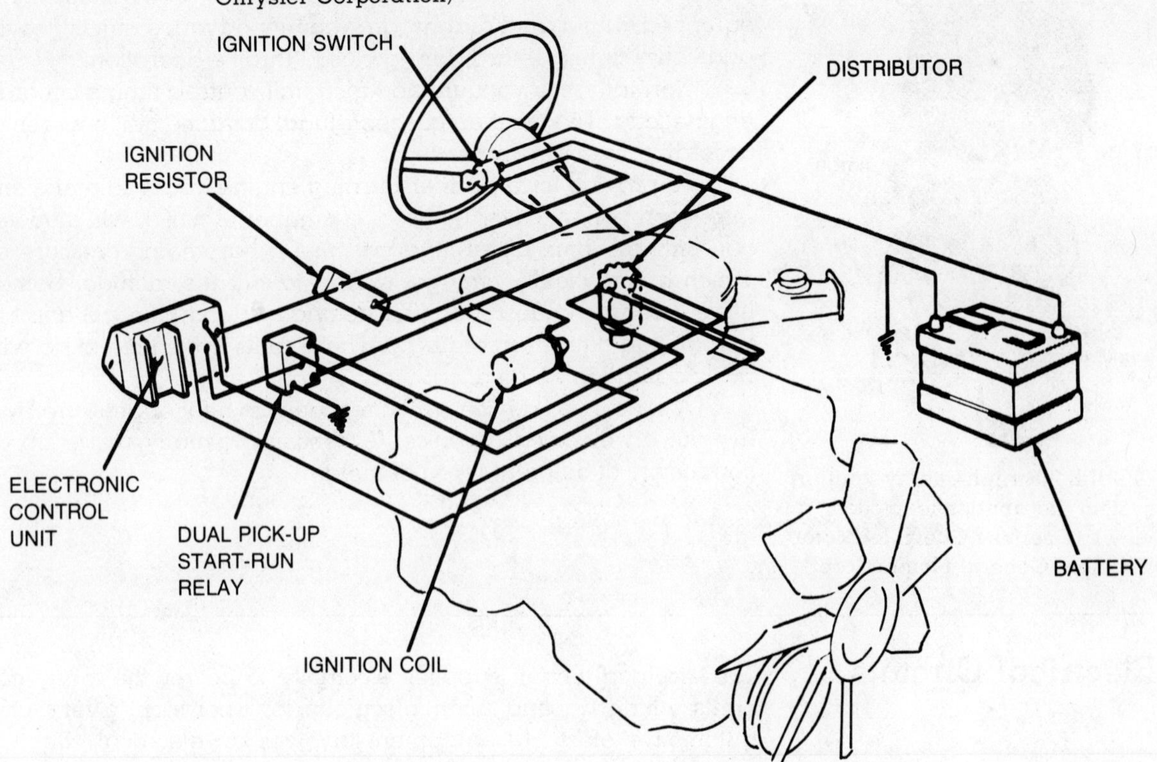

The secondary (high voltage) circuit is made up of the following units:

Secondary windings of the ignition coil	Distributor cap
Spark plugs	High tension wires
Rotor	

If a capacitor is located in the distributor it is not part of the ignition system; it is for radio noise suppression. Some electronic ignition systems will use a resistance wire or resistor unit while others will not. Figure 3-4 is a line drawing of an electronic ignition system used on some Chrysler products.

Spark Timing

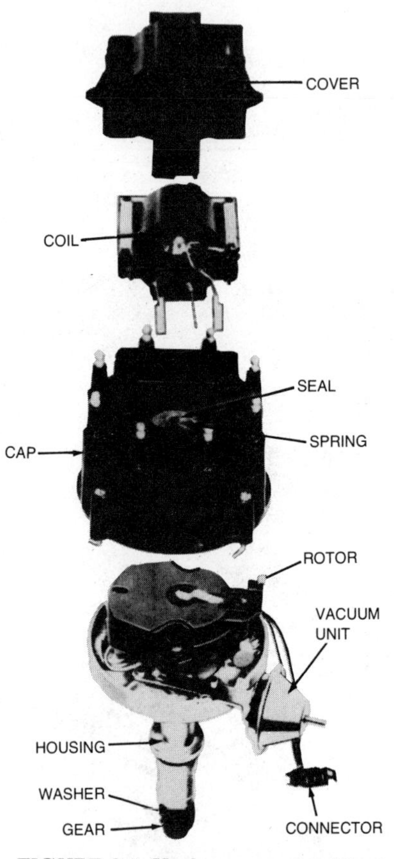

FIGURE 3-5 High-energy ignition system distribution (exploded view). (Courtesy Chevrolet Motor Division, General Motors Corp.)

Some method must be used to control spark timing (advance and retard). Most of the conventional distributors using contact points have both a vacuum advance unit and a mechanical advance unit. The vacuum control unit uses a diaphragm which is activated by vacuum to provide ignition timing advance or retard. The mechanical advance unit depends upon centrifugal weights to advance ignition timing according to engine RPMs. Figure 3-5 is an exploded view of a high energy ignition (HEI) distributor which uses an integral coil and a vacuum advance unit.

Some of the electronic distributors also use vacuum and centrifugal weights to regulate ignition timing. However, there are many variations as to how the timing is regulated on the different makes and models of vehicles. Some distributors use only a vacuum control while others have only a mechanical advance unit. Some distributors are equipped with a dual diaphragm vacuum advance unit to provide for additional timing retard during closed throttle operation.

Normally, the vacuum advance unit controls timing according to engine load. The mechanical centrifugal advance unit governs timing according to engine speed.

To provide for a cleaner burning engine (reduced emissions) different components may be used, a number of which will involve ignition timing. Some distributors will use a barometric pressure sensor which automatically changes timing to suit the altitude. Some may have a sensor to detect engine detonation (spark knock) and retards the ignition timing accordingly. These units have little to do with the basic operation of the distributor.

A sensor is a device which responds to heat or pressure by sending out an electrical impulse. A sensor is usually made up of two conductors of different types of metal.

Electrical Circuits

The electrical circuit supplies electricity to power the many components which depend upon electricity for operation. Every piece of automotive electrical equipment involves an electrical circuit using some kind of conductor. The most common conductor is copper wire covered with an insulating material. There must always be a complete circuit before electricity can flow. Because the battery is the primary source of electrical energy, all circuits leave and return to the battery, either directly or indirectly. For this reason it is essential to have a good battery in the vehicle before attempting to find electrical problems.

To reduce the amount of wiring needed for a complete circuit, the metal parts such as the engine, frame, and metal body parts are used as conductors. These metal parts are referred to as ground. For this reason any bare spot (place where the insulation is off the wire) on a wire that comes in contact with metal, will result in a "ground." This will be a shorted circuit when current is flowing. It also means that the metal case or housing of most electrical units must have a clean and tight mounting contact. Any loose or dirty connections or broken strands in stranded wire will create a resistance to current flow. A simple voltage drop test can be made to locate high resistance without disturbing the connections. The prods of a low reading expanded scale (0-5) voltmeter tightly pressed against the terminals on either side of the connection will indicate if there is a resistance when current is flowing. In low amperage circuits any reading of 0.01 volt or more indicates above normal resistance. Resistance of over 0.02 volt at the battery cables and terminals indicates a poor connection.

Switches

A switch of some type is usually part of a circuit used to control an operating unit. Some circuits, in addition to having a switch to control the particular component, will also be connected through the ignition switch so that current will flow only when the ignition switch is "on" or in the accessory position. The radio circuit is an example of this type circuit.

FIGURE 3-6 Cutaway view of a starting motor and solenoid. (Courtesy Oldsmobile Division, General Motors Corp.)

A solenoid switch is generally used in the starting motor circuit. In this case the solenoid, a magnetic switch, is used to connect a heavy current load from the battery to the starting motor. The solenoid is activated by a low amperage current supplied from the "start" section of the ignition switch. Other solenoids may be used to activate various units on command, such as to open and close circuits or, in some cases, to increase or decrease fuel flow.

Figure 3-6 is a cutaway view of a starting motor and solenoid. The solenoid is used to shift the starting motor pinion into engagement with the flywheel ring gear and connect the starting motor to the battery.

Circuit Protection

To protect a circuit from burning insulation off wires and possibly melting the wire as well as damaging an operating unit should a short circuit develop, a fuse, circuit breaker or fusible link will generally be inserted in most circuits. A fuse is a metal conductor having a low melting point which melts and breaks the circuit should a short occur in the circuit. The fuse is replaceable simply by removing and inserting a new fuse in the fuse holder after the trouble in the circuit is corrected. Figure 3-7 shows a fuse panel which contains the fuses, circuit breakers, and a receptacle for the directional signal flasher and hazard flasher. Also shown is a miniature fuse of the blade terminal type. This type of fuse is used in most of today's electrical systems. This fuse is blown.

A circuit breaker uses moveable contact points operated by a bimetal strip (like a thermostat) which will automatically open the contacts and break the circuit when an overload occurs. When the problem no longer exists the circuit breaker contacts close and normal operation is restored.

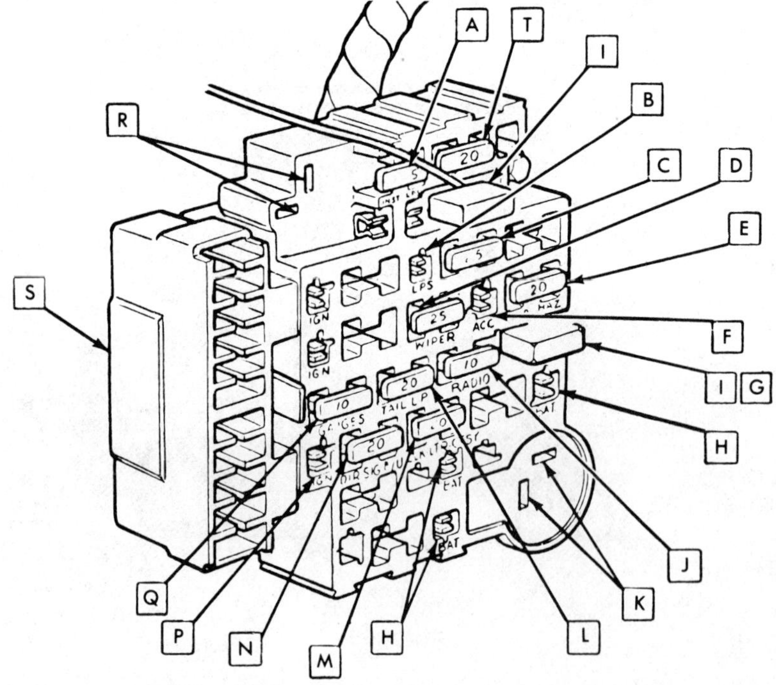

FIGURE 3-7
Typical fuse panel and common type of fuse. (Courtesy Chevrolet Motor Division, General Motors Corp.)

I CIRCUIT BREAKER
A FUSE-INST PANEL LAMPS
B RECEPTACLE-LAMPS
C FUSE-HEATER & A/C (C60)
D FUSE-WINDSHIELD WIPER
E FUSE-STOP AND TRAF HAZARD LPS
F RECEPTACLE-ACCESSORY
G POWER ACCESSORY
H RECEPTACLE-BATTERY
J FUSE-RADIO (U63)
K RECEPTACLE-DIR SIG LP FLASHER
L FUSE-TAIL LAMPS
M FUSE-CLOCK, CIG LIGHTER AND CTSY LAMPS
N FUSE-DIR SIG AND BACK-UP LAMPS
P RECEPTACLE-CRUISE CONTROL (K30) REAR WINDOW DEFOG (C50) (ALL IGN CONTROL)
Q FUSE-GAUGES
R RECEPTACLE-TRAF HAZ FLASHER
S FISHER BODY CONNECTOR
T FUSE-INSTALLED WHEN USING LD5 AND L26 ENGINE

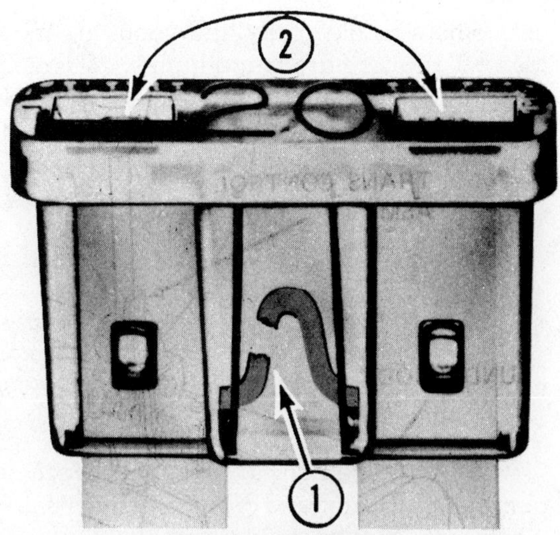

TO TEST FOR BLOWN MINI-FUSE:
① PULL FUSE OUT AND CHECK VISUALLY.
② WITH THE CIRCUIT ACTIVATED, USE A TEST LIGHT ACROSS THE POINTS SHOWN.

FIGURE 3-7 (cont.)

A fusible link is a section of wire having a low melting point. When the circuit is shorted (overloaded) and heats up, the link melts and opens the circuit. The section of wire containing the fusible link must be cut out of the circuit and replaced with a new link. The fusible link is used in place of a fuse in circuits which carry heavier loads than a headlight or stop light circuit. Figure 3-8 shows a fusible link repair. A clean and tight connection must exist between the new link and the wires. A link kit will usually contain a repair sleeve which must be tightly crimped.

FIGURE 3-8 Fusible link repair. (Courtesy Oldsmobile Division, General Motors Corp.)

FUSIBLE LINK INSTALLATION

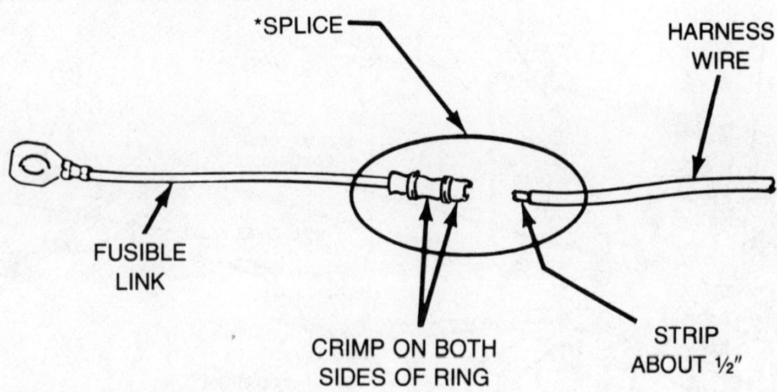

* If original splice had 2 harness wires than 2 fusible links must be installed.

Emission Controls

Emission control mandates have brought about the use of numerous components which aid in the reduction of engine exhaust emissions. A number of these components depend strictly on engine vacuum for operation. Some depend upon vacuum, heat, and electricity for actuation, others on electricity and vacuum, and still others solely on electricity. Variations are found in the different makes and models of vehicles. Figure 3-9 is a line drawing showing the major components of an emission control system. This system does not incorporate an electronic emission control unit.

Examples of units which depend solely upon vacuum include:

Vacuum controlled heat valve
Vacuum controlled choke valve
PCV positive crankcase ventilation system
Air management system which includes an air injector reactor pump with diverter and check valve system. Some diverter valves may incorporate a solenoid.

Air management system which includes an air injector reactor pump with diverter and check valve system. Some diverter valves may incorporate a solenoid.

The thermostatically controlled air cleaner depends upon heat and vacuum, as does the exhaust gas recirculation valve.

In the area of electrical-electronic control for emission reduction, the major activating component is usually a sensor. In general when a

FIGURE 3-9 Basic emission control system components. (Courtesy Chrysler Corporation)

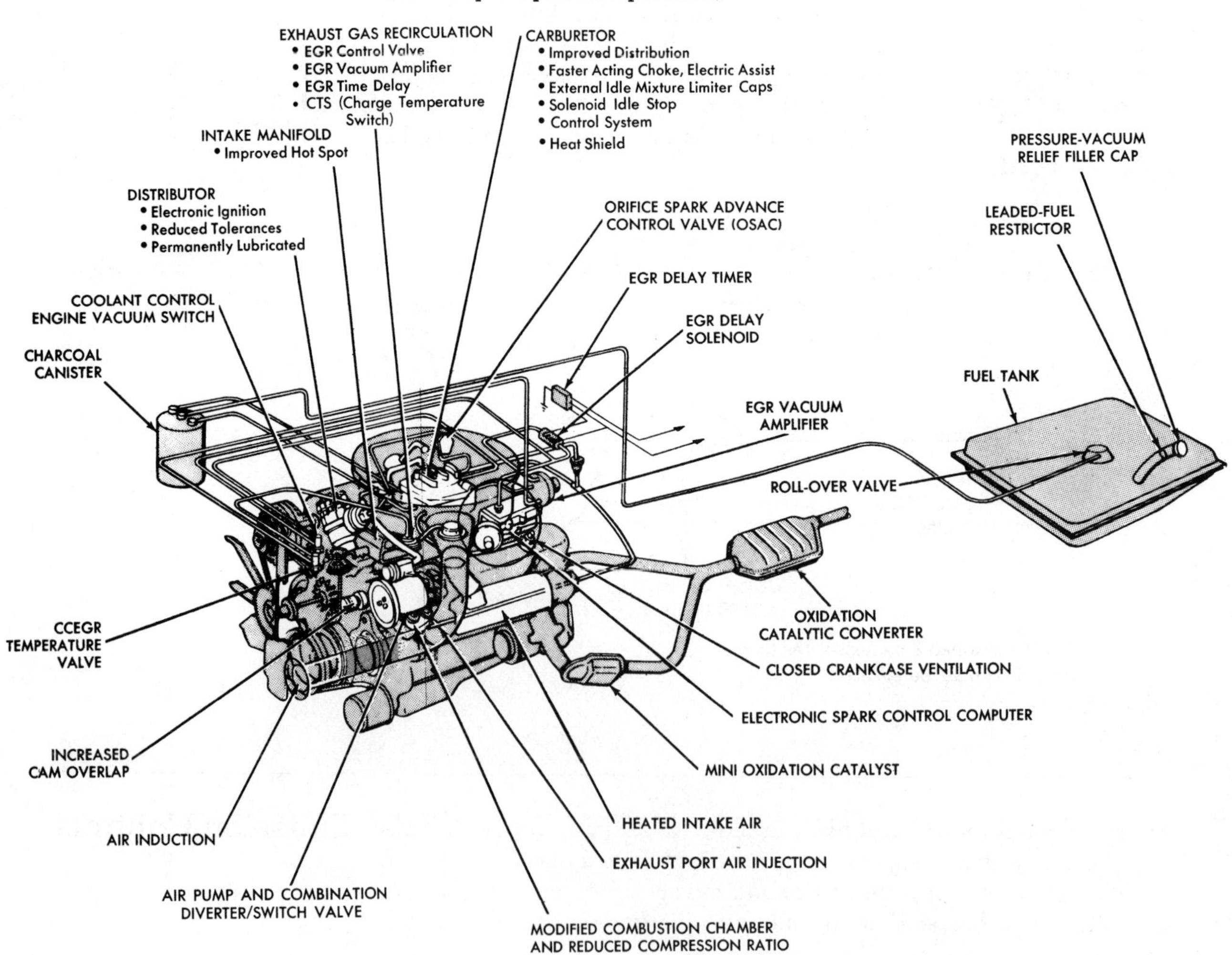

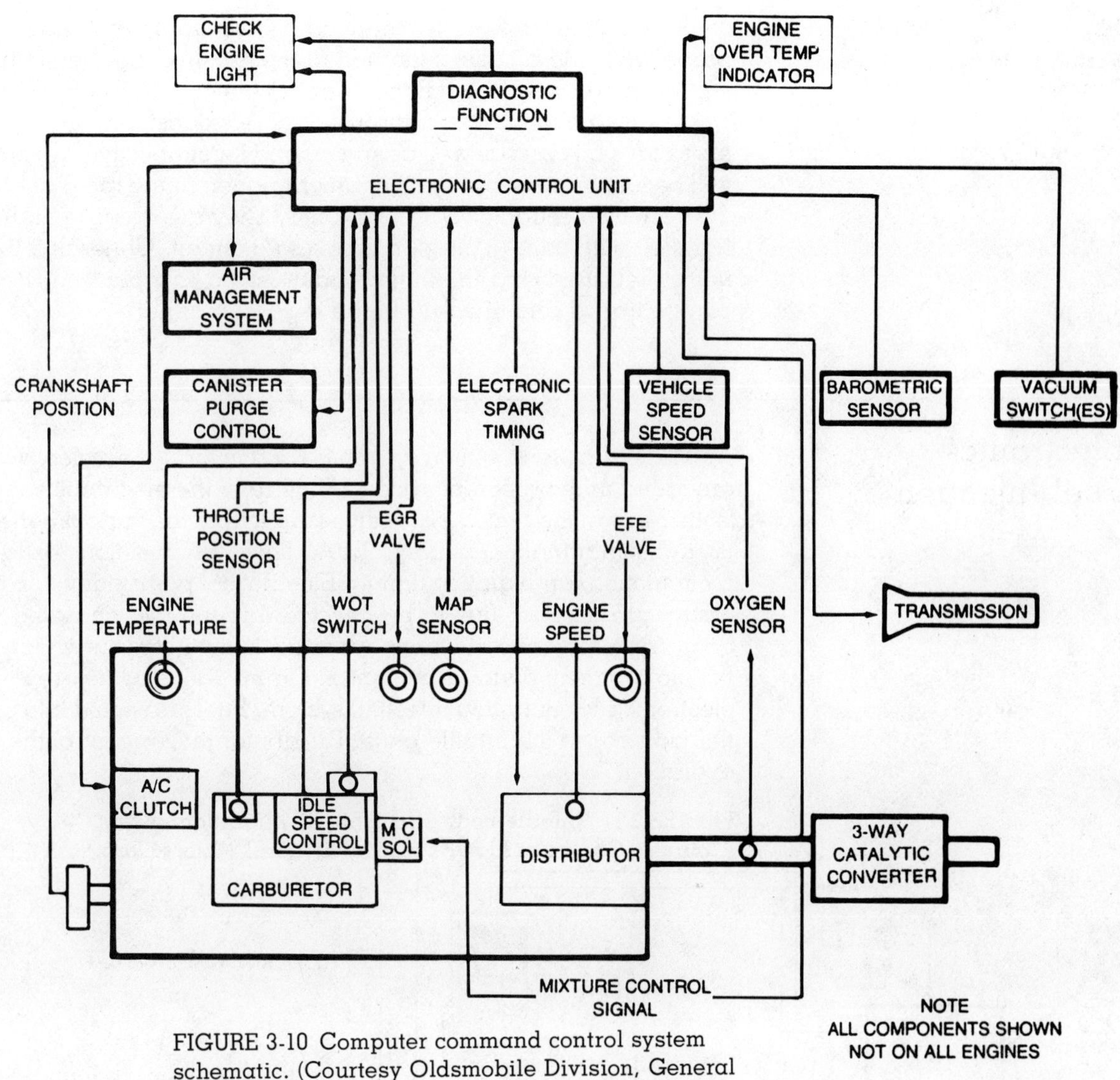

FIGURE 3-10 Computer command control system schematic. (Courtesy Oldsmobile Division, General Motors Corp.)

computer control system is used, sensors send signals to the electronic control module which monitors the voltage from the different sensors and sends a control signal to operate the particular component used to modify operating conditions.

The computer-controlled catalytic converter is a fuel management system that controls exhaust emissions by regulation of the air-fuel ratio and a special catalytic converter which lowers the level of oxides of nitrogen, hydrocarbon, and carbon monoxide. The basic components include an electronic control module, an exhaust gas oxygen sensor, an electrically controlled carburetor, a special type catalytic converter, an engine coolant temperature sensor, a throttle position sensor, and usually a "check engine" telltale light. Figure 3-10 is a schematic of a computer command control system indicating the flow of information to the electronic control unit and from the control unit to the different components.

Although we are primarily concerned about the electrical components, because of the interrelationship with vacuum controlled units the various vacuum operated units cannot be ignored. For an emission control system to function properly both the vacuum operated and controlled units as well as the electrical-electronic units must function properly. To do a satisfactory job of troubleshooting the vacuum system must be considered along with the electrical-electronic systems.

Printed circuits are being used more extensively by manufacturers to save on costs as well as space, and for simplicity. Printed circuits will be found in back of the instrument panel, in the radio as well as in the various electronic control modules. They are delicate and must be handled with care to prevent breaking a circuit. Generally, they cannot be repaired and the entire circuit board is replaced. The circuits can be traced and checked in the regular manner.

Electronic Fuel Injection

An electronic fuel injection system is used in many vehicles. Variations are found in the different systems. Basically the electronic control unit is the heart of the system. It receives input from the various sensors and uses the information to control fuel flow, air injection, exhaust gas recirculation, and ignition timing. Electric fuel pumps develop the necessary pressure for fuel to be injected into the fuel charging system. Some systems have solenoid-operated injector valves which control fuel flow to the individual cylinders. Figure 3-11 is a line drawing of an electronically controlled injection system. Fuel is injected into the throttle body above the throttle plate. Distributor pulses control the injector operation.

FIGURE 3-11 Throttle body electronic fuel injection system. (Courtesy Chevrolet Motor Division, General Motors Corp.)

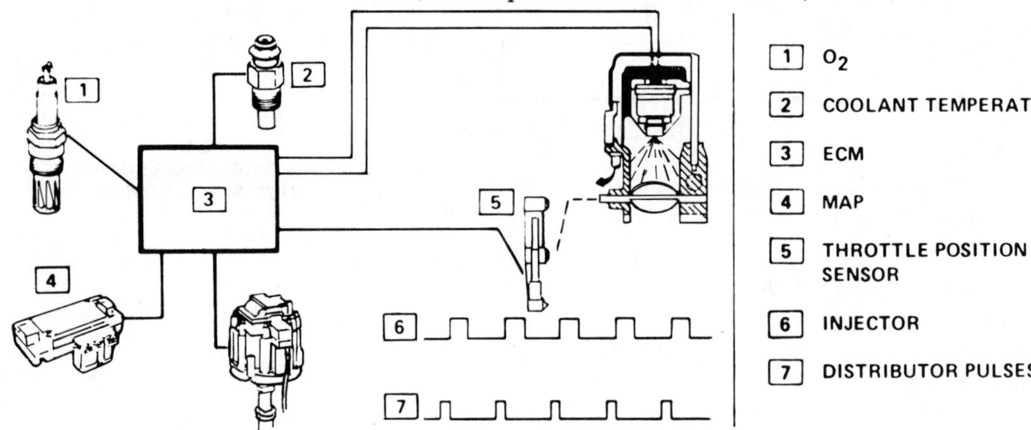

Most of the electronically controlled units, fuel injection, electronically controlled emission systems, etc. are complex systems which demand precise operation. Many of the components cannot be serviced and the entire unit must be replaced. Of major importance is being able to identify the component which is faulty, being able to trace the circuit, and being able to check the flow of electricity. This is one of the main factors in troubleshooting.

Electrically Operated Components

Certain electrically operated components may be incorporated in the regular fuel system such as an electric bowl vent solenoid, inertia switch, electrically heated choke, an antidiesel solenoid, an electric fuel pump, and solenoid-controlled metering rods. An electrically operated cooling system fan is used on some engines.

Electricity is involved in the air conditioning and heating systems to operate fans, controls, temperature controls, and the operation of the air conditioning compressor switch. Signaling devices such as oil pressure, coolant temperature, windshield washer solution level, seat belt buzzer, and ignition switch buzzer all depend upon electricity for operation.

The entire lighting system operates by electricity, as do most of the accessories such as radio, horns, electronically operated light beam control, rear defroster, windshield wipers, and windshield washers.

Simple Testing Tools

Simple tools are all that is necessary to troubleshoot a circuit. A jumper wire, which can be made from an insulated 14 or 16 gauge wire 2 to 4 feet long with alligator clips on both ends, is a valuable tool and can be used to bypass a switch or an open circuit.

A DC voltmeter having a 0 to 18 volt range is used to measure circuit voltage. The negative lead of the voltmeter is connected to a good ground and the positive lead to the point to be measured. A good circuit should have a reading close to battery voltage.

An ohmmeter is used to measure resistance between two points. Because an ohmmeter is powered by a battery, it can also be used to check circuit continuity. An ohmmeter is an essential tool for checking computer control units and electronic ignition components.

A test lamp employing a 12 volt bulb in a socket with two leads can be used to check if voltage is reaching the unit being checked. It is connected in the same manner as a voltmeter.

A self-powered test lamp which is a bulb, battery, and a set of test leads wired in series can be used to check for a continuous circuit. When connected between two points of a continuous circuit the lamp will glow. It is used for a continuity check or a ground check. An ohmmeter can be used for the same purpose. When using a self-powered test lamp or an ohmmeter make sure the power is off in the circuit being checked. Figure 3-12 shows the diagnostic tools needed to check the electronic fuel injection system.

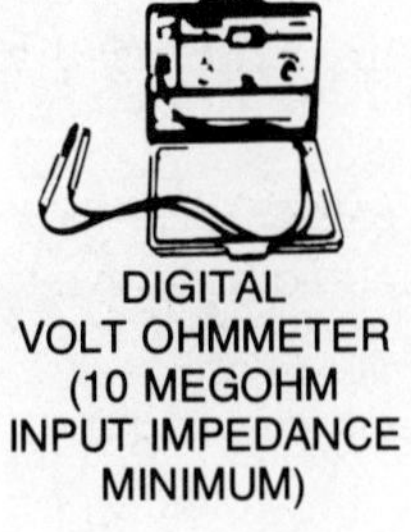

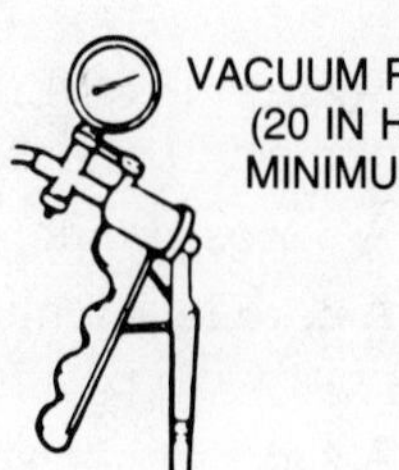

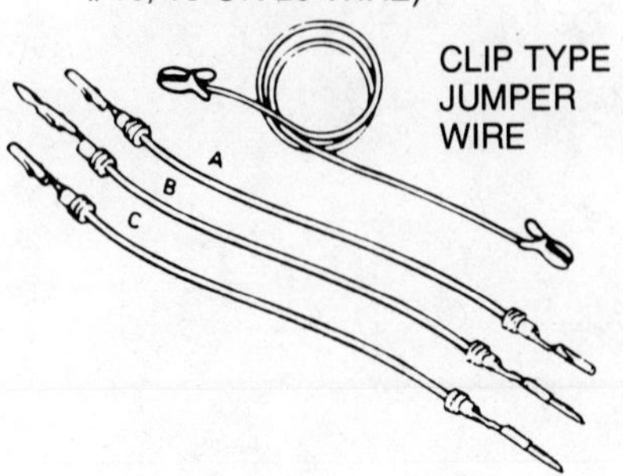

FIGURE 3-12 Diagnosis tools needed to check many of the electronic fuel injection systems. (Courtesy Chevrolet Motor Division, General Motors Corp.)

Checking Circuits

The various electrical accessories used throughout the vehicle are all checked in much the same manner. First, determine whether electricity is reaching the particular unit and if it is properly grounded to provide a complete circuit. If in doubt about the circuit, connect a wire directly from the battery to the unit, thus bypassing the complete circuit, including the switch. If sufficient current is reaching the unit and it is properly grounded and still does not operate, the unit must be repaired or replaced.

A fuse that continually blows is an indication of a shorted circuit. Electricity is flowing to ground rather than to the unit it is supposed to flow through. To find the short, turn off everything powered through the fuse. Disconnect other units powered through the particular fuse, such as motors; or if lights, remove the bulb or bulb connection. Turn on the ignition switch if the circuit is powered through the switch. Connect one lead of the test lamp or voltmeter to the hot end of the blown fuse holder. Connect the other lead to a good ground. If power is reaching the fuse holder the test lamp will glow or the voltmeter will read battery voltage. If the voltmeter shows considerably less than battery voltage it could mean there is a high resistance in the circuit such as a loose or dirty connection. Disconnect the test lamp lead or voltmeter lead from the ground and reconnect it to the load side of the fuse. If the test lamp is off or the voltmeter reads '0" the short is in the disconnected equipment or circuit. If the light comes on or the voltmeter shows a reading, the short is in the wiring. You can find the short by disconnecting the circuit connectors one at a time until the light goes out or, if a voltmeter is used, there is no reading. If the test shows no short in the wiring, reconnect the units which were disconnected, one at a time until the lamp comes on or the meter shows a reading. This is the unit that is shorted and needs to be serviced. Checking circuits is very much an elimination process.

While there are a large number of different components electrically operated, some very simple, others more complex, the process of troubleshooting can become a routine procedure by using a systematic approach. A simple step-by-step procedure will permit a person to locate exactly where trouble exists.

Summary of Basic Automotive Electricity

1. Electrical flow is the movement of electrons within a circuit.
2. There must be a complete circuit in order for electricity to flow.
3. Fuses, circuit breakers or fusible links are used to protect most circuits from overload.
4. A series circuit is wired negative to positive.
5. A parallel circuit has all units connected negative to negative and positive to positive.
6. A short circuit is usually the unintentional grounding of a circuit.
7. A switch is a device used for opening, closing or changing the path of current flow in an electrical circuit.
8. A conductor is usually a wire that allows for the easy flow of electricity. Most electrical wires are made of copper. Spark plug wires have a nylon thread impregnated with carbon.

9. An insulator is a nonconductor of electricity.
10. Voltage is electrical pressure (potential) (EMF).
11. Amperage is the volume of electrical flow.
12. An ohm is the term used to measure the resistance to electrical flow.
13. A voltmeter is always connected parallel to the circuit.
14. An ammeter is always inserted into the circuit.
15. An ohmmeter directly indicates the resistance in a circuit, wire or electrical component.
16. An ohmmeter has its own battery; therefore it does not require an outside source of electricity.
17. A voltage drop test is used to locate resistance in a circuit.
18. A direct current (DC) flows in one direction only.
19. An alternating current (AC) is constantly changing from positive to negative and back again.
20. Numerous electrical units depend on magnetism for their operation.
21. All magnets have a north and a south pole.
22. Unlike magnetic poles attract one another; like magnetic poles repel one another.
23. When electricity flows through a wire a magnetic field is created around the wire.
24. Winding the wire in the form of a coil increases the magnetic lines of force surrounding the wire.
25. Inserting an iron core in the coil strengthens the magnet.
26. A solenoid is an electromagnet having an iron core which is moveable. It is used to engage the starting motor drive pinion with the flywheel. The core moves when the coil is energized.
27. A starting motor depends upon magnetism for its operation. It converts electrical energy to mechanical energy.
28. The battery and generator are the sources of electricity in the automobile. It is a 12 volt system.
29. A generator is used to charge the battery in an automobile. It converts mechanical energy to electrical energy.
30. Induction is the process by which an electrical conductor becomes electrified when near a charged body.
31. The principle of self-induction is defined as the inducing of a voltage in a current-carrying wire when the current in the wire itself is changing (ignition coil).
32. An induced current is a current generated in a conductor as it moves through a magnetic field or as a magnet field is moved across a conductor.
33. The ignition system, through induction, converts a 12 volt current to approximately 25,000 volts and delivers it to the spark plug at a predetermined time.
34. A capacitor (condenser) absorbs electricity, stores it and discharges it back into the circuit.
35. A resistor is used to limit current flow.

36. Transistors and diodes are used to regulate (control) generator output.
37. A diode acts as a one-way switch to current flow.
38. Diodes are used in an AC generator to convert alternating current to direct current.
39. A battery can only be charged with a direct current.
40. A transistor is a type of switch. It is used in the distributor in place of contact points. Transistors made possible the development of the computer.

Certain electronic components used in the different emission control systems help to insure more efficient power plant operation. Some of the more common units and terms are defined as follows:

A SENSOR is a device sensing a condition and relaying the information to a control device. The sensor supplies the input signals required for the operation of the computer control unit.

A MODE is a particular state of operation.

A TRANSDUCER is a device for changing one form of energy into another. A transducer may be used to change electrical energy into vacuum, hydraulic or mechanical energy.

The DIGITAL COMPUTER is an automatic electronic component used to perform calculations. The purpose is to reduce engine emissions. This is done by selecting the best air/fuel ratio of the exhaust gases entering the catalytic converter. The computer compares the data from the various sensors with the programmed calibration data stored in the (PROM) Programmable Read Only Memory. This data is a record of the engine operating standards which produce the least amount of engine emissions and the most efficient engine performance. The computer then signals to activate the different components in such a way as to bring about the best operating conditions with minimum emissions.

An AMPLIFIER is an electronic device (usually a transistor) used in a circuit to strengthen or increase the electrical input signal.

A CONTROL MODULE is similar to an integrated circuit made up of a printed circuit, including resistors, capacitors, diodes, and transistors.

4 Battery Service

This chapter discusses the purpose of the battery, how batteries are rated, how to maintain the battery and, of major importance, how to test the battery to determine if it is serviceable.

Two factors are of primary importance when evaluating battery problems. Does the battery have the capacity to satisfy the load requirements and, secondly, what is the state of charge? The battery may be in good condition internally (have the needed capacity), but unless it has the necessary charge (high specific gravity reading of the electrolyte) it will not perform in a satisfactory manner.

The state of charge is checked with a hydrometer. The maintenance free battery has a built-in indicator (hydrometer). The battery having removable cell caps is checked with a battery hydrometer which measures the specific gravity of the electrolyte. This indicates the amount of acid in the electrolyte which is available to react with plate material. This can only be checked if the electrolyte is above the top of the plates. If it is not, add water and charge the battery before testing.

The capacity of the battery is determined by placing a load on the battery and measuring the voltage. This may be referred to as the high rate discharge test.

General Description

The storage battery is considered the "heart" of the electrical and ignition system. The battery and charging system are the sources of all electric current required by the automobile and are part of every electrical circuit. The battery is the source of electricity for starting the engine, operating the electrical system when the engine is not operating, helping to control the voltage in the electrical system and providing electricity when electrical demands exceed the output of the charging system.

From this brief introduction you can readily see that the battery plays an important part in the operation of the automobile. The automobile cannot operate without a good battery. Before any electrical troubleshooting can be done effectively it must be established that the battery is in satisfactory operating condition.

The battery is a group of connected electro-chemical cells which convert chemical energy into electrical energy. When the battery is connected to current-consuming devices such as the headlights, starting motor, air conditioner, and heater, chemical reaction takes place between the chemicals on the plates of the battery cells and the electrolyte. This chemical reaction causes electrons to flow from the battery to the completed circuit and back to the battery. Electricity is the flow of electrons. Figure 4-1 shows a cutaway section of a maintenance-free battery.

FIGURE 4-1 Maintenance free battery. (Courtesy Chrysler Corporation)

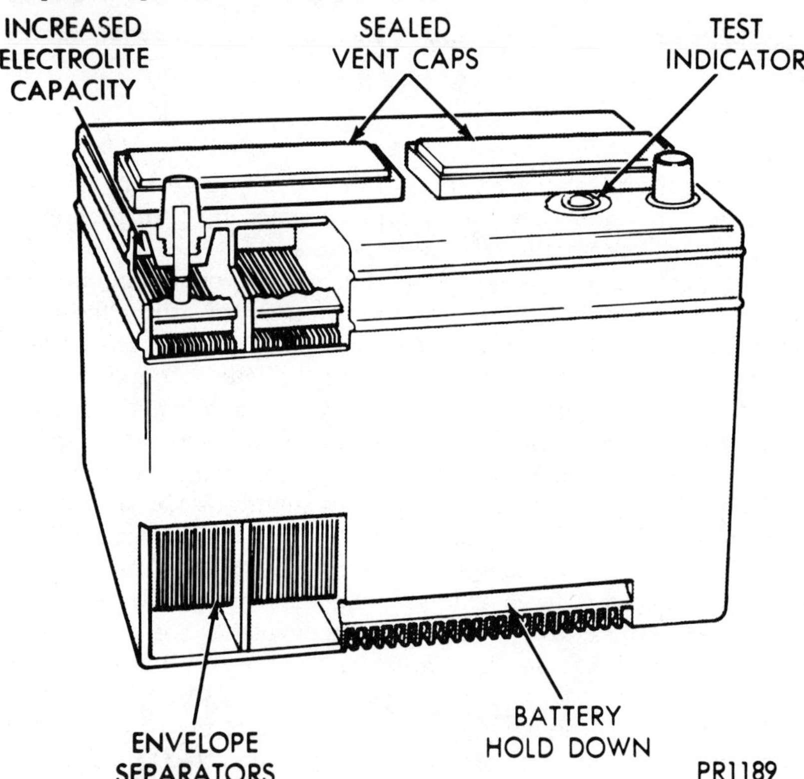

The capacity of the battery to produce current is limited. The capacity depends upon the area of plate surface in contact with the electrolyte, the number of plates in a cell, and the concentration of sulphuric acid in the electrolyte. After most of the plate surfaces have reacted with the electrolyte, the battery is discharged and will no longer be able to produce current. Before it can function properly again it must be recharged.

A battery is recharged by forcing a direct current from an outside source through the battery in the opposite direction to the current flow during discharge. This reverses the chemical reactions within the battery so the battery reverts to the original chemical contents. Recharging takes place whenever the engine is running unless there is trouble some place or an excessive load is being placed on the electrical system.

A fully charged cell will have about 2.1 volts. This is true regardless of the size of the cell or the strength of the electrolyte. When six cells are connected in series, a 12 volt battery is formed. Gasoline-powered automobiles are equipped with 12 volt batteries and electrical systems. Diesel-powered automobiles will use two 12 volt batteries for operating the starting motor. The electrical system is still a 12-volt system.

Batteries are available in various physical sizes and electrical ratings to meet the needs of the different vehicles. The physical size (dimensions) of a battery is usually expressed in terms of group numbers and letters which have been established by the Society of Automobile Engineers (SAE) and the Battery Council International (BCI). Electrical ratings are expressed in terms of volts, cold cranking power, and reserve capacity.

Batteries are sold on a warranty basis for a fixed number of months. This will vary from 12 to 48 months depending upon the capacity of the battery. If a battery proves defective within the warranty period, credit is allowed toward the purchase of a new battery.

Battery Ratings

Battery ratings are used as a means of indicating the type of service the battery should perform. The ability of the battery to crank the engine effectively for a reasonable period of time is most important. The ratings given for most batteries indicate the capability of the battery to provide a specified amperage for a given period of time and temperature without the voltage dropping below a designated point.

The ratings most commonly used are labeled as the cold cranking power or cold power rating and the reserve capacity rating. Some manufacturers may specify a peak watt rating which is a compilation of the cold cranking power and the voltage. While there may be some different ratings, the cold cranking rating and the reserve capacity ratings are accepted as the most informative to the purchaser.

Cold Crank Rating

The cold crank rating or cold power current rating is used to describe the capacity of the battery during cold weather conditions. It is determined by discharging a battery for 30 seconds at 0°F (−18°C) without the terminal voltage dropping below 7.2 volts. The number of amperes discharge then becomes the rating number.

To provide enough starting power in cold temperatures a 12-volt system will generally require one ampere for each cubic inch of engine displacement. A 200 cubic inch engine would require a battery with a cold cranking rating of at least 200 amperes. Most batteries will be rated within a range of 250 to 500 amperes.

Reserve Capacity Rating

The reserve capacity rating is a safety rating as well as a capacity rating. The rating number indicates the number of minutes the battery will supply electrical energy to operate the ignition, lights, windshield wipers, and other equipment in the event of a charging system failure. A battery with a reserve capacity of 120 minutes indicates that the vehicle will operate two hours with a charging system failure. Reserve capacity is determined by applying a 25-ampere discharge on the battery at 80°F (27°C) until the minimum terminal voltage is 10.5 volts. Most batteries will be within the 60- to 125-minute range.

Maintenance-Free Battery

Most vehicles are equipped with a maintenance-free battery. As the name implies, it is maintenance-free, having no removable cell caps, and water never needs to be added. The maintenance-free battery has more electrolyte in the cells than a regular battery. With the small amount of water that is normally used there is no need to periodically add water; therefore, the top is permanently sealed with vents located in the battery cover. A special chemical composition inside the battery reduces the production of gases to an extremely small amount during normal charging voltages.

The advantages of the sealed (maintenance-free) battery are: No addition of water needed for the life of the battery; overcharge protection against gassing. The battery will not accept too high a voltage charge; reduced self-discharge; more capacity for the size and weight than a conventional battery.

A charge indicator located in the top of the battery cover permits determining the level of the electrolyte and the state of charge. When the test indicator (a form of hydrometer) shows a green dot or any green appearance the battery is in a serviceable condition. The battery can be charged and tested. If the indicator is dark, with no green visible and there is a cranking complaint, charge the battery and make a load test to determine its condition. When the indicator shows clear or light yellow, it means the electrolyte is below the bottom of the hydrometer. This may be the result of excessive charging, a cracked case, a worn out battery or that the battery has been tipped over. Replace the battery. Do not try to jump start or charge the battery.

Older batteries and a few of the new ones have removable cell caps. This permits the addition of distilled water should the electrolyte level become low. Electrolyte must cover the top of the plates at all times. This type of battery permits the state of charge of each cell to be tested with a hydrometer.

Battery Heat Shield

An insulated plastic heat shield is used on some installations. The shield is made of polypropylene with a urethane foam insulation molded on the inside surface on the side facing the engine. The purpose of the shield is to keep the battery cooler. Outside cooling air enters the cover through an opening in the yoke, flows around the battery and exits through openings in the top and around the bottom of

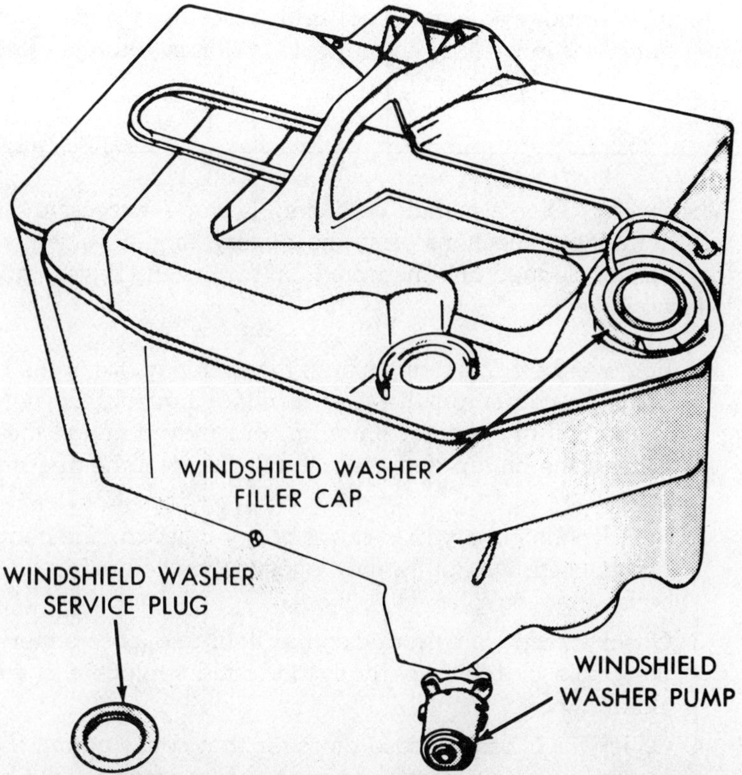

FIGURE 4-2 Battery heat shield which includes the windshield washer reservoir. (Courtesy Chrysler Corporation)

the cover. The shield must be removed when servicing the battery. The windshield washer reservoir is incorporated into the heat shield on some installations. Figure 4-2 shows a battery heat shield which incorporates the windshield washer reservoir along with the washer pump.

Common Causes of Battery Failure

A battery is not designed to last forever; however, with proper care you can generally get several years of satisfactory service. If the battery tests good but fails to perform satisfactorily, it indicates the battery is not charged. Some of the more common reasons are:

1. Accessories left on over night, lights, radio, etc.
2. Slow average driving speed for short periods of time.
3. The electrical load is greater than the generator can handle for the type of driving—generally short trips with much starting and stopping while using the air conditioner, heater, radio, defroster, and lights.
4. Defects in the charging system such as generator drive belt slippage, electrical short circuits, faulty generator and/or regulator.
5. Battery abuse, such as failure to keep terminals clean and tight. Failure to keep the top of the battery clean and dry.
6. Allowing the battery to freeze, which may crack the case and/or loosen the active material on the plates. A battery in a discharge state will freeze if the temperature drops below the freezing point.

In freezing weather do not add water to a battery unless the vehicle is to be used so the water will mix with the electrolyte.

Visual Inspection and Maintenance

Whenever problems such as corrosion, leakage, excessive dirt or suspected faulty connections exist, the battery should be removed from the vehicle, cleaned and inspected. To service the battery proceed as follows:

1. Remove the cable clamps from the battery posts or the bolts that hold the cables on the side terminal battery. Do not pry the clamps off or hammer on them; this may damage the battery. Spread the clamp and then lift off. Remove the negative cable first.
2. Remove the battery hold-down bolt or bolts and the heat shield if one is used. Do not tip the battery when removing as this may cause the electrolyte to spill out.
3. Check for dirty or corroded connections and loose battery posts. If the cable clamp is partially corroded replace the cable and clamp.
4. Check for a broken case or cover that could permit the loss of electrolyte. If a defective case or cover is found, or a broken or loose post, replace the battery.
5. Inspect the battery carrier for damage caused by acid leaks.
6. If acid damage is present clean the area with a solution of warm water and baking soda, a teaspoon of soda to a quart of water.
7. Clean the top of the battery with the same kind of solution.
8. Clean the inside surfaces of the terminal clamps with a terminal cleaning tool.
9. Clean the battery posts with a suitable tool. If a tool is not available the clamp and battery post can be cleaned with emery paper. Figure 4-3 shows the use of a battery post cleaning tool. The other end of the tool is used to clean the battery cable terminal.
10. When installing the battery in the carrier do not overtighten the hold-down bolts as it may damage the battery. About 36 in. lbs. of torque is enough when a torque wrench is used.
11. Install the heat shield if one is used.
12. Install the battery cables. If the clamp type connector is used make sure the top of the clamp is flush with the top of the post. Install the negative cable first. Tighten the bolts securely.
13. Coat all connections with a light mineral grease after tightening.
14. If the battery has removable cell caps, remove them and check the level of the electrolyte. The level should be to the bottom of each vent plug hole (cap). There usually is some type of indicator located below where the cap seats to show the correct electrolyte level when adding distilled water. It is very important that the top of the plates in each cell be kept covered with electrolyte. When necessary, add distilled water or water containing no minerals to obtain the correct electrolyte level.

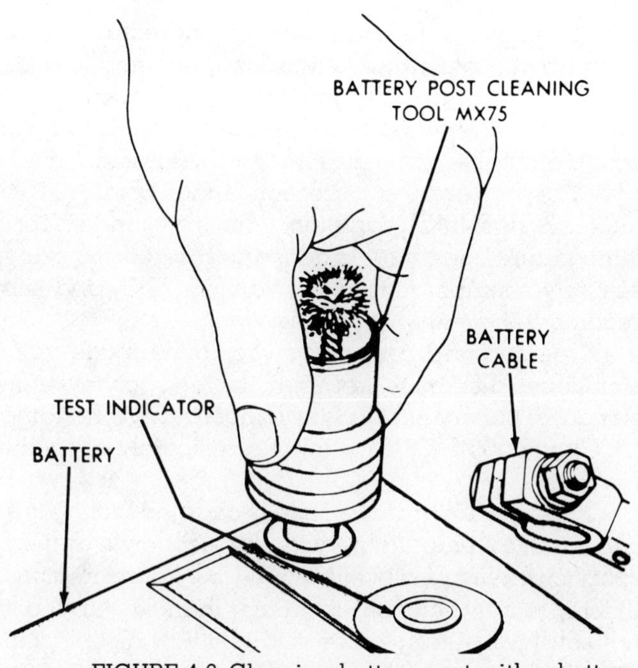

FIGURE 4-3 Cleaning battery post with a battery cleaning tool. (Courtesy Chrysler Corporation)

Battery Testing

Battery tests are made to determine the state of charge of the battery and the battery capacity. The state of charge indicates if the battery is charged and to what extent. The battery capacity (load test) is used to determine if the battery has the capacity to take care of the electrical needs of the vehicle.

State of Charge

The state of charge of a battery can be checked with a hydrometer if the battery cells have removable caps. The maintenance-free battery has an indicator (form of hydrometer) built into the battery cover.

The electrolyte in a battery contains approximately 35 percent sulphuric acid and the remainder distilled water. The amount of acid in the solution is in terms of specific gravity and measured with a hydrometer. The specific gravity changes as the battery is charged and discharged because the acid chemically combines with the plate material in the battery during discharge. While undergoing a charge the acid is driven from the plates.

When distilled water has been added to the battery to bring the electrolyte up to the correct level, the solution should be thoroughly mixed before attempting to check the state of charge. Always charge the battery before taking a hydrometer reading.

While the specific gravity reading of the electrolyte will vary according to the amount of acid in the solution, it also will vary with the battery temperature. As a result, no hydrometer reading is correct unless the temperature of the solution has been checked and a correction made. The hydrometer float is generally calibrated at 80°F

(27°C). Temperature corrections are necessary for accurate readings because the electrolyte expands (becomes less dense) when it is heated and shrinks (becomes more dense) when it is cold. Most hydrometers will have a built-in thermometer along with a scale to indicate the number of points to add or subtract for correct readings.

The temperature correction is four points (0.004) specific gravity for each 10°F (6°C) variation from the standard of 80°F (27°C). The temperature correction is added to the specific gravity reading if the electrolyte temperature is above 80°F (27°C) and subtracted from the reading if the temperature is lower.

Temperature corrections should be made whenever there is a significant difference between the electrolyte temperature and the standard battery electrolyte temperatures. Readings between 60°F (16°C) and 100°F (38°C) will not significantly affect the specific gravity reading.

The specific gravity of a fully charged battery is from 1.260 to 1.280 corrected for temperature with the electrolyte at the proper level. The specific gravity of all cells should be approximately the same. If the difference between cells is greater than 50 (0.050) points the battery is not satisfactory for service and should be replaced. Figure 4-4 is a drawing of a hydrometer used to check the specific gravity (state of charge) of a battery. The right hand drawing illustrates how the reading is taken at the electrolyte level.

After prolonged charging, if the specific gravity of all cells is not at least 1.230 the battery is not in good condition and may not provide satisfactory service. When the specific gravity is less than 1.225 the battery should be recharged. The following chart shows the capacity of a battery as it relates to the state of charge.

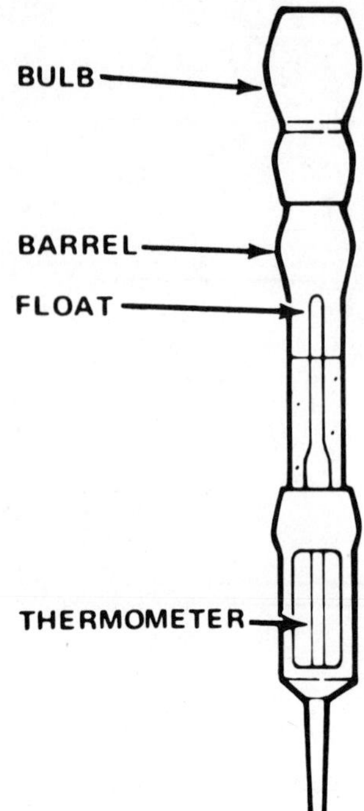

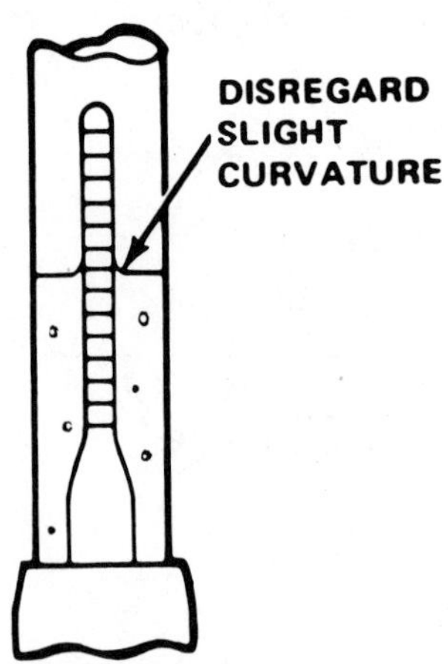

FIGURE 4-4 Hydrometer. (Courtesy American Motors Corporation)

STATE OF CHARGE AND BATTERY CAPACITIES	
Fully Charged	1.260 - 1.280
75% Charged	1.225 - 1.235
50% Charged	1.190 - 1.200
25% Charged	1.155 - 1.165
Discharged	1.125 and under

The hydrometer consists of a glass tube with a flexible bulb at the top and a short hose at the bottom. A glass float is located inside the glass tube, calibrated to read in specific gravity. A thermometer is usually incorporated in the lower end of the hydrometer so the electrolyte will flow past the thermometer when drawn up into the tube.

Electrolyte is drawn into the tube by the hydrometer and the float can be seen and read as it floats in the solution. The height of the float in the electrolyte indicates the density (weight) of the electrolyte as compared to water. This indicates the specific gravity. The float rides high in the liquid if the specific gravity is high and the float is low if the specific gravity is low. The readings are made on the float at the surface of the liquid.

A discharged battery should not be allowed to remain in freezing temperatures because it may freeze and crack the case and/or loosen the material on the plates. Following is a chart that shows battery freezing temperatures:

SPECIFIC GRAVITY	FREEZING TEMPERATURE	
1.280	−90°F	−68°C
1.250	−62°F	−52°C
1.200	−16°F	−27°C
1.150	5°F	−15°C
1.100	19°F	− 7°C
1.050	27°F	− 3°C

Battery Capacity

Three different methods may be used to check battery capacity or ability to crank the engine. The best method is to use a battery-starter tester. This tester consists of an ammeter, voltmeter, and a variable carbon pile resistor. The ammeter is in series with the variable resistance unit. This permits adjusting and measuring the load placed on the battery. Automobile manufacturers recommend this method of testing and usually specify the load that should be used for testing purposes.

When checking the battery capacity with a battery-starter tester be sure the control knob on the tester is turned off before connecting the tester to the battery. If the battery has side terminals, an adapter should be installed before making the test so as to insure good connections. Connect the test leads to the battery posts or adapter: Positive lead to the positive battery post and negative to negative. The voltmeter lead clips should be connected to the battery posts, not the tester clips. Apply approximately a 225 ampere load for 15 seconds to remove the surface charge. This is done by turning the control knob and watching the ammeter. Remove the load and wait at least 15 seconds before applying a test load for 15 seconds. Without specifications, a test load of approximately 200 amperes should give an accurate test reading. Do not load the battery for more than 15 seconds at any time. For batteries which are rated in terms of ampere-hours (most present batteries do not have this rating) the correct load is three times the ampere-hour rating. If the battery voltage does not drop below the minimum listed according to battery temperature, the battery is good and can be returned to service. At normal temperature (70°F to 80°F) the battery voltage should be 9.6 volts or more. Figure 4-5 shows the hook-up for making a battery capacity test by placing a controlled load on the battery.

Following are listed the minimum acceptable voltages for good service according to battery temperature:

VOLTAGE	TEMPERATURE	
9.6	70°F	21°C
9.4	50°F	10°C
9.1	30°F	0°C
8.8	15°F	−10°C
8.5	0°F	− 0°C
8.0	0°F	Below

If the voltage is less than what is shown on the chart the battery is

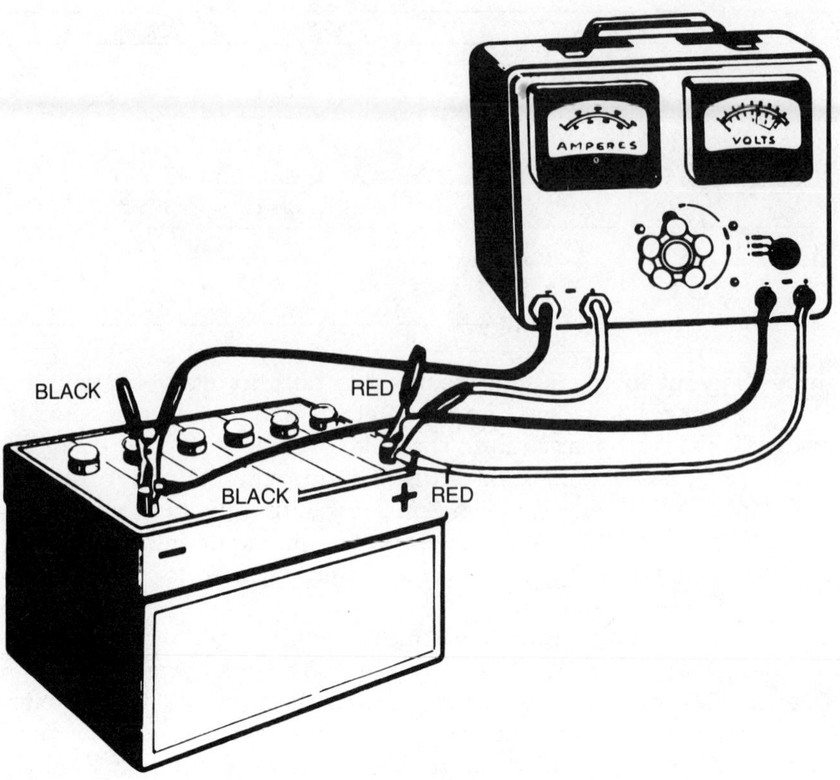

FIGURE 4-5 Making a load (high rate discharge) battery test. (Courtesy Chrysler Corporation)

discharged or defective. If the battery is discharged it should be recharged and then retested.

With a maintenance-free battery, if the indicator shows green an adequate charge exists. If no green is present and the indicator shows black, charging is required. If a clear or light yellow shows, do not attempt to charge, replace the battery.

On the battery with removable cell caps check the specific gravity of each cell. If there is a difference between any two cells of more than 50 points the battery is not satisfactory for service and should be replaced. If the specific gravity is 1.225 or lower, charge the battery and make another capacity test.

A second type of load test is sometimes used in conjunction with a fast battery charger. Some fast chargers have a fixed resistance unit built into the charger. The resistance generally is in the 150 to 225 ampere range. At no time should the load (resistance) be placed on the battery for more than 15 seconds. Many of these chargers will have a scale calibrated to show good (green), fair (yellow) and poor (red) to indicate battery condition. If a voltmeter is used, a serviceable battery should read at least 9.6 volts or better. As with all chargers the positive lead from the charger is connected to the positive battery terminal. Always clean the battery and terminals before making the test.

While the above test is not as accurate or as meaningful as the test using a battery-starter tester it does give a fair indication of the condition of the battery. Before condemning a battery it should be given a good charge and then rechecked. If the battery will not take a charge in a reasonable length of time it should be taken out of service. If the battery will not hold a charge overnight it is not serviceable.

It is possible to obtain an indication of the serviceability of the battery with a minimum of tools and equipment. Inspect the battery for cracks, loose posts and electrolyte level. Check for corroded, loose or dirty terminals. Clean and tighten before making any type of test.

Position the vehicle so the headlights will shine on a wall or reflective surface. Turn on the headlights and crank the engine. Assuming the starting motor has been functioning satisfactorily, the starting motor should crank the engine at a normal speed and the headlights should remain bright. If the lights dim and the starting motor falters or cannot crank the engine, it indicates a poor connection between the battery and starting motor, a weak or damaged battery or a defective starting motor. Check the state of charge and charge the battery if the specific gravity is low or the green dot does not show. If the same condition exists after checking the connections and starting motor amperage draw, replace the battery.

If a voltmeter is available, turn on all the lights, heater and other electrical equipment and crank the engine. Have someone measure the voltage across the battery posts. It may be necessary to disconnect and ground the coil to distributor cable to prevent the engine from starting while making the test. The voltmeter should read 9.6 volts or more. Check the state of charge and charge the battery if the specific gravity is low or the green dot does not show. Repeat the test. If the battery still does not function properly it should be replaced. What is taking place is that the lights and starting motor are acting as a load when checking battery capacity. Open voltage, no load on the battery, means very little. The battery can have an open voltage reading of 12.6 volts but still not function under load. However, if the open voltage is less than 12.6 volts it will not operate under load and probably it will not hold a charge.

Battery Charging

Always clean the outside of the battery before charging. Before charging the battery with removable cell caps, check the level of the electrolyte. If necessary add distilled or mineral-free water to bring the solution up to the indicator ring beneath the fill holes.

Many different types of battery chargers are available, and any of them can be used to charge the battery. Most commercial establishments use a fast charger which starts at a high amperage (30 amperes) and drops off to about 10 amperes after approximately one hour. The lower the charging rate the longer it will take to bring the battery up to full charge. Regardless of the type of charger used, if the battery feels hot or if violent gassing or spewing of electrolyte occurs, reduce the charging rate. To bring a battery to full charge, if a fast rate charger is used, it should be followed by at least 15 minutes of slow charge at 10 amperes or less.

When the battery requires charging (this applies to both types of batteries), charge the battery for about 20 minutes and make a capacity test. If the battery fails, charge again for 20 minutes and test again. If it fails to test up the second time, replace the battery. Always replace the battery with one of the same type to meet manufacturer's specifications for load requirements. If the battery passes the load test continue to charge until the battery is fully charged with the specific gravity at

1.260 to 1.280. In the case of the maintenance-free battery, charge only until the green dot appears.

The charging procedure may vary with different chargers. However, the leads from the charger are always connected to the battery with positive lead to positive battery terminal and negative to negative.

Most chargers automatically lower the rate of charge as the specific gravity reading becomes higher. When charging a battery with a charger that does not automatically cut back, as soon as the battery begins to gas excessively and/or electrolyte spews out, reduce the charging rate.

A battery that has been in a discharged state for a period of time will be slow in accepting a charge. A battery that is cold, below 40°F, should be allowed to warm up for three or four hours before charging.

When charging a maintenance-free battery and the green dot fails to appear after a reasonable period of time, 20 to 30 minutes with a fast charger or six to eight hours with a slow charge (5 to 10 amperes) it may be necessary to tip or shake the battery to make the green dot appear.

Assist (Jump) Starting With Auxiliary (Booster) Battery

If the battery in the vehicle will not crank the engine to enable the engine to start, it is possible to use the battery from another vehicle to assist in cranking the engine without removing the battery from either vehicle. Both batteries must be of the same voltage, normally 12 volts. Do not tow or push a vehicle to start. Damage to the emission system and/or to other parts of the vehicle may result.

Both the booster battery, the one in the vehicle being used to start the car with the discharged battery, and the discharged battery must be handled carefully when using booster cables. Booster cables are heavy insulated electrical cables with heavy clips on both ends. Always use caution when working around and/or handling batteries to prevent serious personal injuries, particularly to the eyes or property damage from such things as battery explosion, battery acid or electrical burns. Short circuiting any battery while it is connected to the automobile electrical system can damage the electrical components.

Hydrogen gas is produced by a battery, particularly while being charged. A flame or spark near a battery may cause the gas to ignite resulting in an explosion.

Battery electrolyte is an acid and spilling should be avoided. Any spilled electrolyte should be flushed with large quantities of water. When working around the vehicle be careful that metal tools or jumper cables do not contact the positive battery terminal and metal parts of the vehicle as a short circuit could result. This could cause a severe arcing (flash) which may damage the cable clip, tools or metal making contact. Severe burns could result.

To use a booster battery proceed as follows:

1. Set the parking brake and place the automatic transmission in "park" (neutral for manual transmission) on both vehicles. Do not let the two vehicles involved touch each other as this could cause a ground connection.

2. Turn off the lights, air conditioning or heater, radio and all other electrical loads on both vehicles.
3. Attach one end of the positive jumper cable to the positive terminal of the booster battery and the other end to the positive terminal of the discharged battery.
4. Attach one end of the negative jumper cable to the negative terminal of the booster battery and the other to a solid engine ground on the vehicle to be started. A generator mounting bracket, an air conditioner compressor mounting bracket or a head bolt should provide a good ground if it is not covered with a thick coat of paint or dirt. DO NOT connect directly to the negative terminal of the battery needing a boost.
5. Start the engine of the vehicle that is providing the jump start (boost).
6. Start the engine of the vehicle with the discharged battery.
7. Disconnect the jumper cables. The negative cable must be removed first from the engine that was jump started.

5 Starting System

In order to start an automobile engine the engine crankshaft must be turned over (cranked) to set the various operating units in motion. An electric starting motor which may also be called a cranking motor or starter is used for this purpose. The starting motor is an electric motor specifically designed for cranking an internal combustion engine at speeds which will result in the engine starting.

The starting motor, while operating on the same principle as any other electric motor, has certain features which make it different from the electric motor used to drive the various pieces of equipment found in the home or factory.

Electricity is supplied to operate the starting motor by a 12-volt storage battery. The starting motor is connected to the engine flywheel through a reduction drive gear arrangement. The operator of the vehicle must be able to engage the starting motor whenever it is necessary to start the engine. The starting motor must be disengaged from the flywheel ring gear as soon as the engine starts.

Because it takes a lot of electrical energy to crank an engine, a gear reduction (ratio) must be used between the starting motor drive gear and the engine flywheel ring gear. By turning the starting motor at about 1,800 RPBs the engine will be cranked at approximately 150 to 180 RPMs depending upon the gear ratio. A ratio of 12 to 15 to 1 is typical.

Because of the heavy load placed on the battery during the starting process, electrical resistance plays a very important part in the entire battery-starter circuit.

The typical automobile starting system includes the battery, starting motor, drive mechanism, remote starter switch, a neutral switch, cables to connect the motor and switch to the battery, and a ground return system. Figure 5-1 is a schematic drawing of a typical starting motor system.

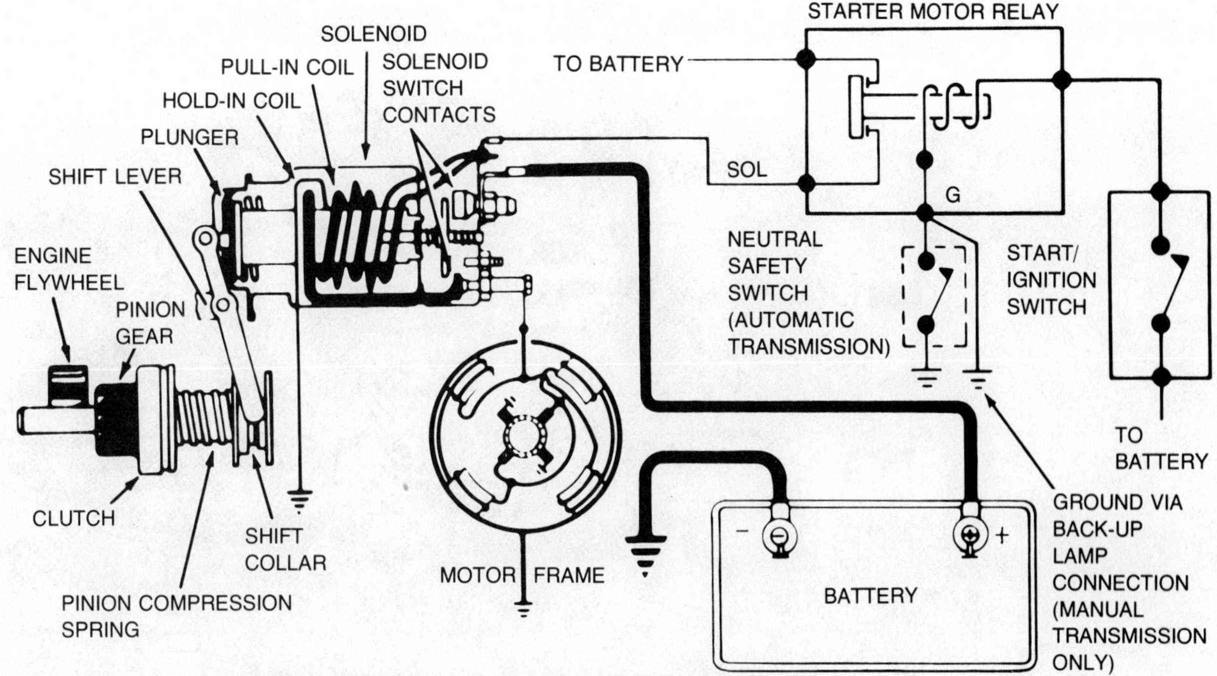

FIGURE 5-1 Starting motor system. (Courtesy American Motors Corporation)

When the starter control switch (turning ignition key) is closed the solenoid is energized, shifting the starting motor pinion into mesh with the flywheel ring gear. The main contacts of the solenoid are closed and battery current is delivered to the starting motor. The starting motor now cranks the engine. When the starter switch is released current stops flowing. The drive pinion disengages from the ring gear and the starting motor no longer operates.

All starting motors used on automobiles are similar in construction and operation although they may vary somewhat in size and shape. The solenoid may be mounted in a different manner but the function it performs is the same for all. In place of a solenoid, on some installations a relay may be used along with a movable starter pole shoe to engage the drive pinion.

Starting Motor Construction

The starting motor assembly is made up of field coils placed over pole pieces which are attached to the inside of the frame (housing). An armature is mounted on bushings in the commutator end frame and the drive gear housing. The armature assembly consists of a stack of iron laminations mounted on a shaft, a commutator assembly and the armature windings. The windings are heavy copper ribbons assembled into slots in the iron laminations. The ends of the windings are soldered to the commutator bars which are electrically insulated from each other and from the iron shaft. Copper brushes are mounted on the field frame or end frame and ride on the commutator bars. Spring tension keeps the brushes in contact with the commutator.

Figure 5-2 is a cutaway view of a typical starting motor with the solenoid enclosed in the starting motor frame (housing).

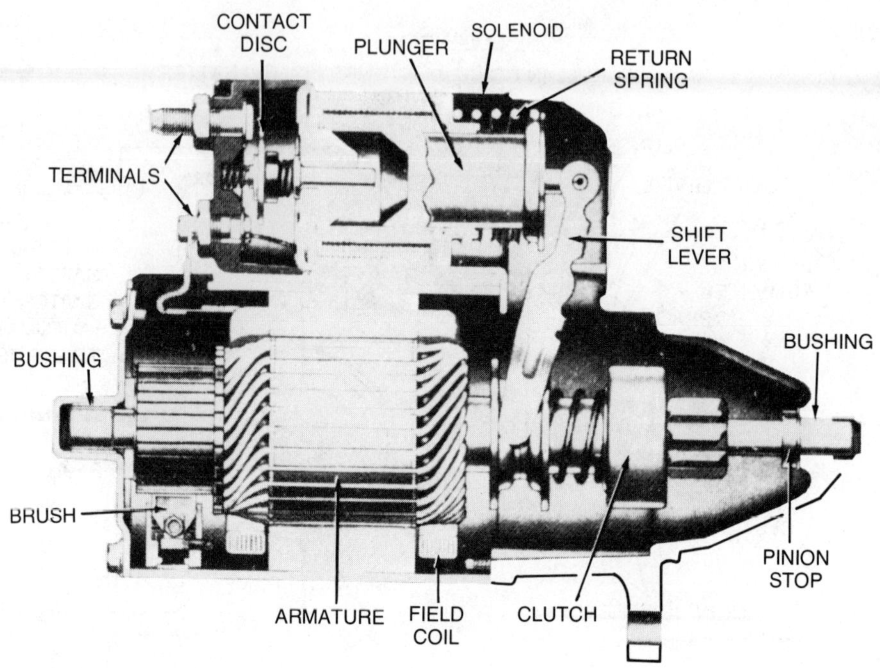

FIGURE 5-2 Integral frame starting motor. (Courtesy Oldsmobile Division, General Motors Corp.)

Drive Mechanism

The drive mechanism is mounted on the armature shaft, generally opposite the commutator. Some starting motors use a reduction gear set. With this type of construction the drive assembly is mounted on a separate shaft. The drive mechanism, sometimes called an overrunning clutch assembly, clutch drive or starter pinion assembly, is engaged with the flywheel ring gear before the engine is cranked. It retracts from the flywheel ring gear when the engine starts.

The drive mechanism is constructed in such a manner that the drive pinion will be locked to the shaft when the starting motor is cranking the engine but will turn freely in the opposite direction when the engine starts. In other words, the engine cannot drive the starting motor.

Starter Solenoid

The drive mechanism is engaged and disengaged by the solenoid or relay. The solenoid which is mounted on the starter frame performs two functions. (1) It provides a low resistance circuit to carry heavy current flow between the battery and starting motor, and (2) it also moves the drive pinion on the starting motor shaft into mesh with the engine flywheel ring gear before the engine is cranked.

The solenoid is made up of two windings, a hold-in coil and a pull-in coil. The magnetism created by the two windings attracts the solenoid plunger into the coil. This movement through a lever arrangement shifts the pinion into mesh with the ring gear and moves the contact disc which closes the circuit between the starter and the battery. When the drive mechanism is shifted into mesh, the pull-in coil is shorted and no current will flow through the coil. The hold-in coil keeps the drive engaged resulting in less current draw than when both coils are energized.

Starter Relay

Another type of starting system utilizes a simple relay in place of a solenoid to connect the battery to the starting motor. With this type of arrangement, a movable pole shoe is used to move the starter drive pinion into engagement with the flywheel ring gear. When the starting motor is not in use, one of the field coils is connected directly to ground through a set of contact points. When the starter is first connected to the battery, a heavy current flows through the grounded field coil, actuating the movable pole shoe located inside the field coil. The pole shoe is attached to the starter drive lever. When the pole shoe is moved, the lever forces the starter pinion into engagement with the flywheel ring gear. When the movable pole shoe is fully seated, it opens the field coil grounding contacts and the starter will operate in a normal manner. A holding coil keeps the pole shoe in the fully seated position while the engine is being cranked. When the current flow stops (starter switch released), a spring retracts the drive pinion from the ring gear.

Starting Motor Operation

The starting motor operates on the principle of magnetic attraction and repulsion. When an electric current flows through the armature windings a magnetic field is created around the coils of wire. At the same time current is flowing through the field coils. This results in magnetic lines of force (magnetic field) traveling from the north pole of the field coil shoe through the armature core on the armature shaft to the opposite south pole of the field coil shoe. The basic motor shown in Figure 5-3, for illustration purposes, shows a loop of wire between pole pieces

FIGURE 5-3 Basic starting motor (illustration purposes). (Courtesy Chevrolet Motor Division, General Motors Corp.)

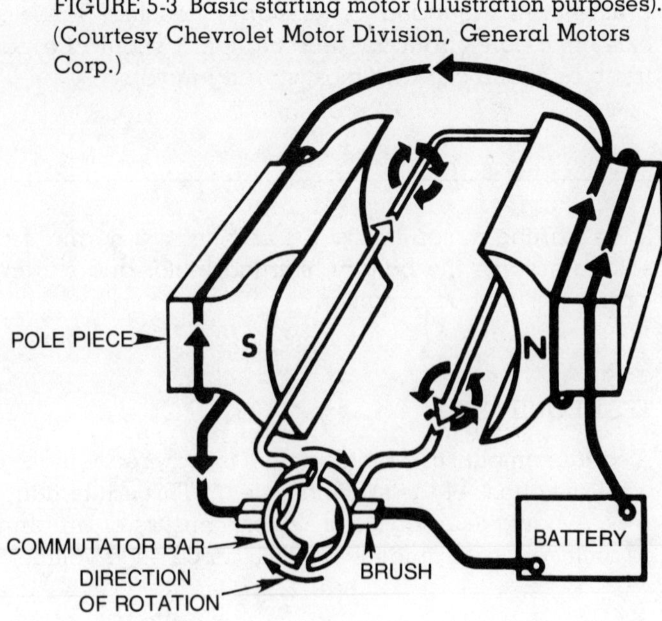

connected to two separate commutator bars. Riding on the commutator bars are two brushes connected to the battery and windings around the pole pieces.

The magnetic field around the armature coils has the same polarity as the lines of force created in the field coils. This causes the coils of the armature to be repelled (like magnetic poles repel one another). Because the armature is mounted on a shaft, it can rotate, and as soon as each armature coil has moved out of the magnetic field set up by the field coil windings it approaches a magnetic field of opposite polarity. The location of the starter motor brushes on the commutator is such that the flow of current is reversed, reversing the magnetic field polarity of the armature. This constant reversal of current flow in the armature coils causes the armature to continually revolve.

In order for the starting motor to function, the armature must be supported on bushings so that it can revolve freely in the housing without excessive free play. The clearance between the armature and field shoes must be kept to a minimum in order to obtain maximum effectiveness of the magnetic lines of force. The armature laminations, however, cannot make contact with the field shoes because any contact between them will short out the starting motor.

The commutator is insulated from the armature laminations and shaft. The armature windings are insulated from one another and the armature slots. Each coil is soldered to a commutator bar with each bar insulated from one another and the armature assembly. The commutator must be smooth and free from foreign matter so a good electrical connection can be maintained between the commutator and brushes.

The field coil windings are insulated from one another and from the housing. One end of each coil is attached to an insulated brush. The other ends of the field coils are connected to a common battery terminal.

Most starting motors have four brushes mounted on the brush holder or housing. The brushes are spring loaded (have spring tension) which keeps them in solid contact with the commutator bars. Two brushes are insulated and attached to the field coils. The other two brushes are grounded to the starter housing. These conditions must exist; therefore, from this information it should be possible to locate troubles which occur in most starting motors.

Starting System Service

If the starting motor cranks the engine at a normal rate of speed it is safe to assume the battery, starting motor and starting motor wiring circuit are in good condition.

TEST EQUIPMENT

A certain amount of test equipment is required to make a complete and accurate check of the starting system. This equipment is as follows:

A battery-starter tester which consists of an ammeter having a capacity of approximately 0 to 600 amperes, a voltmeter of 0 to 40 volt capacity and a variable resistor unit. This type of test equipment is essential in order to accurately check the amperage draw of the starting motor. This is the same type of test equipment used to check battery capacity.

A test lamp to check for continuity and ground in the various circuits is necessary. An ohmmeter can be used for checking continuity, in place of a test lamp.

A heavy cable, such as a booster cable, is needed when connecting directly between the battery and starting motor.

A jumper wire, 14 gauge wire with clips on either end, four or five feet long is useful.

A voltmeter with a low range scale (0 to 5 volts in tenths) is essential for checking voltage drop (resistance) in a circuit.

When repairing or testing an armature, an armature growler is necessary. This is used to check for internal shorts in the armature.

OVERALL INSPECTION OF SYSTEM

Locating troubles in the starting system includes making sure an adequate source of electricity is available (charged battery) and all terminals and cables leading from the battery are in satisfactory condition, clean and tight. There must be a complete circuit from the starter switch section of the ignition switch through the neutral switch to the solenoid relay. The solenoid (relay) must move the drive mechanism into engagement with the engine flywheel ring gear and then connect the battery to the starting motor. The drive mechanism must disengage as soon as the engine starts.

To operate satisfactorily, the amperage draw of the starting motor must be within specified limits. If the engine can turn over freely (no excessive friction), a higher than normal amperage draw indicates problems within the starting motor. Normal starting motor draw (engine turns over freely) should be within a 180 to 200 amperage range.

TROUBLESHOOTING STARTING MOTOR SYSTEM

Normally, a starting motor system gives very little trouble. When problems do occur most of them are due to battery and battery connection malfunctions. Before any units are removed from the starting circuit for repair, a number of checks should be made to isolate the problem. Generally starting system troubles fall within the following categories:

1. Starting motor fails to operate; nothing happens when the switch is turned to the "start" position.
2. Starting motor engages but will not crank the engine.
3. Starting motor cranks the engine slowly.
4. Solenoid clicks but the engine is not cranked.
5. Starting motor spins but does not crank the engine.
6. Starting motor is noisy.

CHECK BATTERY AND CIRCUIT

As the battery is the source of electricity the first place to check when trouble arises in the starting motor system is the battery. This applies in all cases of starting system malfunctions other than the starting motor spinning without cranking the engine, or a noisy starter.

1. Make a visual inspection of the battery case for cracks and leaks. Check for loose, dirty, corroded or eroded battery terminals, broken and/or loose cables at terminals other than battery posts. Check the battery carrier and hold down clamps for looseness or damage.
2. Check the condition and charge of the battery. If the battery has a built-in hydrometer check to see if the green dot is visible. If the dot is visible the battery is charged. If the indicator is dark the battery needs to be charged. If the indicator is light yellow or bright, replace the battery. A load (capacity) test should be made to give a complete indication of the battery condition. This requires a battery-starter tester. If there is a question about the battery, replace it or use a booster battery which is known to be satisfactory. If the starting motor cranks the engine satisfactorily with a different battery the existing battery is at fault.
3. If the solenoid clicks but the engine does not turn over, it indicates the starting circuit is complete; electricity is flowing through the circuit and solenoid. This could indicate a discharged battery, poor connections or a malfunction in the starting motor. A locked engine can also result in the solenoid clicking and not turning over the engine. If there is a question about connections, make a voltage drop test. A resistance reading of over 0.02 for each connection indicates a high resistance and the connections should be removed, cleaned and tightened.
4. With a good battery, battery cables with clean and tight terminals, if there is no response when the starter switch is turned to start position it indicates an open circuit. It will generally be a problem with the neutral switch. Some type of neutral switch is used to prevent completing the starting motor circuit unless the automatic transmission is in neutral or park. On many installations with a manual transmission the clutch pedal must be depressed before the starting motor will operate. If the neutral switch is bypassed and the starting motor now operates, the problem is in the neutral switch. The switch may be out of adjustment so the shift lever will not activate the switch properly. Try moving the shift quadrant through the different ranges. If the starting motor operates in any range it means the switch must be adjusted. If there is no response the switch circuit is probably open.
5. If the battery, battery cables and neutral switch check out satisfactorily, bypass the control circuit by connecting a jumper wire directly from the positive battery terminal to the control terminal on the starter solenoid. This is the small terminal on the solenoid. If the starting motor now operates the problem is in the control circuit. Figure 5-4 shows how to test for open field coils, grounded field coils and the solenoid windings. Another method of checking, if a voltmeter having a 0 to 16 volt range is available, is to disconnect the control wire at the solenoid and connect the negative lead of the voltmeter to a good ground. Connect the positive

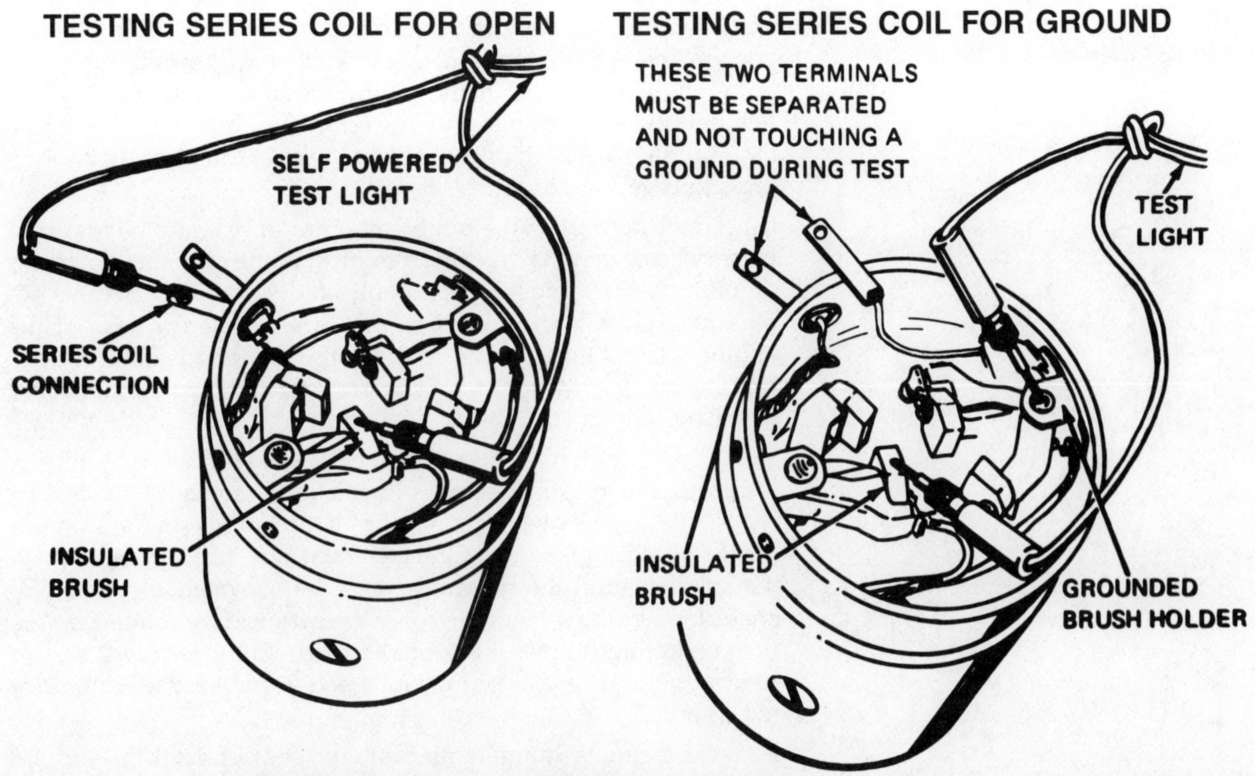

TESTING SERIES COIL FOR OPEN

SELF POWERED TEST LIGHT

SERIES COIL CONNECTION

INSULATED BRUSH

TESTING SERIES COIL FOR GROUND

THESE TWO TERMINALS MUST BE SEPARATED AND NOT TOUCHING A GROUND DURING TEST

TEST LIGHT

INSULATED BRUSH

GROUNDED BRUSH HOLDER

FIGURE 5-4 Testing the disassembled starting motor. (Courtesy Chevrolet Motor Division, General Motors Corp.)

voltmeter lead to the wire which was disconnected from the solenoid. Turn the ignition switch to the start position. If the voltmeter reads battery voltage, the circuit is satisfactory; if not, an open circuit exists in the control circuit which includes the starter switch, the wire leading to the solenoid or the neutral switch is not functioning. A test lamp can be substituted for a voltmeter to determine if there is a complete circuit. Trace the circuit to find where it is open. A jumper wire can be used to bypass the neutral switch. A voltmeter or a test lamp connected to the wire or terminal of the ignition-start switch can be used to determine if current is flowing through the switch when it is turned to the start position.

6. If current is present to the solenoid control terminal but there is no response from the solenoid, check the starting motor. Bypass the solenoid by connecting a heavy cable such as a booster cable to the positive battery terminal. Touch the other end of the cable to the starter terminal at the solenoid. If the starting motor now operates, the problem is in the solenoid.

Testing Starting Motor on Vehicle—Starter Cranks Slowly

1. Check the state of charge and capacity of the battery or substitute a known good battery. Using battery jumper cables (booster) from a vehicle with a good battery is another means of checking to see if the trouble is with the battery or starting motor.
2. If the starter cranks normally with a good battery, replace or recharge the battery. If the starter motor still does not crank the

engine normally, remove, clean and tighten the cable connections at the battery terminals, solenoid, and ground on the engine. High resistance in the supply circuit or connections can result in the starting motor cranking the engine at a slower rate than normal. These connections can be checked for resistance by making a voltage drop test.

3. If this does not correct the trouble, the starter needs to be removed for service or there is an excessive drag in the engine. Too heavy an oil in the crankcase in extremely cold weather will cause engine friction. A hydrostatic lock can cause a heavy drag or the engine will not turn over. A hydrostatic lock is caused by coolant leaking into the cylinders. To check, remove the spark plugs and crank the engine. If coolant has leaked into the cylinders it will blow out through the spark plug holes as the engine is cranked.
4. If the starting motor does not crank but the solenoid chatters or clicks, check the battery and wiring. If the battery and wiring are good, the starter is faulty. On rare occasions, trouble might be in the solenoid and the assembly must be replaced as a unit. To check for a faulty solenoid, bypass the solenoid by connecting the battery terminal on the solenoid to the starter terminal with a heavy cable. If the starter functions in a normal manner, replace the solenoid.
5. If the starter spins (humming noise) but does not crank the engine, the starter drive mechanism is at fault. The starting motor must be removed.
6. Sometimes the starting motor may become noisy and there will be a high-pitched whine during cranking before the engine fires. This may be due to excessive clearance between the starting motor drive pinion and the flywheel ring gear. A high-pitched whine after the engine fires as the key is released may be the result of too little distance between the drive pinion and flywheel ring gear. A loud whoop after the engine fires and a sound like a siren if the engine speeds up and the drive does not disengage immediately can be the result of a defective clutch in the pinion. A rumble or growl as the starter motor is coasting down after starting can be the result of a bent armature shaft. Shims are available for some starting motors to permit shifting the housing in or out to change the mesh of the pinion with the ring gear. Removing the lower flywheel housing will generally permit seeing how the starting motor drive pinion meshes and if there is a bent shaft. The end clearance between the end housing and the drive pinion must be within certain limits or the shift yoke may rub against the clutch collar during cranking. This should be measured against specifications if the starting motor has been disassembled or the solenoid removed. Worn parts or improper installation may cause this condition. There is no adjustment.

Amperage Draw Test

It is a simple matter to check the amperage draw of the starting motor with a battery-starter tester. This will clearly indicate the condition of the starting motor. The engine should be at normal operating temperature. Excessive friction such as a tight engine or heavy oil will increase

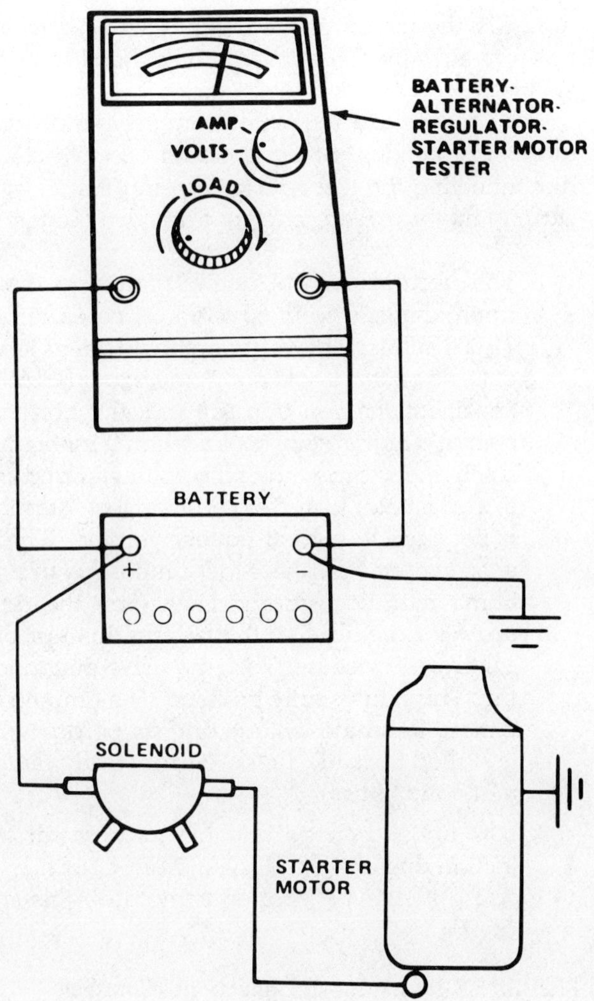

FIGURE 5-5 Starting motor amperage draw test. (Courtesy American Motors Corporation)

amperage draw. Connect the tester according to manufacturer's instructions, making sure the variable resistor control knob on the tester is in the off or zero position. Crank the engine long enough to read the cranking voltage and note. Do not crank for more than 30 seconds. Without cranking the engine, turn the variable resistor control knob on the tester until the voltmeter reads the cranking voltage previously noted. Read the equivalent starter amperage draw on the ammeter and refer to the manufacturer's specifications for current draw limits. If specifications are not available, most systems should draw from 180 to 200 amperes. Figure 5-5 is a schematic drawing of a test hook-up for making an amperage draw test. The tester consists of an ammeter-voltmeter with a variable resistance unit attached to the battery terminals.

Starting Motor No-Load Test—Starter Removed

If a tester is available it is well to make a no-load test after the starting motor has been removed and before disassembly. This will indicate where the troubles may be and what to look for after disassembly.

Before testing, the armature should be checked for freedom to turn. Pry the pinion around with a screw driver. If the armature does not rotate freely the starter should be disassembled without further testing.

To test, make the tester connections according to the manufacturer's instructions. Be sure to shut off the tester before connecting or disconnecting the test cables. Closing the tester switch will cause the starting motor armature to revolve. Use the test results as follows:

1. The normal current draw, including the solenoid, should be approximately from 50 to 95 amperes at approximately 5,700 to 11,000 RPMs. The voltage should be at least 10.6 volts. An indicator is necessary to count the exact RPMs. However, from these specifications you can see that the normal starting motor must spin at a high rate of speed when it is not under load. Figure 5-6 is a schematic drawing of the voltmeter and ammeter hooked to the starting motor to make a no-load test. Normally the resistance unit is not used to control battery voltage. Check the manufacturer's specifications for the exact amperage draw, voltage and RPMs. Some manufacturers may include the amperage and voltage draw for a stall test. To perform this test place the starter motor solidly in a vise and lock the drive pinion to prevent it from turning. This can usually be done by clamping vise grip pliers on the pinion. Read the voltage and amperage when the starting motor is stalled (locked). Rated current and voltage draw indicate normal conditions.
2. Low no-load speed and high current draw indicates too much friction due to tight, dirty or worn bearings. A bent shaft will also cause friction. A shorted armature—this should be checked out

FIGURE 5-6 No-load test connections (Courtesy American Motors Corporation)

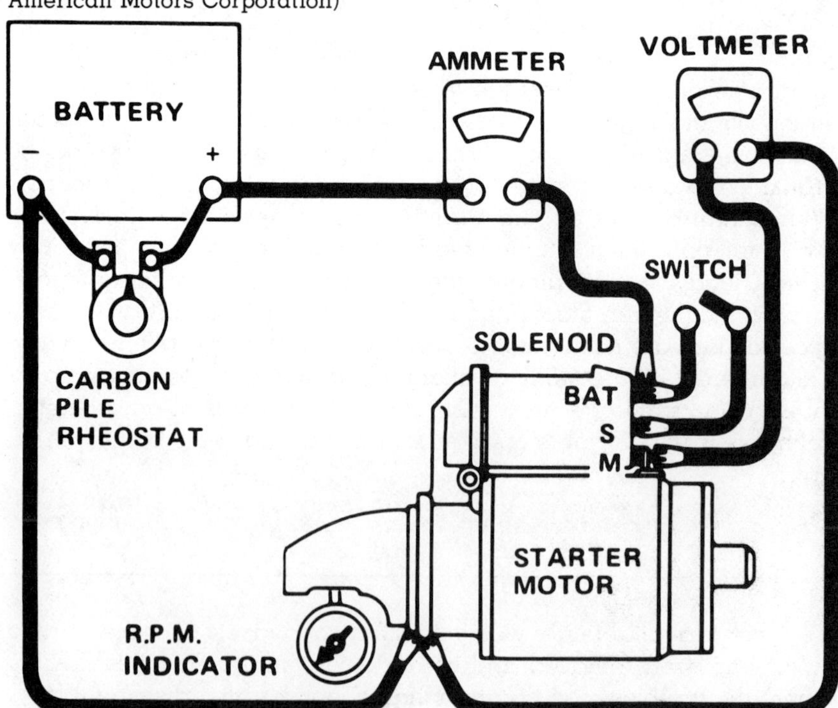

on a growler if suspected. A check for a grounded armature or field coils should be made with a test light.

3. Failure to operate with a high current draw indicates a ground in the terminal or field coils—check with a test lamp or ohmmeter.
4. Failure to operate with no current draw indicates an open field. This can be checked with a test lamp. Check for open armature coils with a test light. Inspect the commutator for badly burned bars. Inspect for broken brush springs, worn brushes and/or high insulation between the commutator bars. This would result in a poor electrical connection. The commutator must be smooth and free from foreign matter in order to maintain a good electrical connection between the commutator and brushes.
5. Low no-load speed and low current draw indicates a high resistance due to poor or defective connections, dirty commutator or open circuits internally.
6. High free speed and high current draw indicates shorted field coils. There also could be a short in the armature windings, this can be checked with a growler.

The disassembly of the starting motor is generally obvious, as is the removal of the unit from the engine.

6 Charging System

The purpose of the charging system is to keep the battery charged and maintain a supply of electricity to meet the operating needs of the vehicle.

The charging system consists of a generator (alternator), battery, charge indicator, regulator, and the necessary wiring. Many late model vehicles are equipped with an integral type charging system which has the regulator unit built into the generator. Regardless of whether or not a separate unit is used or the regulator is encased in the generator housing the function is the same. The generator produces electricity and the regulator limits the charging rate to prevent over charging the battery and/or damaging the generator. Figure 6-1 is a schematic of a typical charging system using a separate electronic regulator and warning indicator lamp.

The generator, sometimes called an alternator, produces alternating current which is converted into direct current by diodes located within the unit. A direct current must be used to charge the battery. The generator is driven through a belt and pulley arrangement by the engine crankshaft. A charge indicator in the form of a warning light or a meter that indicates charge or discharge is incorporated in all installations. When the warning light glows red it indicates the generator is not charging. The charge meter indicates whether or not the generator is producing electricity.

Construction

The generator basically consists of two end frame assemblies, a rotor assembly and a stator assembly. The rotor assembly is supported in the end frame by a ball bearing on the pulley end and a roller bearing or bushing on the slip ring end. Two brushes carry electricity through two slip rings on the rotor to the field coil which is mounted on the rotor

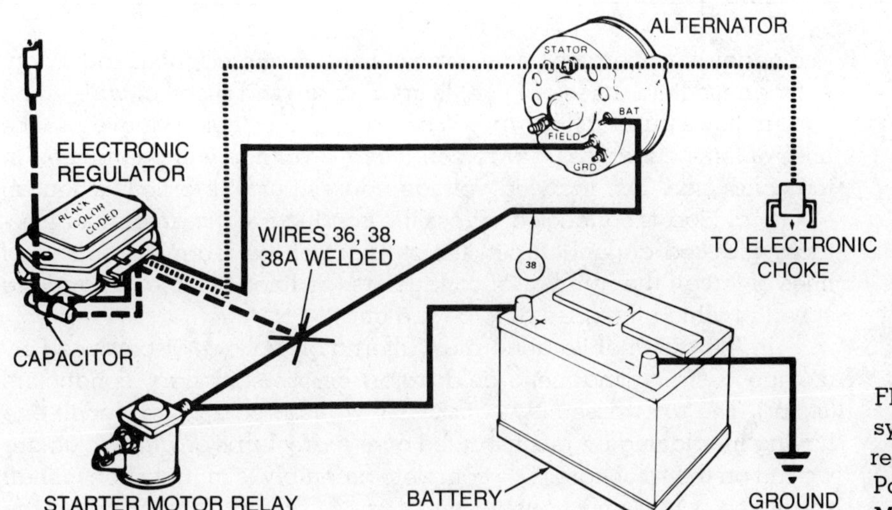

FIGURE 6-1 Charging system with separate electronic regulator. (Courtesy Ford Parts & Service Division, Ford Motor Co.)

shaft. The stator windings are assembled on the inside of a laminated core that forms part of the generator frame. A rectifier assembly containing three positive and three negative diodes is connected to the stator windings. Heavy duty generators may use additional diodes. The diodes change the induced alternating current in the stator windings to direct current which is used to charge the battery and supply direct current to the electrical system. The diodes also act as a one-way switch to prevent the battery from discharging back through the generator windings. Figure 6-2 is a cutaway view of a typical generator. This generator includes a transistorized regulator mounted inside the generator.

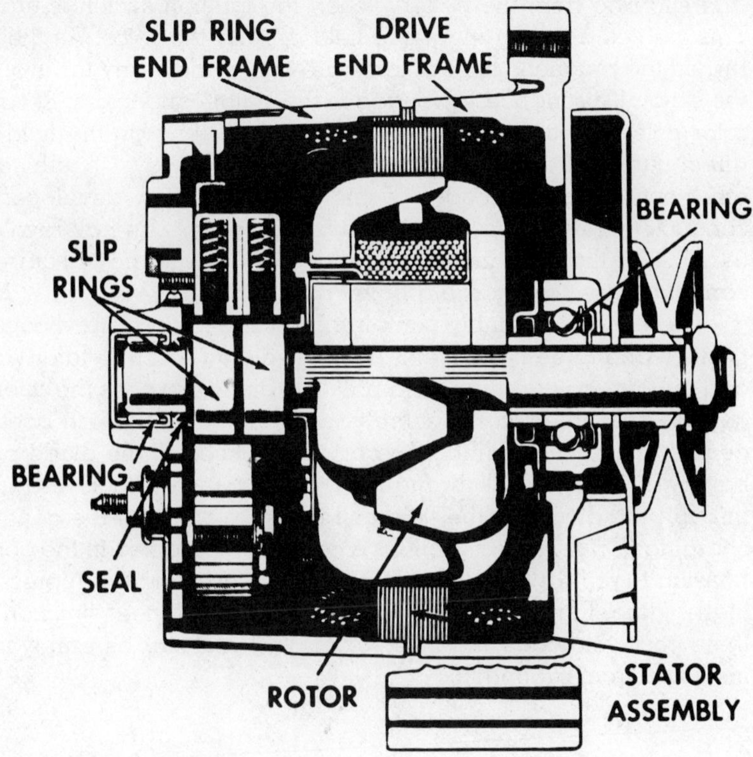

FIGURE 6-2
Cutaway view of a generator with an integral transistorized regulator. (Courtesy Oldsmobile Division, General Motors Corp.)

Operation

The generator operates on the principle of electromagnetic induction. A magnetic field (lines of force) is created around a coil of wire when current flows through the wire. When a magnetic field is moved so the lines of force cut across a wire conductor a voltage will be induced in the conductor. The induced voltage causes current to flow when an electrical load is connected across the conductor. The amount of electricity induced depends upon the strength of the magnet (number of lines of force), the number of conductors the lines of force cut and the speed at which the lines of force are cut.

In the automobile generator (alternator) voltage is produced by moving a strong magnetic field (rotor) across stationary conductors (stator). The rotor assembly consists of two iron pole pieces, each one having interlacing fingers mounted over many turns of wire which are wound on the rotor core. The complete assembly is mounted on a shaft supported in the end housing on bearings and bushings. When the ignition switch is turned to the "on" position, current is supplied to the rotor coil windings through brushes in contact with the slip rings.

The stator assembly is made up of a number of individual steel plates riveted together to form a laminated core for the stator. The rotor revolves inside the stator. Slots are provided in the core of the stator to receive coils of wire. These slots are sometimes referred to as stator teeth. Three separate series of coils of wire are wound around the stator teeth. These coils are arranged in three layers in each stator slot with their relative positions staggered. One end of each winding (series of coils) is connected to a positive and negative diode. A diode is an electrical device which will allow current to flow in only one direction, such as a one-way switch. The other ends of the three windings are joined together to form a common insulated junction called a "Y" connection.

The field coil inside the rotor receives current through the brushes and slip ring from the battery when the ignition switch is turned on. This creates a strong magnetic field around the rotor. As the rotor is turned the magnetic lines of force are cut by the many turns of wire in the stator. This induces a voltage in the stator conductors. Because the rotor pole pieces are externally magnetized through the field coil by direct current from the battery, one pole is always "south" and the other one "north." Because of this the current flow developed in the conductors (stator coils) reverses direction every one-half revolution of the rotor as the field direction changes. This is alternating current and cannot be used to charge a battery.

A rectifier assembly containing, in most cases, six diodes (three positive and three negative) is connected between the stator windings and the generator output terminal. The diode changes the alternating current from the stator assembly to direct current which goes to the generator output terminal. The blocking action of the diode prevents battery discharge back through the generator. Current is also supplied through the diodes to the field coil in the rotor when the generator is charging. On some installations a capacitor is located in the generator housing to protect the diodes from high voltage and to suppress noises in the radio. Figure 6-3 shows a positive rectifier heat sink containing three positive diodes and connectors. The heat sink assembly must be insulated from ground.

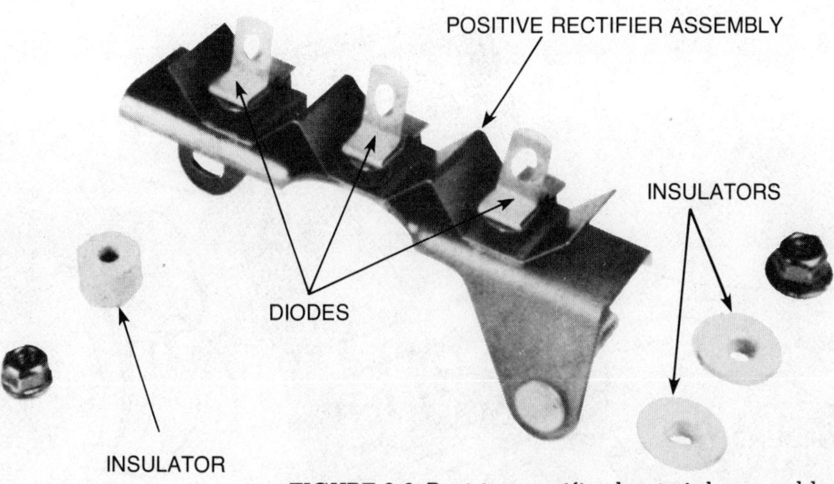

FIGURE 6-3 Positive rectifier heat sink assembly. (Courtesy Chrysler Corporation)

Regulation

The purpose of the charging system is to keep the battery charged and supply electricity to the electrical system. In order to perform satisfactorily, the battery needs to be kept at full charge. Overcharging the battery will greatly shorten its life.

Three things influence the charging rate; the number of conductors which are cut by the magnetic lines of force, the speed at which the lines of force are cut and the number of lines of force present. Of the three factors the only practical means of regulating the charging rate is to control the number of lines of force being produced. Because the field coil inside the rotor creates magnetic lines of force according to the amount of electricity flowing through the coil windings, regulation then becomes a matter of controlling the current flow to the field coils. This is done by means of a transistorized voltage regulator on all charging systems used today.

Regulator Operation

A regulator (limiter) is required because the generator output voltage increases with generator speed. Since enough voltage must be developed at low speeds to charge the battery and operate the electrical accessories, this voltage, if uncontrolled at high generator speeds, would overcharge the battery and damage the accessories. The function of the regulator is to limit the voltage to a safe preset value. The current output of the generator is controlled automatically by inductive reactance. The voltage is limited to a predetermined voltage by controlling the generator field current.

The regulators in use at the present time are of the transistorized (solid state) type. Some are of the integral type having the regulator included in the generator housing while others are a separate unit mounted remotely from the generator. All operate electronically to alternately "turn off" and "turn on" the voltage across the field winding. Basically the transistorized regulator is nothing more than a fast

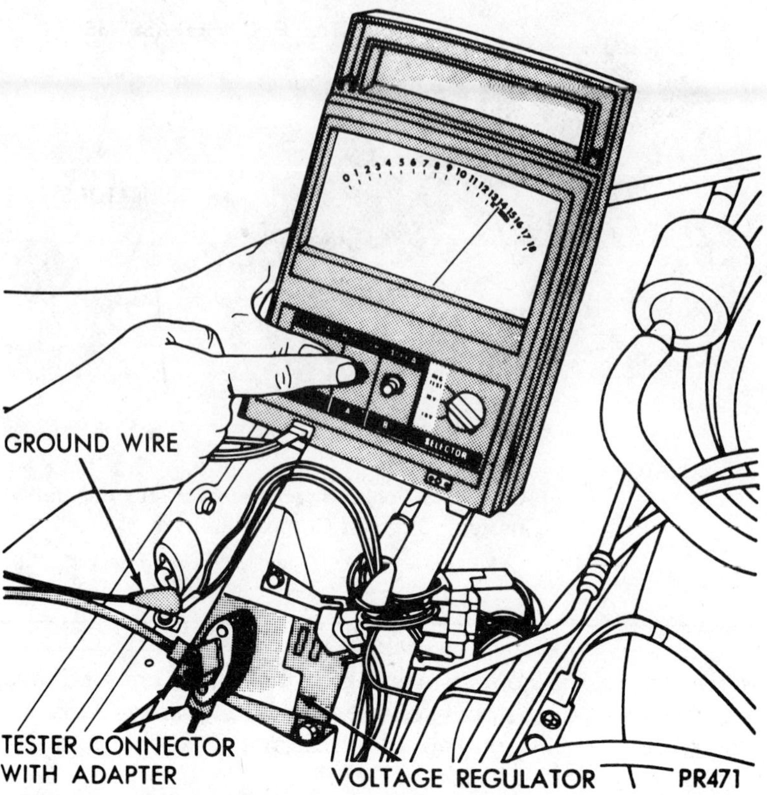

FIGURE 6-4 Electronic voltage regulator tester.
(Courtesy Chrysler Corporation)

acting electronic switch. This switching, between open and closed and back again, can occur at a rate as low as 10 times per second when the electrical demands are high, to as much as 7,000 times per second when the battery is fully charged and the load is light.

The regulator has no moving parts and requires no adjustment. It is made up of several semiconductor components, transistors, diodes, resistors, and capacitors. A heavy duty transistor is in series with the generator field coil. The control circuit which senses system voltage turns the transistor on and off as the load conditions change. Resistors absorb the electrical flow when the circuit is opened.

While a few regulators may have some replaceable components, when problems are located in the regulator the complete unit is usually replaced. The standard regulator is not adjustable. There have been some heavy duty regulators, however, which can be adjusted. On this type of regulator a potentiometer (variable resistor) is used. The charging rate is changed by turning a screw on the potentiometer. Figure 6-4 is a special voltage regulator tester for a specific regulator. By simply depressing buttons it is possible to make a complete test.

Charging System Troubleshooting

The purpose of the charging system is to provide electricity to maintain a fully charged battery and supply electricity to the electrical system when needed. A charging system which functions properly will meet these requirements. Malfunctions may occur in the charging system which can result in an overcharged battery condition, an undercharged battery condition, a no charge condition or a noisy generator.

When trouble is suspected or experienced in the charging system always make a visual inspection of belt tension, all wires and all terminals before making any tests. A fully charged battery should be used when checking generator output.

Overcharged Battery Condition

Too high a charging rate will be indicated by the battery using an excessive amount of water; needing water more often than every three months. Lights and/or fuses burn out frequently. Overcharging of a sealed battery may be indicated by electrolyte spewing out of the vent openings. It may also be indicated in a sealed battery if the battery indicator shows clear or light yellow. This means the fluid level is below the indicator and can be the result of too high a charging rate. The battery should be replaced.

All generators have the capability to overcharge the battery under all normal operating conditions; therefore, a voltage regulator (limiter) is necessary to hold the generator output within specifications. If overcharging is taking place the regulator may be faulty, in need of adjustment if adjustable or replacement if not adjustable. A poor ground between the generator frame and engine, or a poor ground at the regulator base may cause an overcharge condition. A short circuit in the charging circuit wiring can result in a high voltage charging rate. A short or ground in the field windings of the rotor will result in too high a charging rate. The generator must be disassembled to check and correct this condition.

Undercharged Battery Condition

An undercharged battery results in a slow cranking engine. Before checking or servicing the charging system make sure the battery itself is not defective. An undercharged battery can also be the result of a battery drain caused by a short or accessories being left on for a period of time. To determine if there is a short which is causing battery discharge, shut off all electrical components. Remove the clock fuse. Make sure the doors are closed. Disconnect the positive battery cable from the battery terminal. Connect a voltmeter between the positive cable and the positive battery terminal. If there is a voltage reading a short exists in the circuit. Pull the fuses one at a time to locate which circuit is shorted.

An undercharged battery may be due to:

1. Corroded, dirty or loose battery cables or terminals.
2. Loose, dirty or corroded wire connections in the charging system.
3. Drive belt loose, slipping or broken.
4. Regulator not properly grounded.
5. Generator not properly grounded.
6. Resistance in the circuit.
7. Regulator faulty or needs adjustment, if adjustable.
8. Generator faulty.

No Charge Condition

A no charge condition will result in a discharged battery. The no charge condition will be indicated by the charge indicator light remaining on with the engine running. With the ignition switch off, the indicator lamp is off. With the ignition switch on, the indicator lamp should be on; if not there is a faulty bulb or circuit. With the engine running, the indicator lamp is off if the generator is charging. If an ammeter is used to indicate charging the meter will remain on zero and show discharge when a load is placed on the electrical system. A no charge condition may be the result of:

1. A broken or slipping drive belt.
2. A burned out fuse link.
3. An open wire in the charging system.
4. Charge indicator lamp circuit faulty, generator may be charging.
5. Charge indicator meter or wiring faulty, generator may be charging.
6. Generator failure
7. Regulator faulty

Generator Noisy

A noisy generator may be the result of:

1. Loose or worn generator belt.
2. Bent pulley flanges.
3. Loose mounting bolts.
4. Internal generator problems.

Diagnosing Charging Problems

To avoid damage to the charging and electrical system always observe the following precautions:

1. Do not polarize the generator—apply battery voltage directly to the generator output terminal.
2. Do not ground or short across any of the terminals in the charging system unless specified by instructions. To bypass the regulator when testing for output only the rotor field coil is grounded.
3. Do not operate the generator without the output terminal attached to a battery.
4. Make sure the generator and battery have the same polarity.

Figure 6-5 shows the hook-up of a voltmeter, ammeter and variable resistance unit for checking generator output.

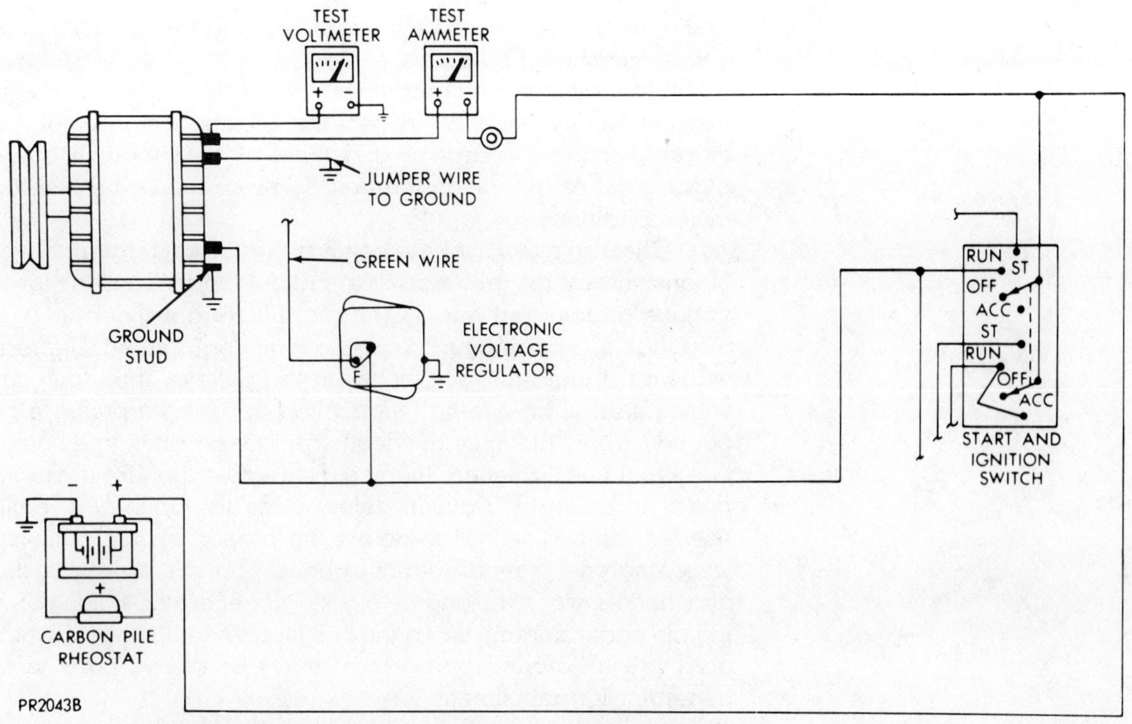

FIGURE 6-5 Generator output test. (Courtesy Chrysler Corporation)

Faulty Indicator Lamp Operation

The charge indicator lamp should operate as follows:

IGNITION SWITCH	ENGINE	INDICATOR LAMP
Off	Stopped	Off
On	Stopped	On
On	Running	Off

If the lamp is on with the switch off, disconnect the two leads from the generator (not the output lead to the battery). If the lamp stays on there is a short between the two leads. If the lamp goes out there is a faulty diode in the generator. Replace the diode unit.

If the lamp is off with the switch on and the engine stopped, the same conditions could be the cause of the problem as well as an open circuit. Check for a blown fuse or fuse link, a burned out bulb or a defective bulb socket. Check the wire between the generator and ignition switch for an open or short circuit.

Generator Output Test

If the indicator lamp and circuit are good but problems occur in the charging system, such as the indicator light does not go out with the engine running, or an indicator meter shows no charge or discharge and/or the battery is not being charged to its full capacity, a generator output test should be made.

Before making an output test, check the tension and condition of the generator drive belt. Inspect the bottom and sides of the belt for cracks, fraying, separation and signs of deterioration due to wear, glaze or oil or grease on the belt. Replace the belt if it shows any of these conditions.

Check to make sure the belt has the correct tension. Several types of tension gauges are available. Follow the instructions for using the various gauges put out by the manufacturers. Lacking a gauge, a reasonable test can be made without any equipment. Depress the belt with your thumb midway between the pulleys. If the belt can be deflected more than one-half inch when applying a pressure of 20 to 22 pounds, about the force needed to replace a crimp type bottle cap, the belt should be tightened. Placing a straight edge, like a yardstick, from pulley to pulley will aid in determining the amount of deflection. If needed, adjust the belt to obtain the proper tension. This is done by loosening one or more retaining bolts. There is usually a slotted arm attached between the engine block and generator which permits rotating the generator unit when the bolt is loosened. Never pry or use force on thin wall areas. Pry against heavy or ribbed parts to move the generator for adjustment.

A slipping belt, when placed under sudden load, such as accelerating, may squeal. Do not overtighten a belt. It places an undue load on bearings and the belt. Figure 6-6 shows the use of one type of belt tension gauge used to check belt operating tension and also for adjusting belt tension.

Before making an output test, always check the wire connections for cleanliness and tightness. If there is a question about the condition of the connections make a voltage drop test.

FIGURE 6-6 Checking belt tension. (Courtesy American Motors Corporation)

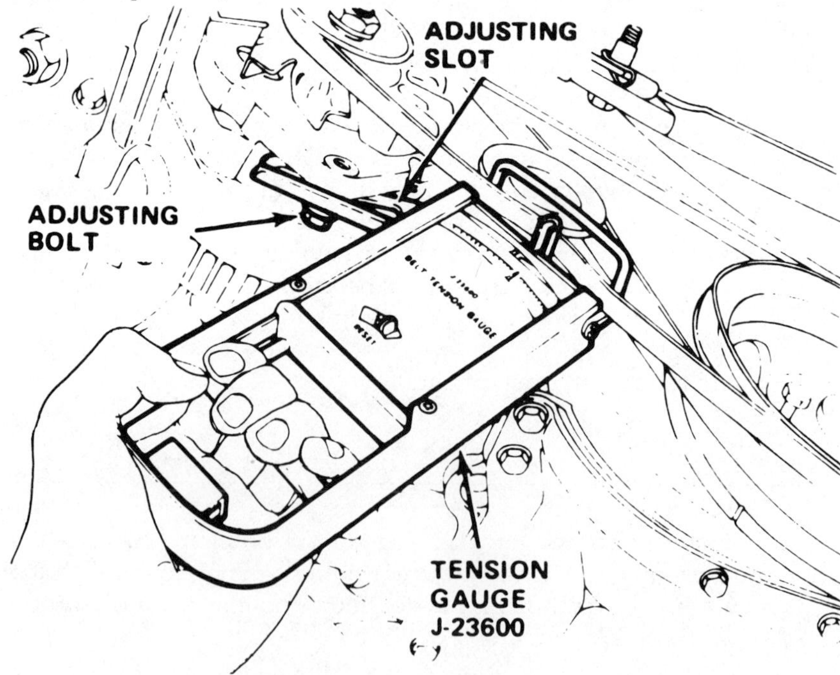

An ammeter is all that is necessary to determine generator output. However, various commercial testers are available for checking the complete charging system. The most common type consists of an ammeter, voltmeter, rheostat, and a variable carbon pile resistor unit. This type unit also is used to check the battery and starting system.

The charging rate of the generator depends upon the demands of the electrical system and is, therefore, regulated to take care of this need. To prevent damage to the electrical system, the generator and regulator are designed to limit charging to a specific rate. When the electrical demands are great, high amperage and low battery, the charging system should produce maximum amperage, assuming the generator is being turned fast enough. To check the charging system capability an ammeter is inserted at the generator output terminal, a load is placed on the system and the engine operated at a high enough rate of speed to obtain maximum charge.

Because the charging rate is controlled by limiting the amount of current flow to the rotor coil, the regulator can be removed from the charging circuit simply by grounding the field coil so no limit is placed on the amount of current flowing to the coil other than generator speed. This enables the generator to exceed charging specifications. The total generator output can be checked by inserting an ammeter in the circuit. The various types of commercial generator-regulator testers can be used to check both amperage and voltage. Most of these testers will have a means of grounding the field and regulating the load placed on the circuit for a convenient and accurate testing procedure.

The output of the charging system is first checked with the regulator in the circuit; if the output meets specifications no further testing is necessary. If the output does not meet manufacturer's specifications, the regulator is bypassed to determine if the generator has the capacity to meet the specific rate of charge.

Although a generator tester is the best and most convenient method for checking output, a reading can be obtained by hooking an ammeter into the circuit. To check with an ammeter disconnect the battery ground cable. Disconnect the battery wire at the generator output terminal. Connect the positive lead of a 0 to 50 ampere range ammeter to the generator terminal. Connect the negative ammeter lead to the wire which was removed from the output terminal. Reconnect the battery ground cable and turn on all the lights, accessories, air conditioner and blowers. If the battery is fully charged, it is well to run the starter for 30 seconds to help discharge the battery. The battery must be partially discharged for the generator to charge at maximum.

Start and run the engine fast enough to obtain a maximum reading on the ammeter. If the output is within 10 amperes of the rated output it is normal. The rated output is usually marked on the generator or regulator. If the current output is not within 10 amperes of the specifications, eliminate the regulator from the circuit and recheck.

If the generator is of the integral type with the regulator built into the generator, insert a screwdriver into the test hole in the end frame. The screwdriver should touch the tab in the test hole and ground against the housing. Figure 6-7 shows the location of the generator test hole. A screwdriver is used to ground the field windings to the housing on a generator with an integral voltage limiter.

On the generator having a separate regulator unit, disconnect the field wire which attaches to the field terminal on the regulator.

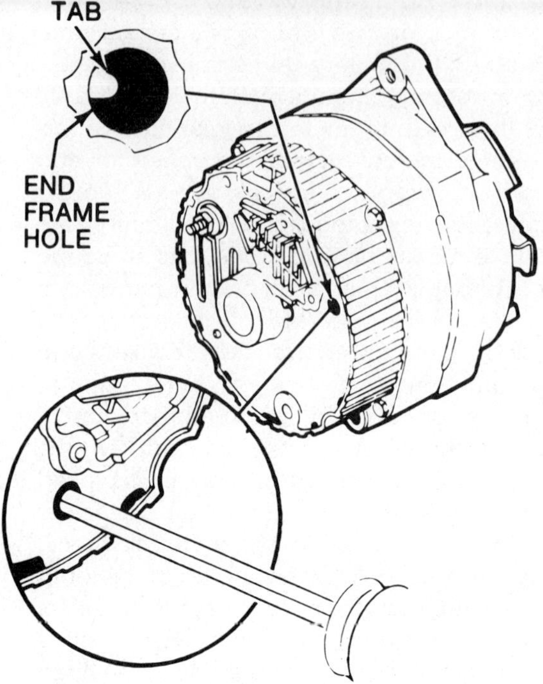

FIGURE 6-7 Generator test hole. (Courtesy Chevrolet Motor Division, General Motors Corp.)

Connect a jumper wire from the generator field terminal to ground. Start and run the engine with the same load and in the same manner as in the previous test. If the output is now within 10 amperes of specifications, the regulator is at fault and should be replaced. In the case of the integral generator, the generator must be disassembled and the regulator unit replaced. If the output is still below 10 amperes of rated specifications the generator needs to be removed from the engine and disassembled.

If a generator-regulator tester is to be used, follow the manufacturer's instructions for test procedures for the particular tester. The generator-regulator tester can place a controlled load on the generator to simulate a discharged battery. The tester can also provide a voltage reading. On some of the older regulators which use vibrating contact points it is possible to change the voltage setting by changing contact point spring tension.

Generator Disassembly and Testing

On the generator using an integral regulator, if the regulator is not performing satisfactorily the generator must be disassembled in order to replace the regulator unit.

On some generators it may be possible to check the condition of the diodes without disassembling the unit. It may also be possible to check the rotor field coil amperage draw without disassembling the unit. However, because there are internal problems and the generator must be disassembled, it will be easier to make a complete test after disassembling the unit.

To service, the generator should be removed from the vehicle.

Before removing, disconnect the negative battery terminal at the battery. Disconnect the leads from the generator. Loosen the adjusting bolts. Remove the generator drive belt. Remove the bolts which retain the generator to the engine.

Many times after it has been established that the generator is faulty, and particularly when special tools such as an arbor press, bearing pullers or pulley pullers are not available, it may be practical to exchange the entire unit for a rebuilt generator.

Before disassembly, scribe a line across the stator and end housing for alignment purposes during assembly. On some generators the brush holder assembly is located in such a manner that the brushes and brush holder can be removed from the end housing before disassembling the unit. Doing this may help to prevent damage to the brush assembly.

Remove the through bolts which hold the assembly together. Separate the end housings from the stator. It may be necessary to tap the end housings with a plastic-tip hammer to loosen the housing from the stator. They may also be pried apart with the blade of a screwdriver. Do not force the housings apart in such a manner that the brushes are damaged. If the pulley and end housing or bearing need to be removed from the rotor shaft, a puller must be used to prevent damage to the different parts. If the rotor is good and the bearing is not worn or damaged there should be no need to remove the pulley and housing from the rotor. Remove the diode assembly and regulator unit if the regulator is built into the housing. The various units can now be tested. Figure 6-8 is a disassembled generator showing the many different components. This generator uses the integral type regulator which is not adjustable.

FIGURE 6-8 Disassembled generator. (Courtesy American Motors Corporation)

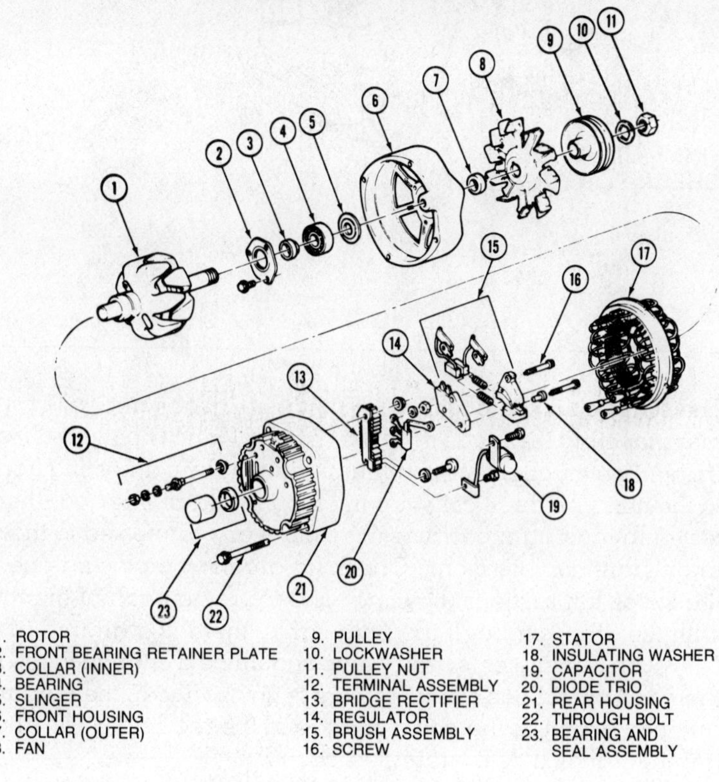

Check Rotor

The rotor is checked for an open circuit, ground or short circuit. A powered test lamp or an ohmmeter can be used to make these checks. When using a test lamp place one probe on each slip ring. The bulb will not light if there is an open circuit. Place one probe on one slip ring with the other probe on the rotor shaft. If the bulb lights there is a short circuit. Check the other slip ring in the same manner. An ohmmeter can be used to make the same tests. Set the selector switch at the X1 scale and calibrate according to instructions for the particular meter. Contact each meter probe with a slip ring. The meter should read approximately 2 to 3.5 ohms. A higher reading indicates a broken wire or a poor internal connection. A lower reading indicates a shorted wire or slip ring. Place one probe on the rotor shaft. The meter reading should be infinite (no deflection). Do this with both slip rings. A reading of other than infinite indicates the rotor is shorted, grounded or has an open circuit. The unit must be replaced. Figure 6-9 shows the procedure for checking the rotor coils for opens and/or grounds with an ohmmeter. A test lamp or voltmeter also could be used.

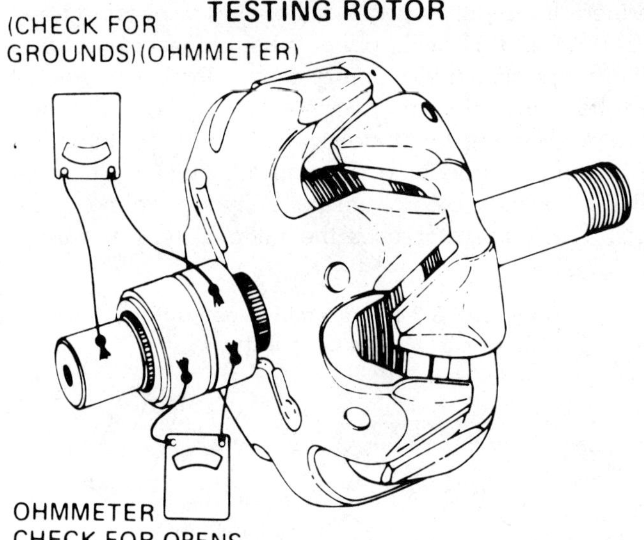

FIGURE 6-9 Testing the Rotor. (Courtesy Chevrolet Motor Division, General Motors Corp.)

Check Stator

The stator coils are checked for complete circuit and for grounds after disconnecting the leads from the diodes. Using a powered test lamp or an ohmmeter, check for continuous circuits by connecting from one coil to the next. All three coils are interconnected at one end, therefore the test bulb must light because the probes are connected to the coil leads in different combinations. Check for ground by placing one probe on the stator laminations (housing) and touching each of the three leads with the other probe. If the bulb lights, there is a ground in a coil.

If an ohmmeter is used, there should be a change in the reading if there is a continious circuit. If there is no change in the reading there is an open circuit. If there is a change in the reading when checking for ground it indicates a grounded circuit.

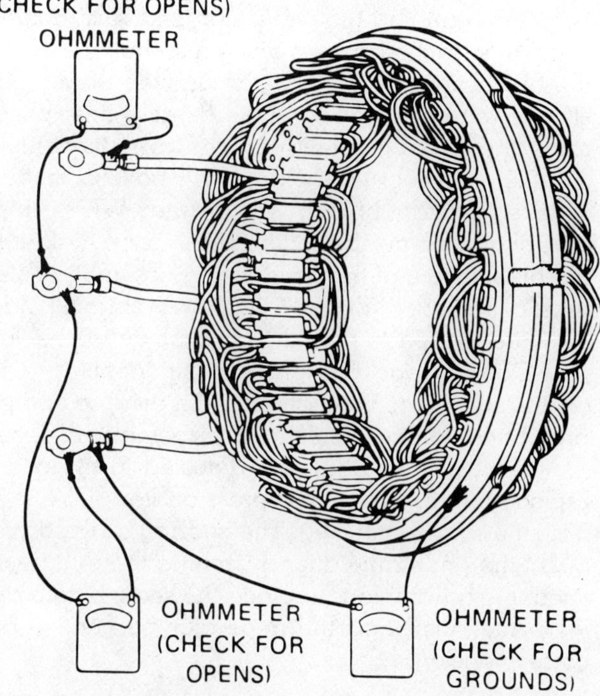

FIGURE 6-10 Checking the stator. (Courtesy Chevrolet Motor Division, General Motors Corp.)

When there is an open or grounded circuit the stator assembly must be replaced. Figure 6-10 shows the procedure for checking the stator coils for open and/or ground with an ohmmeter. A powered test lamp can also be used.

Diode Test

A diode permits current to flow in one direction only and stops flow in the opposite direction. To make an accurate test the diodes should be disconnected from the stator leads. The removal of the diode rectifier, diode heat sink or diode trio is usually obvious. The different manufacturers label the diode assembly differently and will attach them to the housing in a different manner.

While there are diode testers available, an ohmmeter can be used or a 12-volt battery with a test lamp having a 67 (4 candlepower) bulb. To test, contact one probe with the terminal bolt or strap and the other probe to ground (heat sink). Reverse the probes. The bulb should light in one direction and not light in the other. Each diode must be tested separately. When an ohmmeter is used there should be a reading in one direction and no reading (deflection) in the opposite direction. If the ohmmeter scale is set to X to 10 and correctly calibrated, all diodes should show a reading of approximately 60 in one direction and no reading in the other. If any of the diodes are faulty the entire diode assembly should be replaced. Figure 6-11 shows the correct procedure when using an ohmmeter to check each diode. There should be a reading in one direction but no reading in the opposite direction.

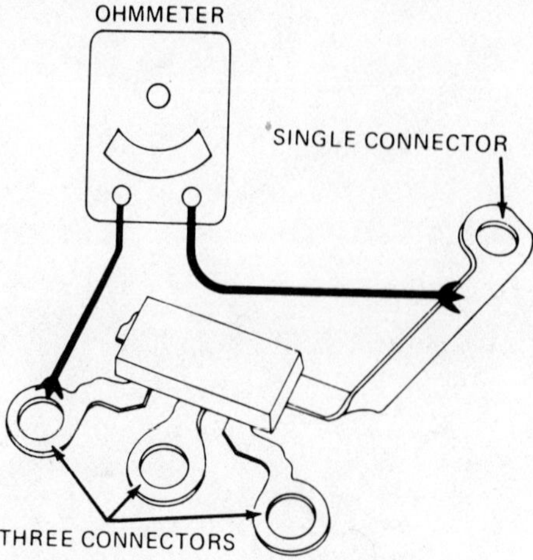

FIGURE 6-11 Checking diode trio. (Courtesy Oldsmobile Division, General Motors Corp.)

Assemble Generator

Before assembling the generator the brush holder should be checked to make sure the brushes and brush holders are properly insulated. If the brushes are worn down or uneven they should be replaced. The slip ring can be cleaned with 400 grit or finer polishing cloth. If the slip rings appear to be out-of-round or worn unevenly they can be trued on a lathe. Some brush holders will have a small hole which can be indexed with a hole in the frame. When this is the case a stiff wire should be inserted through the brush holder into the frame to hold the brushes out of the way during assembly. After assembly the wire must be removed. Figure 6-12 shows a brush holder assembly where a stiff wire is used to hold the brushes out of the way during assembly.

Do not clean any of the components in a solvent. Wipe with a clean rag and/or blow dirt off with compressed air. The bearings are prelubricated and washing in a solvent will destroy the lubrication.

If play or roughness is detected in the bearings they should be replaced. It may require a press and/or puller to remove the bearings from the shaft or housing. The bearing on the drive end can be pressed out of the end frame after detaching the retainer plate. If oil seals are used it is advisable to replace the seals before assembling the unit.

After installing the generator be sure to adjust the belt to the correct tension.

FIGURE 6-12 Brush holder assembly. (Courtesy Ford Parts & Service Division, Ford Motor Co.)

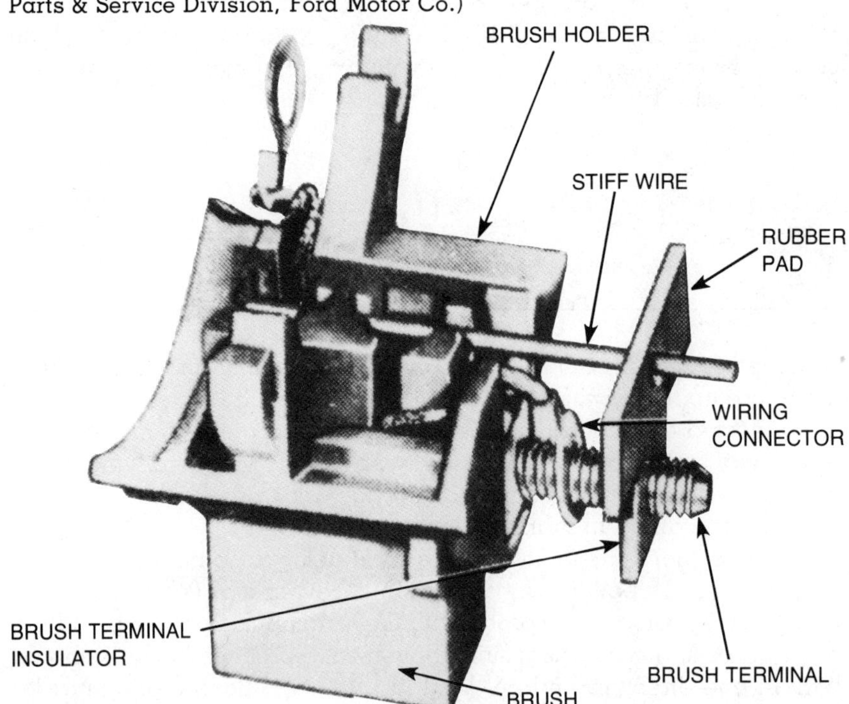

7 Ignition System

The operation of the gasoline engine depends on the burning and expansion of the compressed air/fuel mixture in each cylinder. The air/fuel mixture can not burn and expand unless it is ignited. Ignition is brought about by a spark that is produced by the ignition system. The spark must be of great enough intensity (high enough voltage) to jump the spark plug gap in the combustion chamber against compression pressure. In addition, it must occur at exactly the right time in relation to piston position. Provisions must also be made to vary the time at which the spark occurs in accordance to a number of variables such as engine load, speed, and temperature.

The ignition system must be capable of delivering approximately 40,000 volts to the spark plugs. The system converts the 12 volts supplied by the battery to a high enough voltage to jump the spark plug gap under all load and speed conditions. This is brought about through the process known as electromagnetic induction.

The ignition system consists of the battery, ignition switch, spark plugs, ignition coil, electronic control unit (module), primary and secondary wiring, and the distributor. Most distributors contain a permanent magnet, pole piece, pickup coil, rotor and cap to distribute the spark, as well as some type of electronic control for timing. Today's ignition systems are transistor-controlled and triggered by magnetic pulse. The control unit (module), magnet, pole piece, and pickup coil take the place of the contact points used in earlier model distributors. Certain differences will be found in the various distributors relative to the arrangement of the magnet and control module, as well as the terminology of some components. Some systems will use a resistance wire or ballast resistor unit in the primary circuit to limit the voltage going into the primary circuit when the engine is operating. Regardless, all systems operate in the same manner, developing high voltage in the coil by disrupting the primary circuit to cut magnetic lines of force. Figure 7-1 is a line drawing of a high energy ignition system

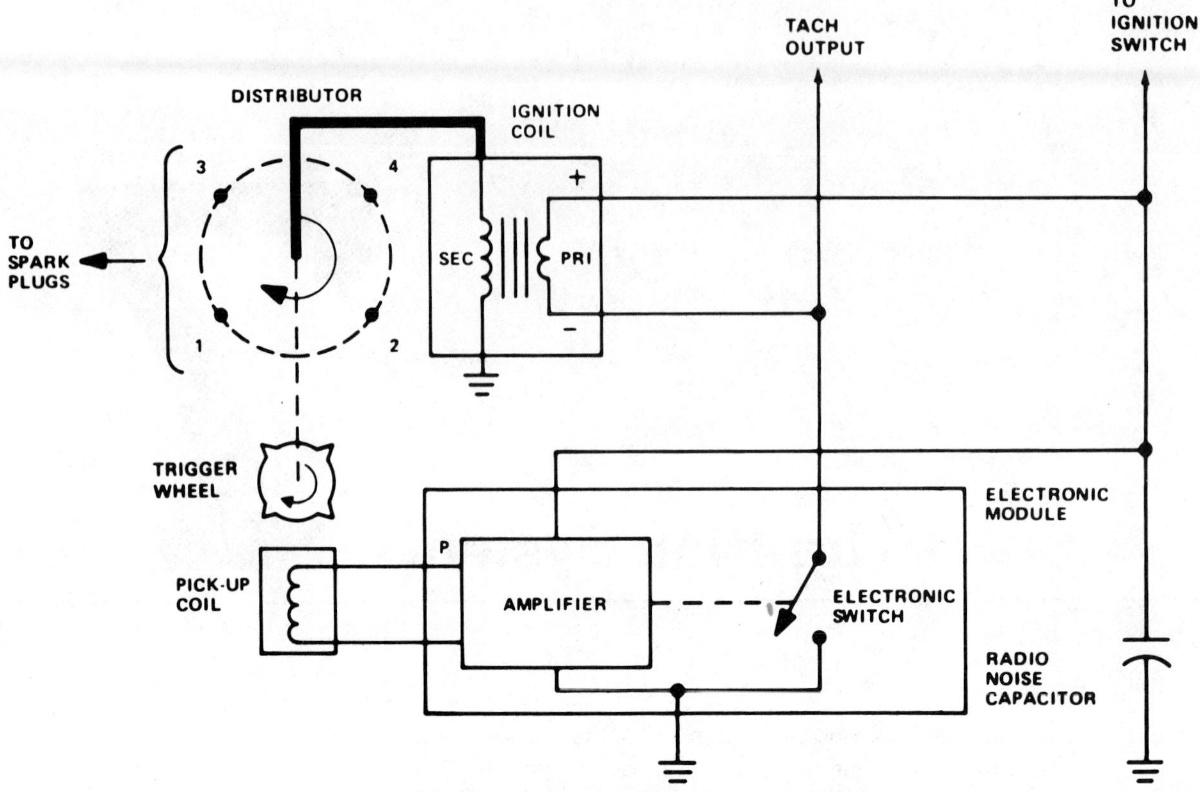

FIGURE 7-1 Electronic ignition system schematic. (Courtesy American Motors Corporation)

(HEI) (Electronic Ignition System) using an integral electronic module. Battery current is supplied through the ignition switch.

The ignition coil is, in effect, a stepup transformer which increases the low voltage output available from the battery to the high voltage needed to jump the gap at the spark plug and ignite the air/fuel mixture in the combustion chamber. The coil is made up of two windings, a primary and a secondary, both wound around a core of soft iron strips or laminations. The primary coil windings are made up of approximately 150 to 200 turns of 20 gauge wire. The secondary windings consist of many thousand turns, 18,000 to 25,000, of very fine wire about 40 gauge. This wire is approximately the size of a human hair.

Basic Components of the Ignition System

All ignition systems function in the same manner and must have the same basic components. These components are:

1. Ignition coil to step up the voltage.
2. Ignition switch to turn the flow of current to the system "on" and "off."
3. Permanent magnets located in the distributor to create magnetic lines of force.
4. A rotating member driven by the camshaft to interrupt the mag-

netic lines of force. This may be labeled a rotor, reluctor or armature.

5. A pickup coil to receive the electrical impulse created by cutting the magnetic lines of force and intensifying the electrical flow.
6. Electronic module made up of transistors, resistors, and diodes to interrupt the electrical flow to the ignition coil windings when triggered by the electrical impulse, and to control distributor dwell.
7. A rotor to carry the secondary voltage from the ignition coil to terminals in the distributor cap.
8. Distributor cap with terminals connected by cables to each spark plug.
9. Advance mechanism to advance and retard the ignition timing by means of vacuum and/or a mechanical centrifugal advance

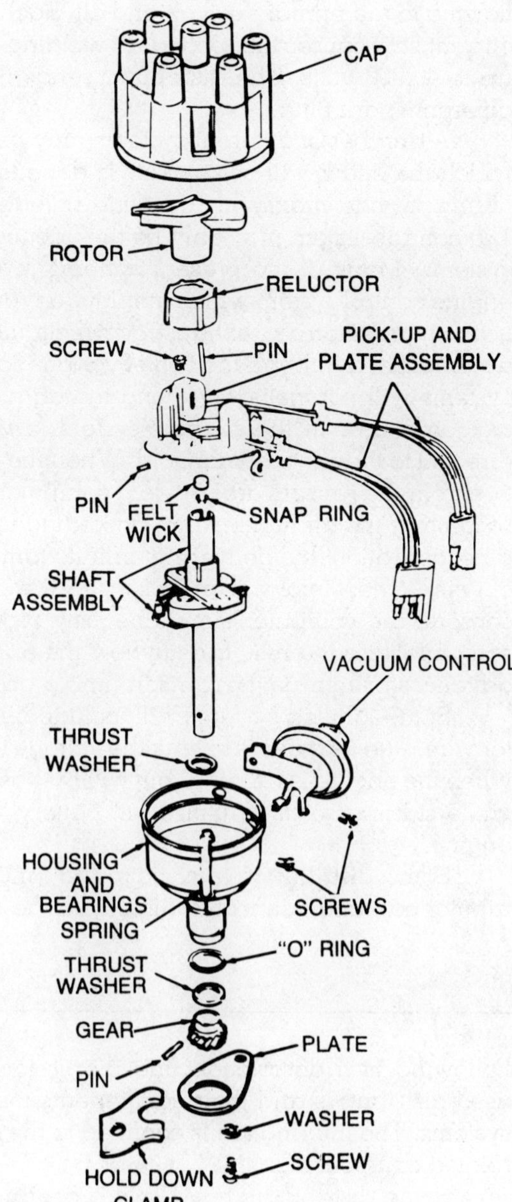

FIGURE 7-2 Disassembled dual pick-up distributor with mechanical and vacuum controls. (Courtesy Chrysler Corporation)

unit. Many of today's distributors depend entirely upon the electronic ignition system for timing retard and advance according to operating conditions. Figure 7-2 is a disassembled view of a six-cylinder dual pickup distributor showing the mechanical advance and vacuum control units.

Operation of the Ignition System

In operation, when the ignition switch is turned on, current flows through the primary winding creating a magnetic field that surrounds both the primary and secondary coil windings. When the engine is turning, the magnetic pickup in the distributor sends an electrical impulse to the ignition module (electronic control unit made up of transistors, resistors and diodes) as each tooth of the rotor, armature or reluctor passes the pickup coil. The module switches the current which is flowing to the primary coil on and off. Each interruption of the primary current flow causes the secondary winding to induce a voltage pulse of up to 40,000 volts. The distributor sends this high voltage out to the different spark plugs.

A number of different systems may be used to control the time at which the spark will occur. This is done to keep emissions to a minimum, provide maximum gasoline mileage and good performance. The control system may only be the vacuum and centrifugal advance systems. Many of the present systems involve a complete electronic engine control system which employs a type of computer to control fuel flow, thermactor air, exhaust gas recirculation, and ignition. This is accomplished through the use of various solenoids and sensors. Other systems will not include varying the air/fuel ratio, but depend on an oxygen sensor in the exhaust system to vary the amount of oxygen directed to the exhaust manifold. When the engine is running, information from the sensors are sent to a computer. Some have the capability of igniting the air/fuel mixture according to the different modes of engine operation by delivering infinite amount of variable advance curves. When information is sent to the computer from the various sensors, the computer simultaneously receives signals from all sensors, analyzes the results as to how the engine is operating, and then advances or retards the ignition timing accordingly.

Some ignition systems will include a ballast resistor unit or resistor wire. The purpose is to limit the voltage to the primary coil windings when the engine is running, but will by-pass the resistance unit or wire while starting so as to utilize full battery voltage while cranking the engine.

Some distributors may have the ignition coil located in the distributor cap and connected directly to the rotor.

Distributor

Following is a description and discussion of the various commonly used distributors and their components found in the different ignition systems. The information is confined to the distributor unit and directly related components.

Some distributors have only a centrifugal advance unit, some a combination mechanical and vacuum advance unit, some a vacuum advance unit only, some a dual vacuum advance-retard unit. Others do not use either, but depend upon an electronic control. The electronic spark control (computer) will be discussed as a separate unit in Chapter 9.

High Energy Ignition System HEI (GMC)

Most HEI high energy ignition systems combine all ignition components into one unit. A few of these distributors have the coil located separately. The high energy ignition system is a magnetic-triggered inductive discharge ignition system, controlled by a transistor. A magnetic pickup assembly located inside the distributor housing contains a permanent magnet, a pole piece with internal teeth and a pickup coil. In operation, when the teeth of the timer core rotating inside the pole piece line up with the teeth of the pole piece, a voltage induced in the pickup coil signals the electronic module to trigger the coil primary circuit. The primary current decreases and a high voltage is induced in the ignition coil secondary winding. This is sent through the rotor and spark plug cables to the spark plugs.

The magnetic pickup coil is mounted on a bearing in the distributor housing and can be rotated by the vacuum control unit to change spark timing. The timer core can be rotated about the shaft by advance weights to provide centrifugal timing advance. When a computer control system is used on this installation, the vacuum and mechanical advance units are eliminated. The pickup coil is connected to the transistors in the electronic control module. The electronic module is connected to the primary windings in the coil.

The module automatically controls the dwell period, stretching it with increased engine speed. The distributor has a long spark duration made possible by the higher amount of energy stored in the primary coil.

FIGURE 7-3 Components of a H.E.I. distributor. (Courtesy Chevrolet Motor Division, General Motors Corp.)

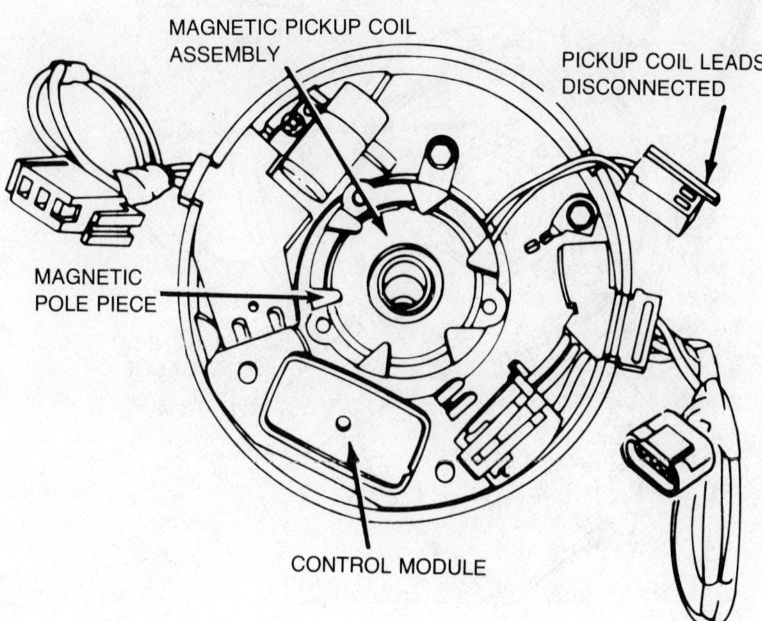

The capacitor (condenser) in the distributor is only for radio noise suppression. This distributor does not use a resistor wire between the ignition switch and ignition coil. Figure 7-3 is a top view of a high energy ignition system showing the various components which make up the distributor.

Electronic Ignition System (Chrysler Corp.)

The electronic ignition system consists of the battery, ignition switch, resistor unit, electronic control unit, pickup coil or coils, ignition coil, distributor, spark plugs, and the necessary wiring. One system uses a dual pickup coil and will have a dual pickup start-run relay. Another distributor of this type has a single pickup coil assembly and is equipped with a dual ballast resistor.

The primary circuit is made up of the battery, ignition switch, ignition resistor, primary windings of the ignition coil, power switching transistor located in the control unit, and a dual pickup start-run relay if dual pickup coils are used. When a dual ballast resistor is used, the compensating side of the resistor is part of the primary circuit.

The secondary circuit consists of the coil secondary windings, distributor cap, rotor, spark plug wires, and spark plugs.

The resistor unit, when used, maintains a constant primary current regardless of the variations in engine speed. During starting, the ignition resistor is by-passed, applying full battery voltage to the primary windings in the ignition coil.

In addition to the two basic circuits, there are two, or if a dual ballast resistor is incorporated, a third circuit is used. When only two circuits are used, one is the pickup coil circuit and the other is the

FIGURE 7-4 Six-cylinder dual pick-up distributor. (Courtesy Chrysler Corporation)

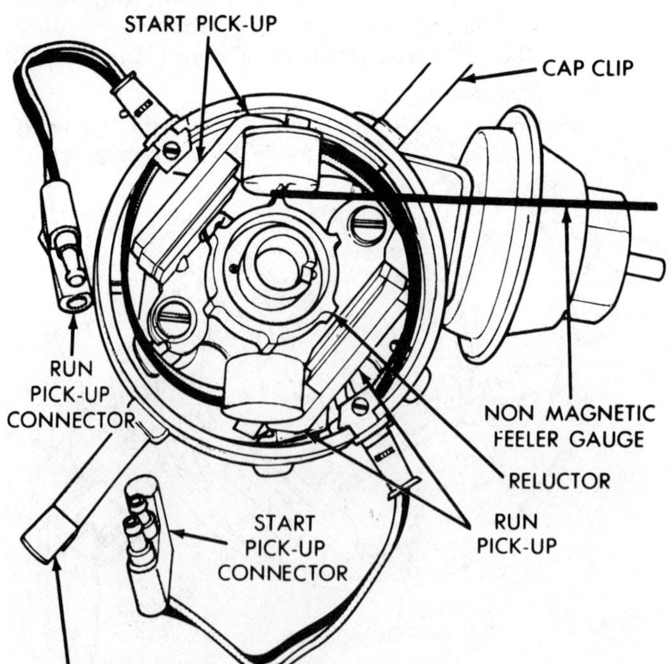

control unit feed circuit. The one circuit operates the circuitry of the control unit, while the pickup circuit is used to sense the proper timing for the control unit. When a third circuit is used it is part of the control unit feed circuit and uses the 5-ohm section of the dual ballast resistor.

The reluctor, rotated by the distributor shaft, produces a voltage pulse in the magnetic pickup each time the spark plug is fired. This pulse of electric current is transmitted through the pickup coil to the power switching transistor in the control unit, causing the transistor to interrupt the current flow through the primary coil windings. The interruption of current flow causes a high voltage to be induced in the secondary coil winding. The high voltage will jump across the spark plug gap and fire the air/fuel mixture.

The length of time the switching transistor allows the flow of current in the primary circuit is determined by the electronic circuitry in the control module. This determines dwell. It is not adjustable.

Some distributors of this type will use a vacuum advance unit that turns the run pickup coil assembly to advance or retard the ignition timing. Some distributors use, in addition to the vacuum advance, a mechanical centrifugal advance mechanism to advance timing according to engine speed. Other distributors depend upon external electronic controls.

Figure 7-4 is an illustration of a six-cylinder dual pickup distributor with the cap and rotor removed. The feeler gauge is used to check the gap between the reluctor and pickup coils.

Dura Spark Ignition System (Ford Motor Co.)

The Dura Spark ignition system primary (low voltage) circuit consists of the battery, ignition switch, primary circuit resistance wire on some installations, primary coil windings, magnetic pickup assembly, and amplifier module. The secondary circuit (high voltage) is made up of the distributor rotor, distributor cap, spark plug wires, and spark plugs. Figure 7-5 is a schematic of the components which make up a Dura Spark system.

With the ignition switch "on" the primary circuit in the ignition coil is energized. When the engine is turning, the distributor armature is rotated by the distributor shaft. This causes fluctuations in the magnetic field created by the pickup coil assembly. As the spokes or teeth on the armature approach the magnetic pickup coil, a voltage is induced. This is sent to the amplifier module, causing the amplifier to interrupt the primary current flow through the coil. When the current flow is stopped, the magnetic field built up around the coil windings will collapse, causing high voltage to be induced in the secondary coil windings. High voltage is produced each time the magnetic field is built up and collapsed. The high voltage flows from the secondary coil windings to the distributor cap where the rotor distributes it to the spark plug terminals in the distributor cap and then to the different spark plugs. This process is repeated for every power stroke of the engine.

This type of distributor is equipped with both vacuum and mechanical centrifugal spark advance control units. The vacuum unit governs ignition timing according to engine load, while the mechanical advance unit governs timing according to engine speed.

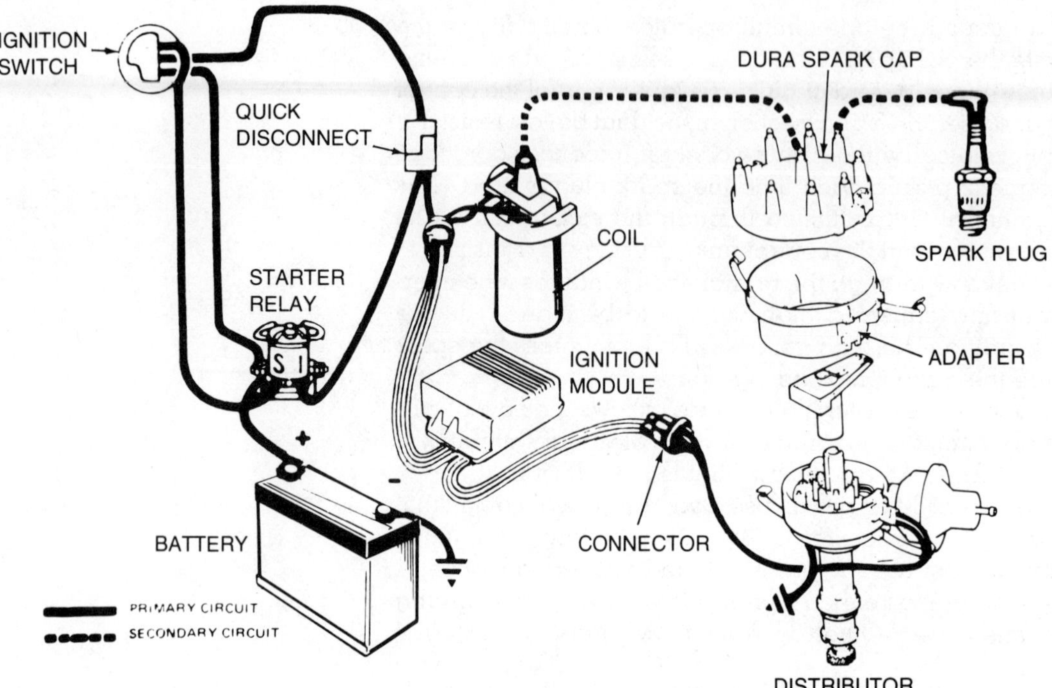

FIGURE 7-5 Typical dura spark system. (Courtesy Ford Parts & Service Division, Ford Motor Co.)

A dual vacuum advance unit is used on some of these distributors. This is to provide additional ignition timing retard during engine closed throttle operation. This occurs at both curb idle throttle position and during engine coast down with closed throttle. Retarding the timing at this time helps to control engine emissions. The dual vacuum advance unit consists of two diaphragms that operate from two different sources of vacuum. The outer (primary) diaphragm is operated by carburetor venturi vacuum to provide advance during normal driving conditions. The diaphragm is connected to the magnetic pickup coil assembly by means of linkage. The inner (secondary)

FIGURE 7-6 V8 dura spark distributor with a dual vacuum advance. (Courtesy Ford Parts & Service Division, Ford Motor Co.)

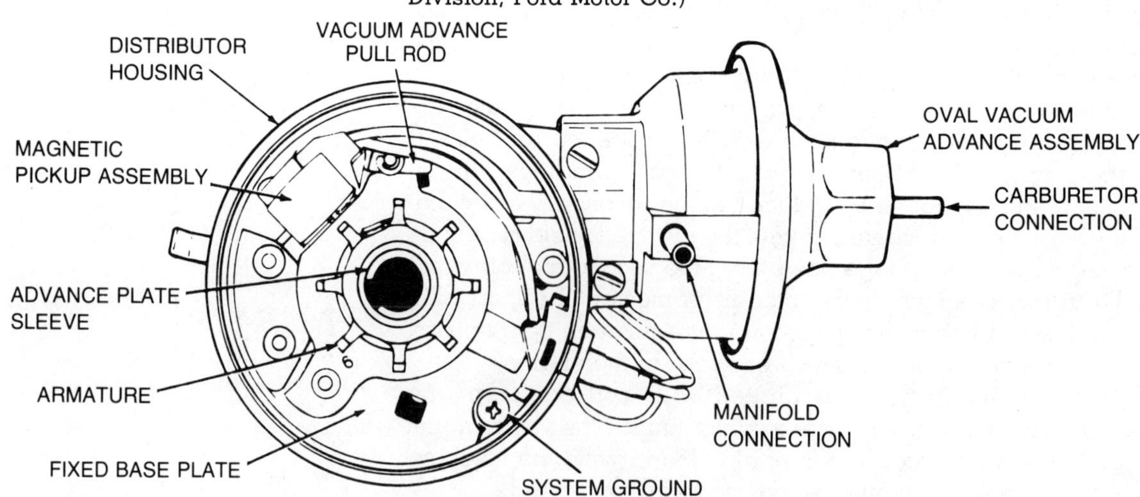

diaphragm operates from intake manifold vacuum and acts to retard the ignition timing. The diaphragm is connected by linkage to the outer diaphragm. Because manifold vacuum is greater than carburetor venturi vacuum during closed throttle operation, the secondary diaphragm will retard the spark. At all other operating phases the larger primary diaphragm operating from venturi vacuum moves the base plate upon which the pickup coil is mounted against distributor shaft rotation, thus advancing spark timing.

The centrifugal mechanical advance unit operates independently of the vacuum advance unit. The vacuum advance unit moves the base plate which mounts the pickup coil. The centrifugal advance changes the position of the armature in relation to the distributor shaft. The centrifugal advance unit is located below the base plate and uses centrifugal weights that move inward or outward with changes in engine speed. As speed increases, the weights move the sleeve and plate assembly ahead of the distributor shaft, thus advancing the position of the armature. The rate of advance is controlled by the calibration of the springs which hold the weights in a retard position. Figure 7-6 shows an eight-cylinder Dura Spark distributor which has a vacuum advance assembly mounted on the housing and an internal centrifugal mechanical advance unit which operates an advance plate sleeve.

Troubleshooting the Ignition System (Failure to Start)

When an engine fails to start, a definite procedure should be followed to locate the problem with a minimum amount of time and effort.

1. To start promptly, the engine must crank at a normal rate of speed. If not, either charge or replace the battery or hook up a booster battery.
2. With the engine cranking normally, check for spark at a spark plug.
3. If spark is present, check for fuel reaching the carburetor.
4. If fuel is reaching the carburetor and there is a normal amount of compression, it is reasonable to expect that the trouble is in the ignition system.
5. Many of the late model vehicles will be equipped with an electronic command module. The device is designed to regulate ignition timing, fuel mixture, and temperature for clean burning. This device should have no bearing on starting the engine.
6. Many vehicles are equipped with an electrical diagnostic connector terminal block. This allows for quick preliminary testing of the engine electrical system and is meant to be used in conjunction with an electronic ignition tester designed for the specific make of engine. These are merely test connections, and have no bearing on the engine starting or running. Vehicles equipped with a computer-controlled emission system will generally have a terminal connection panel which, through the use of special equipment, permits testing of numerous components without disconnecting the unit from the circuit.

When the starting motor cranks the engine at a reasonable rate and the engine does not start it is generally safe to assume there is a problem in the fuel or ignition system. In the majority of cases the trouble will be in the ignition system. It is a simple matter to make a quick check to determine if the ignition system is producing a high voltage spark which is strong enough to jump the spark plug gap.

Quick Check for Spark at Spark Plug

Remove a spark plug wire from one spark plug by twisting the boot that covers the spark plug insulator, while pulling the boot and wire off the plug. Pull only on the boot. Insert a screwdriver blade into the spark plug boot so it contacts the spark plug terminal inside the boot. Hold the screwdriver blade one-quarter inch from a good ground on the engine block. Be sure to hold the screwdriver by the plastic handle and not the metal blade or you may receive an electrical shock. Crank the engine with the ignition switch on the "on" position. If the spark is regular, blue and strong the trouble is probably in the fuel system. If the spark is yellow, intermittent, or there is no spark, trouble exists in the ignition system.

A spark tester consisting of a spark plug solidly attached to an alligator clip (soldered) can be used to check spark instead of using a screwdriver. Attach the alligator clip and spark plug to a good ground on the engine block. Set the spark plug gap to one-quarter inch. Attach a spark plug cable which was removed from one of the engine spark plugs to the test plug. Crank the engine and observe the spark. The spark should jump the gap regularly with a hot blue spark. Figure 7-7 shows the common tools used to perform the more common tests on the high energy ignition and electrical systems. A timing light also is essential.

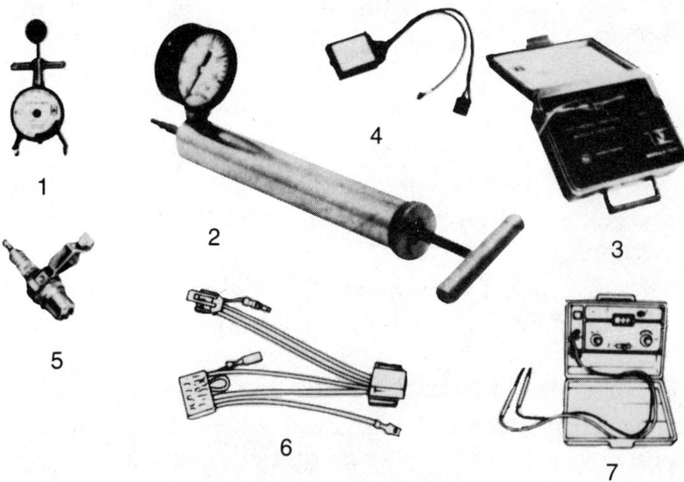

1 DRIVE BELT TENSION GAGE
2 VACUUM PUMP
3 HIGH ENERGY IGN. MODULE TESTER
4 GENERATOR TESTER
5 SPARK TESTER
6 H. E. I. TESTER ADAPTER
7 HIGH IMPEDANCE DIGITAL MULTIMETER

FIGURE 7-7 Common ignition and electrical systems test equipment. (Courtesy Oldsmobile Division, General Motors Corp.)

Quick Check to Determine if Fuel is Reaching the Carburetor

Remove the air cleaner. Hold the choke valve open. Pump the accelerator while looking down the carburetor air horn. If fuel is reaching the carburetor you should be able to see fuel squirting out into the air horn or venturi of the carburetor. If no fuel squirts out, the fuel is not reaching the carburetor.

Problems in the Ignition System

REMEMBER: Always make the simple and easy tests first. It is an elimination process whereby you eliminate as many possibilities as you can with the least amount of work. Work from the simple to the more complex.

Numerous problems may occur in the ignition system which can result in an engine that will not start, is hard to start or will not operate in a satisfactory manner. The major reasons the engine fails to start and/or operates in an unsatisfactory manner are as follows:

1. Open primary circuit due to a faulty ignition switch.
2. A broken wire or poor connection between the battery and ignition switch.
3. A broken wire or loose connection between the ignition switch and coil.
4. A broken wire or poor connection between the ignition coil and distributor.
5. A faulty or broken distributor rotor.
6. A cracked distributor cap.
7. Bad spark plug wires.
8. Short or open circuit in the distributor module.
9. Short or open circuit in the distributor pickup coil.
10. Fouled spark plugs.
11. Reluctor (armature) or (timer core) teeth making contact with the pickup coil.
12. Faulty electronic control module.
13. Faulty resistor wire or ballast resistor coil.
14. Engine wiring wet.
15. Faulty ignition coil.

Visual Inspection of the Ignition System

It is always advisable to make a complete visual check before doing any disassembly work. Inspect all units involved for loose connections, broken or frayed wires, or cracked insulation.

When no spark is present at the spark plugs, another quick check can be made to further check out the primary circuit. Remove the coil high tension wire from the center of the distributor cap. Some of the HET distributors have the coil located in the distributor cap, which eliminates the use of a coil wire. Hold the end of the wire one-quarter inch from a good ground on the engine block. Be sure to hold the insulated part of the wire so you won't get an electric shock. Crank the engine with the ignition switch on. If no spark is present it indicates the problem is in the primary circuit. The primary circuit consists of the battery, ignition switch, resistor unit or wire, primary windings of the

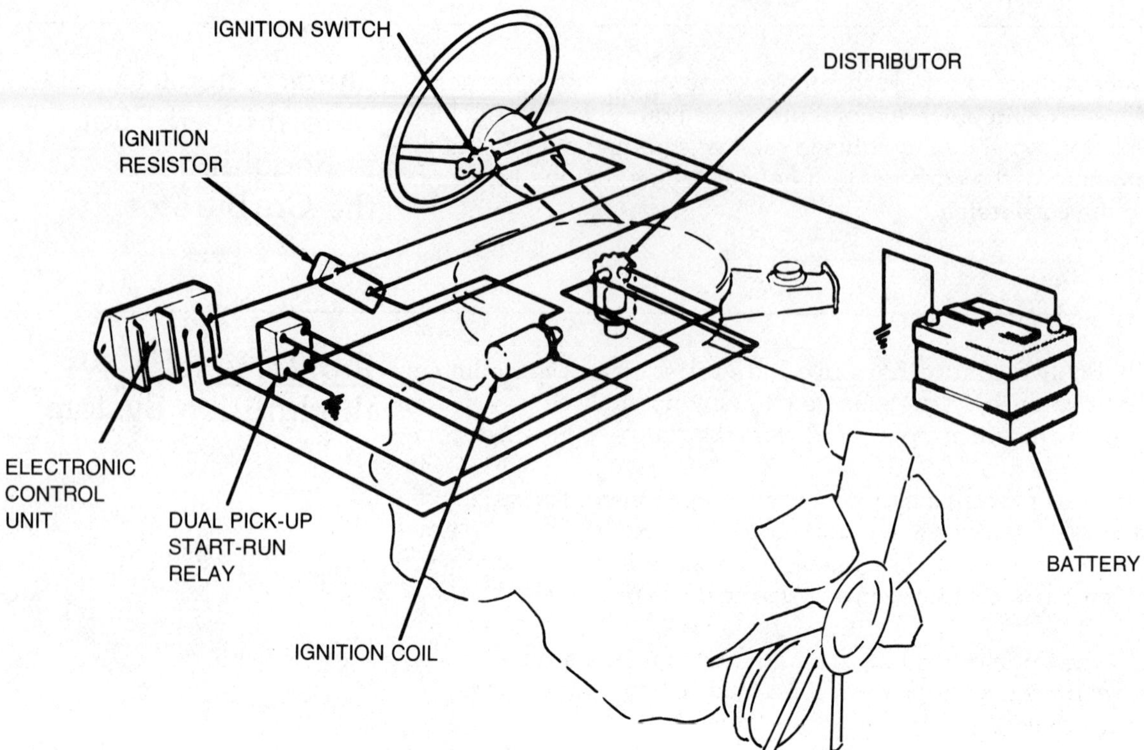

FIGURE 7-8 Primary ignition system. (Courtesy Chrysler Corporation)

ignition coil, pickup coil, control unit (electronic module), and the connecting wires. Figure 7-8 is a drawing of an electronic ignition system showing the components which make up the primary circuit. This system uses a resistor unit to limit ignition voltage when the engine is running.

To check the primary circuit from the battery to the coil, disconnect the primary wire at the ignition coil. Connect one lead of a test lamp or a voltmeter to the wire which was removed from the coil. Attach the other end to a good ground on the engine block. Turn the ignition switch to the "on" position. Crank the engine. The test lamp should light, or if a voltmeter is used, the meter should read battery voltage if the circuit to the coil is satisfactory. If there is no reading or the lamp does not light, the primary circuit to the coil is not complete. Although it is not good practice, the circuit can be checked by momentarily touching the terminal to ground. If an arcing occurs, the circuit is complete.

The problem can be the result of loose connections or broken wires. Examine all wires in the primary circuit. Replace as necessary if the wires are broken or frayed. Clean and tighten all loose connections.

A defective ignition switch can result in current not reaching the coil. To check the ignition switch, bypass the switch by connecting a jumper wire between the wire that goes to the coil and the wire that comes from the battery. If current is now present at the coil the switch is defective. If current does not reach the coil the wire from the switch to the coil may be defective, or if a ballast resistor is used, the resistor may be open. Some vehicles will use a special resistance wire to limit battery voltage to the ignition coil. When this is the case, the resistor wire or ballast resistor unit is bypassed at the ignition switch so full battery voltage will reach the coil when the engine is being cranked.

If current is present to the ignition coil, the circuit from the battery to the coil is satisfactory. If spark is still not present at the center coil wire when the engine is cranked, the problem may be in the ignition coil, pickup coil or electronic module.

If spark is present at the center coil wire but is not reaching the spark plugs, remove the distributor cap and check for cracks and/or carbon tracks. This could result in the spark from the coil following the crack to ground. Check the rotor to make sure it is not broken or cracked.

Check the wires in the distributor cap for a tight fit. Make sure the receptacles in the cap are clean and the ends of the wires are clean.

If either the distributor cap or rotor is damaged the damaged unit should be replaced. When installing a new distributor cap the wires must be replaced in exactly the same location from which they were removed. This is determined by the firing order. The easiest way is to remove one wire at a time from the old cap and install it in the new cap. Both the rotor and distributor cap can only be installed on the distributor shaft and distributor housing properly, because they will seat correctly only in the proper location.

Coil testers are available which can be used to indicate a faulty coil. Many times it is a simple matter to substitute a coil which is known to be good for the coil suspected of being faulty. A coil can also be checked with an ohmmeter.

Check the distributor shaft and/or bushings for wear which results in excessive movement of the shaft in the housing. Excessive free play will permit the reluctor (armature), cam or teeth to rub against the pickup coil block. This will short out the flow of current. Distributor shaft and bushing free play should not exceed 0.006". A dial indicator can be used to measure free play. Bushings are used in the distributor housing to support the shaft. Excessive play can be removed by install-

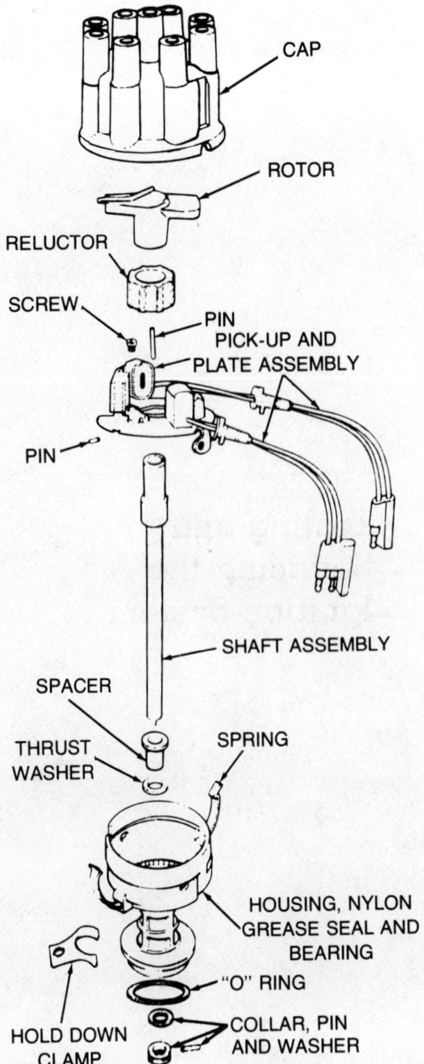

FIGURE 7-9 Disassembled eight-cylinder dual pick-up distributor. (Courtesy Chrysler Corporation)

FIGURE 7-10 Air gap adjustment. (Courtesy Chrysler Corporation)

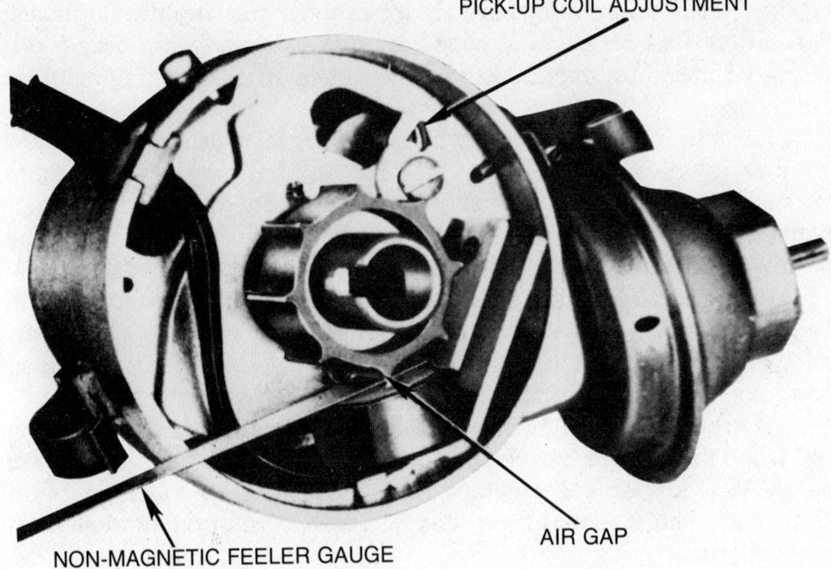

ing new bushings if the shaft is not worn. If the shaft is worn replace both the shaft and bushings. Figure 7-9 is a disassembled view of an eight-cylinder dual pickup distributor which does not use a mechanical or vacuum spark control. The shaft and/or bushing needs to be replaced if excessive free play exists.

On some installations the clearance between the pickup coil and armature is adjustable. The clearance can be measured with a non-magnetic feeler gauge and adjusted to specifications. Too little clearance may result in the armature rubbing the pickup coil block. Too much clearance will weaken the amount of electricity produced. Figure 7-10 shows the pickup coil adjustment for setting the air gap between the pickup coil and the reluctor.

Testing and Servicing the Ignition System

Ignition system troubles are caused by a failure in the primary and/or secondary circuit, incorrect ignition timing and/or incorrect distributor advance or retard. Circuit failures may be caused by shorts, corroded or dirty terminals, defective wire insulation, cracked distributor cap or rotor, defective pickup coil assembly, a defective electronic control module or fouled spark plugs.

Many troubles which result in the engine not starting or not operating properly can be located by mere visual inspection while in other cases the trouble can be isolated by the use of a simple test light, ohmmeter and voltmeter.

To properly service the engine electrical system for maximum performance and economy as well as an efficient way to locate malfunctions, a certain amount of equipment must be used. Service establishments which do a volume of engine troubleshooting and tuneup work use some type of engine performance test unit. Most testers of this type will include a multi-scale voltmeter, infrared exhaust analyzer, tachometer, dwellmeter, ohmmeter, condenser tester, cylinder leakage tester, oscilloscope, coil tester, vacuum gauge, timing light, timing advance tester, a cylinder balance tester, and fuel delivery tester. In addition, a spark plug gauge and feeler gauges will also be needed. Figure 7-11 is an engine analyzer for tuneup and engine diagnosis. The set consists of an oscilloscope for diagnostic service, timing advance light and an expanded-scale tachometer for checking cylinder balance.

If visual inspection along with continuity tests using a 12 volt test lamp or voltmeter fails to isolate the problem that prevents the engine from starting, further tests must be made to locate the specific components causing the trouble. An ohmmeter may be used to check the high tension wires, ignition coil and pickup coil.

Variations in the components which make up the ignition system on the different makes and models of vehicles will be found. However, all systems operate in the same general manner and are tested in basically the same way.

There must be an electrical flow from the battery to the ignition coil when the ignition switch is on and the engine is cranked. This can be checked for continuity with a 12 volt test lamp, a voltmeter or an ohmmeter. There should be a voltage reading of approximately battery voltage.

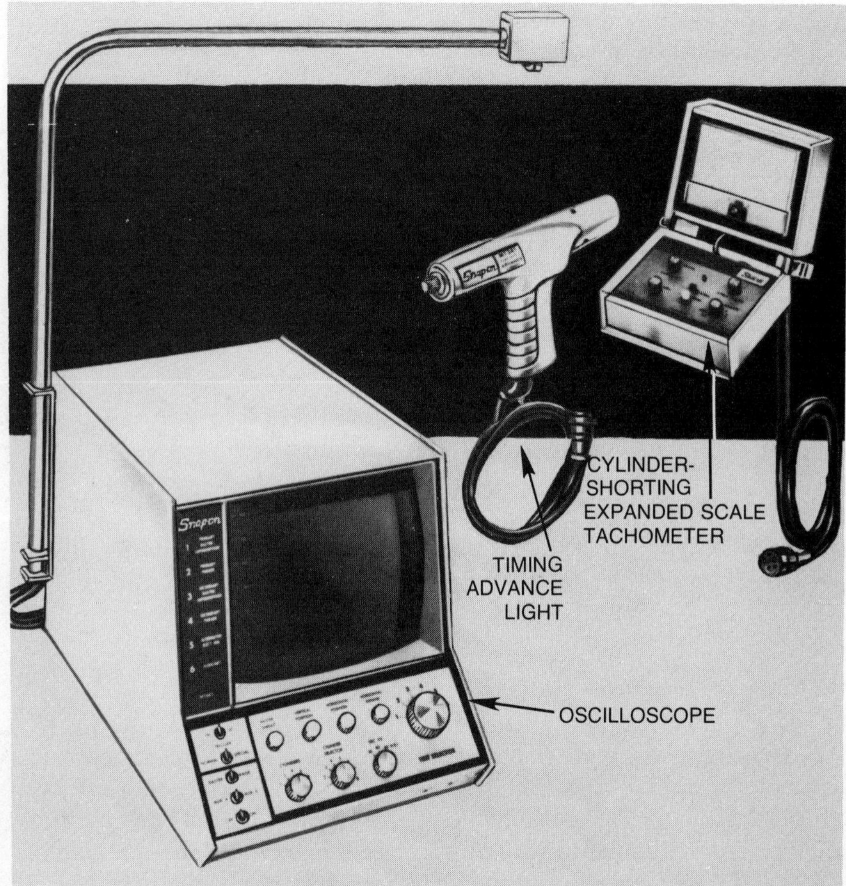

FIGURE 7-11 Engine analyzer set. (Courtesy Snap-On Tools Corporation)

The electronic control module automatically determines the dwell (primary coil windings buildup time) as well as when the primary circuit is interrupted so as to create a high voltage electrical charge to jump the spark plug gap. The module is made up of transistors, resistors, and diodes which necessitates a special tester for the particular make and model of engine.

Because the other units of the ignition system, such as the pickup coil, ignition coil, distributor cap, rotor, and wiring can readily be checked by an elimination process, the trouble can be traced to the electronic control module. When everything else tests satisfactorily, but there still is no spark at the spark plugs, it is safe to assume the module is at fault. No service can be performed on the module; it must be replaced.

Because the pickup coil as well as the secondary windings of the ignition coil are made up of many turns of very fine wire, the practical method to check these components is with an ohmmeter. The ohmmeter is used to check for internal continuity, shorts or ground. All wires have resistance. The size, material and length determine the resistance, therefore manufacturers' specifications will give the resistance range in ohms for the particular component.

The pickup coil is tested by connecting the ohmmeter across the two leads of the coil. Both coil leads must have been disconnected from

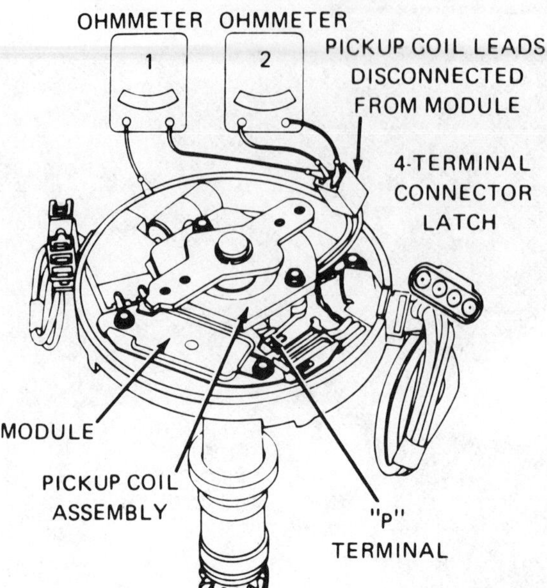

FIGURE 7-12 Checking distributor pick-up coil. (Courtesy Chevrolet Motor Division, General Motors Corp.)

whatever they were connected to. On some General Motors products the meter should read within the 500 to 1500 ohm range, some Chrysler products should read in the 150 to 900 ohm range, some Ford products should read in the 650 to 1300 ohm range while others should be in the 400 to 1,000-ohm range. From this you can see that it is important to check the manufacturer's specifications and replace the coil if it does not meet specifications. No reading indicates an open circuit. Connect one ohmmeter lead to ground and the other to a pickup coil lead. The reading should be infinite at all times (no limit except the needle stop). Check the other pickup coil lead in the same manner. This determines if there is an internal short. Figure 7-12 shows the hookup for checking the pickup coil with an ohmmeter.

The ignition coil can be checked with an ohmmeter if a coil tester is not available. The primary coil range should be between 1 to 2 ohms for most coils. This is checked by connecting the two ohmmeter leads to the two primary terminals on the coil. The secondary resistance should be in the 6,000 to 30,000 ohm range. This check is made by placing one ohmmeter lead on the terminal at the center of the coil tower and the other lead on the distributor terminal of the primary coil.

Spark plug wires may be checked for continuity and/or leakage by placing the ohmmeter leads on each end of the wire. The resistance should not exceed 5,000 ohms per inch.

When a centrifugal advance mechanism is used, its purpose is to advance the ignition timing mechanically, according to engine speed. The unit can easily be checked for operation in the following manner: Twist the distributor rotor in the direction of distributor rotation as far as it will go. Release the rotor. It should spring back to its original position. If the rotor does not come back, the advance mechanism must be repaired. It is usually a problem of broken return springs.

If a vacuum advance unit is used it operates on manifold or carburetor venturi vacuum. The unit consists of a diaphragm enclosed in an air tight compartment. A lever attached to the diaphragm transmits movement to a plate that mounts the pickup unit. If there is a question about the unit it should be checked for leaks. Before checking, make sure the pickup coil assembly, or whatever is actuated by the advance unit, moves freely on its mounting. Check the unit by blowing through the hose connection. If the diaphragm is satisfactory the unit will be airtight. Do not apply high pressure, as it may rupture the diaphragm. Failure of the advance mechanism to operate properly has a very definite affect on engine performance. However, unless the diaphragm in the vacuum control unit is ruptured, malfunctions in either type of advance unit will have no bearing on starting.

Ignition Timing

To obtain maximum engine performance, the distributor must be correctly positioned on the engine to give proper ignition timing. The fuel charge must be ignited at exactly the proper time in relation to piston position. The vibration damper or pulley mounted on the front end of the crankshaft will have a timing mark in the rim. It is usually in the form of a slot cut into the rim of the damper or pulley. A timing plate is located on the timing chain cover. The plate has degree marks stamped on the plate indicating TDC (top dead center) and advance as

FIGURE 7-13 Timing marks. (Courtesy Chevrolet Motor Division, General Motors Corp.)

well as retard. The ignition initial timing test will show when the spark plug for number one cylinder fires in relation to piston position and TDC. Figure 7-13 shows a typical spark timing indicator located on the timing cover with the timing mark on the pulley.

The initial ignition timing check is made in the following manner:

1. If a vacuum advance unit is used on the distributor, disconnect the hose from the vacuum unit and plug the hose. A golf tee usually will serve as a good plug.
2. Connect a power timing light between the number one spark plug and spark plug wire. The wire can be disconnected at either the distributor cap or spark plug, depending upon which is easiest to get at to make the hookup.
3. Connect the timing light to a power source, either the vehicle battery or 110-volt power source, according to manufacturer's instructions for the particular timing light being used.
4. Connect a tachometer to the distributor tachometer connection.
5. Set the parking brake, place the transmission in park or neutral, and start the engine.
6. Loosen the distributor hold-down arm screw just enough so the distributor housing can be rotated by hand in its mounting.
7. Run the engine until normal operating temperature is reached.
8. Set the idle speed to the specifications called for on the Vehicle Emission Control Information label located under the hood. This is very important, because if a centrifugal advance unit is used it will begin to advance timing at a specified speed.
9. Aim the timing light at the timing plate on the chain cover. If the light flashes occur when the timing mark on the vibration damper or pulley is before the specified degree mark as indicated on the Vehicle Emission Control Information label, the timing is advanced. To adjust, turn the distributor housing in the direction of rotor rotation. If the flash occurs after the timing mark is past the recommended degree mark, the timing is retarded. Turn the dis-

FIGURE 7-14 Magnetic timing probe hole. (Courtesy Oldsmobile Division, General Motors Corp.)

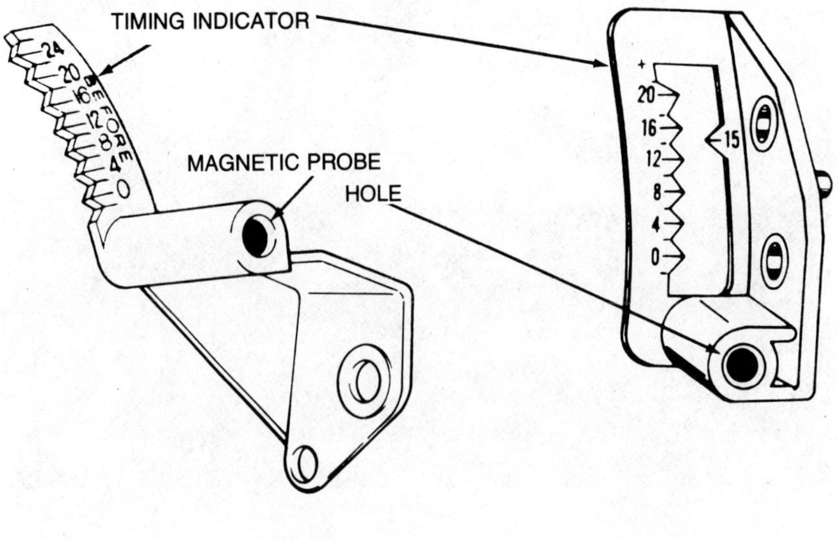

tributor housing against the direction of rotor rotation. Moving the distributor housing against shaft rotation advances timing; with shaft rotation retards timing.

10. Tighten the distributor hold-down arm screw after the timing has been set. Recheck to make sure the distributor housing has not moved.
11. Reconnect the vacuum hose to the distributor vacuum unit.
12. If the idle speed has changed, reset the idle to specifications.

Some engines will incorporate a magnetic timing probe receptacle for use with special electronic timing equipment. Always consult the manufacturer's instructions relative to using test equipment. A regular timing light can be used even if the engine is equipped with a magnetic timing probe receptacle. Figure 7-14 shows the magnetic timing probe hole for two different model engines. The probe hole is located on the engine front cover. A saw slot in the balancer indicates TDC.

Removing Distributor and Retiming

On occasion it may be necessary to remove the distributor from the engine for service, such as to inspect and/or replace the drive gear or to replace the bushings and/or shaft. The position of the reluctor, armature or timer core, and rotor determines when spark will occur and the spark plug which is to be fired. If the engine is not turned after the distributor is removed and the distributor reinstalled with the housing and rotor lined up in exactly the same position from which it was removed, the ignition timing should not have changed.

To remove the distributor, disconnect the vacuum hose from the vacuum advance-retard unit, if one is used. Disconnect the distributor pickup lead wires at the wiring harness connector or ignition switch-battery lead. Unfasten the distributor cap hold-down fasteners, or if latches are used, turn the latches counterclockwise to release. Lift off the distributor cap. Turn the engine crankshaft until the distributor rotor is pointing directly toward the fire-wall. Scribe a mark on the distributor housing and a similar mark on the engine block so the housing and rotor can be reinstalled in exactly the same position from which they were removed. Remove the distributor hold-down cap screw. Carefully remove the distributor from the engine. The shaft and rotor will turn slightly if the distributor gear is attached to the shaft, because the gear is disengaged from the camshaft gear.

Should the engine crankshaft be turned after the distributor is removed, the distributor must be retimed to the engine. To establish basic timing, remove the number one spark plug. Place a finger over the spark plug hole and turn the engine over slowly until compression pressure is felt on the finger. Continue to turn the engine until the timing mark on the pulley or damper is lined up under "0" or TDC on the timing indicator. Turn the rotor so it is aligned near the number one spark plug tower on the distributor cap. Install the distributor on the engine. Insert the hold-down bolt but leave loose enough so the distributor housing can be turned by hand. Install the distributor cap and connect the feed wire or connector. Attach the vacuum hose if it was removed. Start the engine, check and set the timing with a timing light.

Checking Distributor Advance Mechanisms

Ignition timing is extremely critical for efficient operation and reduced exhaust emissions. Most older model vehicles relied upon a centrifugal mechanical timing advance unit and a vacuum advance-retard unit. The mechanical advance operates strictly according to distributor (engine) speed, while the vacuum-operated unit depends upon manifold vacuum and/or carburetor venturi vacuum. Vacuum is determined by engine speed, load, and throttle position.

Some of the present distributors utilize one or both of these timing control units, along with various sensors that feed information into a type of computer which assists in controlling engine ignition timing. Other distributors may not utilize either type of advance unit, but will be entirely controlled by the computer unit. The information is fed into the spark control module which adjusts the ignition timing. Details of this type of equipment will be discussed in Chapter 9.

When vacuum and/or mechanical advance units are used they should be checked for operation when the ignition timing is checked. It is a simple matter to determine whether or not the units are operational when a timing light is being used to check initial timing. With the light hooked up and the distributor vacuum hose disconnected from the vacuum unit, gradually increase the speed of the engine and watch to see if the timing advances as the speed is increased. If there is no advance, the mechanical unit is not operating. Note the speed at which maximum advance occurs. Stop the engine and reconnect the vacuum hose to the distributor vacuum-retard unit. Start the engine and increase the speed to the RPM s at which maximum advance occurred. If the vacuum unit is operating, there will be additional advance.

A timing advance meter can be used to accurately check the operation of both the vacuum advance-retard and the mechanical advance without removing the distributor from the engine. Various manufacturers of electrical test equipment have this type of equipment available. Most manufacturers will label it as a timing advance meter. Always follow the equipment manufacturers' instructions for their particular type of equipment.

Some ignition timing advance meters will incorporate a timing light, a tachometer, and a degree scale. Other timing advance testers will include a timing light and a meter to read degrees of advance. A separate tachometer unit needs to be used with the timing advance meter. Figure 7-15 shows an adjustable timing light which permits accurate checking of timing change with the distributor installed and the engine running. A tachometer is needed to check engine RPM s.

Before testing, operate the engine until it reaches normal operating temperature. To check the degrees of advance of the centrifugal advance unit, disconnect the vacuum hose from the vacuum advance-retard unit and plug the hose. A golf tee will usually serve as a good plug. With the tachometer and timing meter properly connected, start the engine and check the degrees of advance according to engine RPMs. This information will be found in the manufacturer's specifications. As engine speed is gradually increased, the timing mark should move from the original position in the opposite direction of engine rotation. Little or no movement indicates a problem in the distributor that requires attention.

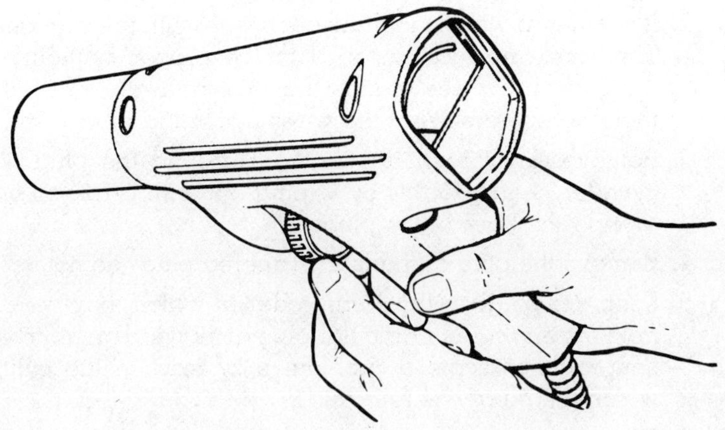

FIGURE 7-15 Adjustable timing advance light. (Courtesy Chrysler Corporation)

To check the vacuum advance-retard unit, reconnect the vacuum hose to the distributor. Gradually increase the engine speed and watch the timing mark move from its original position. On distributors with both vacuum and centrifugal advance units, the total advance should be greater than that observed with centrifugal advance alone. If there is none, or only a little vacuum advance, the unit should be replaced.

Inspect and Service Spark Plugs

Spark plugs normally perform effectively for several thousand miles. Most manufacturers recommend changing plugs every 25,000 to 30,000 miles. This will vary depending upon the type of operation and the specific manufacturer's recommendations. To be assured of maximum performance, it is suggested that the plugs be removed, inspected, cleaned, and the gap reset at 10,000 to 15,000 miles. If the plugs show abnormal conditions they should be replaced.

Occasional or intermittent high speed operation is essential to good spark plug performance, because it provides increased and sustained combustion heat that burns away excessive deposits of carbon and oxides that may have accumulated from frequent idling or continual stop and go slow speed operation.

To service spark plugs, a spark plug socket, generally a thirteen-sixteenths inch is needed. A few engines use a smaller plug requiring a five-eighths inch socket. A ratchet handle and a short extension bar, as well as a spark plug gauge, ignition point file, wire brush, and a small stiff blade to clean between the insulator and base are all that are needed to service spark plugs. Service spark plugs in the following manner:

1. Remove the spark plug wire from the spark plug. To do this, slightly twist the rubber boot that partially covers the spark plug insulator; this breaks the seal. Grasp the boot and pull it from the plug with a steady even pressure. Do not pull on the wire as it can damage it.

2. It may be advisable to mark each wire with the cylinder number. The wires must be installed to the proper cylinder. Write the number on a piece of masking tape and attach it to the wire if there is a possibility of the wires becoming mixed up.
3. Remove any foreign matter from around the plug hole in the cylinder head. Do this by wiping out with a rag or blowing air around the base of the plug.
4. Remove the plug and gasket. Tapered plugs do not use gaskets.
5. Keep the plugs in the same order in which they were removed from the engine. A particular plug displaying an abnormal condition could indicate a problem may exist in the cylinder from which the plug was removed.
6. Clean the exterior of the plug and inspect for cracks in the insulator as well as leakage between the insulator and base.
7. Check for burned electrodes and dirty, fouled or cracked insulators.
8. If new plugs are to be installed, make sure they are the right type for the particular engine. The type of plug is indicated by the number on the plug. This determines the heat range and the reach (how far the plug extends into the cylinder head). Conversion charts are available where plugs are sold that indicate what number of plug fits a particular make and model of engine when using a different brand of plug. Figure 7-16 shows checking the spark plug gap with a gauge. Only the ground electrode is bent to change the gap.

FIGURE 7-16 Checking spark plug gap (clearance). (Courtesy Ford Parts & Service Division, Ford Motor Co.)

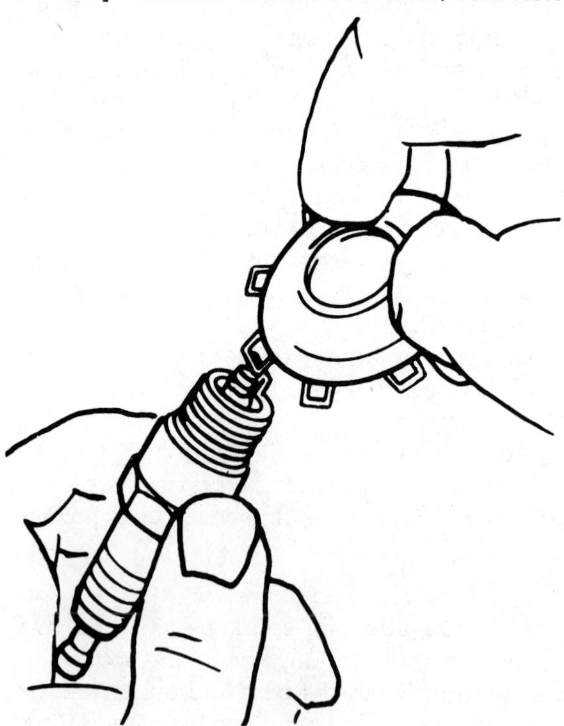

9. When installing new plugs be sure to check the gap and reset if necessary.
10. Gap setting (space between the center electrode and ground electrode) is changed by bending the ground electrode. Spark plugs which have been used are not as efficient as new plugs but by servicing them, engine performance, spark plug life, and reduced engine emissions will generally result. Figure 7-17 illustrates different spark plug conditions. These conditions tell much about engine operating problems.
11. If the electrodes are not burned away, the plugs appear to be of the correct heat range and the insulator is not cracked, eroded or blistered, the plugs can be cleaned, regapped and put back in service.
12. Clean the plug in a petroleum solvent after brushing the outside, including the threads, with a wire brush.
13. An abrasive type cleaner (sand blast) is the best for a good cleaning job. Blow out all abrasive with compressed air after cleaning. Most service stations and garages will have this type of equipment.
14. If a spark plug cleaner is not available use a thin stiff blade that will go down in between the plug shell and insulator and scrape all the deposits loose. Turn the plug upright and shake the deposits out. Repeat until clean.
15. If possible, blow out any remaining deposits with air.
16. Widen the gap by bending the outside (ground) electrode so that an ignition point file may be inserted between the electrodes.
17. File the electrode until all the carbon is removed and the end of the center electrode is flat across the top.
18. Adjust the gap to the correct specifications.
19. Check the gasket to make sure it is seating properly. If no gasket is used (tapered seat) make sure the surface is clean.
20. Install the plugs.
21. Tighten to the manufacturer's specifications with a torque wrench. Most 14 mm plugs are tightened to approximately 25 to 30 ft/lbs.
22. If a torque wrench is not available make sure the plug turns freely in the thread. Tighten the plug finger tight then with a wrench tighten the plug having a tapered seat approximately one-sixteenth turn. A plug using a gasket should be turned approximately one-half turn.
23. Check the spark plug wires. If the insulation is cracked, oil soaked or brittle the wires should be replaced. It is generally advisable to replace the wires as a set.
24. The tower for the wires in the distributor cap as well as the ends of the wires should be clean and fit tightly into the cap. If the distributor cap is dirty it should be wiped off with a clean rag.
25. Reinstall the spark plug wires to the same cylinder from which they were removed.

GAP BRIDGED

IDENTIFIED BY DEPOSIT BUILD-UP CLOSING GAP BETWEEN ELECTRODES CAUSED BY OIL OR CARBON FOULING. REPLACE PLUG, OR, IF DEPOSITS ARE NOT EXCESSIVE, THE PLUG CAN BE CLEANED.

OIL FOULED

IDENTIFIED BY WET BLACK DEPOSITS ON THE INSULATOR SHELL BORE ELECTRODES.

CAUSED BY EXCESSIVE OIL ENTERING COMBUSTION CHAMBER THROUGH WORN RINGS AND PISTONS. EXCESSIVE CLEARANCE BETWEEN VALVE GUIDES AND STEMS, OR WORN OR LOOSE BEARINGS REPLACE THE PLUG.

CARBON FOULED

IDENTIFIED BY BLACK, DRY FLUFFY CARBON DEPOSITS ON INSULATOR TIPS, EXPOSED SHELL SURFACES AND ELECTRODES.

CAUSED BY TOO COLD A PLUG, WEAK IGNITION, DIRTY AIR CLEANER, DEFECTIVE FUEL PUMP, TOO RICH A FUEL MIXTURE, IMPROPERLY OPERATING HEAT RISER OR EXCESSIVE IDLING CAN BE CLEANED.

NORMAL

IDENTIFIED BY LIGHT TAN OR GRAY DEPOSITS ON THE FIRING TIP.

PRE-IGNITION

IDENTIFIED BY MELTED ELECTRODES AND POSSIBLY BLISTERED INSULATOR METALIC DEPOSITS ON INSULATOR INDICATE ENGINE DAMAGE.

CAUSED BY WRONG TYPE OF FUEL, INCORRECT IGNITION TIMING OR ADVANCE, TOO HOT A PLUG, BURNT VALVES OR ENGINE OVERHEATING. REPLACE THE PLUG.

OVERHEATING

IDENTIFIED BY A WHITE OR LIGHT GRAY INSULATOR WITH SMALL BLACK OR GRAY BROWN SPOTS AND WITH BLUISH BURNT APPEARANCE OF ELECTRODES.

CAUSED BY ENGINE OVERHEATING, WRONG TYPE OF FUEL, LOOSE SPARK PLUGS, TOO HOT A PLUG, LOW FUEL PUMP PRESSURE OR INCORRECT IGNITION TIMING. REPLACE THE PLUG.

FUSED SPOT DEPOSIT

IDENTIFIED BY MELTED OR SPOTTY DEPOSITS RESEMBLING BUBBLES OR BLISTERS.

CAUSED BY SUDDEN ACCELERATION. CAN BE CLEANED IF NOT EXCESSIVE. OTHERWISE REPLACE PLUG.

FIGURE 7-17 Spark plug appearance reflects engine operating conditions. (Courtesy Ford Parts & Service Division, Ford Motor Co.)

8

Emission Control Systems

The automobile engine contributes to air pollution because gasoline or diesel oil is used as a fuel. Both types of fuels are basically hydrocarbons and are not completely burned within the engine. When unburned hydrocarbons escape into the air they contribute to contamination (pollution). The federal government has placed limitations on the quantity of three different compounds which are emitted by the automobile engine. These are hydrocarbon HC, carbon monoxide CO and oxides of nitrogen NO_x.

The automobile engine has four sources from which unburned hydrocarbon may be released. They include the crankcase where blowby gases account for approximately 20 percent of the total. The second source is the exhaust system which contributes about 60 percent. In addition to unburned hydrocarbons, exhaust emissions include carbon monoxide and oxides of nitrogen. The remaining 20 percent contaminants come from the fuel tank and carburetor. Evaporation is continually taking place from these units. It is for these reasons that various types of emission control components and adjustments must be incorporated to keep automobile pollution within federal mandated limitations.

Most emission control components are vacuum operated. A few such as the positive crankcase ventilation system and the thermostatically controlled air cleaner depend strictly on vacuum for their control and operation. A few units may use solenoids and/or sensors to activate the vacuum control.

On a number of late model engines, a computer control system electronically controls the exhaust emission system. The actual operation of the emission control unit will be the same on most engines regardless of the type of control units used. The computer control system is discussed in a separate chapter, Chapter 9. Figure 8-1 shows the components of an emission control system which uses an electronic spark control computer.

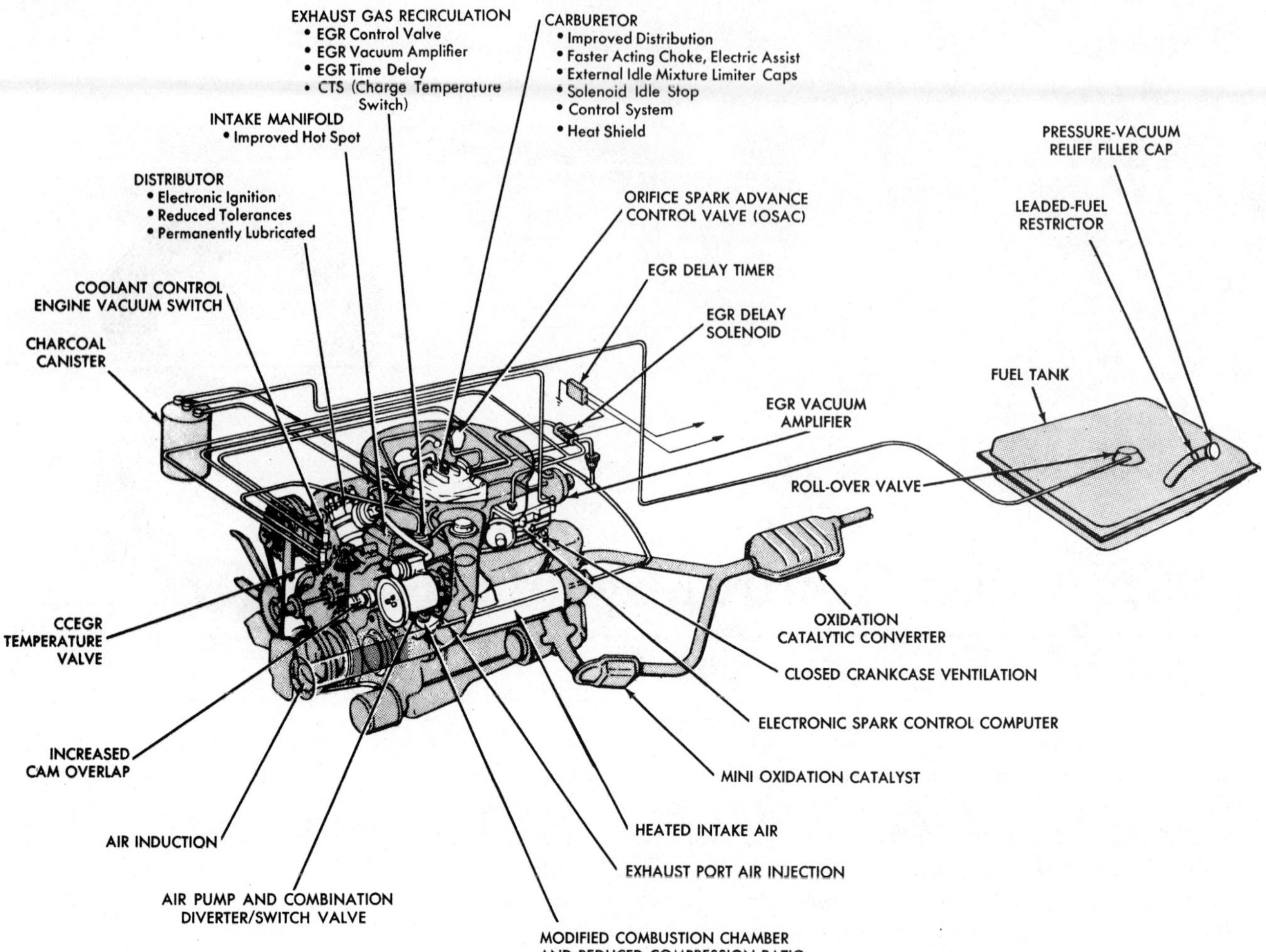

FIGURE 8-1 Components of an emission control system. (Courtesy Chrysler Corporation)

As the operation of most of these emission control units affect overall engine efficiency, whenever preventive maintenance, troubleshooting or diagnostic operations are performed the emission control system components must be taken into consideration. Most of the units are comparatively simple in construction and can easily be checked, serviced or replaced as necessary.

Hoses supply the vacuum used in operating many of these control units and are, therefore, a major factor in performing service work on them. It is easy for a hose to become disconnected, develop a crack, be pinched or cut so that a leak is present. No engine can operate efficiently or smoothly when a vacuum leak exists. Whenever working around the engine check the condition of the hoses and their hookup. The under hood emission control decal will usually show the correct hose hookup and routing, because it is easy for hoses to become disconnected and not reconnected in the correct location. Figure 8-2 is a schematic of the vacuum hose arrangement used with a Ford Motor EEC111 computer-controlled emission system.

Since federal standards for emission controls were first established, many changes have taken place. One reason being that federal regulations have become more stringent and automobile

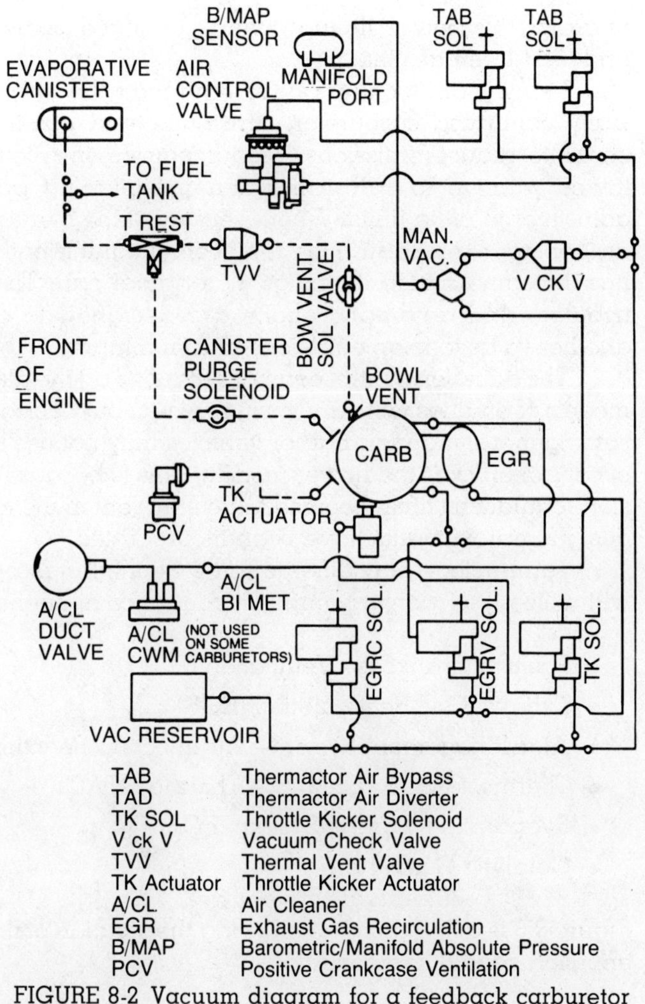

FIGURE 8-2 Vacuum diagram for a feedback carburetor system. (Courtesy Ford Parts & Service Division, Ford Motor Co.)

manufacturers have developed more sophisticated components. More emission control equipment is being used to provide for a cleaner burning engine.

Gasoline is a hydrocarbon and engine designs are such that only a small percentage of the total potential energy in the fuel is utilized. This means that unless checked, there will be a considerable amount of hydrocarbons allowed to escape into the atmosphere.

The purpose of the emission control system is to bring about more complete burning of the hydrocarbons before releasing the exhaust gases into the atmosphere. In addition, present passenger vehicles make use of a catalytic converter in the exhaust system, which further reduces hydrocarbons and carbon monoxide pollutants after the exhaust gases leave the engine.

The development of emission controls has been an evolutionary process throughout the years, starting basically with the positive crankcase ventilation system.

The following changes in engineering design and added components have helped to reduce engine emissions: Changing the combustion chamber design for better burning; higher cooling system temperature; higher idle speeds; idle stop solenoid; controlled vacuum retarding distributor timing control; changed spark advance curve, and lead-free gasoline.

Many manufacturers have equipped the engine with a specifically calibrated carburetor, distributor and possibly the automatic choke to reduce emissions. Manufacturers' instructions must be followed relative to calibration when replacing parts and making adjustments to the units. Whenever any of the mentioned components are replaced, make sure the replacement unit is of the exact type and has the same specifications as the original part. The carburetor, distributor, and automatic choke are designed to complement one another so as to keep emissions at a minimum.

The emission control components used on the different makes and models of engines will vary to some extent but basically perform in the same general manner. Earlier vehicles may not use the same number of control units as the newer models. This is because the federal emission regulations have become more stringent in the last few years and design improvements have been incorporated.

Terminology may differ to some extent, but most present vehicles will utilize the following emission control components:

- Positive Crankcase Ventilation (PCV)
- Exhaust Gas Recirculation (EGR)
- Air Management System—Air Injection Reaction (AIR)
- Thermostatic Air Cleaner—Thermac (TAC)
- Evaporation Control System (ECS)
- Catalytic Converter

Figure 8-3 is a line drawing showing the location of the various engine emission control components.

FIGURE 8-3 Location of engine emission control components. (Courtesy Chevrolet Motor Division, General Motors Corp.)

1 OXYGEN SENSOR (MOUNTED IN EXHAUST MANIFOLD)
2 FUEL PUMP RELAY
3 A/C CLUTCH RELAY
4 MAP SENSOR
5 A/C COMPRESSOR CONTROL RELAY (MOUNTED ON COWL)
6 A/C CYCLING SWITCH
7 OIL PRESSURE SWITCH (NEXT TO DISTRIBUTOR)
8 EST CONNECTOR (FROM DISTRIBUTOR)
9 COOLANT SENSOR
10 POWER STRG. PRESSURE SWITCH (ON PRESSURE LINE)
11 COOLANT FAN RELAY
12 T.C.C. CONNECTOR

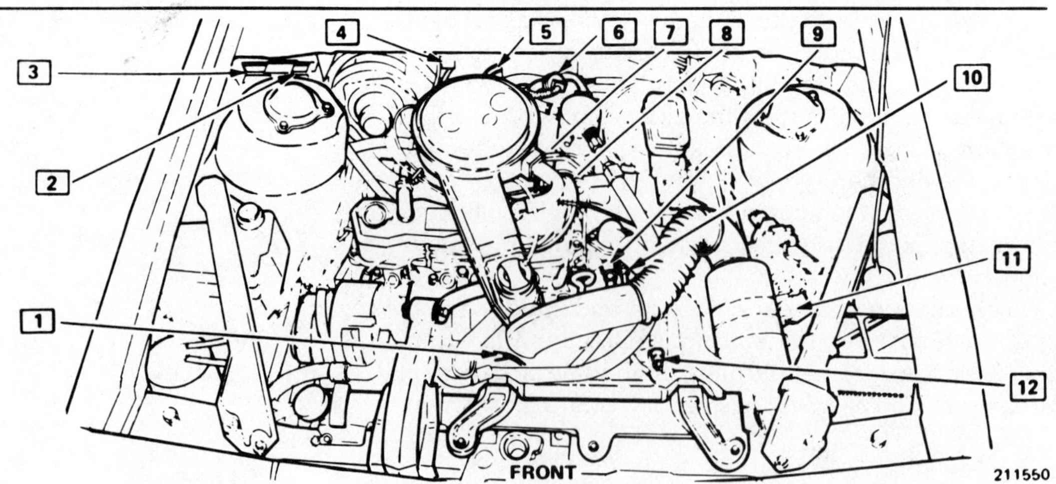

Following is a description of the more common emission control units:

Positive Crankcase Ventilation (PCV)

The PCV valve is located on the valve cover or intake manifold. The valve provides for more complete scavenging of crankcase vapors caused by blowby and movement of air through the crankcase. Ventilating air is drawn from the clean air section of the air cleaner through a tube down into the crankcase. Air and fumes are then drawn up through the PCV valve (a one-way valve) by way of a hose or passageway into the intake manifold. Intake manifold vacuum draws the crankcase fumes through the intake manifold and into the combustion chamber where they are burned.

Basically, because the PCV valve is a one-way valve, vacuum must move through the valve in one direction and close off tightly when the flow is in the opposite direction. A faulty valve results in a slow, unstable idle with frequent stalling. This is the result of the valve being plugged, stuck, or of a restricted air cleaner. The complete system, including the air cleaner and hoses, should be cleaned and a new valve installed. Figure 8-4 illustrates a typical PCV flow system as used on most engines.

FIGURE 8-4 PCV valve flow system—typical. (Courtesy Chevrolet Motor Division, General Motors Corp.)

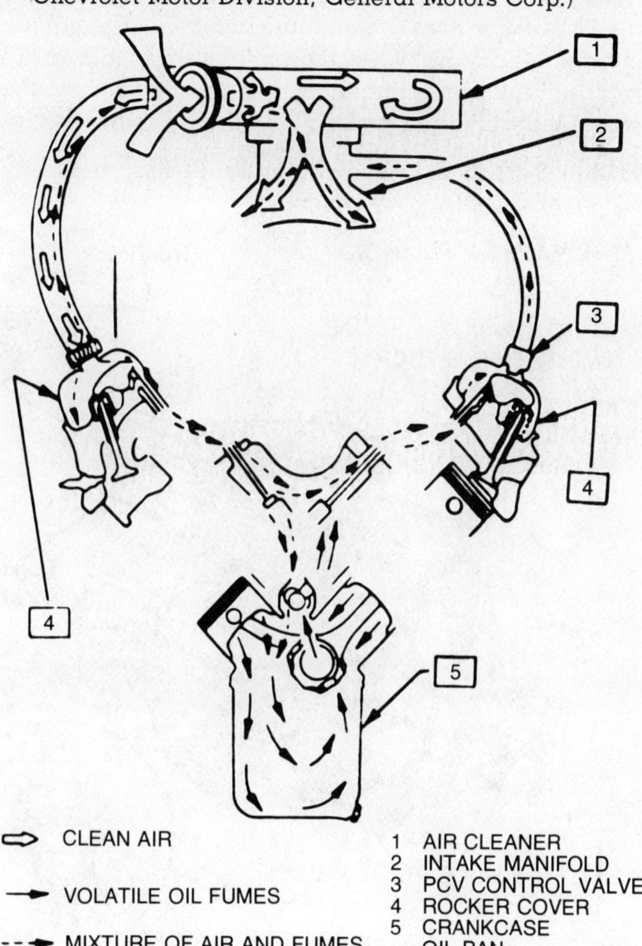

To check the operation of the crankcase ventilation system, with the engine idling, remove the PCV valve from the rocker arm cover. If the valve or system is not plugged a hissing noise will be heard as air passes through the valve and a strong vacuum should be felt when a finger is placed over the valve inlet. Stop the engine, remove the PCV valve from the cover and shake it. A clicking noise should be heard, which indicates the valve is free. Many manufacturers recommend a new PCV valve be installed every 30,000 miles.

If there is oil in the air cleaner the PCV valve may be plugged, or there could be a leak in the system. Clean all hoses, clean or replace the air cleaner element, and replace the valve. Inspect all hoses and connections making sure there are no leaks.

Exhaust Gas Recirculation Valve (EGR)

The oxides of nitrogen, NOx, in engine exhaust emissions can be reduced by lowering the peak flame temperatures during combustion. This can be accomplished by allowing a predetermined amount of hot exhaust gases to be recirculated so as to dilute the incoming air/fuel mixture. The exhaust gas recirculation EGR valve reintroduces small amounts of exhaust gas into the combustion cycle so as to reduce the generation of nitrogen oxide NOx. The amount of exhaust gas reintroduced and the timing of the cycle varies by calibration and is controlled by such factors as engine speed, altitude, engine vacuum, exhaust system back pressure, coolant temperature, and throttle opening. All EGR valves are vacuum actuated. The valve opens and closes a passageway between the exhaust manifold and intake manifold. Intake manifold vacuum draws exhaust gases into the intake manifold when the valve is opened. Figure 8-5 shows a typical exhaust gas

FIGURE 8-5 Exhaust gas recirculation (EGR) system. (Courtesy Chrysler Corporation)

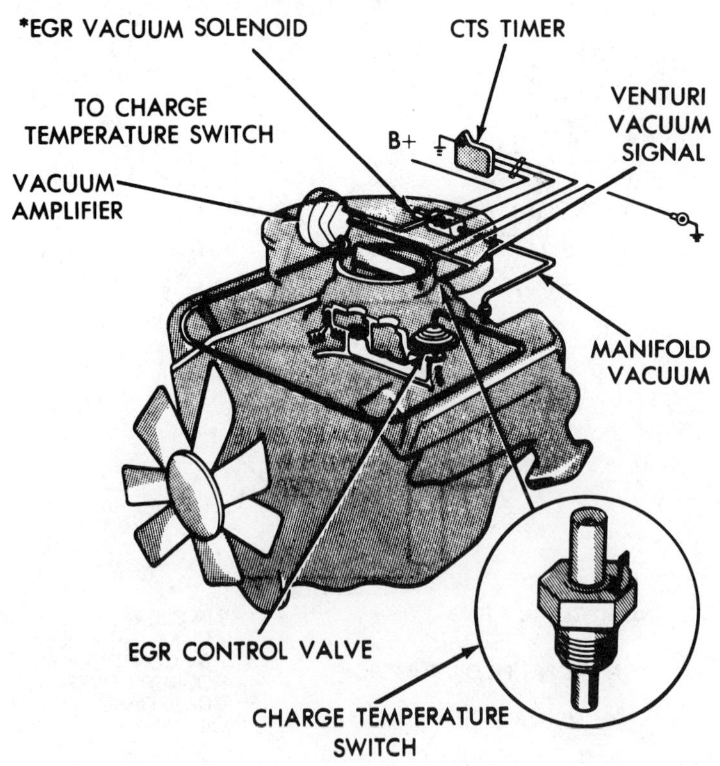

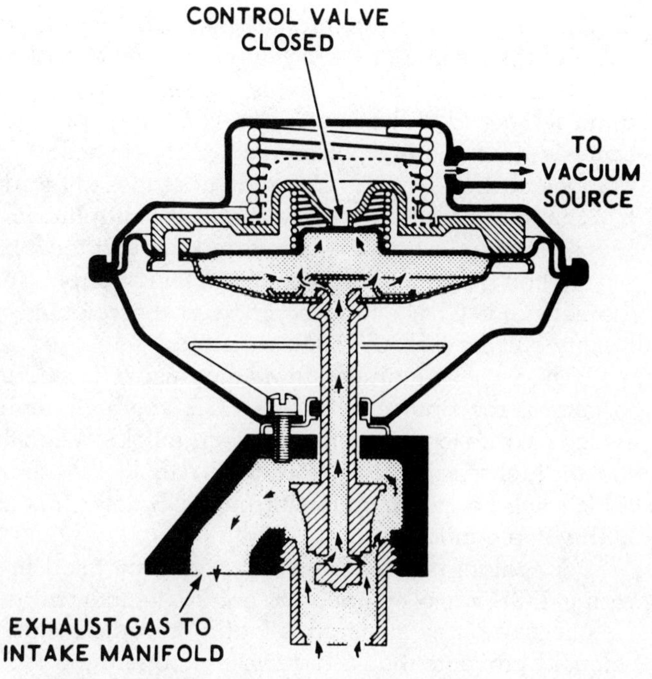

FIGURE 8-6 Back pressure type EGR valve—closed. (Courtesy Oldsmobile Division, General Motors Corp.)

recirculation (EGR) system. The system depends upon engine intake air flow, intake vacuum, temperature, and exhaust gas pressure.

The following information is general, and while certain differences may exist, the basic operation will be very much the same for all valves. A back pressure control valve may be incorporated in some units. A few back pressure valves may be electrically operated. One type of valve uses a small diaphragm control valve inside the EGR valve, which acts as a pressure regulator. The control valve receives exhaust back pressure through the hollow shaft that exerts a force on the bottom of the control valve diaphragm.

In operation, the valve remains closed during periods of idle and deceleration to prevent rough idle. The valve opening is determined by the amount of vacuum received and the amount of back pressure in the exhaust system. Figure 8-6 is a cutaway view of the EGR valve which has a back pressure transducer integrated into the valve.

In order for the system to function properly all moving parts must be free to move and not stick as a result of deposits. All hoses and connections must be tight so there is no leakage.

The operation of the EGR valve is checked with the engine at normal operating temperature. With the engine at normal idle speed, quickly accelerate the engine to approximately 2,000 RPMs. Movement of the valve stem during the period of acceleration should be visible by observing a change in the relative position of the stem of the valve. Movement of the valve stem indicates the control system is functioning. The diaphragm plate should move freely when pushed with a finger; if not the valve must be replaced.

If the valve is not functioning check for vacuum to the valve. This may be done by connecting a vacuum gauge to the end of the hose which was removed from the valve. There should be a minimum of 5 in. hg. vacuum with the throttle open. If a vacuum gauge is not available, place a small piece of paper over the end of the hose while the engine is running. If vacuum is present it will hold the paper tightly against the end of the hose. If no vacuum is present find the reason, such as hose routing not correct, plugged hose, leaking hose, or a plugged carburetor port. Clean all passages to be sure they are open. If vacuum is present to the unit and the diaphragm moves freely by hand, the diaphragm is leaking and the unit must be replaced.

When a solenoid is used, check for a complete electrical circuit to the solenoid. Check the operation of the solenoid unit by applying battery current directly to the solenoid.

The various manufacturers may use different units in the system to control the operation of the EGR valve. A temperature change switch may be located in the intake manifold. When the temperature of the air/fuel mixture is below 60°F. (16°C) the change temperature switch will be closed, allowing no EGR timer function, therefore the EGR valve cannot open.

A coolant control EGR valve may be used in some systems to restrict EGR valve operation to engine temperatures above 75°F.

A time delay solenoid is found on some installations. The delay solenoid prevents the EGR valve from operating for a minimum of 35 seconds, 45 seconds or 90 seconds after the engine starts. Different model engines will have different time delay periods. Check manufacturer's specifications. A test lamp or an ohmmeter can be used to check time delay operation. The light goes out when the solenoid no longer operates.

A vacuum amplifier may be used on some engines. This is to strengthen the comparatively weak vacuum signal received from the carburetor venturi. This is to provide for the necessary vacuum reaching the valve.

Some vehicles may be equipped with an electronic EGR control. This is incorporated in the spark control computer.

A faulty EGR system caused by a leak in the vacuum control system, a leaking diaphragm, or the valve remaining in an open position will generally result in a very rough idle or the engine dies out on return to idle.

Early Fuel Evaporation System (EFE)

Most early fuel evaporation valves are installed at the exhaust outlet where the exhaust pipe is connected to the manifold. The purpose is to direct exhaust gases through the exhaust crossover passage in the intake manifold during cold engine operation. The heating of the intake manifold improves fuel vaporization during the warmup period.

For many years the early fuel evaporation system consisted of a manifold heat control valve operated by a thermostatic spring and counterweight. This type of unit is generally labeled as the manifold heat control valve. Figure 8-7 is a line drawing of a manifold heat valve controlled by a thermostatic spring.

To be assured of positive action and better control, many manufacturers are incorporating a vacuum actuated valve controlled by a thermal vacuum switch. The thermal vacuum switch is located on the engine block and extends into the engine coolant. The switch applies

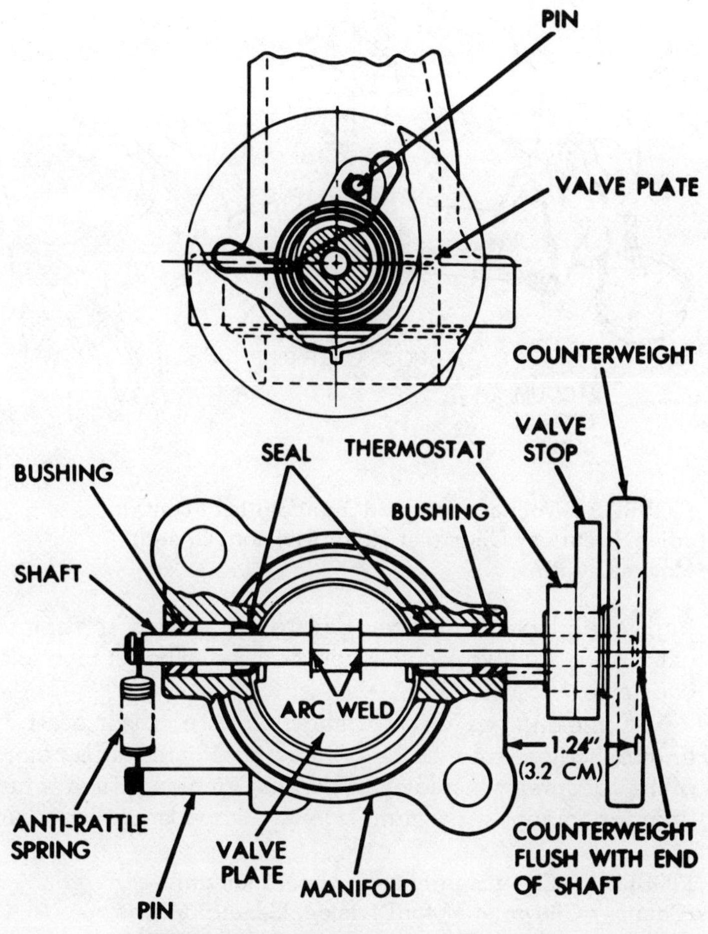

FIGURE 8-7 Manifold heat control valve. (Courtesy Chrysler Corporation)

vacuum to the heat valve actuator assembly to keep it in a closed position until the coolant temperature reaches a predetermined temperature.

To check for operation, the exhaust valve must move freely and the actuator must hold the heat valve in a closed position when the engine is cold. If the actuator unit will not hold vacuum for at least one minute it must be replaced. If the valve binds, try to free it with manifold heat valve lubricant. If the valve cannot be made to operate freely, it must be replaced. To check operation, apply at least 10 in. hg. of vacuum from an external source. Intake manifold vacuum at idle will be over 10 in. hg.; therefore this can also be used for testing.

If vacuum is not reaching the actuator, inspect the hose for damage such as cracks, leaks, deterioration, pinching, or kinks. Check the operation of the thermal vacuum switch. With the engine coolant cold, the vacuum switch must be open. Apply vacuum from an external source or directly from the intake manifold to the inlet port. The engine must be cold, therefore make the test as soon as the engine is started. If there is no vacuum at the outlet port the switch is faulty. When the engine is hot, the switch must close off all vacuum to the actuator and the heat valve must be open. The coolant must be drained if it is necessary to remove the switch. A faulty EFE valve results in poor operation during engine warmup, rough idle, stumble, and lack of

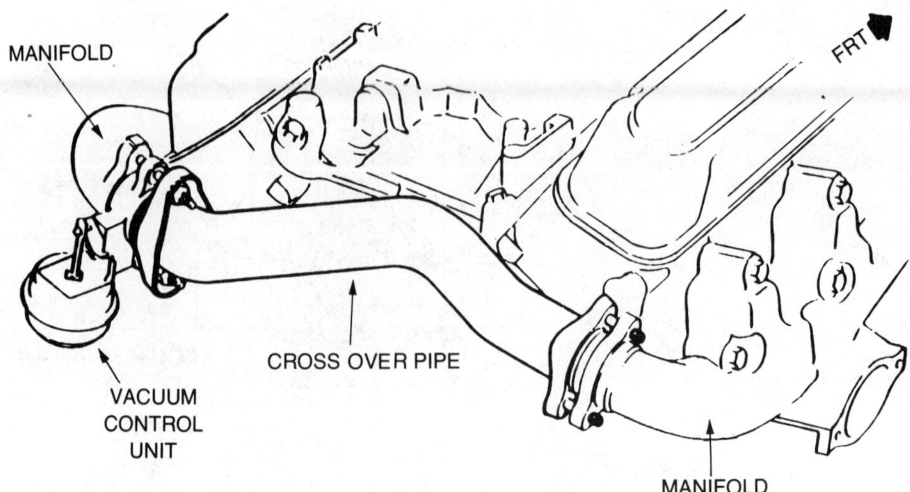

FIGURE 8-8 Vacuum operated manifold heat control valve. (Courtesy Chevrolet Motor Division, General Motors Corp.)

high speed performance. Figure 8-8 shows a vacuum operated exhaust heat valve located between the exhaust manifold and cross-over pipe.

Some engines use a heating element consisting of a ceramic heater grid located beneath the primary bore of the carburetor. This is part of the carburetor insulator. When the ignition switch is turned on and engine coolant temperature is low, voltage is applied to an EFE relay.

FIGURE 8-9 Electric early fuel evaporation unit. (Courtesy Chevrolet Motor Division, General Motors Corp.)

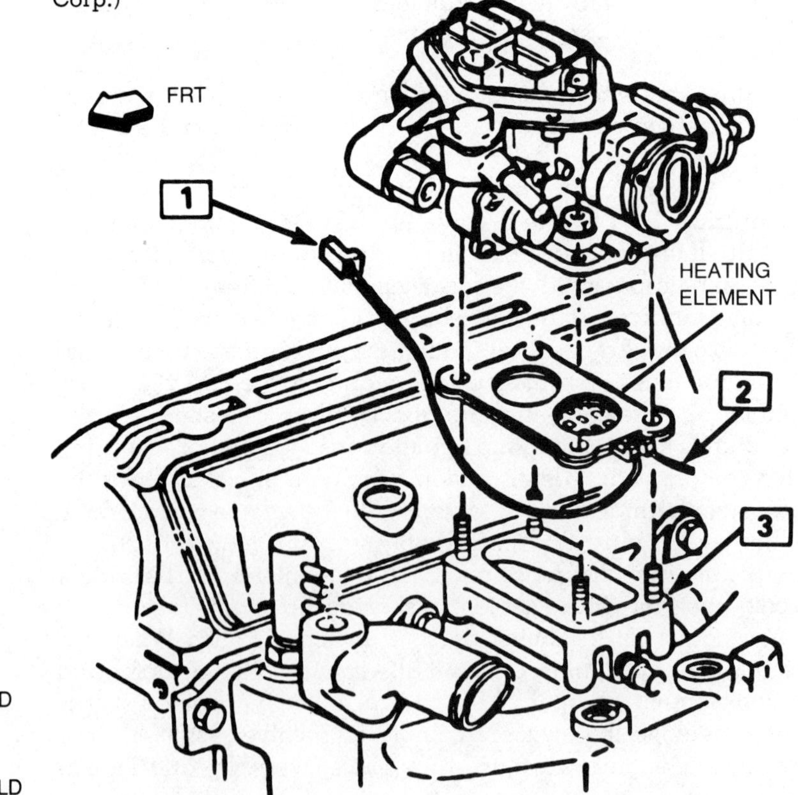

1 TO RELAY

2 TO GROUND

3 INTAKE MANIFOLD

When the relay is energized, voltage is applied to the heater. When the coolant temperature reaches a predetermined level, a temperature control switch de-energizes the relay which shuts off the heater. A solenoid (relay) is utilized to control current flow to the relay.

The carburetor must be removed in order to replace the heater. Always check the electrical circuit and connections before replacing the relay or heating element. Figure 8-9 is an electric early fuel evaporation system which is located between the carburetor and the intake manifold.

Air Injection System

Automobile manufacturers label the various air injection systems differently, such as an air injection reaction system (AIR), air management system, thermactor (thermal reactor), and air supply system, but they all function in much the same manner and basically use the same components.

The air injection system is a method used to reduce the amount of hydrocarbons and carbon monoxide emitted from the engine through the exhaust system. This is done by injecting air directly into the exhaust port of each cylinder. Air added to the hot exhaust gases improves oxidation of the gases before leaving the exhaust system. In addition, some systems are designed to inject air into the catalytic converter.

Most air injection systems utilize an air pump, a management valve which may include a diverter valve as well as an air switching and control valve, an air injection manifold, or passages to the exhaust ports in the cylinder head with the necessary hoses and connections, plus some type of check valve. Figure 8-10 shows an air injection system with a belt-driven air pump used on a V8 engine.

The air pump mounted on the front of the engine is belt driven. Intake air passes through a centrifugal fan filter where foreign matter is separated from the air by centrifugal force. The pump discharges air to a valve arrangement which distributes air according to engine operating conditions. Different controls and valves may be used on the various engines but in general all basically perform in the same manner.

During cold operation, airflow from the pump is directed to the exhaust ports to help reduce the hydrocarbon and carbon monoxide in the exhaust as well as reducing the total amount of exhaust gases. During deceleration and wide-open throttle operation airflow to the exhaust ports is cut off and is directed to the outside through a silencer or to the air cleaner to reduce noise. Excessive pump pressure is also diverted to the outside or to the air cleaner.

After the engine is warmed up, air may be directed to the catalytic converter to provide an oxidizing atmosphere for more effective catalytic operation.

A check valve arrangement is used to protect the air injection system in the event of pump belt failure, abnormally high exhaust pressure, or if the air hose is ruptured. The valve also prevents hot exhaust gases from backing up in the hose or pump in the case of engine backfire.

The valve generally labeled a diverter valve, is sensitive to the sudden change in intake manifold vacuum which activates the valve.

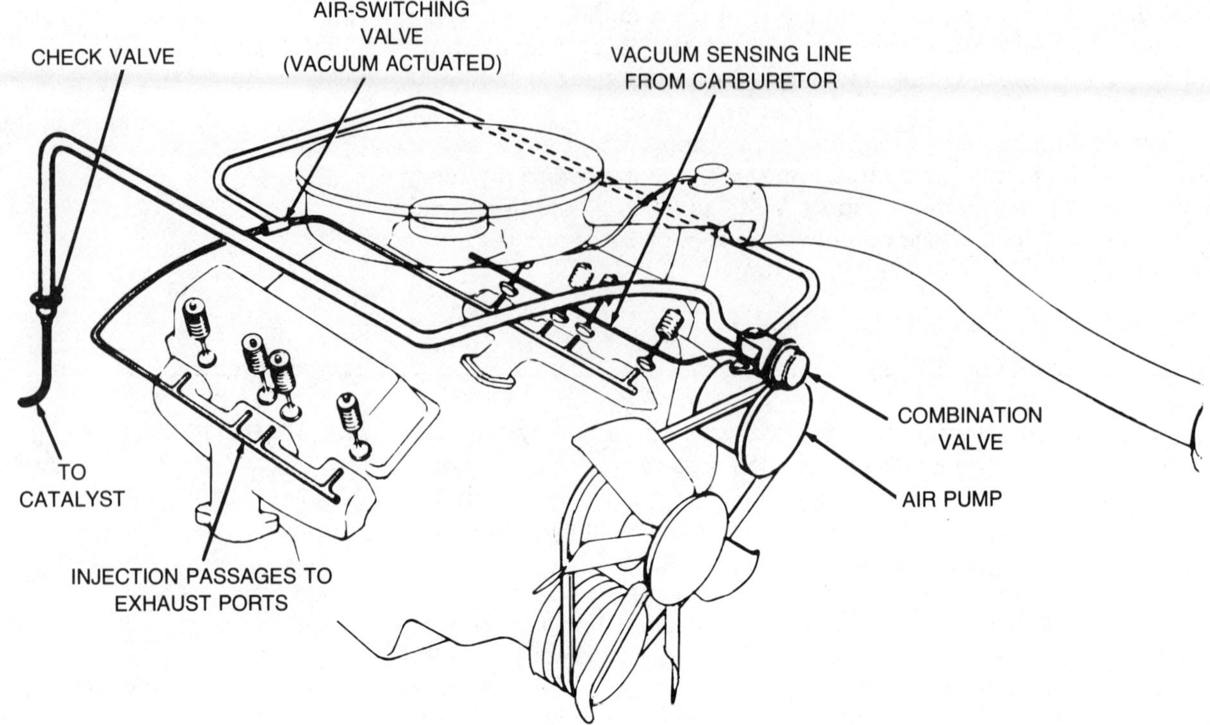

FIGURE 8-10 Air injection system. (Courtesy Chrysler Corporation)

The valve depends upon manifold vacuum for its operation. When an electronic control module is used, a solenoid will control valve operation according to conditions reflecting input from the oxygen sensor, throttle position, coolant temperature, spark advance, exhaust gas recirculation, and engine load.

Many of the late model air injection systems utilizing a computer control are known as closed loop injection systems. In such systems, the oxygen is monitored by means of a sensor and adjustments are made in the air/fuel mixture to provide for cleaner burning.

In open loop, the control system operates without regulated air/fuel mixture, thus a fixed mixture is fed to the engine.

A defective air injection system does not cause poor idle or driveability. When the system fails, check the pump, the valve system, hoses, connections, and the triggering devices.

To check for pump air supply operation, accelerate the engine to approximately 1500 RPMs, remove the output hose and observe the airflow from the pump outlet. If the airflow increases as the engine speed is increased, the pump is functioning. The air injection pump is not completely noiseless. Under normal conditions the noise rises in pitch as speed increases. Excessive pump noise, chirping, rumbling or knocking indicates a leak in the system, pump mounting bolts loose, valve not operating, or pump failure. There is a filter fan behind the pump pulley. To replace the filter fan, remove the pulley. Use needle nose pliers to remove the filter fan. Do not pry off. The fan will usually be broken in the removal process. Install a new filter fan and draw into place by installing the drive pulley. Figure 8-11 shows the removal of the centrifugal filter fan from the air pump to enable replacement of the fan. Removing the fan will destroy the impeller.

FIGURE 8-11 Removing pump centrifugal fan. (Courtesy Oldsmobile Division, General Motors Corp.)

Inspect the drive belt for deterioration, cracks, wear, and adjustment. Inspect all hoses for deterioration or leaks. Inspect all tubes for cracks or leaks. Check all tubes and hoses for routing. A diagram for routing the various hoses will generally be found on the emissions label in the engine compartment.

Connections and hoses can be checked for leaks with a soapy water solution. With the engine running brush the solution where leaks might occur. If there is leakage bubbles will occur.

If a vacuum signal hose is used, vacuum must be present at the point the hose connects to the valve, when the engine is running.

The condition of the check valve can usually be observed after the hose has been removed. The valve must move freely, open in one direction and seal in the other. To check, blow air in one direction and then in the opposite direction. Air must flow freely in one direction and be sealed in the other.

Check the control valve solenoid circuit if a solenoid is used. Vacuum must be present to the control valve.

Pulse Air Injection Reactor (PAIR)

Instead of an air pump, some engines are equipped with a pulse air injector reactor system to help reduce hydrocarbon and carbon monoxide in the exhaust system. This system consists of a pulse air valve and a check valve for each exhaust port. As each cylinder is fired a pulse is created in the particular exhaust port.

The flow of exhaust gas is either positive or negative pressure, depending upon whether or not the exhaust valve is open or closed. If the pressure is positive, the check valve is forced closed and no exhaust gas can flow past the valve into the fresh air supply line. If the pressure is negative (vacuum), the check valve will open and fresh air will be drawn in and mixed with the exhaust gases. During high engine RPMs the check valve remains closed.

An electric or vacuum shut-off valve operated by the computer command control regulates the air supply. When the engine first starts and is operating in open loop, the valve is energized and the fresh air line is open. When the computer command control switches to closed loop, the valve is de-energized and the fresh air line will close.

A deceleration valve is used to prevent backfiring in the exhaust system during deceleration. When deceleration causes a sudden vacuum increase in the vacuum signal line, the pressure differential on the valve diaphragm will overcome the closing force of the spring. This opens the valve and bleeds air into the intake manifold. Air trapped in the chamber above the vacuum diaphragm will bleed at a calibrated rate through the valve portion of the integral check and delay valve, thus reducing the vacuum action of the diaphragm. When the vacuum load on the diaphragm and the spring load equalize, the valve will close, shutting off the air flow into the intake manifold. The check and delay valve provides quick balancing of the chamber pressure when a sudden decrease in vacuum is caused by acceleration rather than deceleration.

If the unit fails and hot exhaust gases pass through, the pulse air valve heat will burn the paint off the valve assembly and the rubber hose will deteriorate. Failure will also be indicated by a hissing noise.

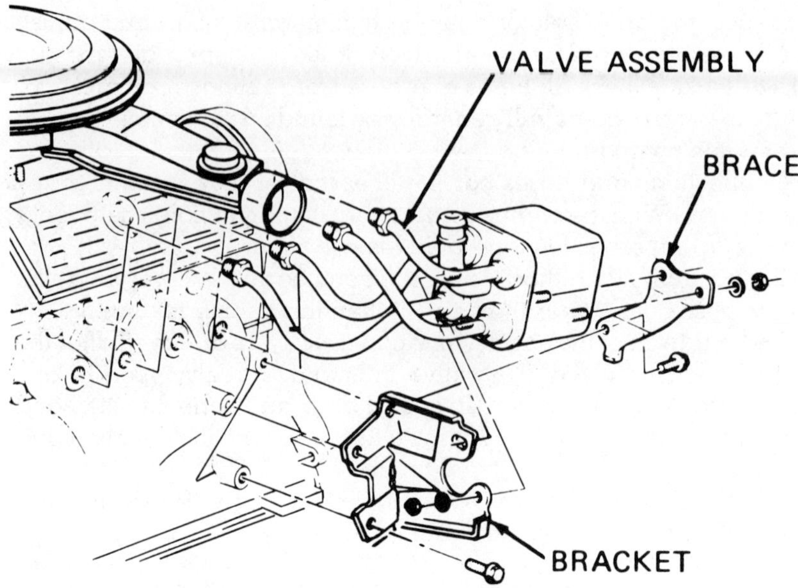

FIGURE 8-12 Pulse air valve assembly. (Courtesy Chevrolet Motor Division, General Motors Corp.)

If the hose to the air cleaner deteriorates, hose particles may enter the carburetor and cause problems. The carburetor will need to be cleaned. If one of the check valves fail, exhaust gas will enter the air cleaner.

Check the operation of the pulse air valve and the hose for leaks and/or cracks. Check the air valve by applying 15-in. hg. vacuum to the valve. There is an allowable drop in vacuum to 5-in. hg. in two seconds. A faster drop indicates a defective valve. Figure 8-12 shows a pulse air valve assembly which uses a check valve for each individual cylinder.

Thermostatically Controlled Air Cleaner

All engines are equipped with an air cleaner to filter the air before it enters the carburetor. In addition, today's engines have a thermostatically controlled air cleaner to control the temperature of the air entering the carburetor whenever the ambient temperature is low. The air is warmed before entering the carburetor.

Various automobile manufacturers may label the unit differently, but they all operate basically in the same manner. Such labels as heated inlet air, thermostatic air cleaner, or cold weather modulator are used.

Cold air does not mix or vaporize as rapidly with the fuel in the airstream as warm air. By pre-heating the cool incoming air, the engine will warm up faster as the fuel vaporizes more rapidly. This makes for more efficient operation with less exhaust pollutants.

A damper assembly in the air cleaner inlet, operated by a vacuum motor, mixes pre-heated and non-heated air before it enters the carburetor. This aids in warming the air before it enters the carburetor. The air is pre-heated by a sheet metal shroud which covers part of the exhaust manifold.

The vacuum motor which opens and closes a damper in the air cleaner inlet snorkel is modulated by a temperature sensor located in the air cleaner. When the temperature is above a prescribed setting, the damper will begin to open. When the air temperature is below the prescribed value, vacuum is trapped in the motor and the damper to outside air remains closed. A hot air duct conducts heated air from a shroud on the exhaust manifold into the air inlet. Figure 8-13 is a line drawing of a thermostatic air cleaner showing the various components which make up the unit. It shows the unit in the hot air delivery mode.

To check the operation of the air cleaner, inspect all hoses and ducts to make sure everything is properly connected. Be sure the hoses are not kinked or plugged, and have not deteriorated. If the engine is warm, remove the air cleaner and allow it to cool. A cool wet rag placed on the sensor will aid in cooling. Reinstall the cool air cleaner. Place a thermometer as close as possible to the sensor. Start and let the engine idle. The damper door should immediately move to close the snorkel passage. When the damper door starts to open the passage, remove the air cleaner cover and check the thermometer. It should read 100° ± 20°F. If the damper does not start to open the snorkel passage, either the vacuum motor is not functioning or the sensor is malfunctioning.

To check the vacuum motor, disconnect the vacuum hose from the sensor which connects to the motor. Apply at least 7 in. hg. of vacuum to the motor hose. Vacuum can be obtained from an outlet on the intake manifold with the engine running at idle speed. The damper door should completely close off the snorkel passage. If not, check the linkage for correct hookup and/or binding, and the damper door for free movement. With vacuum still applied, trap vacuum in the motor by squeezing or folding the hose so it is tightly closed. The damper door should remain closed. If not, replace the motor. The motor can be

FIGURE 8-13 Thermostatic air cleaner. (Courtesy Oldsmobile Division, General Motors Corp.)

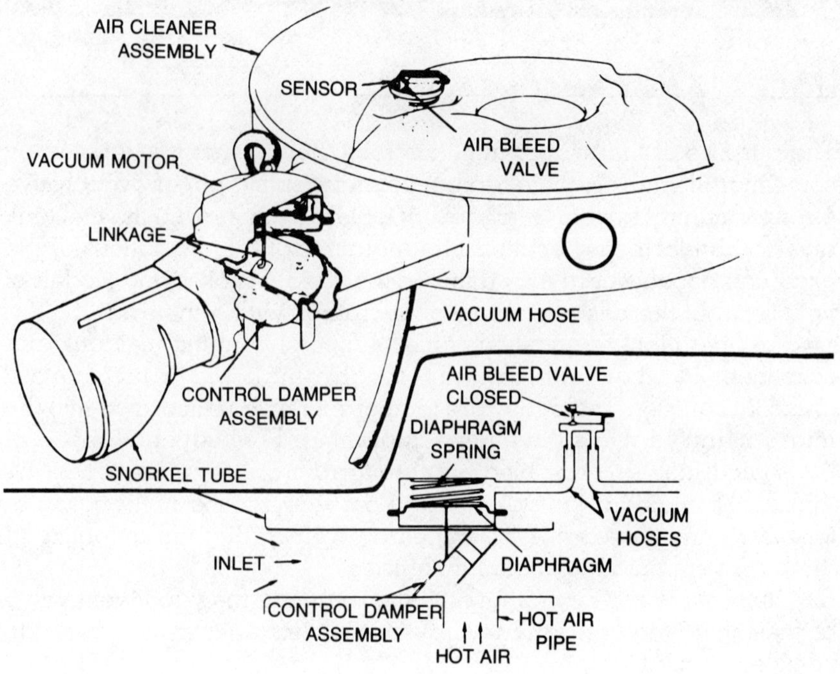

removed by drilling out the two spot welds and enlarging as necessary to remove the restraining strap. The new motor service package will contain the necessary restraining strap and sheet metal screws to secure the new vacuum motor.

If the motor functions satisfactorily when vacuum is applied directly to it, the sensor is faulty and needs to be replaced. To replace the sensor, pry up on the sensor retaining clip and remove the clip and sensor. Install the new sensor and gasket in place and press the retainer clips on the hose connectors. Connect the vacuum hoses.

When servicing the air cleaner, always replace the cleaner element if there is any sign of dirt or other obstructions. Figure 8-14 shows the location of the sensor in the thermostatic air cleaner. Pry up the tabs on the sensor retaining clip to remove the sensor.

FIGURE 8-14 Removing the sensor from the thermostatic air cleaner. (Courtesy Oldsmobile Division, General Motors Corp.)

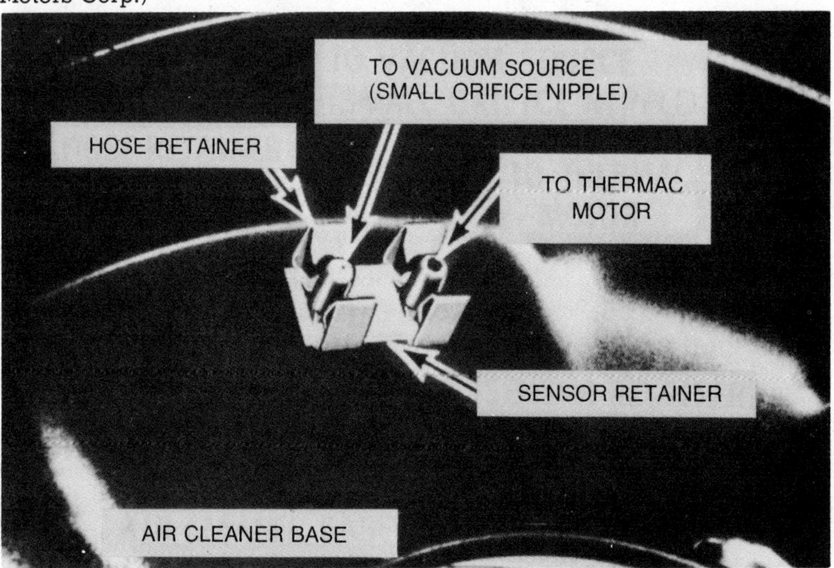

Evaporation Control System

The purpose of the evaporation control system, or as it is labeled by some manufacturers, the evaporative emission system or evaporative emission control system, is to prevent gasoline fumes from the fuel tank and carburetor being emitted into the atmosphere. Variations of the exact components used may differ on the various makes and models of vehicles, but the basic principle of operation will be the same.

In operation, the gasoline fumes (vapors) from the fuel tank and carburetor fuel bowl are carried through vent hoses or tubes into a charcoal canister. There they are temporarily held until drawn into the intake manifold while the engine is running. Fuel vapors trapped in the sealed fuel tank are bled out through an orifice in the top of the tank, to the charcoal canister. Fuel vapors which collect in the carburetor bowl when the engine is stopped are vented through an orifice in the bowl vent, into the charcoal canister.

In some vehicles a roll-over valve is used in the vapor vent valve at the top of the fuel tank to prevent fuel leakage in the event the vehicle is tipped over.

A pressure-vacuum relief fuel filler cap is used on the sealed gasoline tank. The purpose of this type cap is to relieve excessive pressure or vacuum in the fuel tank should a malfunction occur in the system or if the vent lines are damaged. This prevents damage to the tank and other fuel system components.

The charcoal canister stores fuel vapors until they are purged into the engine intake manifold for burning. When the canister is purged depends upon the design of the system and the operating mode. A purge valve is used in most systems to control the conditions in which purging occurs. Generally this is when the engine is restarted.

The canister is an activated carbon storage device which absorbs and stores the fuel vapors that are emitted from the gasoline tank and the carburetor when the engine is not running. When the engine first starts, the fuel vapor is purged from the carbon (charcoal) element by intake airflow (vacuum) and burned in the normal combustion process. Figure 8-15 is a line drawing of a typical evaporative emission control system using the open canister.

FIGURE 8-15 Evaporative emission control system (EECS). (Courtesy Chevrolet Motor Division, General Motors Corp.)

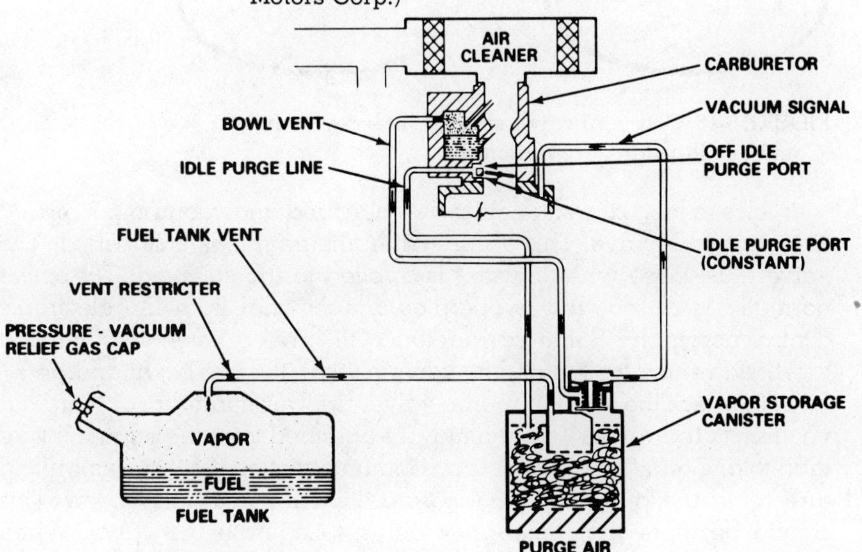

Some canisters are of the closed design, drawing fresh air from the air cleaner, instead of drawing air through a filter located in the bottom of the canister. A few installations may use two canisters, along with two purge valves.

Many canisters have a replaceable filter. It is recommended that the filter be replaced at approximately every 30,000 miles, or more often in dusty areas. Figure 8-16 shows replacing the filter in a charcoal vapor control canister.

A purge valve controls the flow of vapors from the canister to the intake manifold. The valve is vacuum operated and normally closed during regular engine operation. Some are vacuum controlled, and calibrated to close when vacuum reaches a predetermined value. Other systems use a solenoid to activate the vacuum control. The solenoid is energized by a signal from the electronic control module.

When the system is in "open loop" (engine running) the solenoid is energized and blocks vacuum to the purge valve. When the system

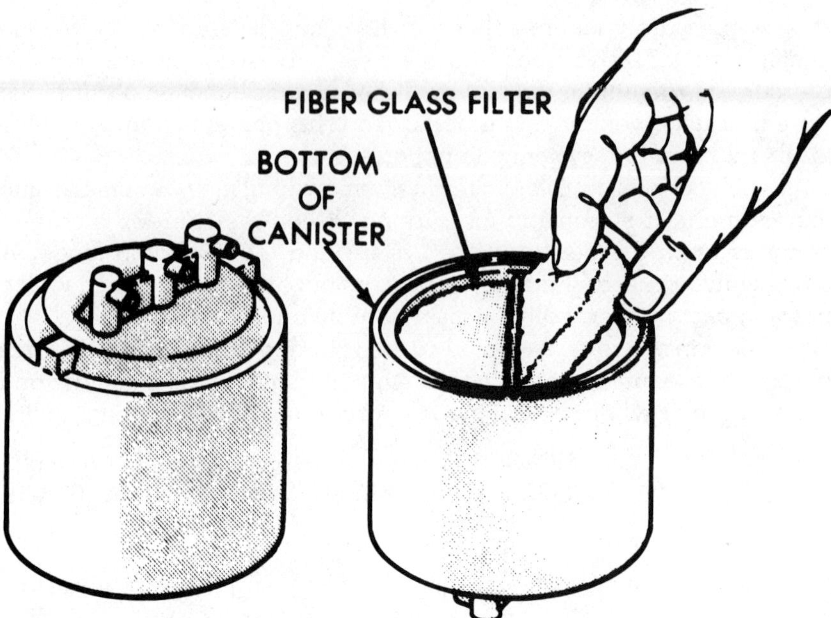

FIGURE 8-16 Charcoal vapor storage filter replacement. (Courtesy Chrysler Corporation)

is in "closed loop" the solenoid is de-energized and vacuum is supplied to operate the valve. This occurs when the engine is first started. The valve must close when current is applied to the solenoid. The valve normally is closed, but is operated by a signal from the electronic control assembly. Some carburetors will have a solenoid-controlled fuel bowl vent valve to regulate venting when the fuel bowl is purged.

To check the vacuum purge valve, apply a minimum of 16 in. hg. vacuum to the valve. Vacuum may be obtained from the engine intake manifold. Connect a hose from a vacuum outlet on the intake manifold directly to the purge valve. Operate the engine at idle speed. This should be more than enough vacuum to operate the valve. When vacuum is applied to the valve, the purge line to the tank vapor line and to the carburetor vent should open so vacuum will be present at both outlets. Replace the valve if it is not functioning properly.

Catalytic Converter

The catalytic converter is an emission control device added to the exhaust system to reduce the levels of hydrocarbon, carbon monoxide and oxides of nitrogen. These are pollutants in the exhaust system which would normally be expelled into the atmosphere.

The converter looks very much like a small muffler. Because the unit becomes extremely hot when the engine has been operating for a period of time, a heat shield may be located between the converter and the floor pan.

The catalytic converter requires the use of unleaded fuel. Using more than one or two tanksful of gasoline which contains lead will destroy the effectiveness of the converter.

The catalytic converter uses a type of material (catalyst) whose presence alters the rate of chemical reaction. By doing so, some of the exhaust gases are reduced to harmless materials.

Some variations occur in the different converters relative to the catalytic materials used. The catalyst in the bead type converter can be replaced. The beads (pellets) are usually coated with platinum and palladium. Some may also use rodium coated pellets.

The catalyst used in a monolith converter is not serviceable. This type converter consists of a structured shell containing a monolithic substrate—a ceramic honeycomb structure through which the exhaust gas must flow.

Some vehicles use a dual-bed converter to lower the levels of oxides of nitrogen, hydrocarbon, and carbon monoxide pollutants to a greater extent. An air supply tube from the air management system delivers additional air between the dual beds of the converter, which causes the second bed to oxidize any remaining hydrocarbons and carbon monoxide to further minimize overall emissions. Figure 8-17 is a drawing showing a cutaway view of a dual-bed catalytic converter as well as an illustration of the flow of exhaust gases through the unit.

To determine if the converter is functioning properly or needs to be serviced or replaced, an infrared exhaust analyzer must be used.

When it is necessary to replace the pellets in the converter using beads or pellets, remove the converter from the vehicle. Remove the plug in the bottom of the converter. This is done by driving a chisel into the center of the pressed plug in the converter and prying the plug out. Be careful not to damage the edges of the converter so the new plug will not leak. A new plug kit will have the necessary bolt and nut arrangement for installing a new plug.

Tip the converter and shake to remove all of the beads. When installing new beads, shake the unit as they are poured, so as to get as many in as possible.

FIGURE 8-17 Construction and flow through a dual bed catalytic converter. (Courtesy Oldsmobile Division, General Motors Corp.)

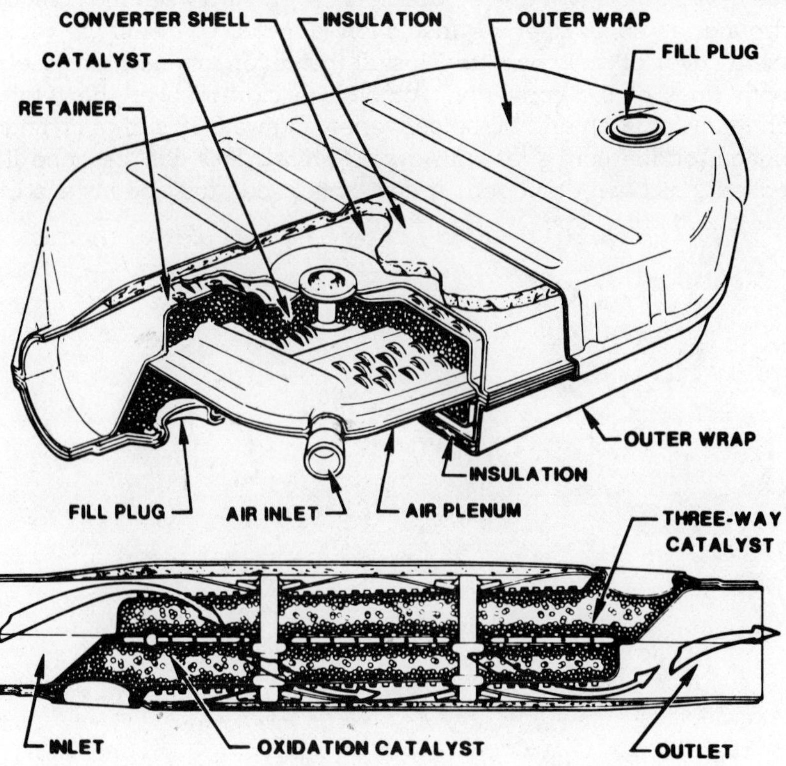

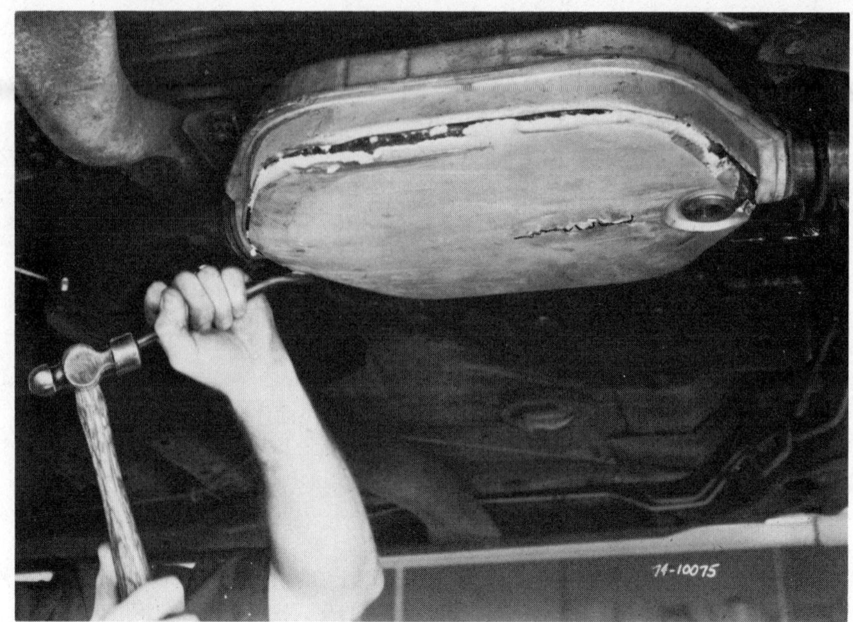

FIGURE 8-18 Removing the damaged bottom of a catalytic converter. (Courtesy Chevrolet Motor Division, General Motors Corp.)

There is a vacuum device on the market which can be used to suck the beads out without removing the converter. It is only necessary to remove the plug from the bottom.

If the bottom of the converter has been damaged or torn away, a new bottom cover replacement kit is available for some types of converters. The outer shell on the bottom of the converter is removed by cutting around the edges with a chisel. Remove the insulation. If the inner shell is good, install a new bottom cover replacement kit. Place the new insulation in the replacement cover. Apply sealing compound around the cover after the insulation is in place. Install the replacement cover on the converter. Install the cover retaining channels on both sides of the converter. Attach two clamps over the retaining channels at each end of the converter. Figure 8-18 shows cutting the bottom off the converter with a cold chisel. This can be done if the bottom has been damaged. A new bottom can then be installed.

Computer Control Systems

The preceding chapter discussed the various engine emission control components that are used by the different manufacturers to meet government environmental protection agency mandates. Many of these control devices have been used on most vehicles for several years. In the majority of cases the units depended upon electricity, heat, and/or vacuum for their control and operation.

Purpose

To provide for greater emission reductions as regulations become more stringent, and to make for better economy as well as engine performance, the different automobile makers developed electrical/electronic control components more sensitive and responsive to engine operating conditions.

In addition to the components which are directly associated with emission control, electronic controls have been incorporated in other areas to bring about improved economy and performance along with less emissions.

Any improvement in combustion results in a cleaner-burning engine and less harmful exhaust emissions. The use of electronics to regulate spark timing, create better air/fuel mixture, provide for transmission torque converter lockup under certain conditions, as well as regulate airflow to the exhaust manifold and/or catalytic converter, has contributed to improvements in automobile engine operations.

The advent of the electronic (transistorized) ignition system which is now used by all American automobile manufacturers was the first general use of an electronic system to improve engine performance. This system was introduced in the mid-sixties. The distributor uses a transistorized control module consisting of transistors, diodes and resistors which act as a switching device in place of ignition contact points. By the elimination of moving contact points, the distributor dwell angle does not change mechanically, and the initial timing remains fixed.

On a number of installations, particularly older vehicles, timing is varied to compensate for changes in load and speed through the use of a mechanical centrifugal advance unit and a vacuum advance-retard unit. Most of the present electronic ignition systems, through the use of sensors, are capable of varying the dwell and timing electronically to better meet engine operating requirements without the use of centrifugal or vacuum units.

Making spark timing sensitive to barometric pressure, engine temperature, detonation, load and speed conditions, then varying the timing accordingly through the use of electronic controls, has further improved the entire engine performance range.

For more efficient engine operation, better performance and reduced exhaust emissions, varying the air/fuel mixture is desireable. With the regular fuel system arrangement, a certain amount of air/fuel ratio change does take place according to different load and speed conditions. There are, however, a number of different operating modes at which time the air/fuel mixture is such that the engine is not obtaining maximum performance. In addition, any time engine efficiency, particularly combustion efficiency, drops off, undesirable exhaust emissions increase.

Engineering advances have resulted in the development of emission control devices, most of which were described in the previous chapter. These, to mention a few, include the exhaust gas recirculation system, catalytic converter, an early fuel evaporation system, an air management system, and a heated air intake. Certain operating conditions relative to temperature, vacuum, barometric pressure, detonation, and air flow, trigger these units and cause them to operate. While these emission control components improve operation and reduce exhaust emissions, to obtain the optimum operational mode, the various units should be coordinated so there will be an interaction between the different components.

The most effective way to bring about this condition is to monitor the conditions under which the engine is operating, and then make corrections and changes to bring about more complete combustion. The more complete the burning of the air/fuel mixture, the better the engine performs with greater operating economy and less undesirable exhaust emissions produced by the engine. The use of electrical, electronic, and vacuum devices makes it possible to vary the air/fuel ratio as well as spark timing, resulting in better performance and less exhaust emissions.

To determine what adjustments or alterations should be made to the air/fuel ratio and spark timing, information must be obtained from the units that affect operation, so adjustments can be made. Various sensors, electrical switches, solenoids and vacuum operated switches may be used to operate a particular component by turning it on or off. Temperature, pressure, or vacuum may be used to direct an electric current to flow to a center which, according to how it is programmed, will then direct a current flow to operate a particular component. This is the basis of the electronic control system, which is a form of computer system.

General Description

Nomenclature relative to the electronic control system used on a great many of today's automobiles will vary considerably. The primary purpose is to reduce the undesirable pollutants emitted by the engine into the atmosphere. This is done by changing the operating mode as dictated by numerous conditions such as temperature, speed, load, by (in most cases) the controlled addition of oxygen to the exhaust system, and varying the air/fuel ratio and spark timing.

The electronic control system may be labeled by the different manufacturers as a feedback system, electronic spark control system, computer command control system, computerized emission control system, electronic engine control system, or a microprocessor control unit. In every case it is a system made up of a number of electronically controlled components. Figure 9-1 is a diagram that illustrates the electronic computer control of the air/fuel mixture according to the oxygen content of the exhaust gas.

Basically, the heart of the system is an electronic control unit consisting of transistors, diodes and resistors, and generally referred to as a computer unit or microprocessor. The unit receives signals from sensors located on different components which make up the system, such as the oxygen sensor, coolant temperature, crankshaft position, spark timing, engine vacuum, atmospheric pressure, and incoming air temperature.

A sensor is a device which senses a condition such as temperature or pressure, and relays this information in the form of a small voltage flow to a control device. Temperature change will create electron movement (electricity) in certain materials when designed for such a purpose.

The control device (computer) unit monitors the mode of operation according to the signals received from the various sensors. The computer is programmed to send out signals in the form of a low voltage

FIGURE 9-1 Basic cycle of computer operation. (Courtesy Oldsmobile Division, General Motors Corp.)

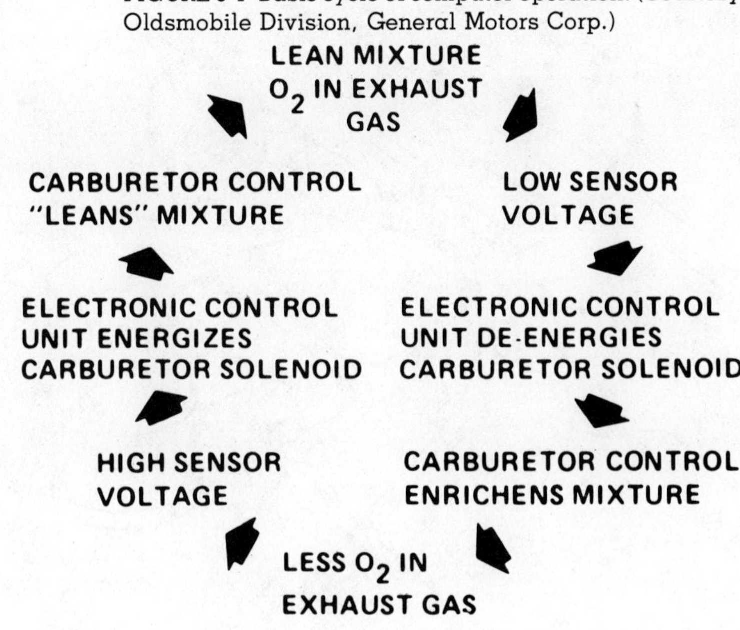

which will cause certain things to happen, such as divert air to the exhaust manifold or catalytic converter, retard spark timing, change carburetor air/fuel ratio, when a change in operation is needed for better operational performance and less emissions. The low voltage current may first be directed to an amplifier which increases the electrical flow. The current flow may be used to trigger a switch, a vacuum diverter, or operate a solenoid to bring about the desired results.

From the preceding chapter one should be aware of certain factors that improve operation. For example, retarding ignition timing helps eliminate detonation, a cold engine will not operate as efficiently as a warm engine, and a rich mixture is needed for better acceleration. These conditions were taken into consideration in the past and are still utilized to some degree on certain makes and models, by the use of vacuum controls, solenoids, and centrifugal advance. This method does not have the precise interrelationship and coordinated action that can be brought about by an electronic control system.

The transistors, diodes, and resistors used in the electronic control system (computer) have no moving parts and therefore are not subject to wear or change. The unit, for the most part, is not serviceable.

One of the important factors that has made possible the utilization of an on-board computer is the refinement and use of the various types of sensors. As stated before, a sensor is a device which senses a condition and relays this information in the form of a low voltage current flow to a control center where it is used to activate or bring about an operational change in another unit. Sensors supply the electrical input signals required for the operation of the electronic control module (computer). Figure 9-2 is an illustration of a MAP manifold absolute pressure, or a vacuum sensor which measures changes in manifold pressure and provides this information in the form of an electrical signal to the EMC electronic control module.

FIGURE 9-2 Manifold absolute pressure MAP or vacuum sensor. (Courtesy Oldsmobile Division, General Motors Corp.)

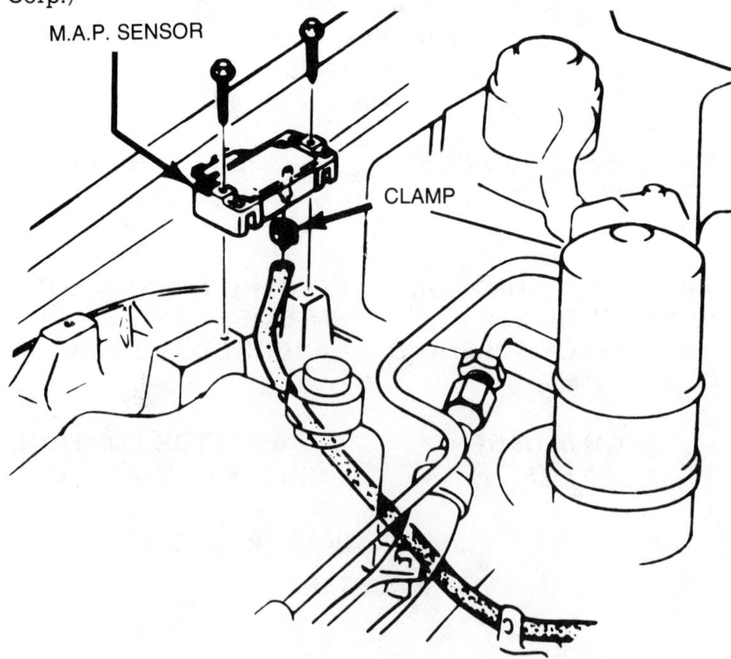

Rather than numerous individual control units located throughout the engine compartment, which determine when certain changes should be made, an electronic control unit (computer) is located in a central place where the signals for the different modes of engine and vehicle operation are delivered. The computer unit sends back signals to change the operating mode according to how the computer is programmed.

Components Included in Computer Control Systems

The underlying reason for developing the computer system is to control exhaust emissions. Basically, regardless of how many or how few units are included in the computer system, the system electronically controls the exhaust emissions by monitoring different engine/vehicle functions, as many as fifteen or more on some vehicles and using this information to control several different operations, nine or more in some instances. The system is designed to make constant adjustments to maintain good performance under all normal operating conditions while allowing and/or assisting the catalytic converter to effectively control emissions.

The computer system which uses a type of digital computer receives input in the form of a low voltage current from various sensors relative to the operating conditions of different components. By monitoring different engine/vehicle operating modes, changes can be brought about that provide for better performance and economy with less engine exhaust emissions.

Sensors supplying input to the computer control may include the following:

- Air/fuel ratio
- Engine RPMs
- Detonation (knock)
- Manifold absolute pressure (measures manifold pressure change)
- Barometric pressures (atmospheric pressure change)
- Vacuum (intake manifold vacuum change)
- Throttle position (position of throttle plates)
- Wide open throttle
- Transmission gear position (signals lockup of converter)
- Idle speed control (signals when throttle lever contacts plunger)
- Coolant temperature (temperature data)
- Oxygen (oxygen content of exhaust gases)
- Park/Neutral (signals when vehicle is in park/neutral)
- Diagnostic link connector
- Crankshaft position

The electronic computer control module receives the signals in the form of a low voltage current from the component sensor. According to how the computer is programmed, signals may be sent to any of the following components:

- Air diverter valve (controls air flow from the air pump to the air selector valve and/or air cleaner)
- Torque converter clutch solenoid valve
- Early fuel evaporation solenoid valve
- Fuel metering solenoid
- Idle speed control
- Spark timing control module
- Exhaust gas recirculation solenoid valve (EGR)
- Check engine light
- Light driving module

Some systems will control ignition timing, air/fuel ratio, and exhaust gas recirculation, but not overall timing. Some systems control only ignition timing.

The present trend is to monitor more components and to make adjustments according to the operating mode.

Operation in General

The computer system includes the various sensors, switches, solenoids, control module, etc., and is programmed by the manufacturer to monitor particular units and direct changes to be made which result in better operation. You cannot separate engine operation and exhaust emissions because the more efficiently the engine operates the less will be the undesirable emissions. The different switches and solenoids, some operated by vacuum, electricity or mechanically may activate a particular unit, but a sensor is involved which transfers the change in operation into the form of a small electrical flow before it reaches the actual computer unit. In the same manner, the information sent out from the computer will be in the form of a small electrical impulse. The electrical impulse will be used to trigger a switch or solenoid, which will change the operating mode.

The sensors that monitor engine conditions send information to the electronic control module (computer) at various voltage levels. These voltage levels are changed by the electronic control module to digital form for processing by the computer unit of the control module. The computer compares the sensor data with the programmed calibration data stored in the (PROM) Programmable Read Only Memory. This data is a record of the engine operating standards that produce the least amount of engine emissions and the most efficient engine operation. The standards vary for the different makes and models of engines and vehicles. The standards (program) cannot be changed in the field.

The computer unit is designed to operate on a very low voltage flow, both input and output. This means that the control for the component involved must be designed to send a low voltage signal to the computer unit and to be triggered by a low voltage signal. Amplifiers may be used in the circuit to increase the signals where necessary.

Sensors may be utilized in a variety of situations. A sensor may be designed to send a signal when coolant temperature exceeds a certain limit. A sensor may be utilized to send a signal when there is a barometric pressure change, a manifold pressure change or to detect detonation in the engine. Switches may be used to send a signal to the sensor, which in turn, sends an electrical impulse to the computer when the throttle plate in the carburetor for example, is wide open, or when the throttle is against the idle stop. The same may apply when the transmission is shifted into neutral/park or the air conditioner unit is turned on or off. An electrical current may be used to signal a motor to cycle, such as used to change the position of the metering rods in the carburetor should the air/fuel mixture need to be changed. An oxygen sensor in the exhaust system which responds to the amount of oxygen in the exhaust system may send a signal to the computer, indicating a shortage of oxygen. The computer will then signal to the air management system calling for more air. The signal may then trigger a switch or solenoid to provide for additional air to be delivered to the exhaust system.

Vacuum plays an important part in engine operation, as well as emission control. Vacuum may be used to trigger electrical signals which are sent to the computer control module by way of a sensor. Signals from the computer control may be used to operate a switch or solenoid to redirect vacuum so as to change operating conditions.

In summary, the computer control module receives low voltage signals from various components which are part of the power plant. According to how the computer is programmed, low voltage signals will be sent out to various units which then trigger some form of switch device to bring about changes. The change may affect different components such as ignition timing being advanced or retarded, air directed to the exhaust ports, air cleaner or catalytic converter. The air/fuel ratio is changed because of a change in barometric pressure or operating mode. The timing is retarded because detonation is occurring; and the idle speed is increased because the air conditioner is operating.

The computer is used on numerous modern fuel injected engines for fuel delivery and metering. It is also used to control the modular displacement engine.

This is a new and expanding control area with the different manufacturers making greater use of computer controls in more and more engines.

The computer unit itself cannot be serviced. Most problems which occur will be in the operating components and are checked and serviced in the usual manner. Sensors, switches, and solenoids cannot be repaired; therefore servicing, for the most part, will be a matter of tracing circuits and isolating the faulty component. Repair usually consists of replacing faulty parts which is a bolt-off, bolt-on procedure.

Operating Principles

Basically all onboard computers operate in the same manner. They all utilize sensors which deliver a low voltage current to the computer. The computer in turn directs a low voltage current signal which is used to trigger a reaction to bring about a change in operating mode. This may be to operate a switch causing a solenoid to operate, cause a vacuum line to be opened, or change distributor timing.

The difference in the various computer installations is the number of units included in the system. Some vehicle manufacturers use the computer system merely to regulate distributor dwell and timing.

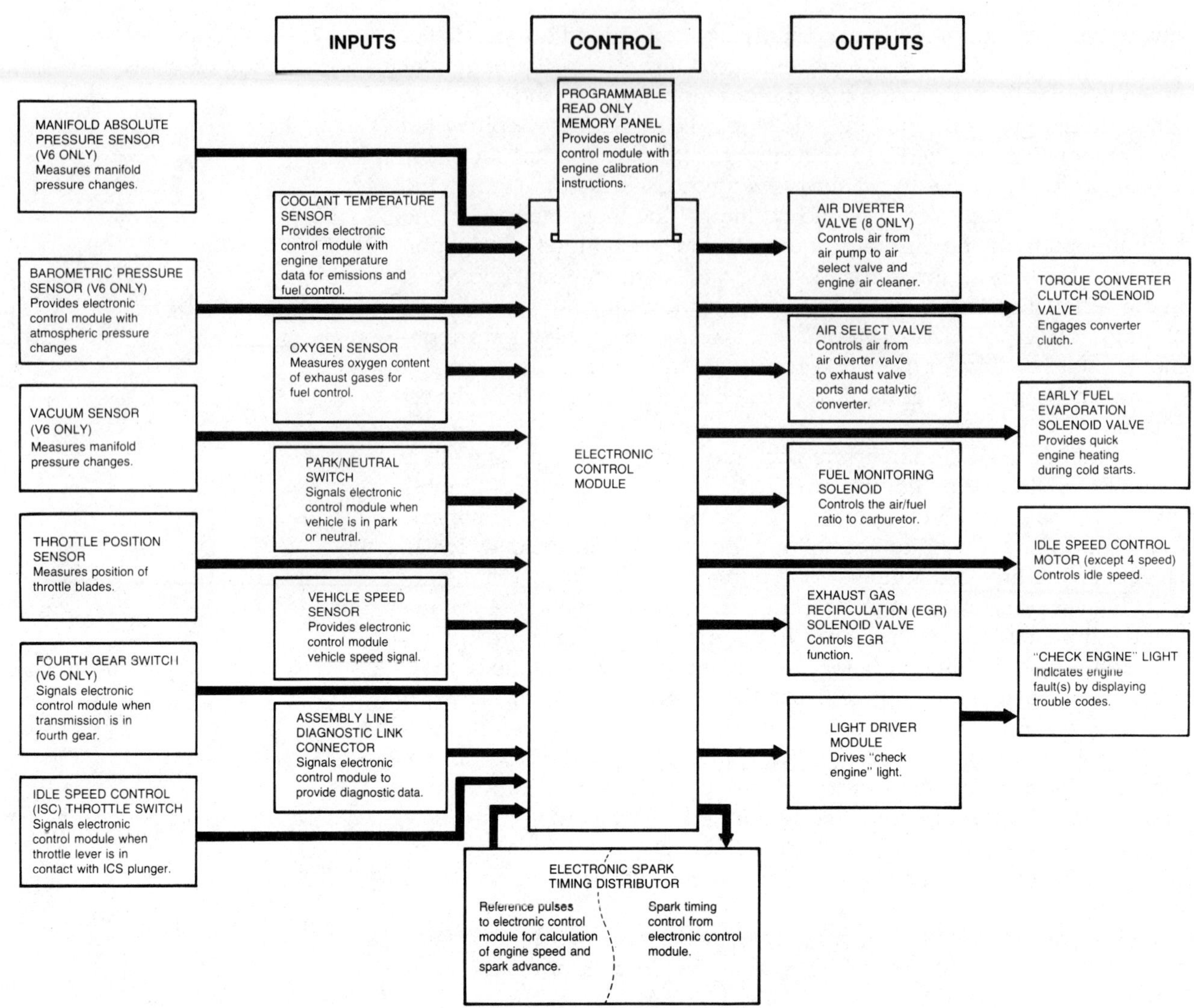

FIGURE 9-3 Computer command control flow chart. (Courtesy Oldsmobile Division, General Motors Corp.)

Other installations may regulate timing and dwell as well as oxygen flow to the catalytic converter, vary the air/fuel mixture, purge the evaporation canister, or lockup the torque converter. Some computer systems incorporate a self-diagnostic feature whereby the computer indicates when a problem exists, or if a problem in operational mode is suspected, the computer can be made to "talk."

If the distributor does not use a vacuum unit or a centrifugal mechanical spark timing control, the timing is electronically controlled. Figure 9-3 is a flow chart of the computer command control of an emission control system managed by a digital computer. It indicates the input to the electronic control module and the output from the control module that influences engine operation.

Difference in Terminology Used by the Various Systems

While the basic operation is the same for all, the various automobile manufacturers will label the computer system differently. Terminology sometimes becomes confusing. In the case of General Motors, the complete system is labeled as the computer command control (CCC), and the actual computer unit which performs the various switching operations is called the electronic control module (ECM). Other manufacturers use different labels. The term microprocessor is used by several manufacturers to designate the actual computer unit. The term computer and module are sometimes used interchangeably.

No attempt is made to pinpoint by make and model exactly which vehicle will use a particular computer control system and the components included in the system due to the continued effort by most manufacturers to expand the use of the system. Vehicles made specifically for California will use different controls than those made for other states.

Different engines will have different requirements and will use different controls. Manufacturers are adapting the computer control system to more components as time goes on.

General Motors products use a system labeled as the computer command control (CCC). The actual computer component which is programmed to control the various components is labeled the electronic control module (ECM).

Figure 9-4 shows the location of the electronic control module (ECM) which is under the instrument panel on most General Motors vehicles.

FIGURE 9-4 Electronic control module (ECM) location. (Courtesy Chevrolet Motor Division, General Motors Corp.)

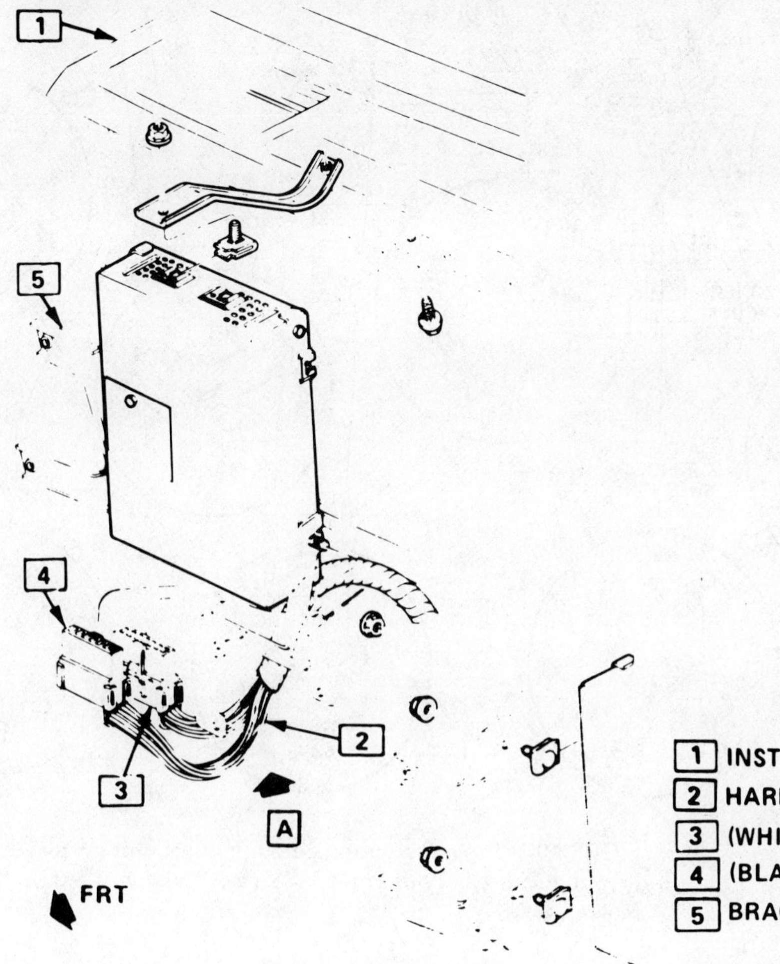

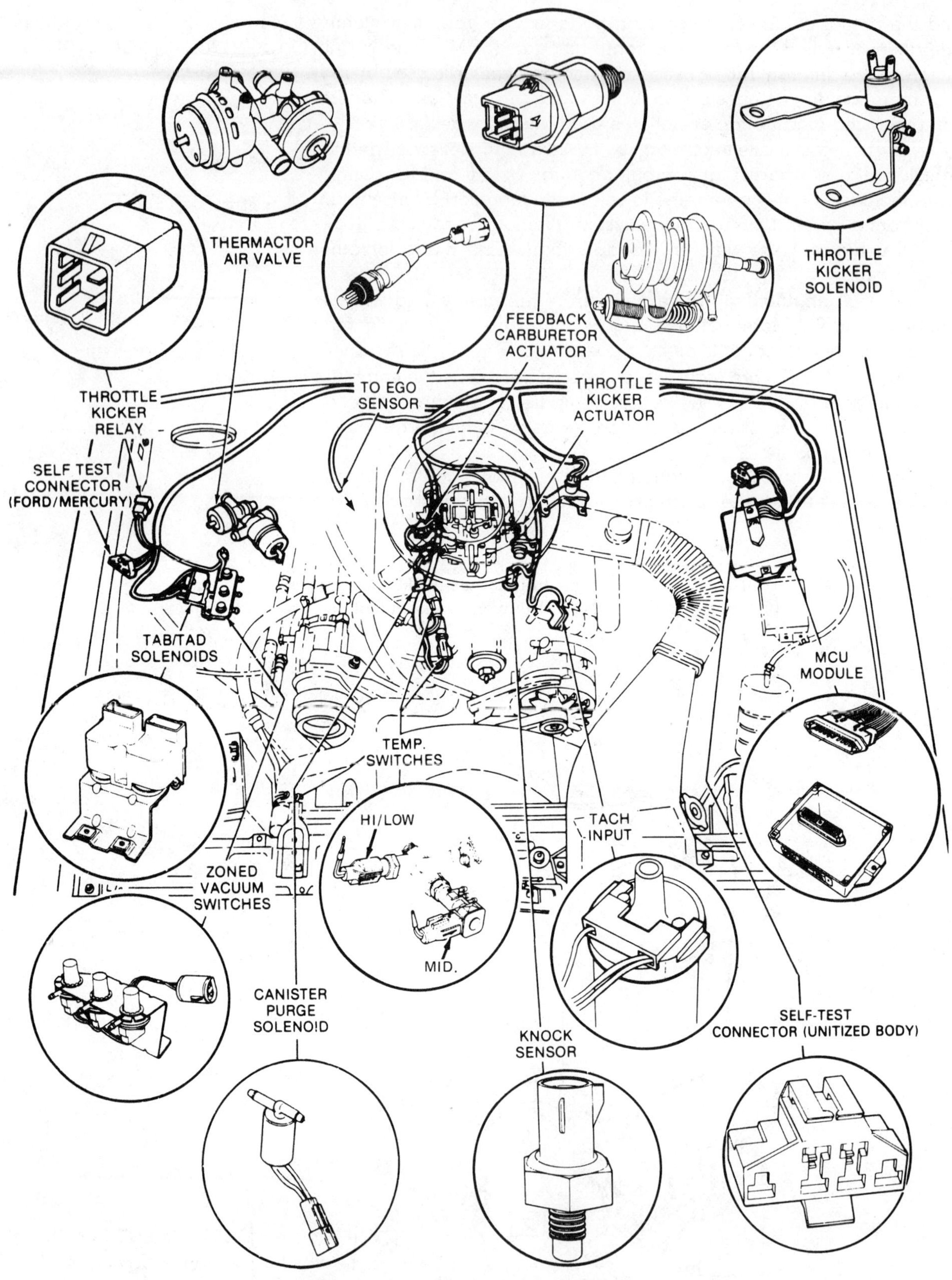

FIGURE 9-5 Typical microprocessor control unit system layout. (Courtesy Ford Parts & Service Division, Ford Motor Co.)

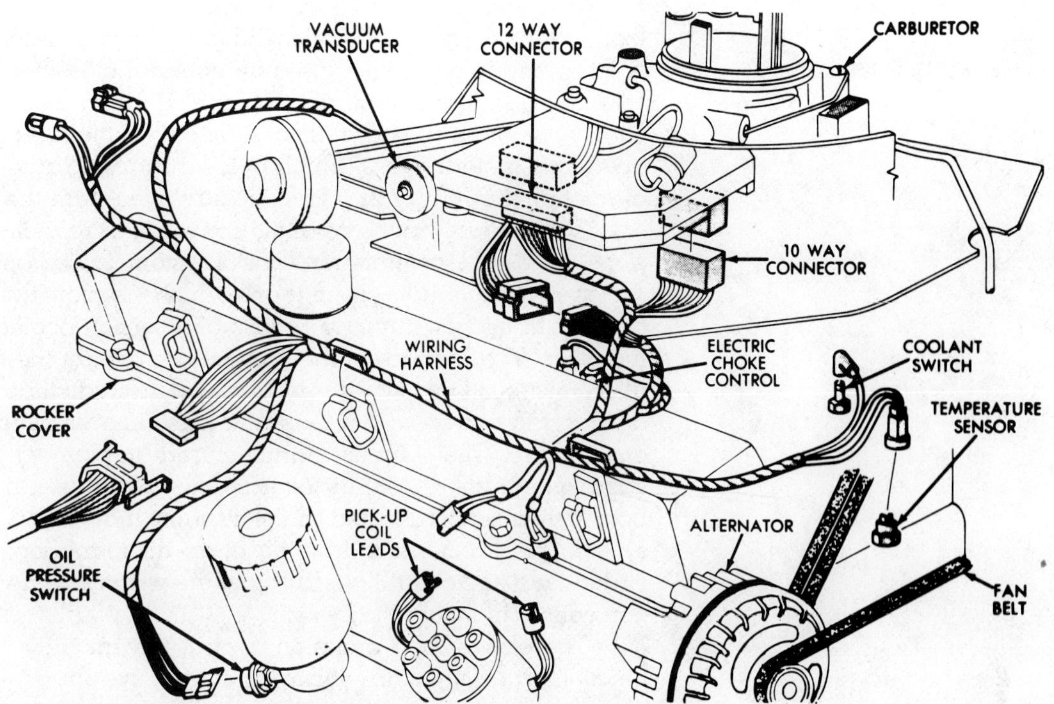

FIGURE 9-6 Switches and sensors for electronic spark control. (Courtesy Chrysler Corporation)

The system found on Ford Motor products may be labeled as the microcomputer control unit (MCU), the electronic engine control system (EEC) and a third, more advanced system, designated as the electronic engine control IV system. A microcomputer unit controls the air/fuel ratio and exhaust gas recirculation. The computer unit is generally referred to as the microprocessor or microcomputer. Figure 9-5 illustrates the electronic control components used on an eight-cylinder Ford Motor product microprocessor control unit.

Chrysler Corporation labels the system an ignition computer. It is a spark control computer and uses a control unit labeled, microprocessor. As the name implies it controls spark timing. Some later model Chrysler products are incorporating an electronic fuel injector system into the microprocessor control along with the spark timing control system. Figure 9-6 shows the switches and sensors used with the computer electronic spark control. The computer is mounted by the carburetor and contains the microprocessor.

American Motors uses the label micro computer unit (MCU), the control unit being a microprocessor. The C4 system used on some engines incorporates a self-diagnostic feature to help localize system malfunctions. Certain engines use a system, computerized emission control (CEC) which controls the carburetor air/fuel mixture. A general term of feedback systems may also be used to identify the control system when a mixture control (MC) solenoid is used in the fuel system.

Closed Loop Emission System

When the computer system is used to assist in the control of the air/fuel mixture delivered by the carburetor along with the control of air being diverted to the catalytic converter, the system is referred to as a closed loop emission system. The closed loop system is used by a number of different manufacturers. One manufacturer classifies this type of carburetor system as a feedback carburetor. Regardless of the label, the carburetor is equipped with a solenoid, sometimes called a motor, operating metering jets which cycle at varying rates to change the air/fuel mixture according to signals relayed from the computer.

To better utilize the catalytic converter in reducing exhaust emissions, a closed loop emission control system is used on many vehicles. A closed loop control system is one which monitors the oxygen content of the exhaust gas through the use of a sensor located in the exhaust manifold. The purpose of the system is to control the variables which affect combustion and, through use of a catalytic converter, break down emissions so as to release the least amount of pollutants into the atmosphere. The various manufacturers implement the closed loop emission control system in several different ways. On all installations however, a sensor located in the exhaust manifold is the heart of the system. Figure 9-7 is a drawing of an air management system with closed loop fuel control operating in the warm engine mode. The oxygen sensor monitors the system.

The closed loop emission control system may be used in conjunction with either an electronic control system or with a computer control system. In most cases it is a part of the computer control system. The simplest system merely includes a sensor which directs the airflow from the air pump to the catalytic converter when there is a shortage of oxygen in the exhaust manifold.

In operation, the sensor generates a voltage according to the oxygen content of the exhaust gases. A decrease in oxygen (richer mixture) results in a higher voltage. As oxygen increases (leaner mixture) the voltage decreases. These voltages are fed to the computer.

FIGURE 9-7 Air management system operating in warm engine mode. (Courtesy Chevrolet Motor Division, General Motors Corp.)

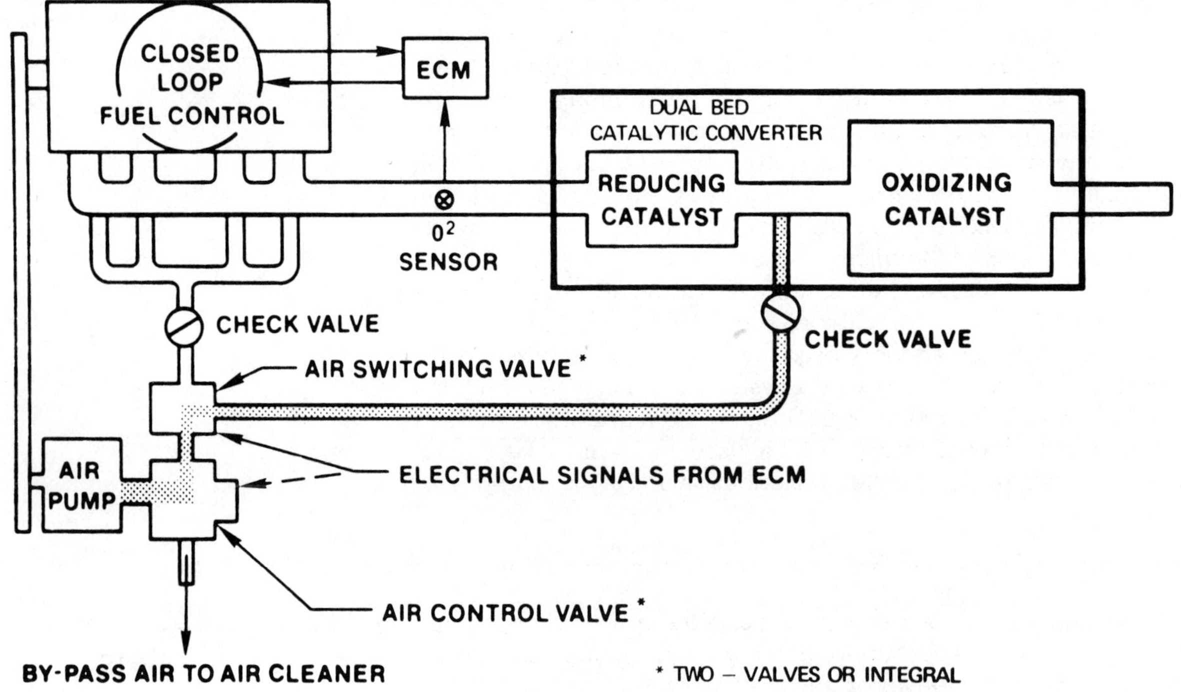

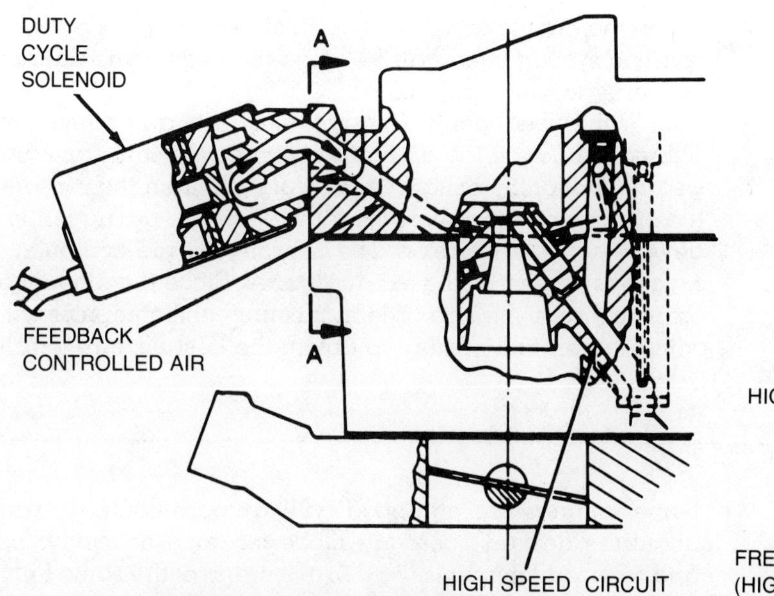

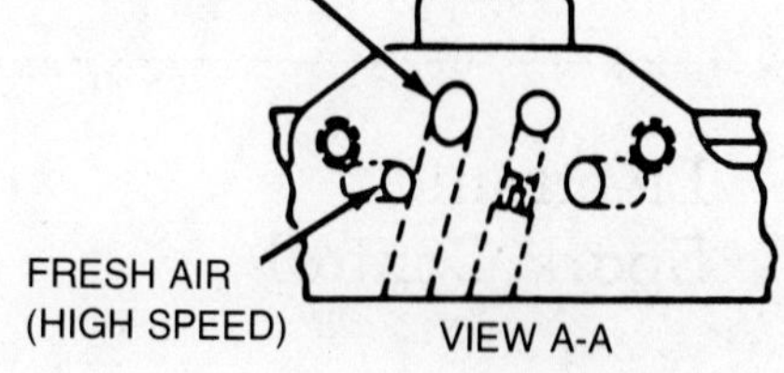

FIGURE 9-8 High-speed system—with O_2 feedback. (Courtesy Chrysler Corporation)

The computer causes the air/fuel mixture to be altered by changing a metering device in the carburetor. The metering device is usually operated by a solenoid or some type of electric motor. It is part of the feedback carburetor installation. Figure 9-8 shows the solenoid used with the feedback carburetor to assist in controlling the air/fuel mixture fed to the engine.

The oxygen sensor does not operate until the exhaust gases are heated to approximately 600°F. When the sensor is not operating, no oxygen diversion to the catalytic converter takes place and the system is in open loop mode. The air/fuel ratio is not controlled by external forces. This is necessary for better cold starting and operation. Other conditions are also used to control the duration of the open loop operational mode, such as the coolant temperature sensor programmed warmup time. Wide-open throttle and power enrichment conditions require richer mixtures, so the unit reverts back to open loop when richer mixtures are called for. When the enrichment requirements have been met, the system reverts back to closed loop if the exhaust gas temperature is high enough to meet programmed specifications.

Different catalytic converters are used according to the particular make and model of vehicle. Some installations use a single-bed converter, some will use a three-way converter which acts on the carbon monoxide, hydrocarbons, and oxides of nitrogen, while a third installation may make use of a dual-bed three-way converter. The first bed is used for exhaust gas reduction and the second bed with injected air from the air injection reaction system to provide oxidation capabilities.

On some installations that include an air injection reaction system (AIR), the system will inject air into either the exhaust ports in the cylinder head, exhaust manifold, or catalytic converter. The system is designed to divert during high speed operation and during deceleration. Air injected into the exhaust ports during cold weather operation helps the converter to reach proper operating temperature sooner.

When the engine is warm, or is in closed loop mode, the air injection reaction system injects air between the beds of the dual-bed catalytic converter to lower emissions.

With a feedback carburetor, electricity and possibly vacuum are utilized to change the air/fuel ratio while the sensor monitors the oxygen content of the exhaust gases. Signals from the sensors are sent to the computer which alters the air/fuel mixture by triggering a metering device in the carburetor. The sensor tells the computer how much oxygen is present in the exhaust gases. Since the amount of oxygen is proportional to the rich or lean mixtures, the computer will adjust the adjust the air/fuel mixture to obtain the best mixture for all operating conditions.

Electronic Spark Control

Some engines are equipped with a spark control module to bring about the desired operating mode for good economy, performance, and reduced emissions. It performs many of the same functions as the computer system. When an electronic spark control module is used for controlling engine ignition spark timing, no vacuum advance-retard unit or centrifugal mechanical advance unit is used with the distributor.

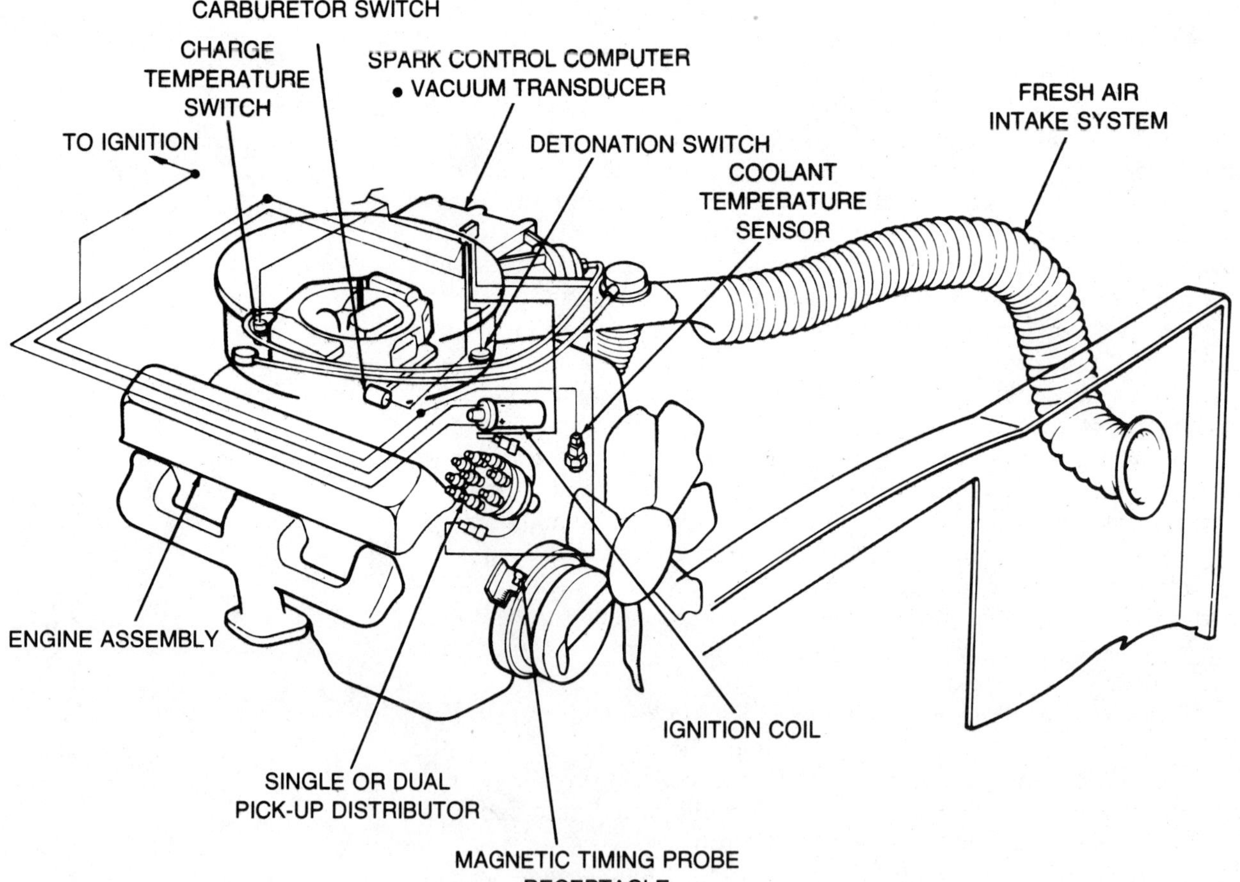

FIGURE 9-9 Electronic spark control system. (Courtesy Chrysler Corporation)

The electronic spark control module performs in the same manner as the computer control system except the catalytic converter is not included in the system. Sensors monitor engine speed, intake manifold vacuum, throttle position, rate of change in the throttle position, inlet air temperature, and engine coolant temperature. The signals from the sensors are interpreted by the electronic spark control module which determines the optimum spark timing and dwell for the existing conditions. The module then triggers the spark to the spark plug at the precise time for maximum performance. Figure 9-9 shows an electronic spark control system which includes a spark control computer.

Factors and Components Affecting Engine Performance

Operating requirements as well as operating conditions, will in many cases, have a direct bearing on vehicle performance. Many times when certain conditions exist, adjustments or changes can be made immediately to bring about better operation.

Numerous conditions have a bearing on vehicle operation which can be monitored through the use of a programmed computer system. Following is a list of factors which have a bearing on engine economy, performance and exhaust emissions. These factors can be monitored and in some cases changed in such a manner that the operational mode of the engine will improve and emissions reduced:

- Barometric pressure
- Coolant temperature
- Intake air temperature
- Intake manifold vacuum
- Throttle position
- Oxygen in exhaust
- Crankshaft position
- Air/fuel mixture
- Spark timing
- Canister purge valve
- Transmission converter clutch
- Exhaust recirculation valve
- Early fuel evaporation
- Manifold pressure
- Battery voltage
- Vehicle speed
- Park/neutral mode
- A/C clutch engagement
- Engine detonation
- AIR management valve

Computer Control Systems Used by Different Automobile Manufacturers

Following is a general description of the computer systems used by the various automobile manufacturers. It presents an insight into the operation of the computer systems in general use at the present time.

While nomenclature varies with the different computer control systems used by the various makes of automobiles you will find that all systems operate very much in the same manner. The difference, in most cases, is the particular components being controlled by the computer system. As the computer control system is a comparatively new system relative to automotive usage and is a very successful method of controlling emissions, its application is becoming greater each year. The trend is to include more components in the different makes and models of vehicles.

If you understand the general operating principles of the system there should be no problem in understanding the operation of a specific system.

General Motors Computer Command Control System (CCC)

General Motors Corporation uses a computer system on various makes and models of vehicles that is labeled the computer command control (CCC) system. It is basically the same on the different makes and models of vehicles, but will vary in respect to the number of units which are controlled by the system.

The computer command control system is an emission control system managed by a digital computer. The purpose of the system is to reduce engine exhaust emissions while maintaining good performance and economical operation. This is done by selecting the best air/fuel ratio for the particular operating condition.

The actual computer unit of the system is the electronic control module (ECM). The system includes, in addition to the electronic control module, various sensors and control devices. The sensors continuously monitor operating conditions and send the data to the ECM in the form of various voltage levels. These voltage levels are changed by the ECM to digital form for processing by the computer. The computer compares the sensor data with the programmed calibration data stored in the Programmed Read Only Memory (PROM). This data is a record of the engine operating standards that produce the least amount of emissions with the most efficient engine performance.

The computer command control system is designed so that most failures will not result in the engine stopping. Figure 9-10 is a schematic of a General Motors computer command control (CCC) system showing the various data sensors and emission controls.

The system has the capability to be programmed to monitor up to 15 different engine/vehicle operating conditions, and with this information, control as many as nine related engine systems. By making constant adjustments it is possible to maintain good vehicle performance under all normal operating conditions while allowing the catalytic converter to effectively control emissions.

In addition, the computer command control system has a built-in diagnostic system that identifies possible operational problems and alerts the driver through a CHECK ENGINE light on the instrument panel. The light comes on when a problem arises in the system and remains on until the problem is corrected. The light is also used with a built-in diagnostic system to aid in locating a problem by flashing a stored code that identifies the possible problem area. A built-in backup system will usually allow continued operation of the vehicle in a near normal manner should problems occur.

The system is designed basically to monitor and control the following features (not all units and controls will be found on all engines):

- Electronic spark timing (EST)
- Electronic spark control (ESC)
- Air injection reaction system (AIR)
- Exhaust gas recirculation system (EGR)

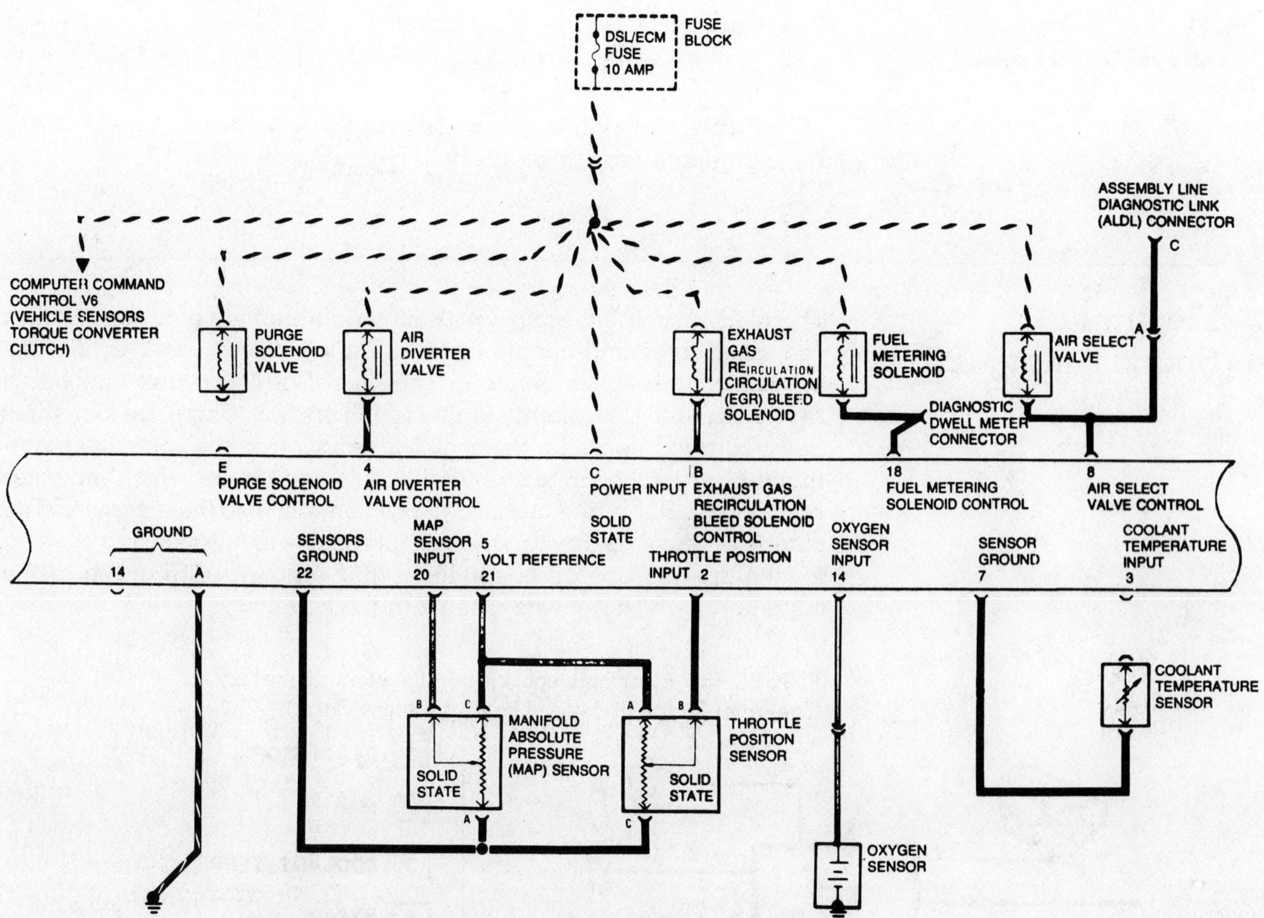

FIGURE 9-10 Schematic of General Motors computer command control system. (Courtesy Chevrolet Motor Division, General Motors Corp.)

- EGR relay
- Early fuel evaporation system (EFE)
- Transmission converter clutch (TCC)
- Electronic control module (ECM)
- Oxygen sensor
- Coolant sensor
- Barometric pressure sensor (BARO)
- Manifold absolute pressure or vacuum sensor
- Mixture control solenoid
- Throttle position sensor
- Catalytic converter
- Distributor reference pulses
- Vehicle speed sensor (VSS)
- ISC throttle switch (ISC)
- Air conditioning "on" signal
- Park/neutral switch (P/N) and back-up lamp
- Battery voltage
- Engine detonation

- Carburetor M/C solenoid signal
- Canister purge valve signal

A brief description of the various components and the effect they have on engine operation follows.

Electronic Spark Timing (EST)

The electronic spark timing is used on all engines equipped with a computer command control system. The electronic spark timing distributor contains no vacuum or centrifugal advance unit and has a seven-terminal high energy ignition (HEI) module. There are four wires going to a four-terminal connector in addition to the connectors normally used on the HEI distributor. A reference pulse which indicates both engine RPMs and crankshaft position is sent to the computer. The computer monitors the signals and determines the proper spark setting for the specific operating condition and sends an EST pulse to the distributor, which delivers a spark to the spark plug.

FIGURE 9-11 Electronic spark timing system. (Courtesy Chevrolet Motor Division, General Motors Corp.)

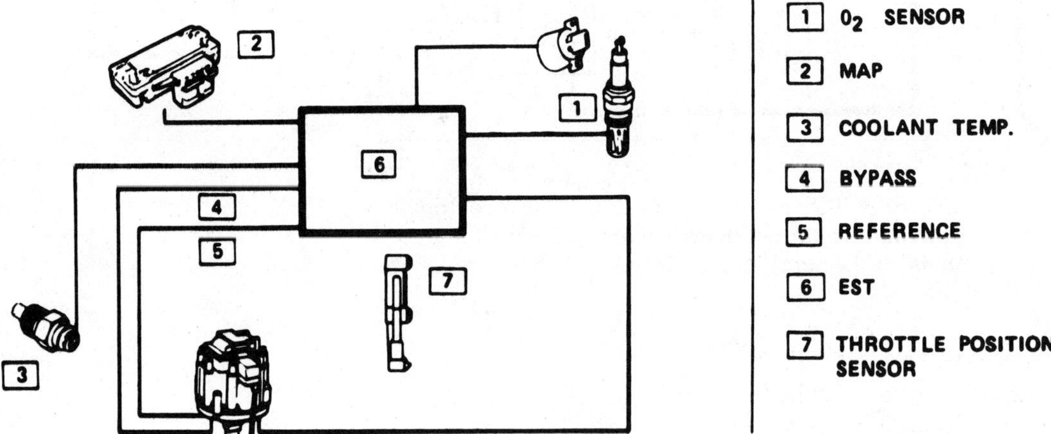

1 O_2 SENSOR
2 MAP
3 COOLANT TEMP.
4 BYPASS
5 REFERENCE
6 EST
7 THROTTLE POSITION SENSOR

Under normal operating conditions the ECM will control the spark advance. However, under certain conditions such as cranking, or when setting initial timing, the distributor can operate without the ECM control. This condition is called "bypass" and is determined by the bypass lead from the ECM to the distributor. When the bypass lead current is high (over 2 volts) such as in normal operating mode the ECM will control the spark. Disconnecting the four-terminal EST connector or grounding the bypass lead causes the engine to operate in the bypass mode. Figure 9-11 is a diagram of the electronic spark timing system. Input to the EST electronic spark timing module determines when spark should occur at the different spark plugs.

Electronic Spark Control (ESC)

Some engines will use the electronic spark control in conjunction with electronic spark timing to retard the spark timing under detonation conditions. A knock sensor signals a separate ESC control to retard the timing when it senses a knock. The ECS controller signals the ECM which reduces spark advance until normal signals are received from the knock sensor.

Air Injection Reaction System (AIR)

An air injection reaction system is used to provide additional oxygen to continue the burning process after the exhaust gases leave the combustion chamber. An engine driven air pump is used to inject air into the exhaust ports in the cylinder head, exhaust manifold, or the catalytic converter depending upon the design of the system. The AIR system operates all the time, but bypasses (diverts) for a short time during high speed operation and deceleration.

When the engine is cold, the computer (ECM) energizes the air control solenoid. This allows air to flow to an air switching valve. When the air switching valve is energized, air is directed to the exhaust ports.

When the engine is at operating temperature or in closed loop mode, the ECM de-energizes the AIR switching valve, thereby directing air between the beds of the catalytic converter. This provides additional oxygen for the oxidizing catalyst to decrease the carbon monoxide (CO) and hydrocarbon (HC) levels while at the same time keeping the oxygen levels low in the first bed of the converter. This enables the reducing catalyst to effectively decrease the levels of oxides of nitrogen (NOX)

If the air control valve detects a rapid increase in manifold vacuum (deceleration), certain operating modes, such as a wide-open throttle, or if the computer self-diagnostic system detects problems in the system, air is diverted to the atmosphere, depending on engine design. This is called diverter mode and is to prevent backfiring in the exhaust system.

Airflow and control hoses transmit pressurized air to the converter or to the exhaust ports by way of internal passages or external piping.

Figure 9-12 shows the routing of the hoses from the air pump through the switching valve and the various check and control valves to the converter.

FIGURE 9-12 Air pump valves and hoses. (Courtesy Oldsmobile Division, General Motors Corp.)

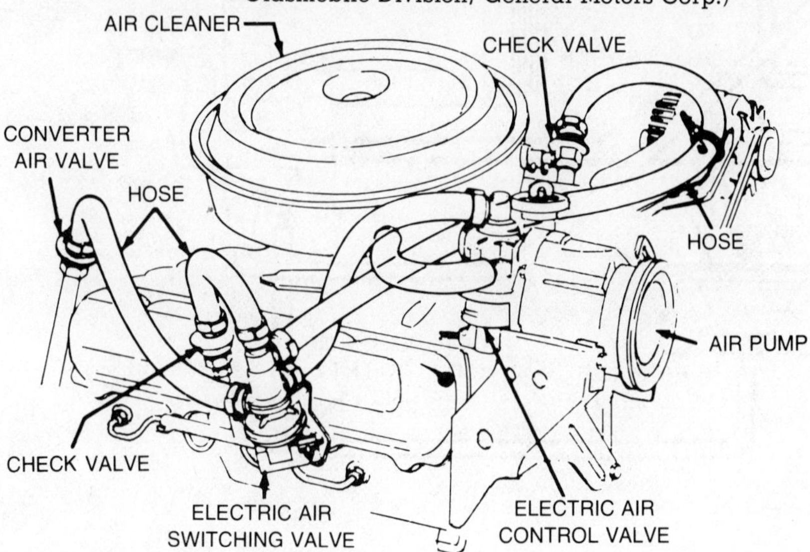

Exhaust Gas Recirculation System (EGR)

The exhaust gas recirculation system meters exhaust gas into the engine induction system through passages in the intake manifold. This lowers combustion temperature, thereby reducing the amount of oxide of nitrogen formed. The amount of exhaust gas admitted is regulated by a vacuum-controlled EGR valve in response to engine operating conditions.

The ECM controls the ported vacuum to the EGR valve by means of a solenoid valve. When the engine is cold, within a specified load range and above a specified RPM, the solenoid valve is energized and shuts off vacuum to the EGR valve. When the engine is warm, the solenoid valve is de-energized and the EGR valve will function.

EGR Relay

When the brake switch is closed (brakes applied) the EGR relay contacts are closed, which completes a ground circuit for the EGR solenoid. With the EGR solenoid now energized, the vacuum signal to the EGR valve is blocked, thus preventing EGR valve operation.

Figure 9-13 is a schematic of the EGR exhaust gas recirculation system which reduces oxides of nitrogen emissions from the engine exhaust by directing exhaust gases into the intake manifold, which reduces combustion temperatures.

FIGURE 9-13 Exhaust gas recirculation (EGR) system. (Courtesy Oldsmobile Division, General Motors Corp.)

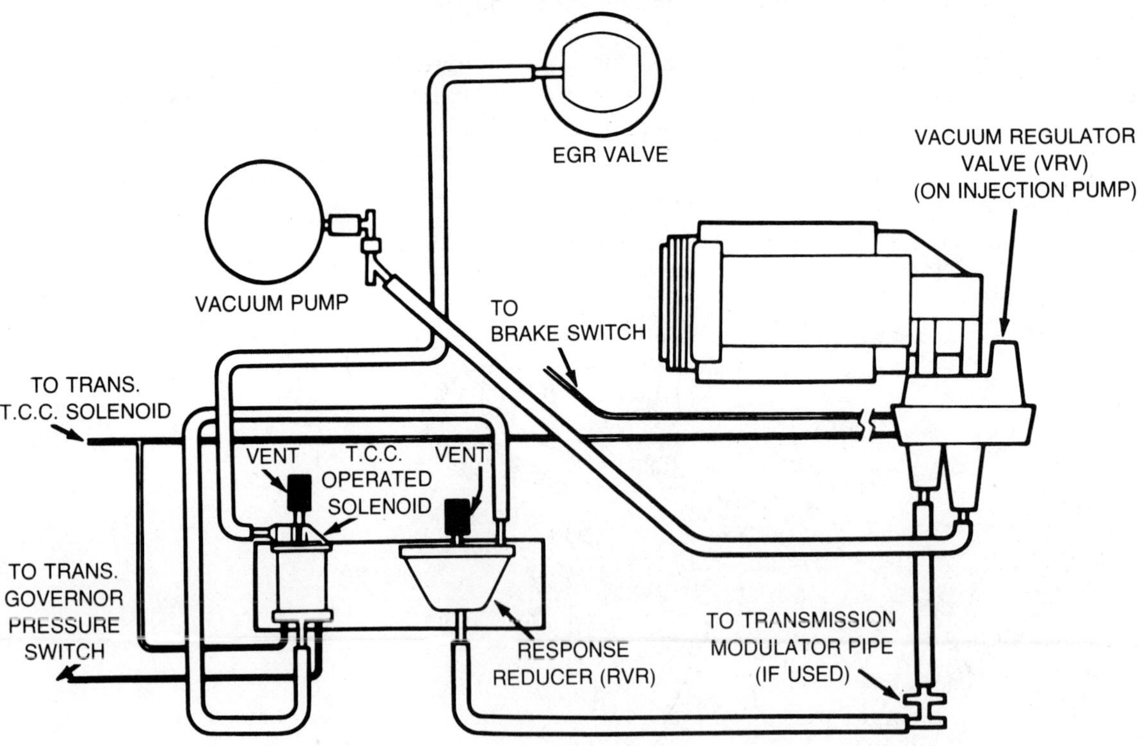

Early Fuel Evaporation System (EFE)

The early fuel evaporation system provides a source of rapid heat to the engine intake system when first starting a cold engine. The vacuum servo EFE system operates a valve to increase the exhaust gas flow under the intake manifold during cold engine operation. The vacuum-operated valve is controlled by an electrically operated solenoid valve that directs vacuum to the EFE valve. This occurs when engine coolant temperature is below the calibrated value of the thermal vacuum switch setting or as programmed by the ECM computer.

Transmission Converter Clutch (TCC)

The computer ECM controls an electrical solenoid located in the automatic transmission. When the vehicle reaches a pre-determined speed, the computer energizes the solenoid that allows the torque converter to mechanically couple the engine to the transmission. When operating conditions indicate the transmission should operate as a regular torque converter, the solenoid is de-energized. This will occur on deceleration.

Oxygen Sensor

The oxygen sensor protrudes into the exhaust stream and monitors the oxygen content of the exhaust gases. The difference between the oxygen content in the exhaust gases and that of the outside air generates a voltage signal to the ECM computer. The computer monitors this voltage and depending on the value of the voltage received, issues commands to adjust for richer or leaner conditions. The computer will not recognize the sensor signal until the sensor temperature reaches 600°F (360°C). Figure 9-14 is an oxygen sensor which protrudes into the exhaust flow, monitors the oxygen content of the exhaust gases and sends a voltage signal to the ECM to adjust the air/fuel mixture.

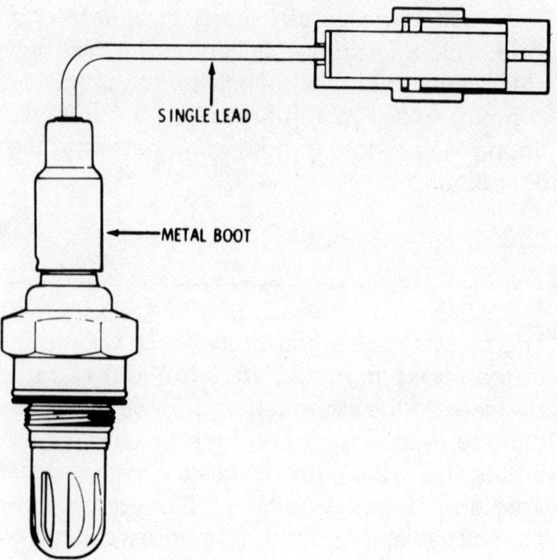

FIGURE 9-14 Oxygen sensor assembly. (Courtesy Oldsmobile Division, General Motors Corp.)

Coolant Sensor

The coolant sensor is mounted in the engine cooling system. It has a high resistance when the coolant is cold and low resistance when the coolant is warm. The coolant sensor supplies temperature information to the computer that is used to control the air/fuel ratio through the M/C mixture control solenoid that provides good cold start and driveability. It also has input that affects the air management system, the EGR system, the EST control, and other systems that are temperature-dependent. Figure 9-15 is a coolant sensor. The lower end extends into the cooling system. The sensor supplies coolant temperature information to the (ECM) electronic control module.

FIGURE 9-15 Coolant sensor and connector. (Courtesy Chevrolet Motor Division, General Motors Corp.)

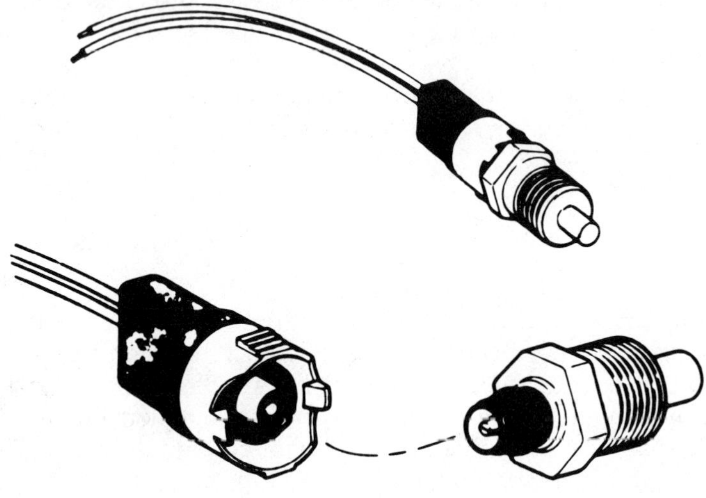

Barometric Pressure Sensor (BARO)

The barometric pressure sensor senses changes in barometric pressure. This information is sent to the computer (ECM) by means of an electrical signal that reflects changes in weather and/or altitude. The computer uses this information to adjust the air/fuel ratio and spark timing to maintain good engine performance under varying operating conditions.

Manifold Absolute Pressure (MAP) or Vacuum Sensors

The manifold absolute pressure or vacuum sensor measures changes in the intake manifold vacuum (lack of pressure). This information is provided to the computer in the form of an electrical signal. A pressure change reflects the need for adjustments in air/fuel mixture and spark timing (EST) that are necessary for good vehicle performance under varying driving conditions. The vacuum sensor is a good means of measuring engine load. It provides a low voltage when manifold vacuum is low (engine under load) and a high voltage when manifold vacuum is high (closed throttle).

Mixture Control Solenoid (MC)

The air/fuel ratio of the carburetor is controlled by an electrically operated solenoid which operates dual metering rods in the float bowl. The metering rods supplement the fuel supplied to the idle and main systems by varying the air/fuel ratio within a precalibrated range. The M/C solenoid, in addition, regulates the air/fuel ratio through the use of an idle air bleed circuit that operates in conjunction with the metering rods.

The computer controls the operation of the solenoid. The de-energized solenoid allows a richer air/fuel mixture while the energized solenoid allows a leaner air/fuel mixture. The solenoid cycles on/off 10 times per second. Figure 9-16 shows a mixture control M/C solenoid. The solenoid controls the air/fuel ratio by moving the metering rod or rods according to engine requirements.

FIGURE 9-16 Mixture control solenoid. (Courtesy Chevrolet Motor Division, General Motors Corp.)

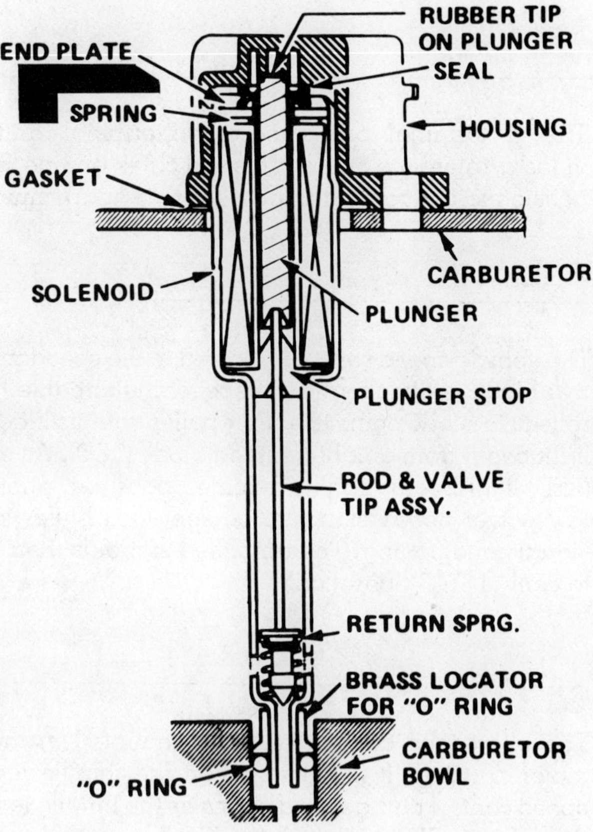

Throttle Position Sensor

The throttle position sensor is located in the carburetor body and is operated by the accelerator pump lever. The sensor operates in very much the same way as a fuel tank sending unit, by electrically signaling any change in position. This informs the computer of the position of the throttle. Figure 9-17 is a throttle position sensor which is operated by the accelerator pump lever on the carburetor. The sensor operates much like a fuel tank sending unit, electrically signaling the ECM of any change in the throttle position.

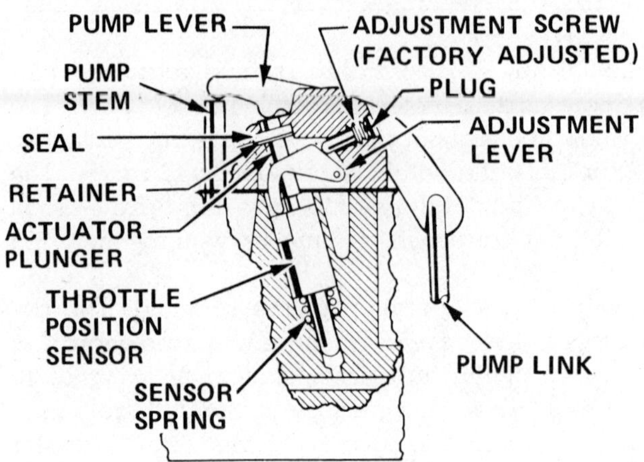

FIGURE 9-17 Throttle position sensor. (Courtesy Oldsmobile Division, General Motors Corp.)

Distributor Reference Pulses

The "R" terminal, one of the seven terminals on the HEI module, provides a reference pulse. This indicates engine RPMs and crankshaft position to the computer for electronic spark timing (EST) purposes.

Vehicle Speed Sensor (VSS)

The vehicle speed sensor is located in the speedometer frame. A reflective blade is attached to the speedometer cable, head assembly. The reflective blade spins like a propeller with its blade passing through a light beam from a light-emitting diode (LED). As each blade enters the (LED) light beam, light is reflected back to a photo cell. This causes a low power speed signal to be sent to a buffer for amplification and signal conditioning. The amplified signal is then sent to the computer to control TCC operation.

Idle Speed Control Throttle Switch (ISC)

The idle speed control switch is mounted in the idle speed control motor housing. It is closed when the throttle lever contacts the idle speed control plunger and opens as the throttle lever moves away from the plunger. When closed, the ISC controls idle speed. The motor cannot react if the switch is open.

Air Conditioning "On" Signal

A 12-volt signal is supplied to the computer when the air conditioning compressor is engaged and a zero volt signal is supplied when the compressor is off. The computer uses this information to send an idle speed control extended pulse in anticipation of the added load of air conditioning.

Park/Neutral Switch (P/N) and Backup Lamp

The park/neutral switch is connected to the transmission gear selector. It is closed when the selector lever is in park or neutral. When closed it retards ignition timing. It also affects torque converter clutch and idle speed control operation.

Computer Controlled Coil Ignition (CCCI)

On some late model General Motors engines the conventional electronic distributor and ignition coil have been replaced with a module containing three double end coils with a spark plug wire attached to the ends of each. This applies to the V6 type engine. Each coil fires two spark plugs at a time. One at the completion of the compression stroke, as usual, and the other end of the coil firing the spark plug of the cylinder which is just completing the exhaust stroke. This firing has no effect on engine operation. A camshaft position sensor provides information for the operation of the sequential fuel injection system. A sensor at the crankshaft pulley signals the computer relative to firing position. The computer triggers the correct coil which sends a high voltage current to the spark plug in the cylinder ready to be fired. One spark ignites the compressed fuel charge while the other fires harmlessly into the exhaust of another cylinder.

The distributorless ignition system is labeled as the Computer Controlled Coil Ignition (CCCI) system. The CCCI microprocessor uses data from the camshaft and crankshaft position sensors to determine the correct spark timing information. A detonator sensor is included in the system for timing modulation. Spark energy to the ignition coils is provided by the electronic control module ECM.

Ford Motor Company Computerized Emission Control System

Ford Motor Company uses different computerized engine control systems on the various model vehicles and will use different labels. One system is labeled the Electronic Engine Control system (EEC); another system is the Microprocessor that is generally referred to as the Microprocessor Control Unit (MCU). Some California engines using central fuel injection are equipped with a system called EECIII Electronic Engine Control. As requirements change and improvements are made to the system, labeling will undoubtedly be changed so as to distinguish the systems.

The essential difference between the EEC system and the MCU system is in what each controls. The EEC system controls ignition timing, exhaust gas recirculation EGR, and the air/fuel ratio. The MCU system controls the air/fuel ratio and exhaust gas recirculation EGR. It does not control timing, but on some model engines the system will control spark timing when detonation occurs. On engines having the EEC system, no vacuum advance unit is used on the distributor.

The labels (terminology) used by the manufacturer may change with the different makes and models of vehicles as more components are added to the system. Following is a brief description of the terms or labels as set forth by the manufacturer.

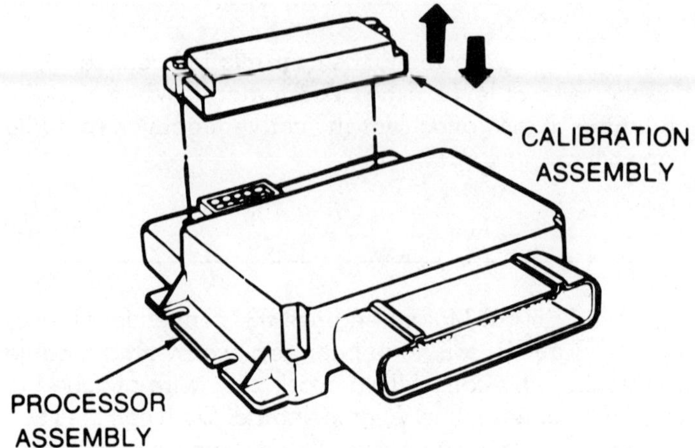

FIGURE 9-18 Calibration and processor assembly. (Courtesy Ford Parts & Service Division, Ford Motor Co.)

The electronic control assembly (ECA) is part of the electronic engine control system, consisting of a calibration assembly containing the computer memory and thus, its control program and a processor assembly that is computer hardware. The processor plugs into the vehicle wiring harness. Figure 9-18 shows a calibration and processor assembly used in the EECIII system equipped with either an electronic fuel injection system or a feedback carburetor.

The electronic engine control (EEC) system is a computer directed system of engine control to reduce emissions. Various models are in use, each controlling different components. The EEC I controls engine timing; the EEC II controls engine timing and fuel through the use of the feedback carburetor (FBC); the EEC III with a FBC is a descendent of the EEC II; the EEC III also controls timing and air/fuel ratio with the electronic fuel injection system. The EEC IV model provides instantaneous and accurate fuel metering. It also controls the duration and spark timing by using data sent to the microcomputer from six sensors which monitor air flow to the engine, incoming air temperature, coolant temperature, throttle position, exhaust gas oxygen content, and crankshaft position. Using this information, the computer unit determines the correct amount of fuel mixture and the proper timing to maintain optimum engine performance.

The microprocessor control unit (MCU) is an integral part of the electronically controlled feedback carburetor system using a three-way catalytic converter. Various sensors are used to monitor the operational mode. The MCU is widely used by Ford products for the control of the air/fuel ratio. It is important to remember that diagnosing and servicing will not differ basically with the addition of more components to the control system.

Electronic Engine Control System (EEC)

The electronic engine control system (EEC), through input from several sensors, uses the information to control fuel flow, thermactor air, exhaust gas recirculation, and ignition. The electronic control assembly (ECA), that is the computer unit, consists of a calibration assembly containing the computer memory and thus its control program, plus the processor assembly which receives input signals from the different sensors. The assembly sends out signals to the various components according to how the unit is programmed.

On engines equipped with central fuel injection, the EEC system is used to control the fuel injection as well as the fuel pump. With the ignition switch in start or run position, the EEC power relay applies voltage to the fuel pump relay. When controlled by the ECA, the fuel pump relay operates, supplying a current flow to the fuel pump through the inertia switch. With high engine vacuum the ballast bypass relay is energized and the normally closed contact points are opened. Current flows through the ballast resistance wire and the electric fuel pump runs at a normal speed. When vacuum is low, as in starting or wide open throttle, the fuel pump vacuum switch opens,

FIGURE 9-19 Schematic of a EEC111 system. (Courtesy Ford Parts & Service Division, Ford Motor Co.)

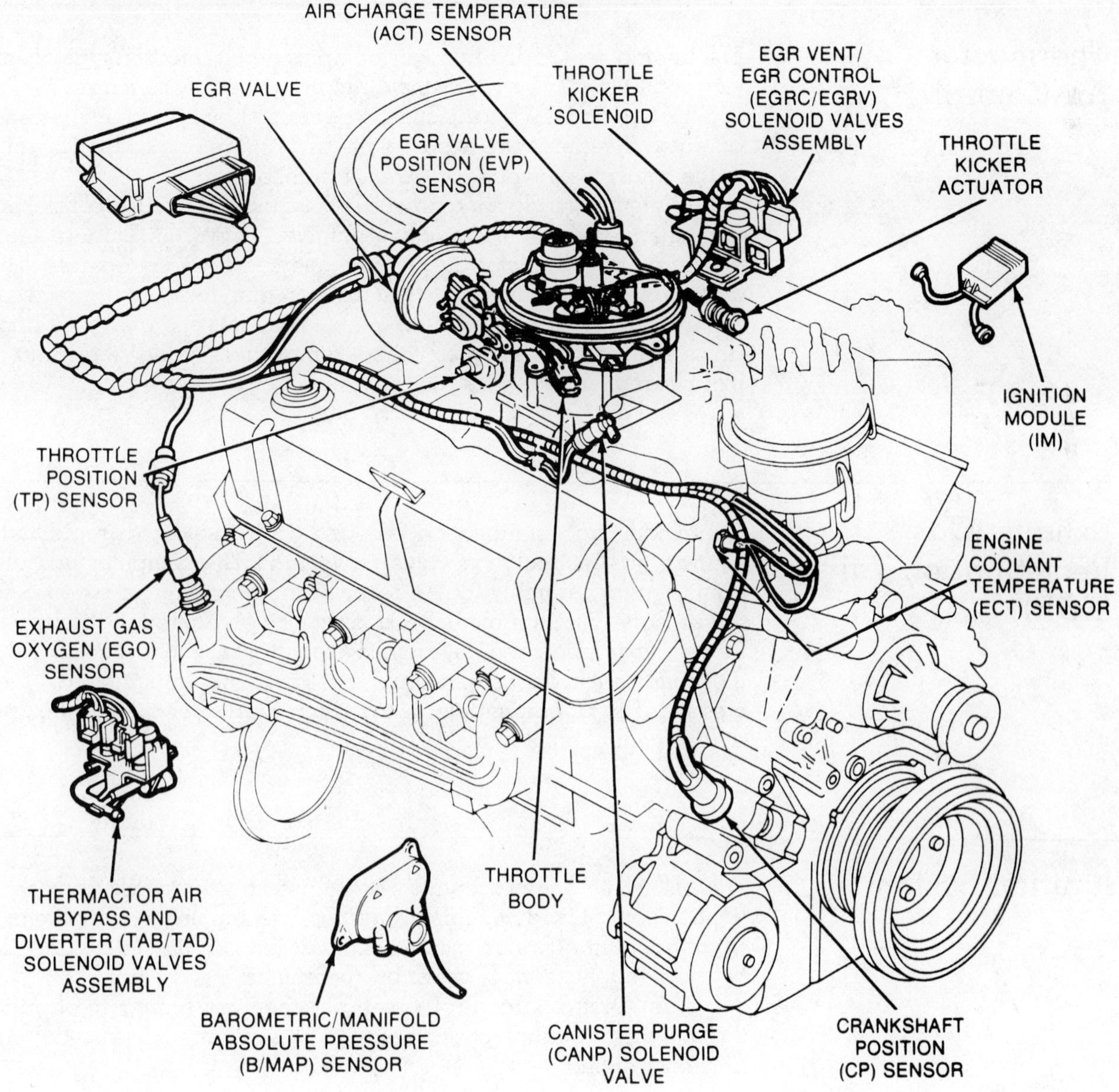

de-energizing the ballast bypass relay. The contact closes and bypasses the ballast resistance wire. Full battery voltage is now applied to the fuel pump which operates at a faster speed.

The more common California engine uses a carburetor. Fuel metering to fit engine requirements with reduced engine emissions is accomplished through a carburetor actuator stepper motor. Information received from the exhaust gas oxygen sensor and other sensors by the ECA will position the carburetor stepper motor in one of 100 possible positions to best regulate the air/fuel mixture.

On both installations a throttle kicker solenoid is used to provide additional throttle opening when required. This occurs at high or low engine coolant temperatures, at high altitudes, or whenever the A/C system is operated. Figure 9-19 shows the various sensors, solenoids and control units used with the EECIII system on an engine equipped with electronic fuel injection.

Thermactor Air Control

The thermactor (basically an air pump) is an air injection type of emission control system, such as the air management system used by General Motors and the air injection system used by Chrysler. A solenoid operated diverter valve is part of the unit and regulates the flow of air to the catalytic converter or exhaust manifold.

With the thermactor air diverter solenoid in normal (operate) position, thermactor air flows to the catalytic converter. During engine warmup the thermactor air diverter solenoid does not operate. Thermactor air is then diverted to the exhaust manifold.

When the thermactor air bypass solenoid is operated, thermactor air is immediately dumped to the atmosphere rather than into the exhaust manifold or catalytic converter.

Exhaust Gas Recirculation Valve (EGR)

The exhaust gas recirculation vent and control solenoids regulate the exhaust gas recirculation valve movement. The computer unit electronic control assembly (ECA), receives information from seven different sensors. The unit also checks existing valve position through the EGR valve position and determines if the present exhaust gas flow into the combustion chamber should be increased, maintained or decreased. The ECA then determines which EGR solenoids will be operated to control emissions.

Ignition System

The electronic engine control system uses a special distributor and ignition control module. This distributor does not use a magnetic pickup or vacuum advance mechanism. All ignition timing is controlled by the electronic control assembly (computer).

The electronic control assembly receives timing information through the crankshaft position sensor. This information is used to control spark timing.

Sensing Devices

Numerous sensing devices are used to determine engine operating conditions. The sensing devices provide the electronic control assembly with throttle, pressure, temperature, and exhaust gas information.

The throttle position sensor sends signals to indicate partially open throttle, closed throttle or wide-open throttle to the computer.

The manifold absolute pressure sensor provides the computer with manifold pressure information which is related to speed, load, and throttle position.

The barometric pressure sensor indicates atmospheric pressure. Atmospheric pressure changes with altitude.

The exhaust gas oxygen sensor sends varying voltages to the computer relative to the oxygen content of the exhaust gas. High oxygen content indicates a lean mixture, lack of oxygen indicates a rich mixture. A lean mixture burns hotter than a rich mixture.

The manifold change temperature sensor senses the temperature of the air being drawn into the intake manifold.

The canister purge solenoid controls the flow of gasoline vapors from the canister to the intake manifold during various engine operating modes.

Microprocessor Control Unit (MCU) Feedback Carburetor Control

The microprocessor control unit MCU system controls the air/fuel ratio through a feedback carburetor control and the exhaust gas recirculation system (thermactor air control) in response to various signals received by the MCU (computer) from the different sensors. Figure 9-20 is a schematic of the vacuum system and the electrical system which provides the control for the MCU microprocessor control unit.

The heart of the system is the microprocessor control unit, that is basically a transistorized series of switches that turn functions on and off. It receives signals from various components, analyzes these signals relative to engine operation, and sends out signals to other components to change the operating mode.

The thermactor air control system consists of an air pump driven by a belt, with an air diverter solenoid and a bypass solenoid. The solenoids are triggered by voltage received from the MCU. When the thermactor air diverter solenoid is in normal operating position, thermactor air flows to the catalytic converter. During engine warmup the thermactor air diverter solenoid does not operate. Thermactor air is then diverted to the exhaust manifold. When the thermactor bypass solenoid is actuated, thermactor air is immediately dumped to the atmosphere rather than to either the catalytic converter or exhaust manifold.

The feedback carburetor control system operates in either an open or closed loop mode. In open loop mode the air/fuel mixture is not controlled by the MCU. The air/fuel ratio metering operates in the same manner as a regular type non-feedback carburetor.

In closed loop, the air/fuel mixture is controlled by the MCU in response to feedback information received from the exhaust gas sensor and other sensors in the system. The carburetor air/fuel mixture change (fuel metering) is now controlled by the carburetor actuator

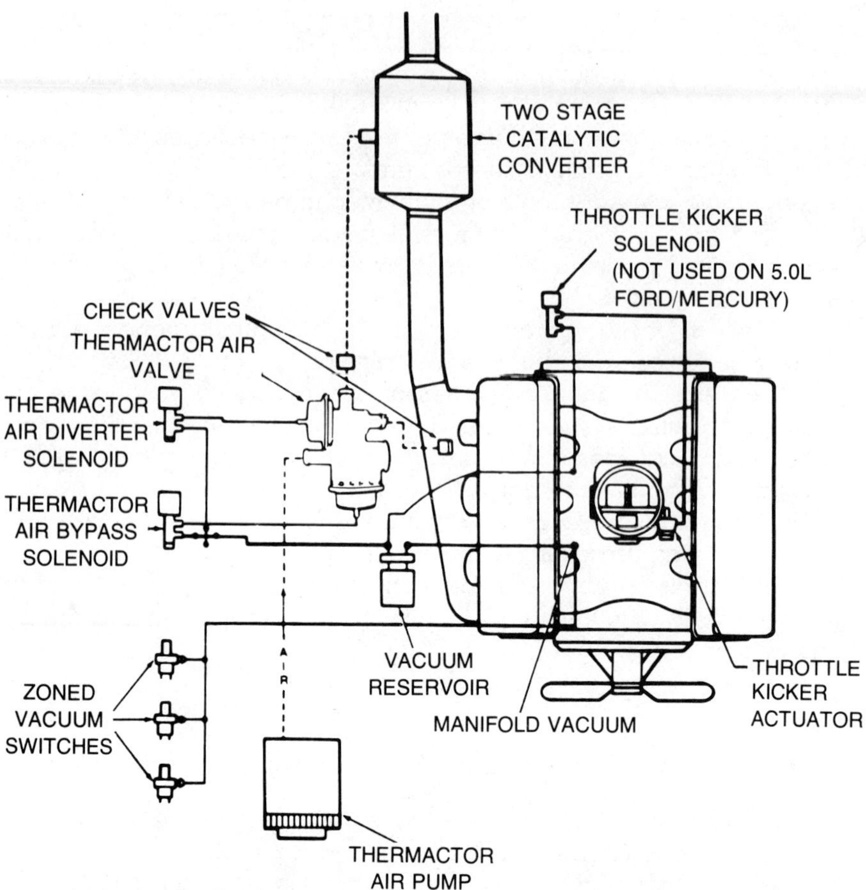

FIGURE 9-20 Schematics of the vacuum and electrical MCU system. (Courtesy Ford Parts & Service Division, Ford Motor Co.)

stepper motor. The stepper motor is connected directly to the metering rods to control fuel flow in as many as 100 different possible steps or positions. The fully extended position provides the richest mixture—less air for the amount of fuel. There is also a throttle kicker solenoid which is operated through the throttle kicker control relay to slightly open the throttle plates when a signal is received from the MCU or from the A/C system.

Various sensing devices are used to determine the different engine operating conditions. The sensing devices provide the MCU with engine temperature, throttle position, and vacuum information. The MCU monitors the air/fuel ratio by means of the exhaust gas oxygen sensor. A lean exhaust gas mixture will show a high oxygen content, while a rich mixture shows a low oxygen content. Heat is the actual sensing factor, the more oxygen the higher the temperature.

When the idle tracking switch closes, the MCU goes into closed loop position. This could be considered as being in the cruising range. During idle and deceleration the switch opens and the MCU signals for an open loop mode of operation.

The electric ported vacuum switch closes when the coolant temperature is above 128°F. This signals the MCU to go to a closed loop operating mode if other factors are in compliance for closed loop.

Zoned vacuum switches operate at various levels of manifold vacuum. They trigger the MCU to control the output solenoids for a

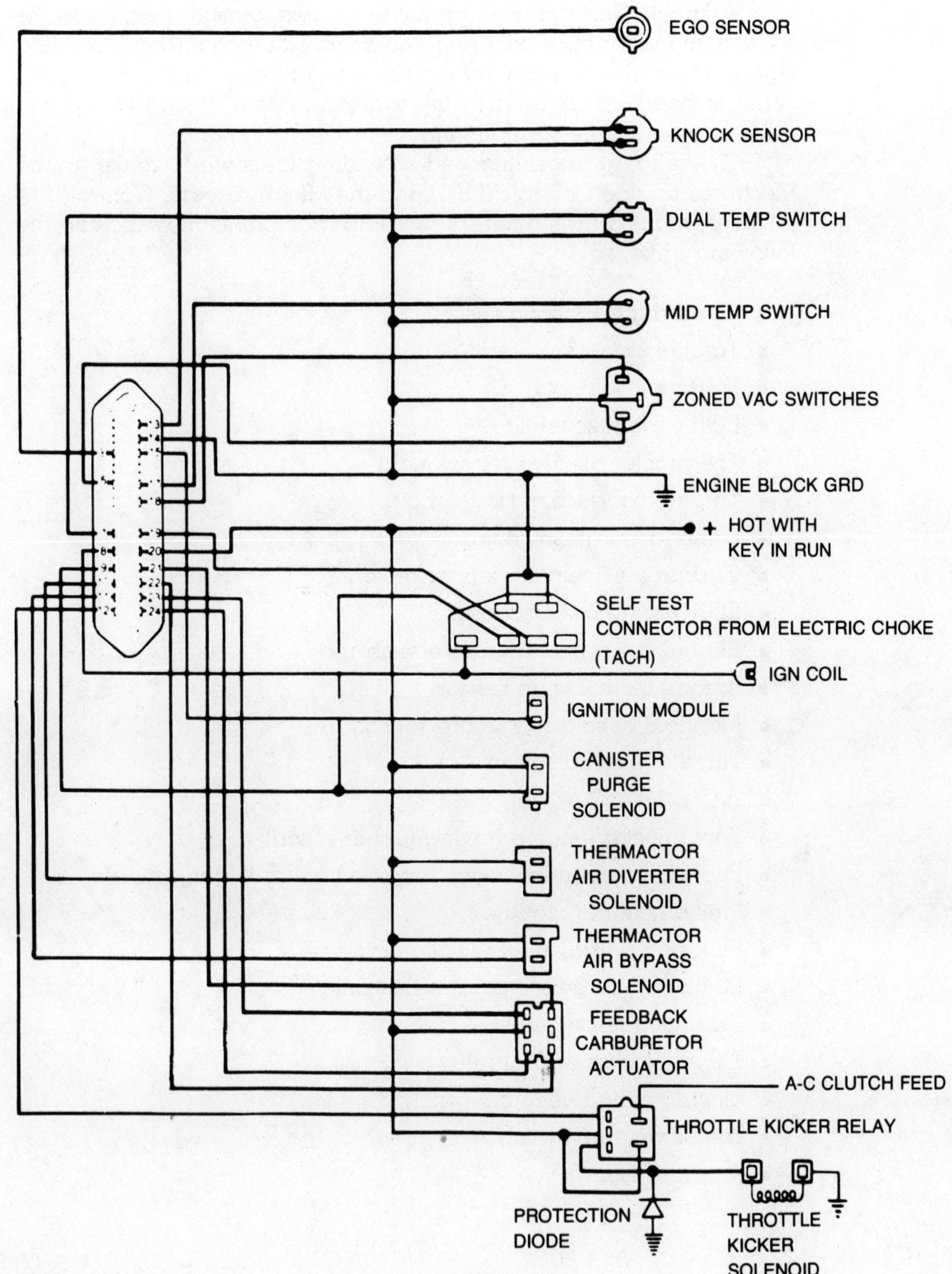

FIGURE 9-20 (cont.)

wide-open throttle position, a crowd enrichment (acceleration under load) and a cold start.

The coolant hi/low switch is normally closed. The switch opens below 55°F and above 235°F. This switch and the electric ported vacuum switch establish various temperature zones for different modes of system operation, according to operational needs.

A canister purge solenoid controls the flow of vapors from the canister to the intake manifold during the various engine operating modes.

A knock sensor is used on some models to send a signal to the MCU when detonation occurs in the combustion chamber. The MCU signals the carburetor to vary the ratio, usually to enrich the mixture. When a computer is used in the ignition system, it signals the distributor to retard the spark timing.

The sending, receiving and activating units which make up the Electronic Engine Controls (EEC) and the Microprocessor Control Unit (MCU) systems on the different model power plants may include the following units:

- Crankshaft position sensor
- Throttle kicker solenoid
- EGR vent solenoid
- EGR control solenoid
- Thermactor air diverter solenoid
- Thermactor air bypass solenoid
- Canister purge solenoid
- Carburetor actuator stepper motor
- EGR valve position sensor
- Engine coolant temperature sensor
- Barometric pressure sensor
- Manifold absolute pressure sensor
- Throttle position sensor
- A/C pressure switch
- Fuel injector (engine having fuel injection)
- Fuel pump vacuum switch (engine having fuel injection)
- Ignition control module
- Fuel pump relay (fuel injection system)
- Manifold charge temperature sensor
- Exhaust gas oxygen sensor
- Throttle kicker control relay
- Electric ported vacuum switch
- Zoned vacuum switch
- Knock sensor

Computer System Used on Chrysler Products

Certain models of Chrysler Corporation vehicles use an electronic fuel control system consisting of a spark control computer, various sensors, and a specially calibrated carburetor along with a dual pickup distributor. The purpose of the system is to bring about a better air/fuel mixture for more complete burning. This results in less exhaust emission. Figure 9-21 is a line drawing of the components used with the spark control computer used on many Chrysler products.

The heart of the system is the spark control computer. It provides the capability of igniting the air/fuel mixture according to different modes of engine operation. This is done by delivering an infinite amount of variable advance curves.

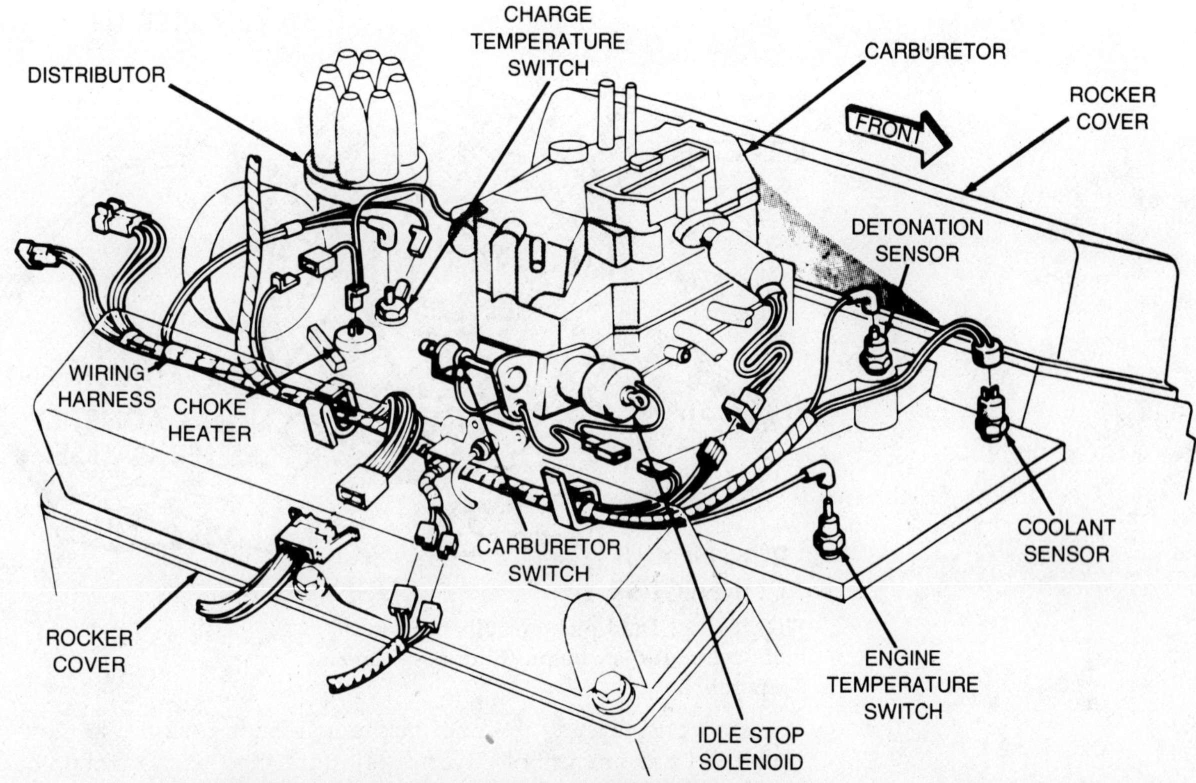

FIGURE 9-21 Electronic spark control system used on some Chrysler products. (Courtesy Chrysler Corporation)

The computer simultaneously receives signals from the various sensors, analyzes the signals relative to engine operation, and then advances or retards the spark timing to best fit engine requirements. A microprocessor (electronic module) located within the computer processes the signals from the sensors for accurate spark timing. The computer determines the exact instant when ignition is required according to operating conditions, and directs the distributor to ignite the air/fuel mixture.

The amount of spark advance is determined by two factors, engine vacuum and engine speed. When spark occurs depends on operating conditions. Advance according to vacuum will be available when the carburetor switch is open. The amount of advance is programmed by the computer and is proportioned according to the amount of vacuum and engine RPMs. Advance according to speed will be provided by the computer when the carburetor switch is open and is programmed to engine RPMs.

On this particular design, seven sensors may be involved in supplying the computer with the necessary information to fire the spark plugs at the right instant. Two pickup coils are located in the distributor housing, a start pickup coil and a run pickup coil. Figure 9-22 shows a distributor which uses dual pickup coils as part of the electronic ignition system. A feeler gauge is used to check the clearance between the pickup coils and the reluctor.

The two functional modes of the computer are start and run. The start mode functions only during engine cranking and starting. The run mode functions only after the engine starts and during engine operation. The two pickup coils will not operate simultaneously. During

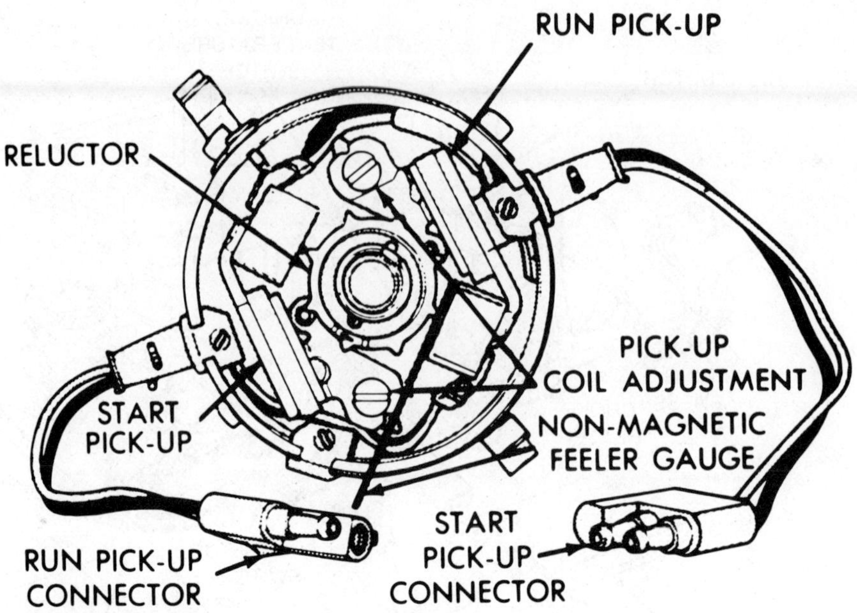

FIGURE 9-22 Dual pick-up coils used in an eight-cylinder distributor. (Courtesy Chrysler Corporation)

cranking and starting the one pickup coil feeds a signal to the computer. A fixed amount of advance is established as the pickup coil is permanently attached to the distributor housing plate. The run pickup coil mode is bypassed.

After the engine has been started and during engine operation the run pickup coil signals feed the computer. The amount of advance is determined by the computer. This is based on information received from the various sensors. The start pickup coil will take over should the run pickup coil fail. However the engine will remain in the start operational mode.

The pickup coil provides a reference signal. When this is received by the computer, the maximum amount of spark advance is made available. Based on data from the different sensors, the computer determines how much of the maximum advance is needed at that particular time.

The different sensors send signals to the computer. A coolant sensor may be located in the cylinder head or intake manifold. It provides a signal when the engine has reached a predetermined temperature. This information is necessary to prevent changing the air/fuel ratio until the engine reaches operating temperature.

A vacuum transducer is located on the spark control computer and signals the amount of engine vacuum. Engine vacuum is a determining factor in ignition as well as bringing about a change in the air/fuel ratio.

A carburetor switch located on the end of the carburetor idle stop tells the computer when the engine is operating at idle. When the curb idle switch contacts the throttle lever ground, any spark advance will be canceled. The carburetor idle system will then be in operation.

A detonation sensor protects the engine from detonation (spark knock). The sensor is mounted in a branch of the intake manifold. It is tuned to a frequency that is characteristic of engine detonation. When knock frequency is detected, the detonation sensor sends a low voltage signal to the computer. The computer will then retard the timing. The amount of retard is directly proportional to the strength and frequency of the detonation condition. When the detonation condition is removed, spark timing is advanced to the original value.

An oxygen sensor is located in the exhaust manifold. It signals the computer how much oxygen is present in the exhaust gases. Since the amount of oxygen is proportional to rich and lean mixtures, the computer will adjust the air/fuel ratio to a level that will maintain operating efficiency. The oxygen sensor is not used on all Chrysler computer installations, only on engines equipped with a feedback carburetor.

A change temperature switch is located in the intake manifold. When the intake (air/fuel mixture) charge temperature is below approximately 60°F (15°C) the change temperature switch will be closed, allowing no exhaust gas recirculation (EGR) valve timer function, no EGR valve operation, and will switch the air injection upstream into the exhaust manifold. The charge temperature switch will open when the intake charge temperature is above approximately 60°F (15°C), thus allowing the exhaust gas recirculation EGR timer to time out, the exhaust gas recirculation valve to operate, and will switch the air injection downstream into the exhaust system.

Chrysler Corporation has expanded the number of computer-controlled units used on more recent models. An electronic feedback carburetor is used on some engines. Incorporated in the computer system on some other engines is a throttle body fuel injection system in place of the conventional carburetor. The electronically controlled throttle body injector system monitors strategic sensors and electronically controls fuel injection. The injector nozzles replace the conventional carburetor, but the air/fuel mixture is still distributed to the individual cylinders by the intake manifold.

An electronic control module monitors pertinent sensors and feeds back the information to the ignition timing control, emission controls, and the air/fuel ratio control, so that it is possible to obtain maximum performance according to operating conditions.

The ability of the computer system to accurately determine the needs of the engine greatly enhances fuel efficiency, particularly during deceleration. The sensors for throttle position, engine RPMs, and manifold pressure indicate to the computer control unit that the engine is decelerating and the air/fuel ratio should be reduced to absolute lean limit.

Elimination of "dieseling" is another function of the computer control system. This is brought about by reducing the air/fuel ratio below the combustible limit at shutdown so that continued running is not possible.

American Motors Corporation Computerized Emission Control System

American Motors Corporation uses different feedback systems which are designed to reduce undesirable exhaust emissions in conjunction with either a dual-bed converter or a three-way catalytic converter, while maintaining performance and fuel economy. The system is individually tailored to fit the needs of the different four-cylinder engines as well as the six-cylinder engine.

In all systems, the primary feedback data is provided by an oxygen sensor located in the exhaust system. The information from the oxygen sensor, plus other sources of information, is used by the electronic control module ECM (microprocessor) to regulate and optimize the air/fuel mixture. This is accomplished by the use of several data inputs and the standard data stored in the Read Only Memory (ROM). The system also contains a Programmable Read Only Memory (PROM) that has stored data unique for the particular engine. These factors are designed into the system by the manufacturer and cannot be changed.

The oxygen sensor provides a variable voltage from 100 to 900 mv (millivolt) to the EMC microprocessor that is basically a voltage analog of the oxygen content of the exhaust gases. As the oxygen content of the exhaust gases increases (lean mixture), the voltage output from the sensor decreases proportionally. As the oxygen content decreases (rich mixture), the voltage output increases proportionally. The microprocessor uses this voltage data to regulate the mixture control (MC) solenoid on the carburetor so as to maintain an optimum air/fuel mixture. The engine must be warmed up to a pre-determined temperature before the oxygen sensor voltage output is acceptable to the microprocessor.

In addition to the oxygen sensor more data senders are used to provide the microprocessor with additional engine operating information. The more data fed into and utilized by the microcomputer unit, the better the engine should be able to operate with less undesirable emissions. Two vacuum operated electric switches, one mechanically operated, one engine coolant operated electric switch and one air temperature operated electric switch are all used to detect and send information to the (MCU) microprocessor unit.

All engines may not have exactly the same number of controls as others, depending on the design features of the engine. Figure 9-23 is a drawing of the C4 system used on AMC vehicles. The E-Cell (emission

FIGURE 9-23 C4 computer-controlled feedback system. (Courtesy American Motors Corp.)

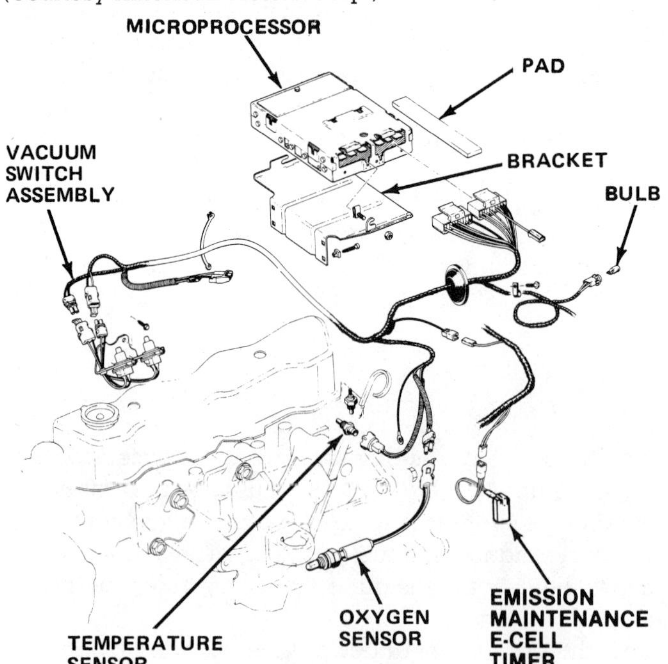

maintenance lamp) illuminates after 1,000 hours of engine operation.

The data senders are used to detect the following: cold engine startup and operation, wide-open throttle, idle condition (closed throttle) as well as partial and deep throttle. Throttle position has considerable effect on engine operation.

A thermal electric switch is located inside the air cleaner and provides a ground circuit for the microprocessor to indicate the need for a cold weather engine startup or an open circuit to indicate normal engine start. Temperature determines the mode of the circuit, either open or closed loop operation.

The coolant temperature switch is controlled by engine coolant temperature and is integral with the intake manifold heater control switch. When the switch is closed it indicates the engine is cold, the temperature is below 135°F (57°C).

A vacuum switch controlled by carburetor ported vacuum has a normally closed electrical contact that indicates a closed throttle. The switch will open at approximately 4 in. hg. vacuum.

Another vacuum operated switch is controlled by manifold vacuum. When the switch is open, it indicates a deep throttle condition (non-cruise operating condition). This switch operates at approximately 10 in. hg.

A wide-open throttle switch is a mechanically operated electrical switch located at the base of the carburetor. The switch indicates when the throttle is wide open.

In addition, included in the system is voltage from the "tach" terminal of the distributor. Until a voltage equivalent to a predetermined RPM is received by the MCU the system remains in the open loop mode of operation—no additional oxygen is fed into the catalytic converter. The result is a normal rich air/fuel mixture for starting purposes.

A stepper motor (type of solenoid) is an integral part on certain model carburetors. The motor controls the metering pins by varying the size of the idle and main air bleed orifices located in the carburetor body. The motor moves the pins in or out of the orifices in steps according to the voltage received from the MCU. The motor has a range of 100 steps; the normal operating area is mid-range, 40 to 60 steps. When the metering pins are stepped in the direction of the orifices, the air/fuel mixture becomes richer; when stepped away from the orifices, the mixture becomes leaner.

A dual-bed catalytic converter is used with this type installation. The system uses "downstream" air injection. Whether air is injected "upstream" directly into the exhaust manifold or "downstream" into the dual-bed catalytic converter is determined by the MCU (microprocessor). Air is supplied by the air injection system, consisting of a belt driven air pump, diverter (bypass) valve, air control valve, air injection manifold, "downstream" air injection tube, and connecting hoses. The system is designed to supply air at two locations, the exhaust manifold and the dual-bed catalytic converter, according to the signal received from the MCU microprocessor.

There are two primary modes of operation from the feedback system, the open loop and the closed loop. In general, each component in the system will be in the open loop mode of operation, or some variation of it, whenever the engine operating conditions do not conform with the programmed criteria for closed loop operation.

During open loop operation, the air/fuel mixture is maintained at a programmed ratio that is dependent on the type of engine operation involved. The oxygen sensor data is not accepted by any system of the microprocessor during this mode of operation.

The following conditions involve open loop operation: engine start-up, coolant or air temperature too low, oxygen sensor temperature too low, engine at idle speed, carburetor at wide-open throttle and battery voltage low. When all of the input data to the microprocessor conform with the programmed criteria for closed loop operation, the oxygen content output voltage from the oxygen sensor is accepted by the microprocessor. This results in an air/fuel mixture that will be optimum for the current engine operating conditions, and will correct any pre-existing too rich or too lean conditions.

A high oxygen content in the exhaust gas indicates a lean air/fuel mixture. A low oxygen content indicates a rich air/fuel mixture. The ideal air/fuel mixture ratio is approximately 14.7:1.

Recent models are equipped with an ignition-controlling knock sensor to eliminate detonation. A two-barrel feedback carburetor also is used on the computer-equipped vehicles.

Troubleshooting the Computer Control System

When a vehicle fails to perform in a satisfactory manner and/or fuel consumption is higher than normal, and/or the engine produces an excessive amount of emissions, it is only reasonable that the problem or problems be discovered, the cause eliminated, and the trouble corrected.

Locating the problem is generally the most difficult job. Following a regular preventive maintenance schedule as recommended by the manufacturer helps to reduce the chances of problems occurring.

Usually, excessive emissions as well as excessive fuel consumption are the result of engine malfunctions. Therefore, a regular tuneup and troubleshooting procedure should be carried out before condemning the computer control system.

It is best to go through the regular troubleshooting procedure that you would normally follow if the vehicle were not equipped with a computer control system. Always make the simple and more obvious checks first. Look for loose, cracked, damaged, or improperly connected vacuum hoses. Check for loose and/or corroded electrical connections. Determine if there are fouled spark plugs, faulty secondary wires, or electronic ignition system troubles. Check the carburetor and fuel system for malfunctions. The emission system components such as the PCV valve, EGR valve, thermostatic air cleaner, and heat valve should also be checked for satisfactory operation. Internal engine problems resulting in the loss of compression or vacuum will result in faulty engine performance. For an engine to function properly, it must have good compression, proper air/fuel mixture, and the necessary spark delivered at exactly the correct time. All of these factors must be considered in order to have an efficiently performing engine.

Vehicles equipped with a computer control emission system incorporating an air/fuel control system have a built-in self-diagnosis system. While there are specific differences in the self-diagnosis systems used by the different manufacturers, all provide basically the same type of information.

All systems utilize voltage impulses to pinpoint the subsystem in which the trouble exists. One system uses a check engine light located in the instrument panel, which comes on when a problem is present in the system. One system requires that a test lamp be connected across test terminals of the terminal panel. This will indicate whether or not a problem exists in the components included in the system. Another system necessitates connecting a special tester or digital voltmeter across terminals of the computer terminal panel to determine if trouble exists in the system.

When the check engine lamp, test light, or test instrument shows a problem exists, it is possible to activate the self-diagnosis system to provide a readout in the form of code signals to indicate the subsystem where the problem is located.

To get the system to "talk" is a relatively simple matter. There is a close similarity in all of the systems; however, you must follow manufacturer's recommendations in every case for specific instructions. The specific hookup will vary with the different makes of vehicles, the code numbers are not the same, and as previously stated, the method of getting the code display will be different. Therefore, general instructions on getting the diagnostic system to "talk" will follow in general terms which apply to all, and then a description, including the code system will follow. By carefully following this material it should be possible to use the self-diagnostic system to your advantage. The system, if properly activated, will indicate either trouble or no trouble.

When the test lamp instrument indicates a malfunction exists in the system it can go one step further—a trouble code will be, or can be made to display, indicating the subsystem in which the problem is located.

While the trouble code reveals the subsystem where the malfunction exists, it does not specifically indicate the component causing the problem. It does not indicate, for example, whether the problem is the sensor, computer, wiring system, or some other part of the system. The trouble could be any one or more of these components.

Some problems may not show up with the self-diagnosis tests. Following a complete inspection and diagnosis procedure before activating the self-diagnosis system will usually clear up most problems. The self-diagnosis system is a valuable aid, but it is not a substitute for the conventional methods of locating problems.

When it has been definitely established that the trouble is in a specific subsystem, it is possible to pinpoint the component where the malfunction is located through the use of test equipment recommended by the manufacturer. A specific procedure must be followed and checked against exact readings in order for the tests to be meaningful.

Factors to Consider When Troubleshooting

There are several factors to keep in mind relative to troubleshooting the computer control system.

1. Emission control is directly related to engine operating efficiency. The engine must be properly tuned and maintained for efficient operation with minimum emissions.

2. The computer control module for all practical purposes is trouble free. Most manufacturers warrant the unit for five years.
3. The sensors, solenoids and switches which are the main units in the control system are for the most part nonserviceable, therefore when trouble is pinpointed as being in one of these parts the unit must be replaced.
4. Operational signals coming from the computer control module and going to the specific operating components are in the form of voltages, therefore electrical connections, terminals, and wires make up the circuits. These electrical circuits are tested and serviced in the same manner as any other circuit, by using an ohmmeter and/or voltmeter.
5. Vacuum is used to actuate a number of different components in the system. Always check hose routing. This is usually shown on the decal in the engine compartment. Check the hoses for tight connections, cracks, or places where the hoses may be pinched.
6. As the computer control system is primarily designed to reduce and keep exhaust emissions at a minimum, always check out the operation of the exhaust emission system, and service or replace any faulty component before checking the computer system.
7. As with most service adjustments and checks, they should be made only when the engine is at normal operating temperature and the upper radiator hose is warm.
8. Before condemning the computer control system, if the equipment is available, make a complete engine diagnosis using an oscilloscope and infrared emission tester. Make the needed repairs and adjustments before servicing and checking the computer.
9. There is a very similar pattern relative to the self-diagnosis system used on all of the vehicles, but enough of a difference exists so that each make and model must be checked according to manufacturer's recommendations.
10. All self-diagnostic systems use a code system whereby the computer is programmed to send out voltage signals in the form of impulses which are fed to the test instrument or check light when malfunctions occur. The codes and method of obtaining the codes vary with the different vehicles.
11. As with any troubleshooting or diagnosis procedure, it is an elimination process. Start with simple checks and visual observations. Eliminate each possibility for problems as you go along. Become familiar with the location of each component as well as its function.
12. When it is necessary to check using the diagnosis terminal connectors, it is essential that manufacturer's specifications and instructions be carefully followed.
13. To actuate the self-diagnosis system, to get it to "talk," requires very little in the way of equipment. Some systems can be checked with an analog voltmeter and jumper wire, some systems necessitate the use of a test lamp and jumper wire, while another system requires only small jumper wires. However, one system requires a special test instrument in order to get a display of service codes.
14. The self-diagnosis system test indicates the subsystem in which

the problem is located. The test does not indicate the particular unit which is malfunctioning. To pinpoint the exact component which is causing the problem requires additional equipment. Either specialized test equipment made for a particular make of vehicle, or as in most instances, a dwell-tachometer, digital volt/ohmmeter, 12-volt test lamp, vacuum pump, timing light, vacuum gauge, jumper wires, and spark tester. Exact specifications and manufacturer's instructions must be carefully followed.

15. In a great many instances, the self-diagnosis test indicates the subsystem in which the problem exists. It has narrowed the problem to a particular area. It may be possible, if you understand the system, to locate the specific trouble and/or component by way of a normal testing procedure.
16. Of major importance is the ability to diagnose a computer-related function.

Computer Control System Self-Diagnostic Units

The computer control system, as the name implies, is strictly a control system. The computer unit (control module) receives signals from different components which affect performance and exhaust emissions. The computer unit, in turn, directs control signals to the different components in the system. The signals cause the various selected units to be turned "off" or "on" according to how the computer control unit is programmed.

The computer control unit (module) is made up of transistors, diodes, and resistors and is not serviced in the field. The complete assembly must be replaced if malfunctions occur within the unit.

The calibration assembly or PROM, is programmed to tailor the electronic control module to meet the requirements for the particular model vehicle. It can be replaced should malfunctions occur. If the unit is functioning properly, but the electronic control module is faulty, the calibration assembly can be removed and reused in the replacement computer assembly.

The computer control unit has no moving parts to wear or change, and it will usually perform in a satisfactory manner over a long period of time.

The components which actually perform the different emission control functions are, for the most part, the same as those used on vehicles not equipped with a computer control system.

Because the computer control unit (module) is relatively trouble free, when problems do occur that might be related to the computer system, always be sure to check for loose or damaged vacuum hoses and loose, frayed, or corroded electrical wires, and/or connections, before making further checks.

General Motors, Ford Motor Company and American Motors vehicles equipped with a computer control system that includes an air/fuel ratio control have a self-diagnostic check system utilizing a code system to establish the particular subsystem in which troubles may exist. Although the check system is not completely infallible, it is a good indicator and should be utilized.

The computer control system should be considered as a possible source of trouble only after all the normal tests, inspections, and corrections have been made that would normally apply to an engine without a computer control system.

A brief overview of the different self-diagnosis systems follows. Each individual make will then be discussed in more detail relative to the code system in use.

General Motors Computer Controlled Emission System

General Motors products equipped with a computer command control (CCC) system have a CHECK ENGINE warning light on the instrument panel. This is automatically illuminated whenever the on board computer calculates something is not functioning correctly. However, many common engine problems may also trigger the check engine light.

Whenever failure to start, stalling when the engine is cold or when the air conditioner is turned on, hesitation on acceleration, surging, rough idle, overheating at idle, detonation, engine miss, higher than normal fuel consumption, higher than normal emission levels, or hard starting occurs, a normal diagnosis procedure should be performed as the initial step.

If the computer system is suspected, it is a good idea to make a quick check by looking for loose and/or damaged vacuum hoses, loose and/or corroded electrical wires or terminals, as well as damaged wires that connect the various components to the computer.

FIGURE 10-1 Under dash connector. (Courtesy Chevrolet Motor Division, General Motors Corp.)

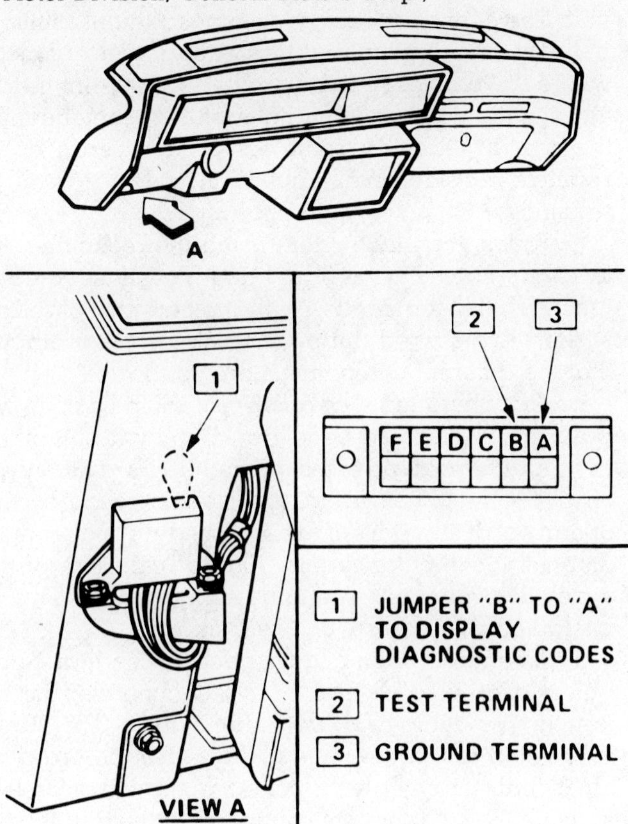

When the check engine light comes on, it is possible to obtain a service code by connecting the test code terminal to the ground test terminal. The trouble code test terminal is mounted in the terminal connector unit located under the instrument panel. The ground terminal is also located in the test terminal unit. By connecting the test terminal to the ground terminal the check engine lamp will flash a code signal, according to where the trouble exists in the system. Figure 10-1 shows the trouble code test lead terminal mounted in a terminal connector located under the instrument panel. A jumper wire must be used to connect terminal "B" "A."

The trouble code will indicate a malfunction in a specific circuit. As the self-diagnosis system does not detect all possible problems, the absence of a code does not always mean there are no problems in the system. The self-diagnostic code system is displayed by intermittent voltage signals sent out from the computer system.

Ford Motor Computer Controlled Emission Systems

A number of different Ford Motor vehicles are equipped with a computer control system. Two basic types of computers may be found, according to the make and model of vehicle. The electronic engine control (EEC) system, or the microprocessor control unit (MCU), may be used on the different Ford products. There are various models of EEC systems that may perform different functions, some operating more components than others.

Both types of electronic control systems include self-diagnostic functions in the form of numerical service codes stored in the computer unit. The service codes are displayed by intermittent voltage signals.

The EEC system requires a special tester to locate the subsystem where the problem exists and then to pinpoint the specific component causing the problem. An analog volt-ammeter can be used in place of the special tester for some tests, but it is an exacting process and requires considerable practice in order to accurately interpret the readings.

To test the EEC system using the recommended equipment, the following should be kept in mind. A self-test procedure used in conjunction with a quick test will indicate the problem area. When the self-test is triggered during a quick test, the computer unit will verify that the different components are connected and operating properly, or are not operating. The quick test will indicate in what area there is a problem. This should be followed up by a pinpoint test.

A different type of test procedure as well as equipment is used to check out the MCU system. A self-test procedure is utilized to verify the operation of the system. The procedure makes use of the on board diagnostic computer system. Figure 10-2 shows the self-test connector which is located in the engine compartment. This is for checking the microprocessor control unit system.

A self-test automatic readout device that converts service code pulses into two-digit display is recommended for easy and accurate testing. An analog DC voltmeter with a 0 to 20 volt range may be substituted to test the system. A self-test program is utilized during a functional test to verify the correct operation of the feedback carburetor system. The MCU system controls only the air/fuel ratio and EGR oper-

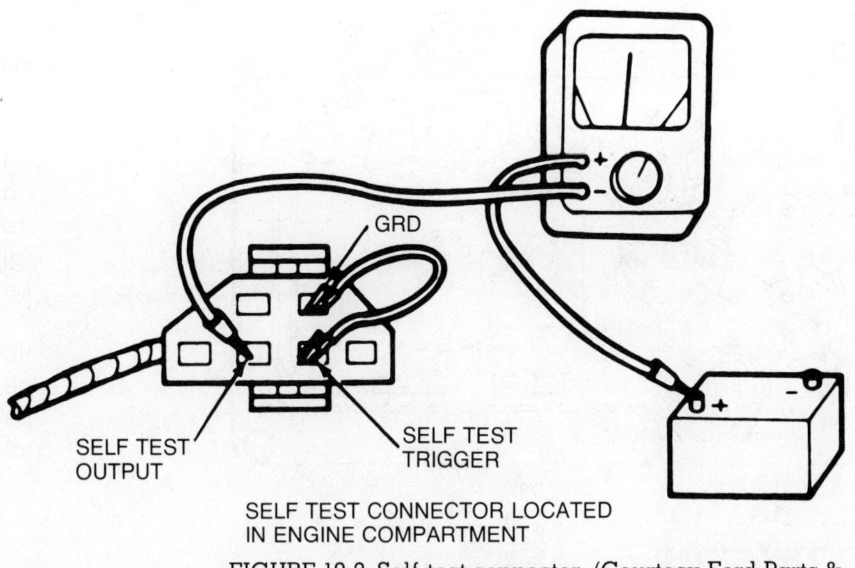

FIGURE 10-2 Self-test connector. (Courtesy Ford Parts & Service Division, Ford Motor Co.)

ation. If a problem is detected, a code will appear which indicates that a subroutine test should be made. Subroutine tests will pinpoint the exact faulty component.

American Motors Computer Controlled Emission System

American Motors vehicles equipped with a computerized emission control CEC system use an integral self-diagnostic system within the electronic control module. The unit detects problems that are most likely to occur in the emission control system.

In addition, an emission maintenance lamp is located in the instrument panel. The lamp illuminates after 1,000 hours of engine operation indicating that the oxygen sensor should be replaced. After replacing the sensor, the E-cell timer must be replaced. This is done by removing a printed circuit board from its enclosure and inserting a replacement timer. The timer is located in the passenger compartment under the instrument panel. Figure 10-3 shows the location of the emission maintenance timer in the printed circuit of the instrument cluster. It is connected to the wiring harness leading to the feedback system microprocessor.

When trouble is suspected in the control system, a 12-volt test lamp is inserted in the test circuit of the control terminal panel. The diagnostic system will cause the test lamp to be illuminated if a fault exists. When the trouble code test pigtail wire, located on the control terminal panel under the instrument panel, is manually connected to ground, the test lamp will flash a trouble code as to where the problem exists. The trouble code is then set in the memory of the computer where it will remain until the trouble is corrected and the battery negative cable disconnected and reconnected. Figure 10-4 shows the electronic control module terminals which are labeled. The manufacturer's instructions relative to test connections and sequence must be carefully followed in order to make a meaningful test.

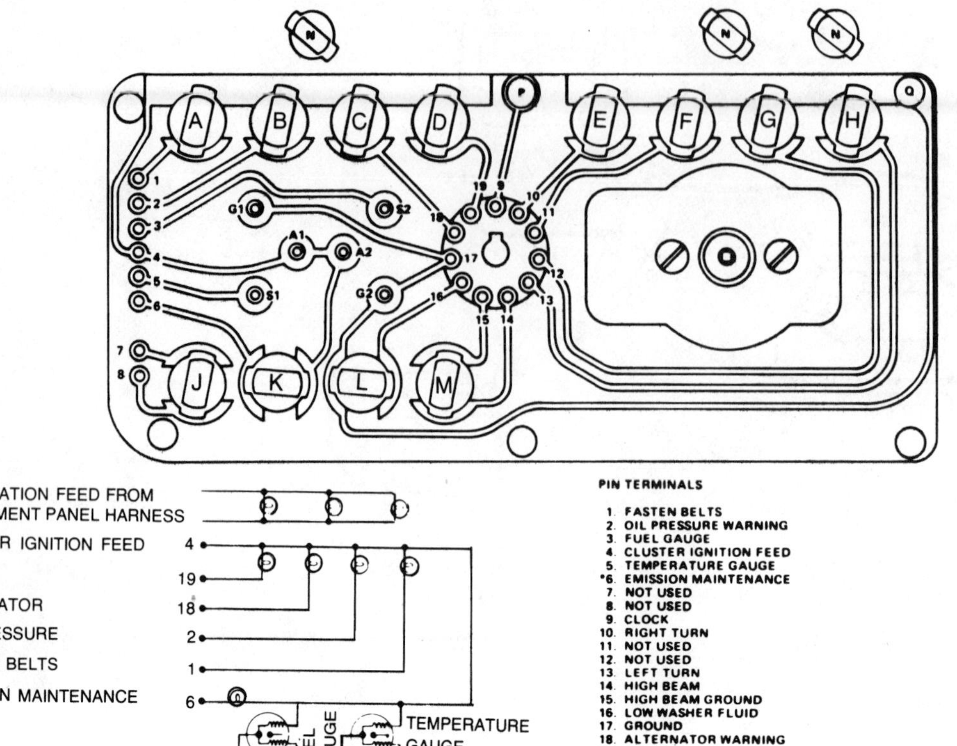

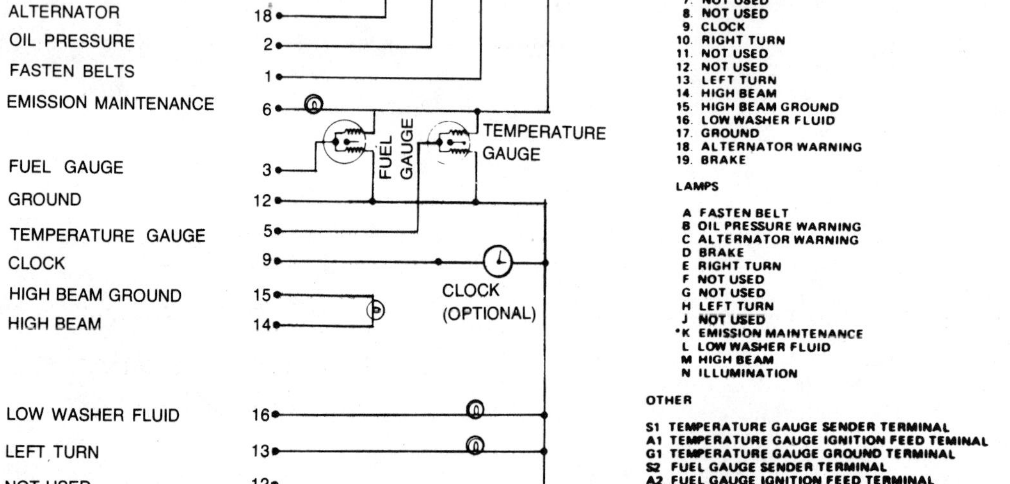

FIGURE 10-3 Instrument cluster circuit board. (Courtesy American Motors Corporation)

How Different Systems "Talk"

GENERAL MOTORS SYSTEM

In the case of General Motors products equipped with a computerized emission control system, the check engine lamp will come on should a problem occur. The problem may or may not be in the computer controlled area. It is also possible that some problems may not register through the self-diagnosis system. A specific code can be made to register on the check engine light by connecting across to ground the different circuits. The code is registered by intermittent flashes of the lamp.

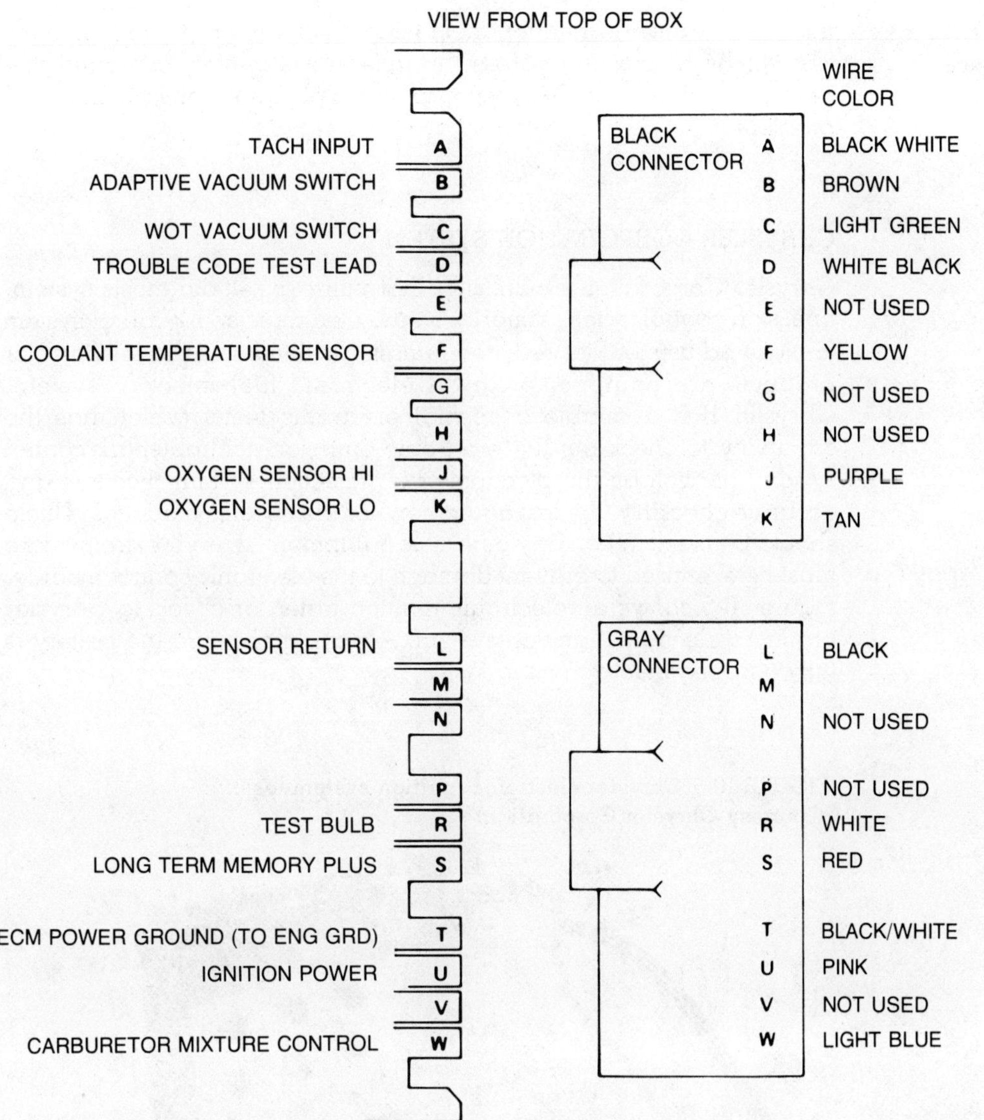

FIGURE 10-4 AMC electronic control module (ECM) terminal connections. (Courtesy American Motors Corporation)

FORD MOTOR SYSTEM

On Ford Motor products, in order to determine the system in which the problem exists (to get the diagnosis system to "talk"), a test instrument specifically designed for Ford Motor products should be used. However, a digital voltmeter, in some cases, if properly used, will indicate the system in which the problems are located.

AMERICAN MOTORS SYSTEM

American Motors products, equipped with a self-diagnosis system as part of the computer system, necessitate hooking a 12 volt test lamp into the computer terminal panel to find out if there is a problem in the system. By connecting across the different terminals to ground it is possible to obtain a coded response which pinpoints the location of the problem.

CHRYSLER CORPORATION SYSTEM

Chrysler Corporation products do not utilize a self-diagnosis system. Emission control relies primarily on the electronic spark conrol system to make adjustment for reduced emissions. Some late model Chrysler products are equipped with an electronic fuel injection system. Chrysler has available a special electronic tester which has the capability to check out the electronic emission control (spark control system) as well as the electronic fuel injection system. For fast and accurate checking, the test equipment for the specific model of vehicle should be used. When any other test equipment is used, extreme care must be exercised to prevent damage to the electronic control module. Figure 10-5 shows an electronic ignition tester for checking Chrysler product's electronic ignition system. Always make sure the battery is fully charged before making tests.

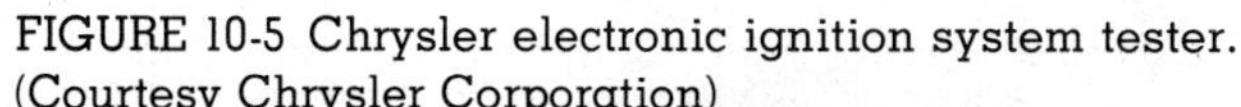

FIGURE 10-5 Chrysler electronic ignition system tester. (Courtesy Chrysler Corporation)

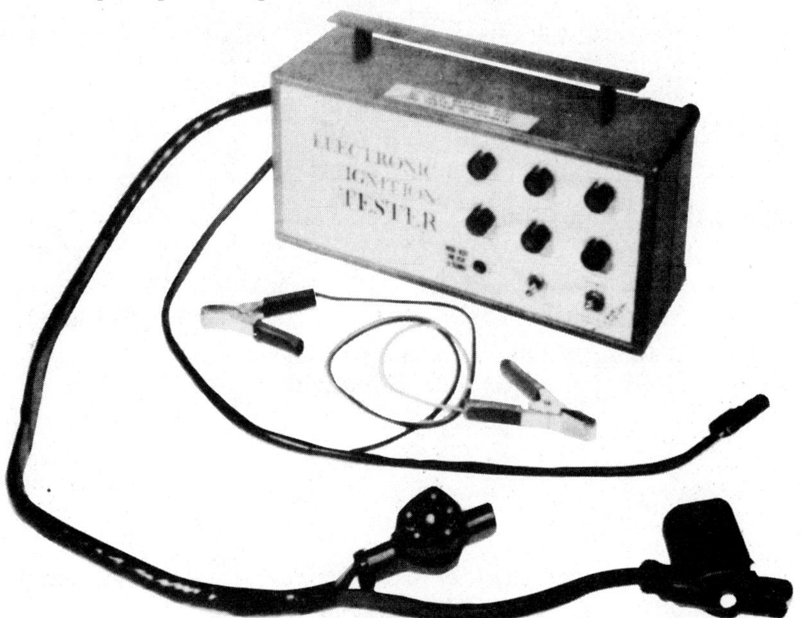

General information relative to the specific systems according to the different makes of vehicles follows. The information must be general because not all makes and model vehicles will have the same emission control components. As time goes on, the different manufacturers are including more components in the system, as well as making changes to the system. This information should enable you to activate the various self-diagnosis systems in order to identify the subsystem in which the malfunction is located.

GENERAL MOTORS COMPUTER COMMAND CONTROL SYSTEM

When the computer command control system is functioning properly, the check engine light will come on and stay on momentarily until the engine is started. If the light does not come on, the fuse, lamp, or circuit is faulty. If the light does not go off after the engine starts, there is undoubtedly a problem in the computer command control system. When the check engine light stays on, a signal in the form of a trouble code is locked into the memory of the electronic control module EMC. The trouble code is in the form of electrical impulses.

The number of codes programmed to be retained in the computer varies with the different makes and models of vehicles. Some may retain only seven or eight trouble codes while others may retain as many as sixty-two. Most of the computer command control systems are programmed to retain 18 or 19 trouble codes. On a limited number of models, once the engine is turned off, the code is wiped out. On these installations it is well to check for the trouble codes before stopping the engine.

When the check engine light stays on, in order to get a code display it is necessary to ground the test lead terminal mounted in the terminal connector panel. The connector terminal unit is located under the instrument panel. The number of terminals in the terminal connector will vary with the make and model of vehicle. One terminal is "test" another is "ground." It may be necessary to refer to the manufacturer's specifications in order to identify the terminal locations.

Connecting the "test" lead to "ground" with the ignition switch on should cause the check engine light to flash a code 12, indicating the self-diagnosis system is working. A code 12 consists of one flash followed by a short pause, then two flashes in quick succession. After a longer pause the code will repeat two more times. Figure 10-6 is a drawing of the ECM (electronic control module) terminals as used with the General Motors (CCC) computer command control system.

When the engine is started and the check engine light stays on, if the test terminal is grounded, the trouble code will flash three times and then repeat itself until the ground is removed or the problem corrected. If more than one problem exists, each trouble code will flash three times. The trouble code will flash in numerical order (lowest number code first).

The trouble codes indicate the subsystem in which the problem is located. It does not tell which component in the subsystem is at fault.

The check engine light will be on only if the malfunction exists in the areas listed. If the trouble clears up, the light will go out but the trouble code(s) will be set in the computer unit. A code stored will be cleared from the computer if it does not recur within 50 engine starts.

If the test terminal is grounded with the engine running, the system will enter the field service mode. In this mode the check engine light will indicate whether the system is in open or closed loop. Open loop is indicated by the light flashing approximately twice each second. Closed loop is indicated by the light flashing approximately each second.

The trouble code numbers indicate problems as follows:

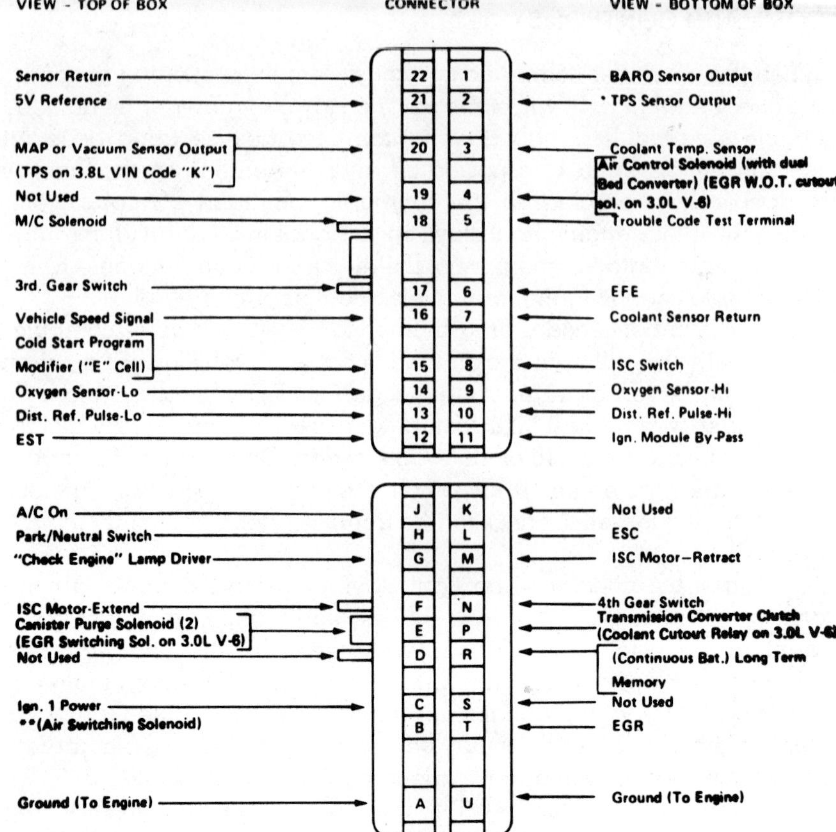

FIGURE 10-6 ECM terminal identification. (Courtesy Chevrolet Motor Division, General Motors Corp.)

12 No reference pulses to the computer. This code is not stored and will flash only to indicate the system is in operation. Normal code with ignition on, engine not running.

13 Oxygen sensor circuit. The engine must run for at least five minutes at part throttle, under load, before the code will set.

14 Shorted coolant sensor circuit. The engine must run for at least two minutes before this code will set.

15 Open coolant sensor circuit. The engine must run for up to five minutes before this code will set.

21 Throttle position sensor circuit. The engine must run for up to 25 seconds at specified curb idle speed before the code sets.

23 Open or grounded mixture control solenoid circuit.

24 Vehicle speed sensor circuit. The vehicle must operate for up to five minutes before this code will set.

32 Barometric absolute pressure circuit low.

34 Manifold absolute pressure (vacuum sensor circuit). The engine must run up to five minutes at specified curb idle speed to set the code.

35 Idle speed control switch circuit shorted. Run at one-half throttle or more for over two seconds.

41 No distributor reference pulses at specified engine vacuum. This code stores.

42 Electronic spark timing bypass circuit grounded.

43 Electronic spark control retard signal for too long, causes a retard in the electronic spark timing signal.

44 Lean oxygen sensor indication. The engine must run for five minutes in closed loop at part throttle before the code will set.

44 and 45 (at same time) faulty oxygen sensor circuit.

45 Rich system indication. The engine must run for five minutes in closed loop at part throttle and road load before the code sets.

51 Faulty calibration unit (PROM) or installation. It takes up to 30 seconds before the code sets.

54 Shorted mixture control solenoid circuit and/or faulty computer.

55 Grounded throttle position sensor circuit, faulty oxygen sensor or computer.

FORD MOTOR ELECTRONIC ENGINE CONTROL SYSTEMS

Both the electronic engine control EECII system and the microprocessor control unit MCU system have a self-test feature included in the computer unit that can be activated by connecting into the unit terminal panel. The self-test information from the computer is in the form of voltage impulses. Because the EECII system includes more components in the computerized control system than the MCU system, a more complex testing procedure requiring special equipment is necessary.

The MCU system regulates exhaust emissions primarily by controlling air/fuel ratio during closed loop operation of the feedback carburetion system. By connecting a special self-test readout tester or an analog voltmeter to the self-test connector in the engine compartment it is possible to obtain a readout of the various circuits and components which make up the computerized emission control system.

When a failure is detected in either system a service code will be displayed indicating the pinpoint tests to make in the case of the EECII system, or the subroutine tests to be made in the case of the MCU system.

CHECKING THE FORD EECII SYSTEM

The ignition system used on an engine equipped with the EECII system uses a special ignition module and ignition coil. The distributor does not have a magnetic pickup or advance unit. All ignition timing is controlled by the electronic assembly (ECA) computer.

As with all vehicles equipped with a computer control system, the system is comparatively trouble free. Therefore, when operational problems occur, a complete diagnosis procedure of the ignition system, emission control system, fuel system, and engine components should be performed in the same manner as if the vehicle was not equipped with a computer control system. This will usually correct the problems.

In the process of checking the ignition timing, it should be noted that if the engine operates with a fixed 10° BTDC spark timing, and the EGR and thermactor systems do not operate, the EEC system is operating in the fail-safe mode. This indicates a problem exists in the EEC system. When this occurs, it will be necessary to make a complete electronic diagnosis of the EEC system. The same procedure is used for checking the EECII system, whether the engine is equipped with electronic fuel injection, or a feedback carburetor system.

Two special testers, a EECII tester and a DVOM (digital voltohmmeter), are needed to make the system "talk"—indicate where the problem exists. If the vehicle is equipped with an electronic fuel injection system, an electronic injector adapter harness and an electronic fuel injection pressure gauge are required. In addition, for complete testing, a tachometer, vacuum pump, jumper wires, vacuum gauge, a timing light, and a spark tester are needed. Figure 10-7 shows the special testers needed for convenient testing of the EECIII electronic emission control system.

FIGURE 10-7 Testers for the EEC111 system. (Courtesy Ford Parts & Service Division, Ford Motor Co.)

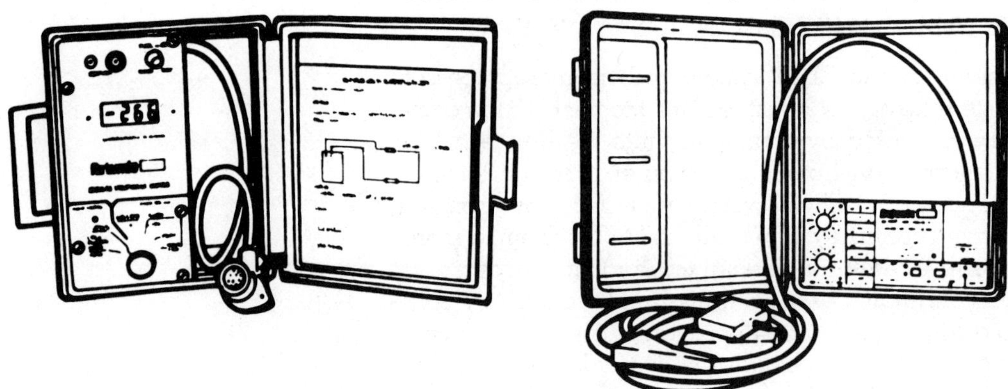

The self-test capability is in the computer memory. When the self-test is activated in conjunction with a quick test, the electronic control assembly performs the electronic engine control system tests to verify that the different actuators and sensors are connected and operating properly.

Determining the specific component that is causing the problem is not possible without the use of detailed instructions and specifications for the particular make and model of vehicle. Without this specific information and equipment, it is better to use the conventional ways of troubleshooting to locate the problems.

Before hooking up the equipment to diagnose the system, make a complete visual inspection for damage to the wiring harness, electrical connections, and all engine vacuum hoses. Check all sensors, actuators, and pulse ring lobes for physical damage. Turn off all electrical loads. Start the engine and idle until the upper radiator hose is hot. Check for vacuum leaks and any leaks around the exhaust manifold and/or EGO sensor. Shut off the engine and hook up the equipment.

To activate the self-test and make the quick test, the DVOM meter is placed inside the EECII tester and plugged into the unit. Disconnect the wiring harness connector from the electronic control assembly. Connect the electronic fuel injection adapter, or feedback carburetor adapter, into the electronic control assembly. Connect the tester into the adapter and reconnect the wiring harness according to the manufacturer's instructions. Figure 10-8 shows the DVOM (digital-volt-ohmmeter) installed in the case of the EECII tester. This equipment is used to make the self-test and quick test.

If the tester lamps come on with the ignition off, check for a short between the vehicle battery and electronic control assembly power circuit, or an open circuit in the electronic control assembly ground circuit. Turn the ignition switch to run and hold the test light button in. All lights on the tester panel should light up.

Follow the manufacturer's instructions for making the quick test. The procedure will call for the use of a timing light, vacuum pump, and measuring the voltage of many of the components included in the system.

The EECII tester uses lights to display the service codes. The service codes are a series of pulses on both of the thermactor solenoid (TAB and TAD) lights at the same time. The pulses represent two digit numbers. Each light is on for one-half second and then off one-half second for each count. The solenoid lights are off for a full second between numbers and for a full five seconds between service codes. An example of the service codes are as follows:

12 Idle speed incorrect RPMs
21 and/or 43 Engine coolant temperature sensor ECT
22 Manifold absolute pressure sensor MAP
23 Throttle position sensor TP
24 Air change temperature sensor ACT
31 Exhaust gas recirculation position sensor EGR
32 Exhaust gas recirculation valve closed
41 Fuel lean—stepper motor

FIGURE 10-8 DVOM installed in the EEC11 tester case. (Courtesy Ford Parts & Service Division, Ford Motor Co.)

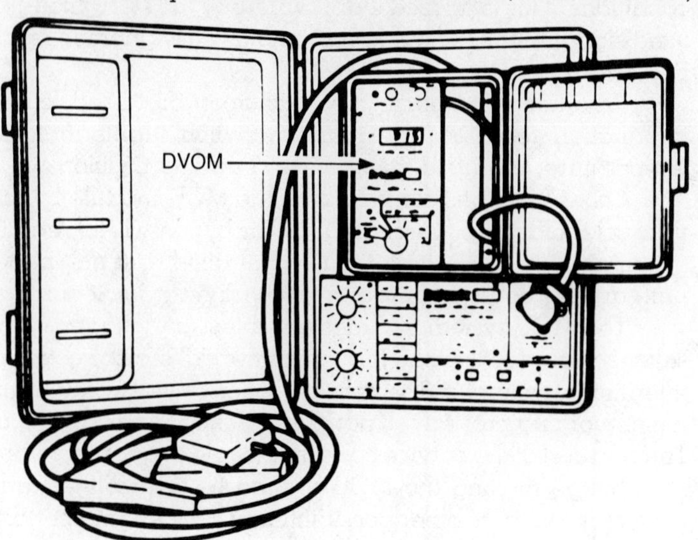

42 Fuel rich—stepper motor
43 Engine coolant temperature sensor ECT
44 Thermactor air operation

If the vehicle passes the quick test the subsystem is functioning normally and the problem exists elsewhere. If a step in the quick test sequence fails, run the pinpoint tests specified by the quick test. The pinpoint tests can be made using the same test equipment. A very specific procedure must be followed as recommended by the manufacturer and checked against exact readings, in order for the tests to be meaningful.

Pinpoint tests are made only as indicated by the quick test. When a pinpoint service operation is completed, go back to the beginning of the quick test and run the series of tests again, to make sure the problem has been corrected.

It is difficult to distinguish whether it is the processor assembly or the calibration assembly when the pinpoint test indicates problems in this area. Replace either one of the units and retest. If this does not correct the problem replace the other unit.

This has been general information which should point out the fact it is essential that special test equipment must be used, as well as the manufacturer's specifications and test procedures. With the necessary equipment, specifications, and test sequence information, it is a simple matter to completely and accurately diagnose and service the system.

CHECKING THE FORD MCU SYSTEM

The microprocessor control unit (MCU) is primarily a system to control the air/fuel ratio so as to keep emissions at a minimum. The fuel control "loop" system consists of an exhaust gas oxygen (EGO) sensor, microprocessor control unit (MCU), and a fuel control solenoid. The EGO sensor senses whether the exhaust gas is rich or lean relative to the best possible performance. This signal is sent to the MCU module, which in turn signals the fuel control solenoid (stepper motor) to bring about a mixture change that will make possible ideal engine operating conditions. This is "closed loop," whereby the MCU module sends out a fixed signal to the fuel control solenoid. This ignores the input from the EGO sensor.

Whether the system goes into open or closed loop is based on information received from various switch inputs that sense coolant temperature, manifold vacuum, and throttle position.

Other functions controlled by the MCU module by means of vacuum solenoids, are the thermactor air bypass (TAB), and the thermactor air diverter (TAD) valve. Also controlled, but not in the calibration unit, are the canister purge, and spark retard solenoid.

The MCU system includes a self-test (self-diagnosis) function. The self-test message is in the form of numerical service codes presented as intermittent voltages. The service codes reveal whether the MCU system is working properly. If not, the codes will indicate the trouble area. The purpose of the service code is to locate the particular trouble area.

Before making the MCU diagnostic test (self-test and functional test), make sure all other possibilities of poor engine performance have been carefully checked out. Visually inspect everything for obvious malfunctions that may cause poor engine performance, poor mileage, and/or excessive emissions. Check, adjust, or service what is necessary to restore normal vehicle operation. This includes electrical troubles, vacuum leaks, ignition system malfunctions, fuel system areas not included in the MCU system, internal engine problems, and emission control malfunctions. As the MCU is comparatively trouble free, everything else should be checked out before attempting the more involved diagnosis.

If the engine does not start, or the problem only occurs when the engine is cold, the self-test feature of the MCU cannot be used.

All tests should be made with the engine at normal operating temperature, upper radiator hose hot. All MCU systems have a low temperature switch that sends signals to the computer. If a cold engine performance problem exists and all conventional problems have been eliminated, the low temperature switch should be tested. Each size engine requires a different testing procedure. The switch used on the eight-cylinder engine is tested during the self-test diagnostic sequence. Some are electrical switches while others are combination vacuum and electrical.

Cold temperature switches are designed to open when the engine is cold and close when the engine is hot. This can usually be checked with an ohmmeter.

The MCU system cannot be checked if the engine will not start and run. If the engine will not start and everything else apparently is all right, there could be a short in the wiring harness of the control system. To check, disconnect the horseshoe-shaped connector from the top of the ignition coil. Disconnect the plug that attaches the ignition control module to the horseshoe connector and distributor. Measure the resistance between the terminal on the horseshoe connector marked "tach," and ground. If the resistance is greater than 1,000 ohms, the MCU is not the cause of the engine not starting. If resistance is less than 1,000 ohms, disconnect the MCU module from the wiring harness and check the resistance again. If the resistance is still less than 1,000 ohms, the fault is somewhere in the circuit. If the resistance is greater than 1,000 ohms with the MCU module disconnected from the wiring circuit, the MCU control module is at fault. The MCU control module cannot be repaired, it must be replaced. Figure 10-9 is a schematic showing the ignition system components of the Ford Dura Spark III system.

The MCU system including the control module carries a 50,000-mile/5-year warranty, whichever comes first. Performing unauthorized service durıng this period may void the warranty.

As previously stated, the MCU system has builtin self-test capabilities that may be utilized if the engine is in an operational condition.

The self-test is utilized in conjunction with the functional test to verify the proper operation of the feedback carburetor system. Only the self-test and functional test need be performed if the system is operational. If, while making the functional test, a failure is detected, a service code will be given directing the operator to the subroutine test to isolate the specific problem. The subroutine tests are to be used only in conjunction with and as the result of a functional test.

To check the MCU system, to get it to talk, one of two instruments are necessary. A self-test automatic readout instrument, which pro-

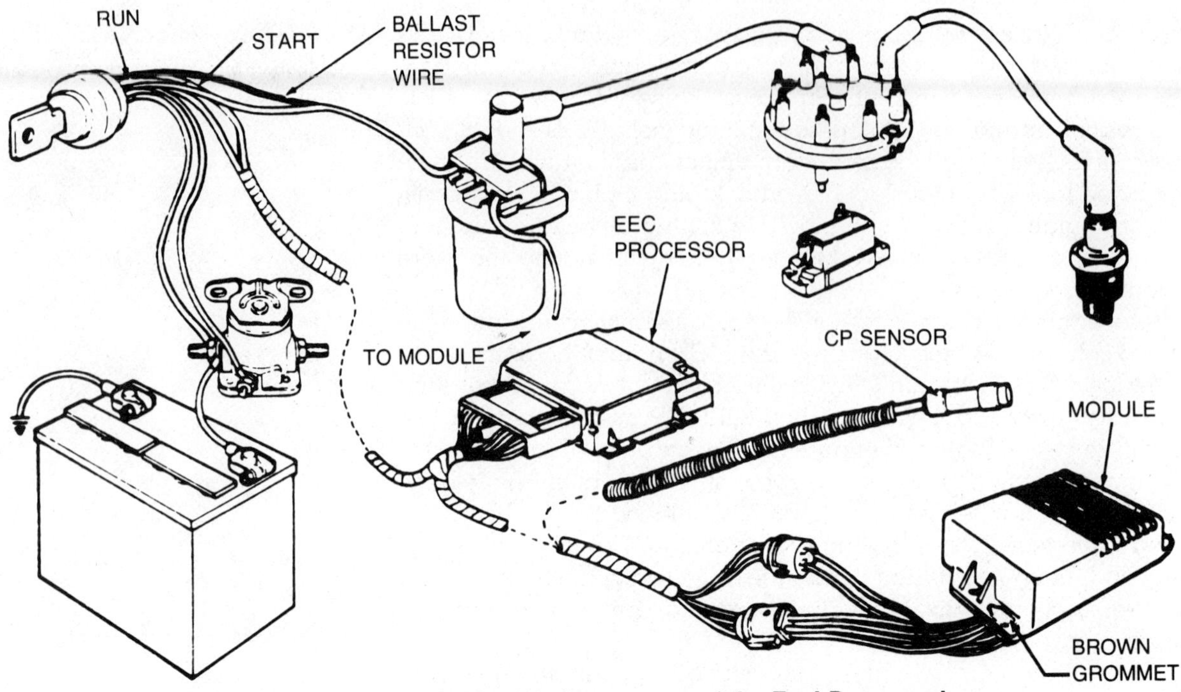

FIGURE 10-9 Components of the Ford Dura spark ignition system. (Courtesy Ford Parts & Service Division, Ford Motor Co.)

vides a digital readout, is the most convenient and accurate unit to use. It provides a service code number indicating the source of trouble when a problem exists in the system.

If a special test instrument is not available, an analog voltmeter with a 0 to 20-volt DC scale may be used. A jumper wire is needed, as well as an ohmmeter with a 0 to 500K ohm scale, vacuum gauge, remote starter switch, and a steel rod or three-eighths in. extension, and hammer, which are used to check the knock retard system.

When a voltmeter is used, it will be necessary to count the pulses of the voltmeter needle in order to read the service code. The first pulse, or series of pulses, is equivalent to the first digit of the two digit service code. There is then a pause followed by another pulse or series of pulses which is equivalent to the second digit of a two digit code. As an example of a code 23 (throttle position sensor), the needle of the voltmeter would rise for one-half second, drop to 0 for one-half second, rise for one-half second, drop to 0 for two seconds, then rise for one-half second, drop to 0 for one-half second, rise for one-half second, drop to 0 for one-half second, rise for one-half second, drop to 0. After four seconds the cycle will repeat itself. Figure 10-10 illustrates the pulse display on the voltmeter while making an on board computer diagnostic check.

Following is a list of service codes. The number indicates the subsection in which the problem exists. Not all engines will be equipped with the same emission control units, therefore the list will not apply to all models. Also, there will be units in the emission control system which are not included in the self-test system. The self-test program is utilized with the functional test. If, when performing the test a failure is detected, a service code indicates the system in which the problem is located.

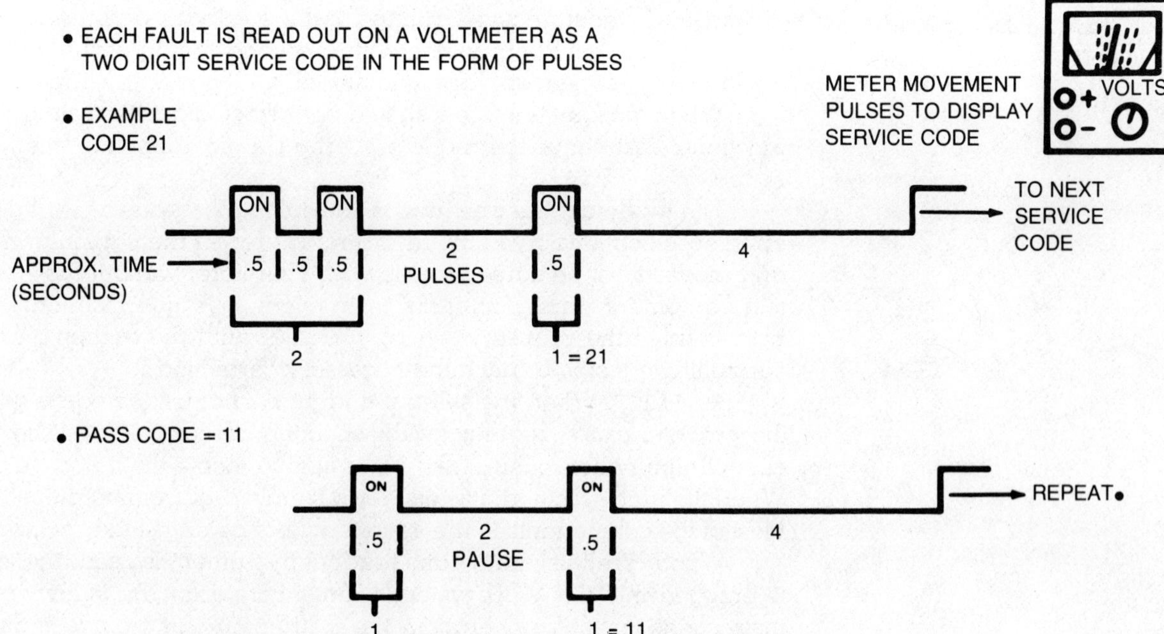

FIGURE 10-10 Example of a service code display on a voltmeter. (Courtesy Ford Parts & Service Division, Ford Motor Co.)

11 System operational
12 Idle speed incorrect
21 and/or 43 Engine coolant temperature sensor
22 Manifold absolute pressure sensor MAP
23 Throttle position sensor TP
24 Air change temperature sensor ACT
25 Knock detection system inoperative
33 Running test
41 Fuel always lean EGO
42 Fuel always rich EGO
44 Thermactor check
45 Thermactor air diverter check (always upstream)
46 Thermactor air bypass check (always not bypassing)
51 or 61 Low temperature switch
52 or 62 Idle tracking switch
53 or 54 Wide-open throttle position WOT
56 Closed throttle—vacuum switch
63 Wide-open throttle
66 Closed throttle—vacuum switch

When the trouble has been isolated to a particular area, as indicated by the service code displayed while making the functional test, the subroutine test procedure must be followed. This is comparable to the pinpoint tests made to the EECII system.

The subroutine test requires additional equipment including a tachometer, vacuum pump, timing light, feedback carburetor actuator, a 12 volt test lamp, watch with a second hand, torque wrench, 1⅛-inch-deep socket, and a voltmeter with a 10 meg. input impedance.

When the fault is found it should be corrected and the self-test and functional test sequence made to verify the problem has been corrected.

The manufacturer's sequence for making the tests, as well as the exact specifications given by the manufacturer for the particular make and model must be carefully followed. Therefore, without the special test equipment, manufacturer's instructions and specifications, it is best to have the unit serviced by a dealer with the equipment and capability to test and make the necessary corrections.

REMEMBER: When the self-test and functional test pinpoints where the problem exists, regular troubleshooting procedures and the process of elimination often make it possible to locate the defective unit. When the unit is located, it is usually a simple replacement procedure. Most of the components in the system cannot be adjusted or repaired.

When a self-test automatic readout instrument is used, the tester is plugged into the MCU system self-test connector. By following the instructions for meter operation, the instrument will provide a digital signal code which indicates if the system is operating satisfactorily. If not, it will reveal which component or subsystem is at fault. Figure 10-11 shows the self-test connector located in the engine compartment. The self-test automatic readout test provides a fast and simply way of locating operational problems.

To use an analog voltmeter, make sure the ignition switch is off. Connect a jumper wire between the self-test trigger and ground of the self-test connector. Attach the positive voltmeter lead to the battery positive post, and the negative lead to the self-test output of the self-test connector. Set the selector switch of the voltmeter to the 0-20 DC scale.

If testing a 4- or 6-cylinder engine, disconnect the charcoal canister hose from the canister purge valve and plug the hose with a golf tee.

When testing a V8, engine remove the PCV valve from the valve cover. In the case of a V8 engine equipped with a vacuum delay valve (a wafer shaped two-color valve spliced into a vacuum line in the air pump control system), a tee and restrictor are part of the thermactor vacuum control line. The restrictor is uncapped during the test.

To conduct a self-test on a V8 engine, with the engine warm, start the engine and operate for two minutes, then shut it off. Restart the engine immediately and allow it to idle. The voltmeter should pulse four times (40). The throttle kicker will increase engine speed. On engines equipped with a detonation sensor place a three-eighths in. extension bar or rod on the manifold near the base of the knock sensor. Lightly tap the bar with a hammer for 15 seconds as soon as code 40 (4 pulses) occur. Within 90 seconds the throttle kicker will retract. If a code 11 occurs, the system is operating satisfactorily. If other codes appear, a subroutine test must be made to isolate the problem.

When testing a 4- or 6-cylinder engine connect the test instrument or analog voltmeter in the same manner as for the V8 engine. The test instrument should flash 88, then 00. To receive service codes, press the push button on the test instrument. Turn the ignition key from off to on.

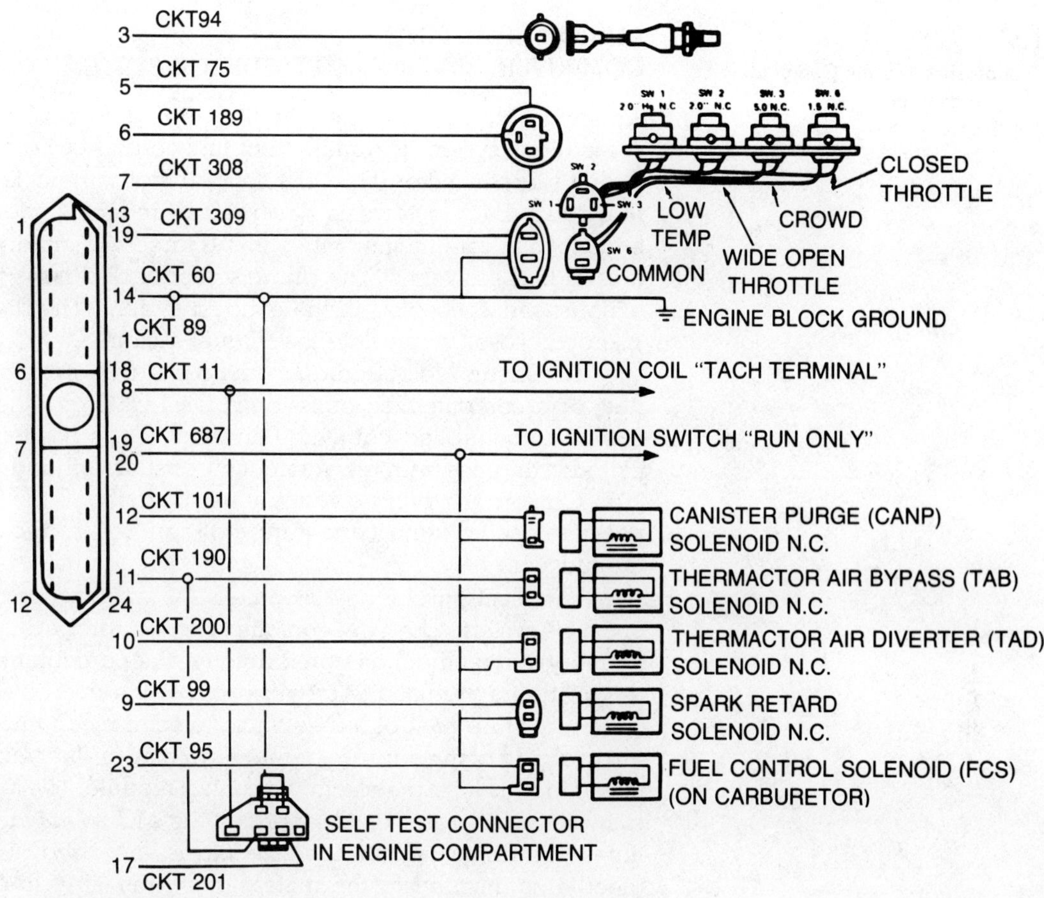

FIGURE 10-11 Schematic of electrical components that feed information to the computer. (Courtesy Ford Parts & Service Division, Ford Motor Co.)

The service code will occur after five seconds. If any number other than 11 occurs, it will be necessary to conduct further tests. If service code 11 shows, start the engine and increase the speed to 3,000 RPM. Watch for 20 or 30 on the test instrument, two or three pulses on the voltmeter. If code 11 reappears, the basic system is performing satisfactorily. If a different service code appears, it is necessary to follow the exact testing procedure using additional equipment as specified by the manufacturer.

If code 11 or pulses indicating 11 appear during slow and fast idle speeds, it is safe to assume there are no problems in the system.

When a code or pulse for a code indicates a malfunction, a different code or pulse may show itself during the repeat cycle. This indicates more than one malfunction.

The subroutine tests involve checking specific circuits for resistance, some circuits for voltage and the amount of vacuum present at certain components. Here again, checking for loose or poor electrical connections and the condition of the wiring, may locate the problem. The same applies to vacuum lines, cracks in the hoses and/or loose connections which may allow vacuum to leak. Always check for these conditions, even if you are not going to make the detailed tests. You may find the problem.

AMERICAN MOTORS COMPUTER CONTROLLED FEEDBACK SYSTEM

American Motors products may use three different feedback systems. A feedback system is a method of fuel control using a computer controlled stepper motor (type of solenoid) that varies the carburetor air/fuel ratio. Each system is designed to reduce undesirable exhaust emissions in conjunction with either a three-way catalytic converter or a dual-bed converter. The primary feedback data is provided by an exhaust sensor located in the exhaust system. The data is used by a microprocessor to regulate the air/fuel mixture.

American Motors products may use a C4 system on some engines, or a computerized emission control CEC on other engines. The computer controlled catalytic converter C4 is used on certain four-cylinder engines with an automatic transmission and vehicles sold in

California having a manual transmission. The C4 system incorporates a self-diagnostic feature that can be used to localize system malfunctions.

The electronic control module ECM (microprocessor) is the brain of the C4 system. The ECM contains a PROM (programmable read only memory) circuit that has stored data for the particular engine. Various data senders are used to provide data to the microprocessor.

A mixture control MC solenoid (electro-mechanical device) is an integral part of the carburetor that regulates air/fuel mixture according to commands from the electronic control module. The ECM functions as a switch to energize or de-energize the MC solenoid as many as 10 times per second. When the solenoid is energized, the metering rod (needle) is inserted in the metering jet, resulting in a lean mixture. When the solenoid is de-energized the needle is withdrawn from the jet, resulting in a rich air/fuel mixture. The air/fuel mixture is determined by the length of time the solenoid is either energized or de-energized (dwell). This is controlled by the information which the ECM receives from the various sensors and data senders, that in turn, is sent out to the MC solenoid. Figure 10-12 illustrates the time span for a rich

FIGURE 10-12 Mixture control (MC) solenoid on-off cycle. (Courtesy American Motors Corporation)

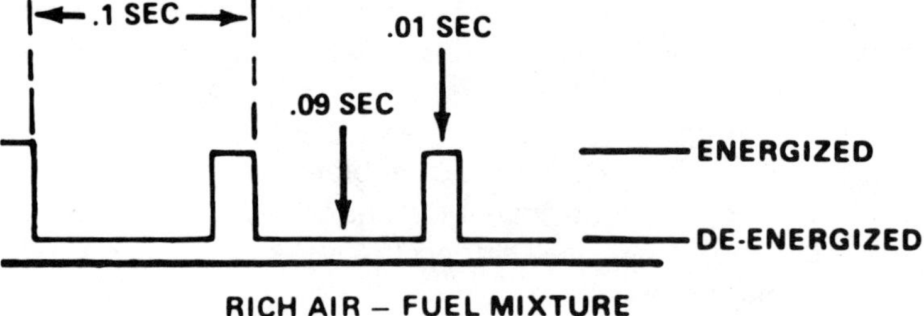

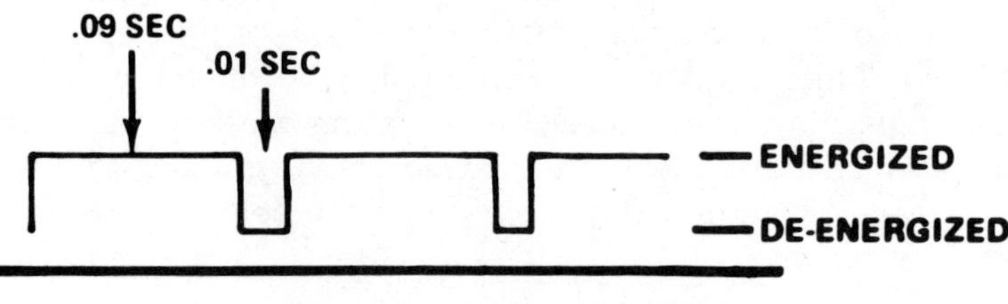

and a lean mixture. The length of time the solenoid is energized determines how lean the mixture will be.

The C4 system should be considered a source of trouble only after all normal test procedures, inspections, and corrections have been made that would apply to a vehicle not equipped with a computerized emission control system.

An integral self-diagnostic system is incorporated in the C4 system to detect problems. The diagnostic system will illuminate a test bulb when a test lamp is connected to ground and to the trouble code test pigtail. The test wire (pigtail) is located under the instrument panel beneath the heater assembly.

As a routine test, the test bulb will illuminate when the ignition switch is turned on and the engine is not running. When the test wire is grounded, the light will flash code 12 (one flash followed by two flashes), indicating the diagnostic system is working. The code will replay three times until the ignition switch is turned off or the engine started.

When the test wire is grounded with the engine running, if a problem exists the trouble code will flash three times. If more than one trouble exists, the second trouble code will flash three times after the first code. A trouble code indicates a problem in a specific circuit. Trouble code 14, for example, indicates a problem in the coolant temperature sensor circuit.

Following is a list of trouble codes which may be displayed in the form of flashes, along with the specific troubles which the flashes indicate. The engine should be at normal operating temperature before making these tests.

Code 12 No RPM (tach) voltage to the EMC.

Code 13 Oxygen sensor circuit. The engine should be operated for approximately five minutes before this code will flash.

Code 14 Short circuit within coolant temperature sensor circuit. The engine should operate for two minutes before this code will flash.

Code 15 Open circuit within coolant temperature sensor. The engine must operate for approximately five minutes at partial throttle before this code will flash.

Codes 21 & 22 (at same time) WOT wide-open throttle switch circuit has short circuit.

Code 23 Carburetor MC solenoid circuit has short circuit to ground or open circuit.

Code 44 Voltage input to ECM from oxygen sensor indicates continuous lean mixture. The MC solenoid is regulated to produce continuous rich mixture. The engine must operate approximately five minutes at partial throttle with a torque load, and the system in closed loop operation before this code will flash.

Codes 44 & 45 (at same time) Faulty oxygen sensor.

Code 45 Voltage input to ECM from oxygen sensor indicates continuous rich mixture. MC solenoid is regulated to produce continuous lean mixture. The engine has to operate approximately five minutes at partial throttle with a torque load, and the system in closed loop operation before the code will flash.

Code 51 Faulty calibration unit (PROM) or installation.

Codes 52 & 53 Test bulb off, intermittent ECM problem. Test bulb on, faulty ECM.

Code 54 Faulty MC solenoid and/or ECM.

Code 55 Faulty oxygen sensor circuit or ECM.

The self-diagnostic system does not detect all possible troubles. The absence of a trouble code does not always indicate there are no malfunctions in the system. An operational test should be performed when there is a complaint of poor engine performance or fuel economy after performing the usual troubleshooting and diagnostic tests.

To make a system operational test, a certain amount of equipment is needed. This includes a dwell meter, test lamp, digital volt-ohmmeter, tachometer, vacuum gauge, and jumper wires. Most dwell meters are acceptable, but if the meter, when hooked into the system, causes a change in engine operation, it should not be used. The dwell meter is used to determine the air/fuel mixture dwell (solenoid controlling the metering pin operation). During closed loop operation at both idle speed and partial throttle, the dwell meter should vary between 10 and 50 degrees, indicating the mixture is being changed according to input voltage from the computer.

The operational tests are specialized and the exact procedure recommended by the manufacturer of the vehicle as well as the manufacturer's specifications must be carefully followed for the test to be meaningful. The test procedure varies with the different models. The electronic control module terminal connections are used for testing purposes on the C4 system.

Figure 10-13 shows the dwell meter connected into the mixture

FIGURE 10-13 Dwell meter connection. (Courtesy Oldsmobile Division, General Motors Corp.)

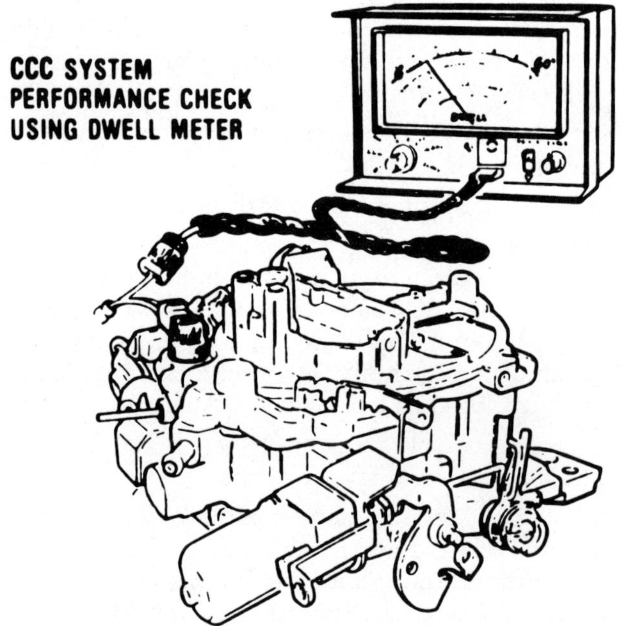

control solenoid circuit. Keeping exhaust emissions at a minimum depends to a great extent upon the mixture control.

The C4 operational tests and trouble code diagnosis include the following:

- Dwell fixed between 5 and 10 degrees
- Dwell fixed between 10 and 50 degrees
- Dwell fixed between 50 and 55 degrees
- Self-diagnostic circuit test
- Adaptive vacuum switch circuit test
- Make the different trouble code tests numbers 12, 13, 14, 15, 21 and 22 together, 22, 23, 44, 45, and 51 to 55

The CEC system does not incorporate a self-diagnostic system. Instead, a fixed sequence of diagnostic tests (operational tests) should be performed to isolate the troubles. The steps in each test will provide a systematic evaluation of each component.

A dwell meter, digital volt-ohmmeter, tachometer, vacuum gauge, and jumper wires are necessary to diagnose system problems. The diagnostic connections permit checking many of the various units by connecting the test equipment to the diagnostic connector terminals. Figure 10-14 illustrates the procedure which is used when beginning the AMC C4 operational test. The exact procedure found in the shop manual for the specific model must be followed if the tests are to be meaningful.

The feedback operation of the CEC system is as follows. When the system is in closed loop mode the microprocessor control unit MCU causes the mixture control MC solenoid to vary the air/fuel mixture in reaction to the voltage input from the oxygen sensor located in the exhaust manifold. Open loop mode of operation occurs when starting the engine; when the engine is cold or the air cleaner air is cold; when the engine is at idle speed, accelerating to partial throttle or decelerating from partial throttle to idle speed; or when the carburetor is either at or near wide open throttle. When any of these conditions occur, the mixture control MC solenoid provides a predetermined air/fuel mixture ratio for each condition. All open loop operations are characterized by predetermined air/fuel mixture ratios.

The four-cylinder CEC diagnostic tests which must be made with the engine at normal operating temperature include the following:

- System operational test
- Coolant temperature switch circuit test
- Vacuum switch circuit test
- Engine RPM (tach) voltage test
- Mixture control MC solenoid circuit test

The diagnostic tests for the six-cylinder engine CEC system include:

- Initialization test
- Solenoid-vacuum switching
- Solenoid-vacuum idle speed relay switch

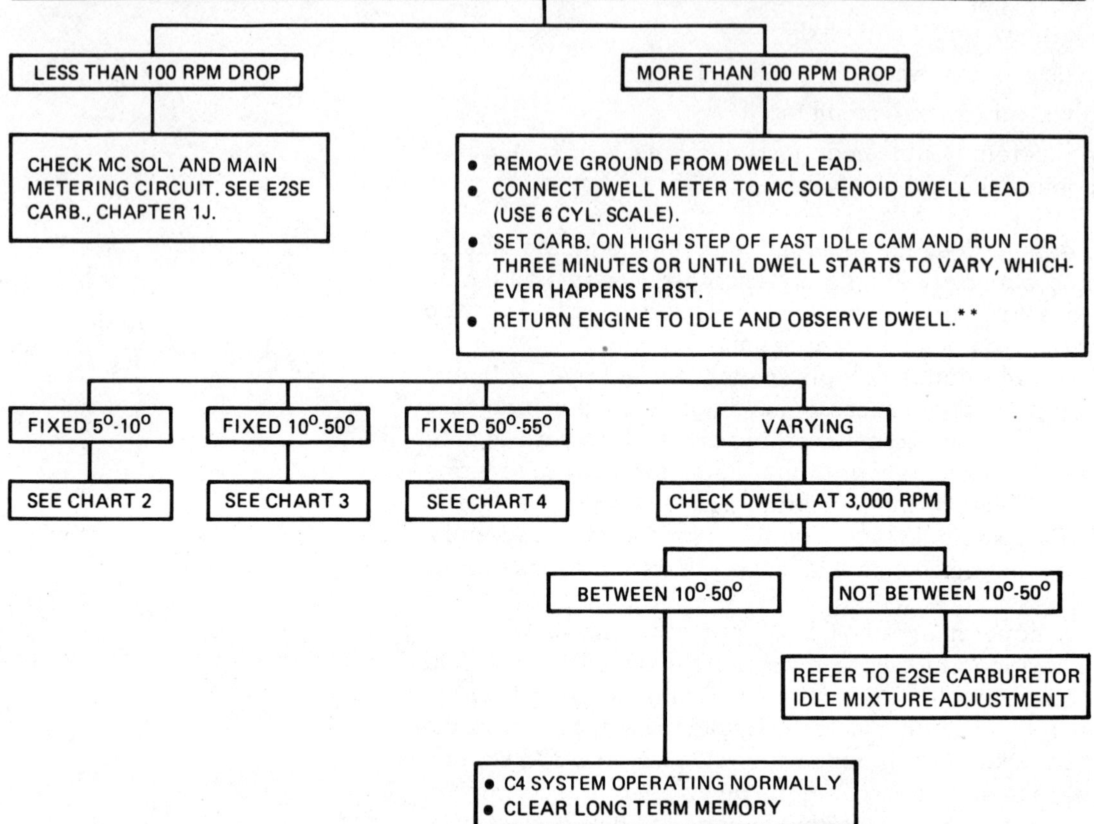

**OXYGEN SENSOR TEMPERATURE MAY COOL AT IDLE CAUSING THE DWELL TO CHANGE FROM VARYING TO A FIXED INDICATION BETWEEN 10°-50°. IF THIS HAPPENS, RUN THE ENGINE AT FAST IDLE TO HEAT THE SENSOR.

FIGURE 10-14 AMC C4 system operational test. (Courtesy American Motors Corporation)

- Open loop switch test
- Closed loop operational test
- Electronic ignition test
- Oxygen sensor and closed loop test
- Air injection system test
- Diverter solenoid test
- Upstream solenoid test
- Idle speed control system test

Figure 10-15 shows the different components which make up the CEC (computerized emission control) system used on many AMC six-cylinder model engines.

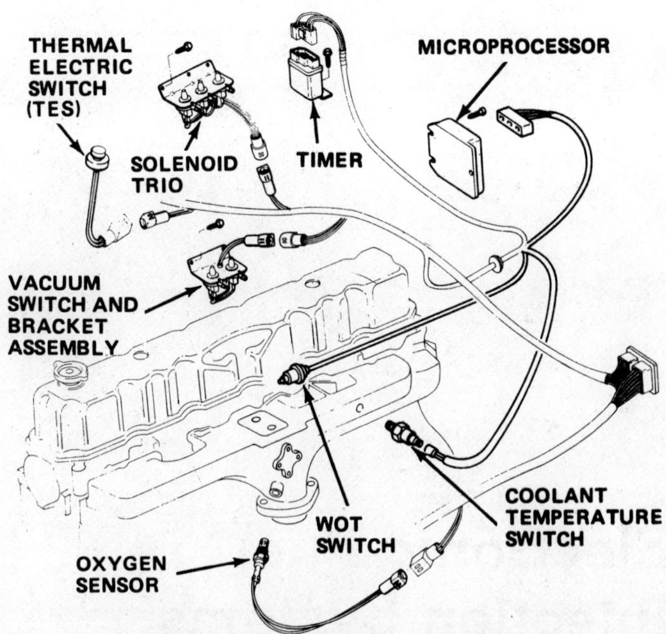

FIGURE 10-15 CEC system (six-cylinder engine). (Courtesy American Motors Corporation)

Testing the Various Systems

The self-test (self-diagnosis) systems used by the different manufacturers are very helpful in locating troubles. However, in order to fully utilize the test system, special equipment is needed in every case. Along with equipment, a specific procedure must be followed and manufacturer's specifications must be used for the particular model being tested. To utilize the complete test procedure, it will be necessary to use the manufacturer's service manual for the specific vehicle being serviced.

As previously mentioned, the regular troubleshooting and diagnostic procedures used to check out a vehicle not equipped with a self-test system should be followed. This will usually locate the trouble. Furthermore, the components which make up the emission control system are activated, in most cases, by electricity and/or vacuum.

It is usually a comparatively simple matter to check the electrical circuits as well as the vacuum circuits. Because the electrical signals which are used to trigger the computer and the various sensors are comparatively weak, it is best to use an ohmmeter to check the different circuits. A heavy current flow may damage the circuit and/or components in the circuit.

11 Electronic Fuel Injection Systems

Many manufacturers are utilizing, on some models, an electronic fuel injection system as a means of reducing exhaust emissions and providing for better economy while still maintaining satisfactory performance.

The fuel injection system used on a gasoline engine must not be confused with the diesel injection system. The diesel engine ignites the fuel charge by heat created from high compression. There is no external ignition system. The diesel engine draws in air to fill the cylinder during the intake stroke. A carburetor is not needed. The fuel system injects fuel into the cylinder in the form of a fine spray against compression and, therefore, requires a high pressure injection pump.

The purpose of a carburetor is to mix gasoline and air in the proper ratio for combustion under all operating conditions. It must control the distribution of the air/fuel mixture to insure uniform amounts of fuel to all cylinders. It must also keep exhaust emissions to a minimum with performance and fuel economy at its maximum.

One of the weaknesses of the carburetor is that there must be a constriction in the form of a venturi in the carburetor air intake to increase the velocity of the incoming air. This creates a vacuum which is needed to draw fuel from the fuel bowl through the metering jet and mix the fuel with air. Such a restriction limits the amount of mixture passing into the cylinder, therefore power is lost at high speed. The carburetor supplies fuel to the moving airstream. Different load and speed conditions will require different air/fuel ratios. The carburetor is not always capable of meeting these requirements efficiently.

Types of Gasoline Injection Systems

There are three general types of gasoline injection systems. They are the direct type, in which fuel is injected directly into the combustion chamber; the port type, where fuel is injected into the intake valve port;

and the third type is the throttle body type of injection system, whereby fuel is injected into the throttle body above the throttle plate or plates.

The direct, or combustion chamber injection system, is not used on any current production four-stroke cycle automobile gasoline engines. The port type injection system is used to some extent. The throttle body injection system is being utilized at the present time on a number of makes and models of engines. The throttle body injection system offers cost savings over other systems, because the manifolding and basic component layout remain mostly unchanged from the regular carburetor system.

THROTTLE BODY INJECTION SYSTEM (TBI)

Most present engines that are equipped with fuel injection use an electronic injection system that utilizes the principle of throttle body injection. Basically, it is a fuel metering system where the amount of fuel delivered by the injector to the throttle body is determined by a signal supplied from the electronic control module ECM. The ECM monitors various engine and vehicle conditions, and uses this information to calculate fuel delivery time (pulse of the injector), so that fuel is metered into the intake air stream according to engine demands.

The air/fuel ratio is monitored and adjusted automatically, according to changes in environmental and engine conditions. The engine and environmental parameters, such as intake air, throttle position, engine speed, engine manifold vacuum, vehicle speed,

FIGURE 11-1 Electronic fuel injection functional command components. (Courtesy Chrysler Corporation)

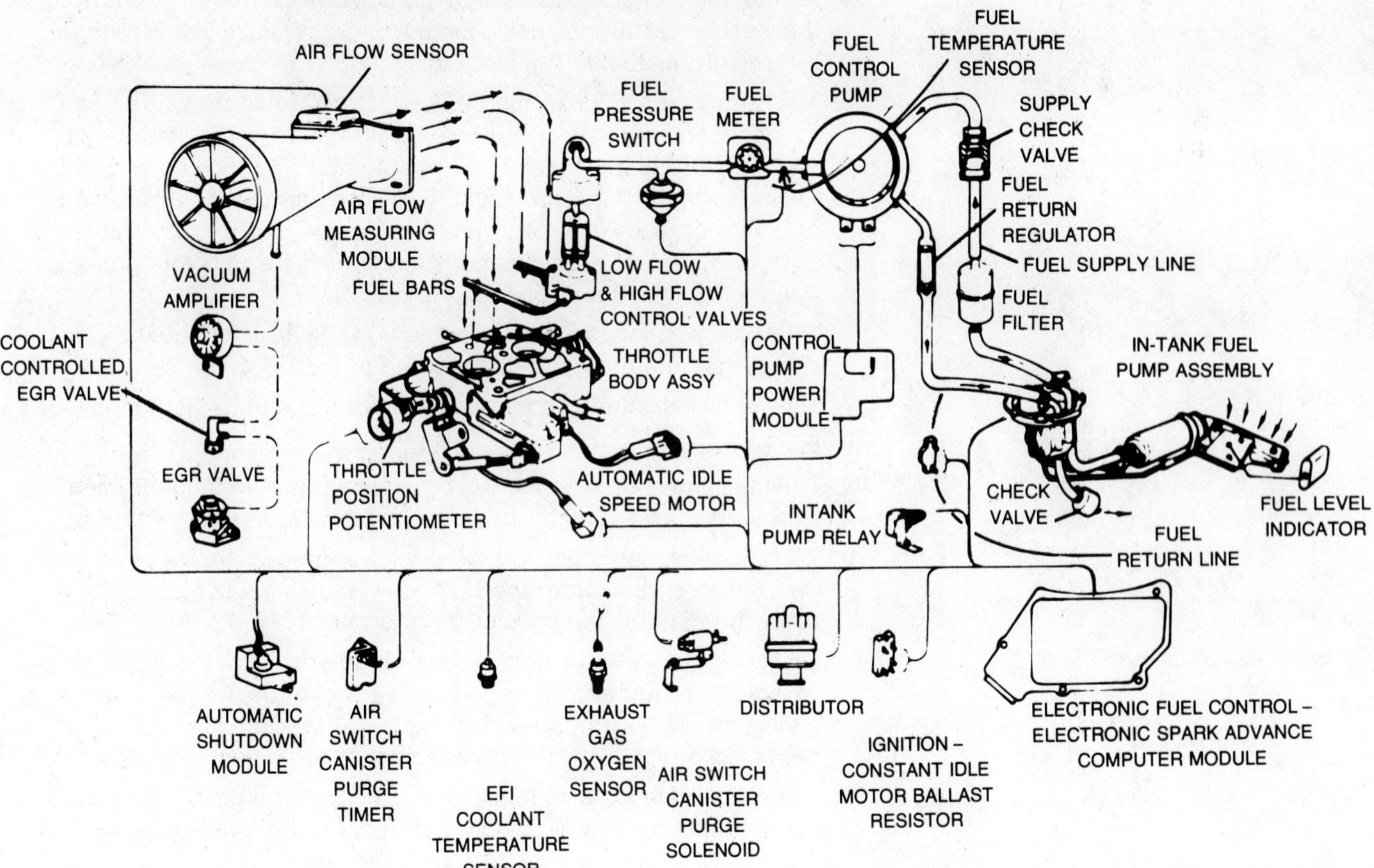

exhaust oxygen level, air intake temperatures, and altitude, are determined by sensors. The output from the sensors is processed by the ECM to provide predetermined optimum fuel quantities that will have low emissions and maximum performance. This amount of fuel is then injected into the air stream.

In all systems, fuel is delivered under pressure from the fuel tank to the fuel delivery unit (injector assembly). Figure 11-1 is a schematic of an electronic fuel injection system showing the different components which have a bearing on the operation of the system by feeding information to the control module.

The basic operating principles and purpose of the present electronic fuel injection system used on the different makes and models of engines are all very much the same. Certain specific components will not be used however, by all makes and models of engines.

CHARACTERISTICS OF THE TBI SYSTEM

Following is a list of characteristics which are common to the electronic gasoline fuel injection system of the throttle body injection design.

1. The purpose of the system is to mix air and fuel in the proper ratio to meet all operating demands.
2. An attempt is made to keep exhaust emissions to a minimum while maintaining satisfactory performance.
3. The air/fuel mixture is distributed uniformly from cylinder to cylinder.
4. An electric fuel pump located in the fuel tank is used to pressurize the system and supply fuel to the injectors. A return line is used to return surplus fuel to the fuel tank.
5. The fuel injector looks much like a carburetor that has been stripped of everything but the throttle bore. The float bowl, mechanical choke, accelerator pump, and high and low speed fuel metering systems are not utilized. The remaining units consist of a throttle body with the throttle plate or plates to control air flow, and the fuel body assembly containing the injector or injectors, along with a fuel pressure regulator.
6. A throttle position sensor is mounted on the throttle plate shaft to signal the amount of throttle opening to the ECM.
7. The air/fuel mixture is controlled by sensing engine demands.
8. In the case of closed throttle, the fuel flow to the engine is shut off.
9. The injection system controlled by an electronic computer system is able to closely match the air/fuel mixture to engine demands.
10. Various sensors monitor different vital engine operating modes, and based on this data, the ECM determines the correct air/fuel ratio and controls the injector input accordingly.
11. The injector nozzle or nozzles are mounted in the throttle body assembly, or hydraulic support plate, above the throttle plate or plates, in such a manner that fuel, in the form of a spray, is delivered directly into the air stream.
12. The electronic fuel injection system is an integral part of the computer control system. It is included in the self-diagnostic system.

13. With the carburetor fuel bowl eliminated, brake stalls, turn cut-outs, fuel boiling and dieseling is no longer a problem.
14. The ECM causes the injector to deliver the precise amount of fuel needed to start and run a cold engine.
15. The electronic control module is the heart of the system.
16. Carburetor-equipped engines having a computer controlled emission system will utilize a solenoid operated mixture control. It is activated and controlled by signals from the electronic control module. The electronic fuel injection system replaces the carburetor and mixture control solenoid.
17. The electronic control units, such as sensors, solenoids, and vacuum operational switches, along with the self-diagnosis system, will be basically the same whether an electronic fuel injection system is used, or a carburetor system.

Basically, all electronically controlled throttle body fuel injection systems operate in the same general manner. As with the computer controlled emission system, however, certain differences exist, such as operational modes, components involved, diagnosing, and servicing procedures. Following is a brief description of the specific characteristics of the injection systems that are used by the different makes and models of engines.

GENERAL MOTORS ELECTRONIC FUEL INJECTION SYSTEM (TBI)

The most common fuel injection system used on General Motors products is the electronic throttle body injection system, whereby the amount of fuel delivered by the throttle body injector TBI is determined by an electrical signal supplied by the electronic control module ECM. The ECM monitors various engine and vehicle conditions needed to calculate the fuel delivery time (pulse width) of the fuel delivered by the injector.

The basic throttle body injector assembly is made up of two major assemblies, a throttle body containing the throttle valve (plate) or valves (plates) to control air flow, and a fuel body assembly with an integral pressure regulator and fuel injector to supply the necessary fuel. Figure 11-2 is a schematic of the throttle body type of electronic fuel injection system.

The injector "on" time is determined by various inputs to the ECM. By increasing injector pulse rate, more fuel is delivered, thereby enriching the air/fuel ratio. Decreasing the injector pulse rate leans the air/fuel ratio.

Electrical pulses are sent to the injector in two different modes, synchronized and nonsynchronized. In the synchronized mode, the injector is pulsed once each distributor reference pulse. Figure 11-3 shows the injector pulses "on time" when fuel is delivered from the injector nozzle into the throttle body. The injector pulses are synchronized with the distributor pulses.

In the nonsynchronized mode of operation, the injector is pulsed every 12.5 milliseconds or 6.25 milliseconds, depending upon the calibration of the unit. The pulse time in the nonsynchronized mode is completely independent of distributor reference pulses. Nonsynchronized mode results only under the following conditions:

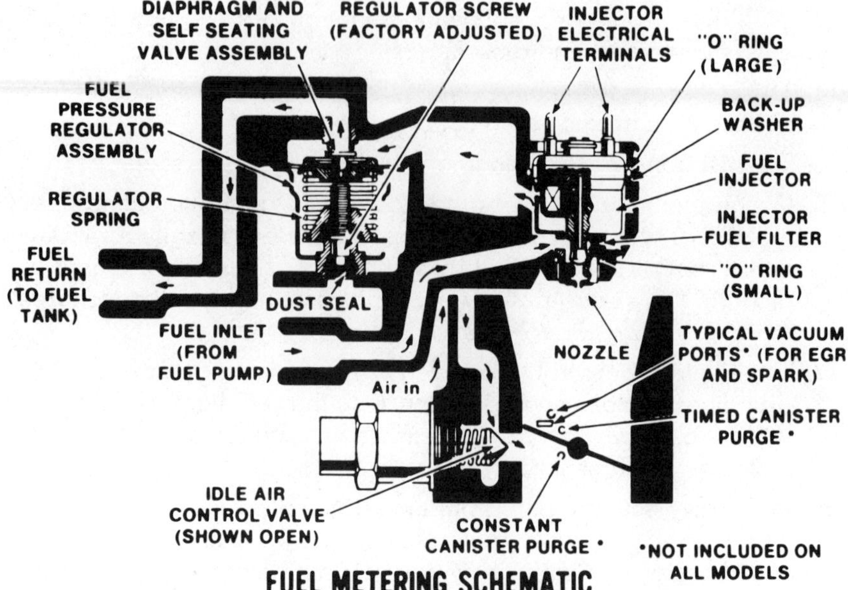

FIGURE 11-2 Schematic of throttle body fuel injection. (Courtesy Chevrolet Motor Division, General Motors Corp.)

1. Fuel pulse width too small to be delivered accurately by the injector.
2. During delivery of prime pulses. (Prime pulses charge the intake manifold prior to or during starting.)
3. During acceleration enrichment.
4. During deceleration enleanment.

Figure 11-4 shows the injector pulses and the distributor pulses. The pulses are not synchronized. The pulse width determines the amount of fuel delivered into the manifold.

The fuel injector unit is solenoid-operated, receiving its operating signal from the ECM. The fuel is supplied by an electric pump located in the fuel tank. The fuel passes through an inline fuel filter to the injector assembly. To control fuel pump operation, a fuel pump relay is used.

FIGURE 11-3 Synchronized mode of operation of the single throttle body injector system. (Courtesy Chevrolet Motor Division, General Motors Corp.)

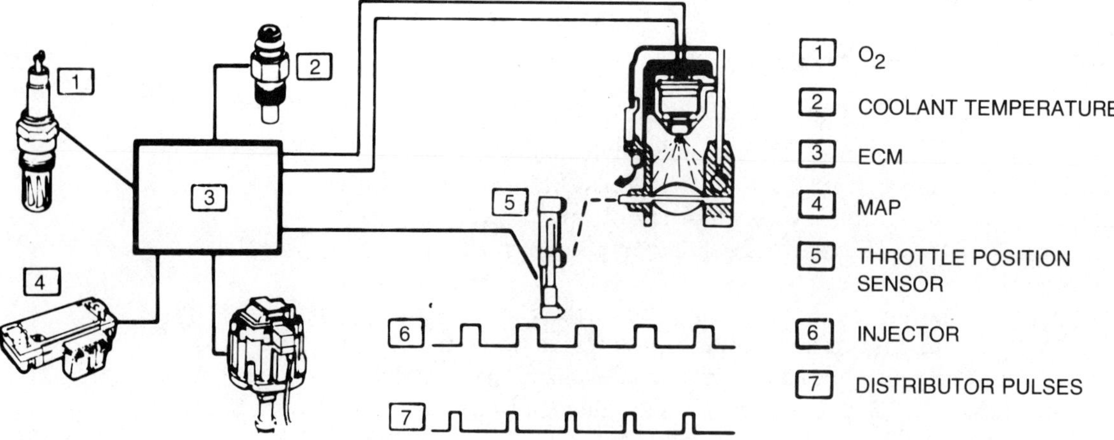

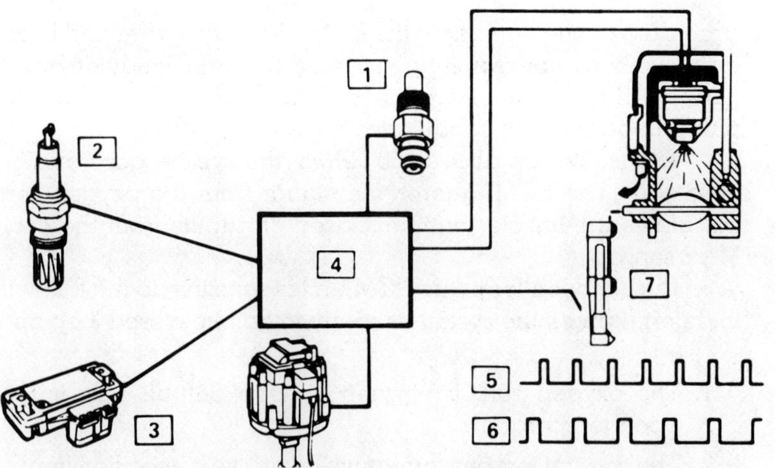

1 COOLANT SENSOR
2 O_2
3 MAP
4 ECM
5 INJECTOR
6 DISTRIBUTOR PULSES
7 THROTTLE POSITION SENSOR

FIGURE 11-4 Nonsynchronized mode—single throttle body system. (Courtesy Chevrolet Motor Division, General Motors Corp.)

When the ignition switch is turned to the on position, the fuel pump relay activates the fuel pump for 1.5 to 2.0 seconds to prime the injector. If the ECM does not receive reference pulses from the distributor at this time, the ECM signals the relay to turn off the pump. The relay will once again activate the pump when the ECM receives distributor reference pulses. During normal operation, the fuel pump pressurizes the system to approximately 10 psi.

The incoming fuel is directed to the lower end of the injector assembly, which has a fine screen filter surrounding the injector inlet. The ECM unit activates the solenoid that lifts the normally closed ball valve off its seat. The fuel under pressure is then injected in a conical spray pattern at the walls of the throttle body bore above the throttle plate or plates. The excess fuel passes through the pressure regulator before being returned to the fuel tank.

The pressure regulator is a diaphragm-operated relief valve with air cleaner pressure on one side and injector pressure on the other side. The function of the regulator is to maintain a constant pressure drop across the injector throughout the operating load and speed range of the engine.

The throttle body portion of the throttle body injector unit may have ports located above, below, or at the throttle plate or plates. These ports (openings) generate vacuum signals for the exhaust gas recirculation (EGR) valve, the manifold absolute pressure (MAP) sensor, and the canister purge system.

The throttle position sensor (TPS) is a variable resistor used to convert the angle of throttle opening into an electrical signal that is sent to the ECM. The ECM uses this signal as a reference point for throttle valve position.

An idle air control assembly (IAC) is mounted in the throttle body and is used to control idle speed. Electrical input signals from the ECM to the (IAC) assembly are determined by the idle speed requirements for the particular operating conditions.

The ECM unit monitors idle speed, and depending on the engine load, moves the IAC core in the air passage to increase or decrease air bypassing the throttle valve to the intake manifold for control of idle speed.

In addition to controlling the air/fuel mixture for idle speed according to idle demands, the ECM also is programmed to control the air/fuel mixture for cranking, to clear a flooding condition, for acceleration enrichment, deceleration enleanment and, control of the fuel pump under certain conditions.

At first startup above 600 RPMs, the system goes into open loop operation. The ECM ignores the signal from the oxygen sensor and calculates the injector ontime, based on inputs from the coolant and MAP sensor.

During open loop, the ECM unit is sensitive to the following items in determining if the system is ready to go into closed loop operation.

1. The oxygen sensor varying voltage output. This is dependent upon temperature.
2. The coolant temperature must be above a specified temperature.
3. A specified time has elapsed since start-up. The specified values are all stored in the PROM unit of the ECM. When these conditions have been met, the system goes into closed loop operation. In closed loop, the ECM will modify the injector pulse width (injector "on" time), based upon the signal from the oxygen sensor. The ECM will decrease the "on" time if the air/fuel ratio is too rich and will increase the "on" time if the air/fuel ratio is too lean.

The basic operation of the electronic fuel injection system (EFT), and the computer command control CCC system is very similar. The main difference is that in the case of the (CCC) system, operational signals from the ECM are sent to the carburetor mixture control MC solenoid that cycles a metering rod (pin) or rods (pins) to control the amount of air/fuel mixture supplied to the intake manifold.

With the electronic fuel injection system, the voltage signals from the ECM are sent to the injector to control the air/fuel mixture. In the case of either installation, information from the same components, such as the oxygen sensor, temperature sensor, and MAP, are sent to the ECM. That, according to how it is programmed, will send out signal voltages to the carburetor control or fuel injector control that will result in the most efficient operation. Electronic spark timing EST is used on all engines.

Because of the similarities of the components, the diagnosing procedure is basically the same. The check engine light will come on when a problem occurs in a unit included in the self-diagnostic system of the computer.

As on the engine equipped with a computer command control system, the electronic fuel injection system should be considered a possible source of trouble only after a regular diagnosis and correction procedure has been carefully carried out that would apply to a vehicle without a computer system. All wiring in the system should be completely checked for faulty, dirty, and/or loose wire connections. Check all vacuum hoses for leaks and proper connections.

When there is a no run situation, check for spark at the spark plugs. If a good spark is present at regular intervals while cranking, check for fuel. This is done by observing the injector while cranking the engine with the air cleaner removed.

The check engine light will come on if malfunctions are present under certain conditions within the computer system. The check engine light is located in the instrument panel. It requires up to five seconds to come on when a problem arises. If the malfunction clears up, the light will go out, but the trouble code or codes will be stored in the computer memory. The code will clear up after 50 starts if the problem does not recur. On some models, the memory can be cleared by disconnecting one battery cable for a minimum of 10 seconds.

Engine performance diagnosis, when an engine check light is part of the computer system, involves three main categories: (1) the diagnostic circuit check that includes the circuits that are part of the computer trouble code system; (2) the driver's complaint check; and (3) a system performance check.

As discussed in chapter 10, TROUBLESHOOTING THE COMPUTER CONTROL SYSTEM, a trouble code system is incorporated as a self-diagnosis tool in the computer system. The self-diagnosis feature can be made to "talk" when properly activated. This procedure was explained in Chapter 10. The trouble code system is much the same for all vehicles except that the number of components used will vary from model to model.

The equipment needed to check the system does not require special testers. Basically, a tachometer, dwellmeter, test light, ohmmeter, digital voltmeter, vacuum pump, vacuum gauge, and jumper wire will be about all that is necessary to make the different tests.

The trouble code display indicates only the system where the trouble is located. It requires a special test procedure to isolate the specific component causing the problem.

Because electrical circuits are involved, and the amount of current flow is small, exact measurements are essential. Each circuit and component will have a specific value relative to resistance. Whether or not the circuit is complete also is important. Different ECM connectors will be found on the various installations.

Figure 11-5 is a diagram which identifies the electronic control module terminals (connectors) used on General Motors products equipped with an electronic fuel injection system.

For the reasons given previously it is essential that the testing procedure and specifications set forth by the manufacturer be carefully observed and utilized. In the majority of cases, a carefully carried out testing and troubleshooting procedure, such as that used to locate problems on vehicles without a computer system, or where the problem is not in the computer system, will isolate the problem.

When the check engine light is on and a trouble code indicates a problem, a choice must be made. Either take the vehicle to a dealer who has the equipment, specifications and ability to make a complete check, or procure a manufacturer's shop manual that gives the procedure to follow, along with the necessary specifications. A shop manual for the particular model vehicle is a very essential tool when performing many of the different tests. In most cases, when the trouble has been located, it will be a matter of replacing the faulty component, which is usually a simple operation.

Some General Motors products have used a somewhat different type of electronic fuel injection system. While terminology (label) may vary to some extent with different makes and models of engines/vehicles, the basic electronic control system is much the same. The engine operating mode is monitored and the air/fuel mixture is electronically metered to best meet engine requirements.

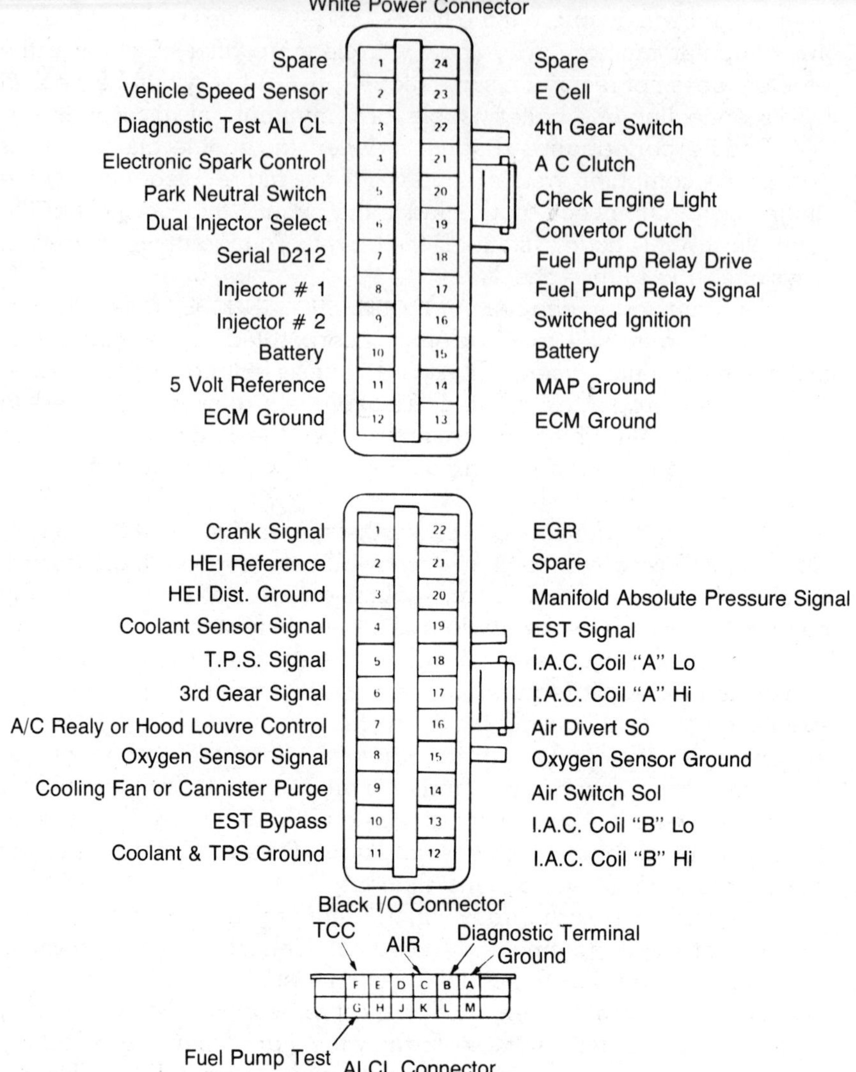

FIGURE 11-5 Electronic control module connector identification (fuel injection). (Courtesy Chevrolet Motor Division, General Motors Corp.)

GENERAL MOTORS ELECTRONIC PORTED INJECTION SYSTEM

This system differs from the throttle body injection system in that electrically actuated fuel metering valves spray a predetermined amount of fuel into the engine. The metering valves (injectors) are mounted on a fuel rail and attached to the intake manifold with the metering tips directed toward the head of the intake valve. This type of design is commonly known as a ported injection system. Figure 11-6 shows the components of the ported type electronic controlled fuel injection system. Their relationship to one another is also illustrated.

The injector opening is timed in accordance with engine frequency (timing) so the fuel charge is present prior to the intake stroke of each cylinder. Depending upon engine design and requirements, the injectors may all be energized at one time, one after the other, timed with the opening of each intake valve, or they may be energized in groups.

The amount of air entering the engine is measured by monitoring the intake manifold absolute pressure (vacuum), inlet air temperature, and engine RPMs. This information permits the electronic control unit (ECU) to compute the flow rate of air being inducted into the engine, and as a result, the flow rate of fuel required to achieve the desired air/fuel ratio for the particular operating mode. The ECU converts the input information into an injector pulse width (dwell) which opens the injectors for the needed duration and at the exact time with respect to the cylinder firing sequence.

The electronic fuel injector system is made up of four major subsystems, (1) fuel delivery; (2) air induction; (3) sensors and (4) an electronic control unit. The function of these separate subsystems is integrated into the operation of the complete system. Figure 11-7 is an illustration of the fuel delivery system as well as a drawing of the air induction setup which makes up the ported electronic fuel injection system.

The fuel delivery system includes an in-tank boost pump, a chassis-mounted constant displacement fuel pump, a fuel filter, fuel rails, an injector for each cylinder, a fuel pressure regulator, fuel supply lines, and return lines.

The air induction system includes the throttle body assembly, fast idle valve assembly, and intake manifold.

The sensors are electrically connected to the ECU and operate independently of each other. Each sensor transmits a signal to the ECU relative to a specific engine operating condition. The following sensors are used; manifold absolute pressure, throttle position switch, temperature, and speed sensor.

FIGURE 11-6 Ported electronic fuel injection system. (Courtesy Cadillac Motor Car Division, General Motors Corp.)

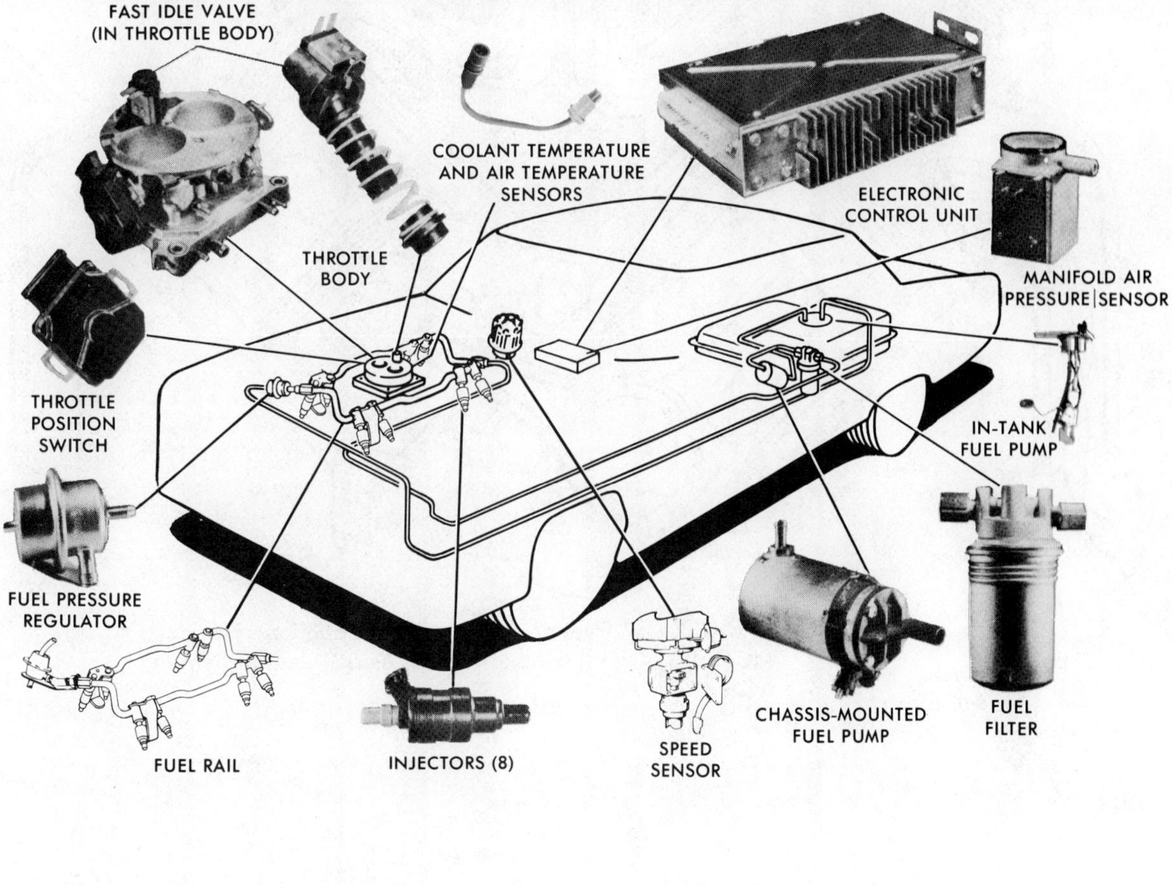

FAST IDLE VALVE (IN THROTTLE BODY)

COOLANT TEMPERATURE AND AIR TEMPERATURE SENSORS

ELECTRONIC CONTROL UNIT

THROTTLE BODY

MANIFOLD AIR PRESSURE SENSOR

THROTTLE POSITION SWITCH

IN-TANK FUEL PUMP

FUEL PRESSURE REGULATOR

CHASSIS-MOUNTED FUEL PUMP

FUEL FILTER

FUEL RAIL

INJECTORS (8)

SPEED SENSOR

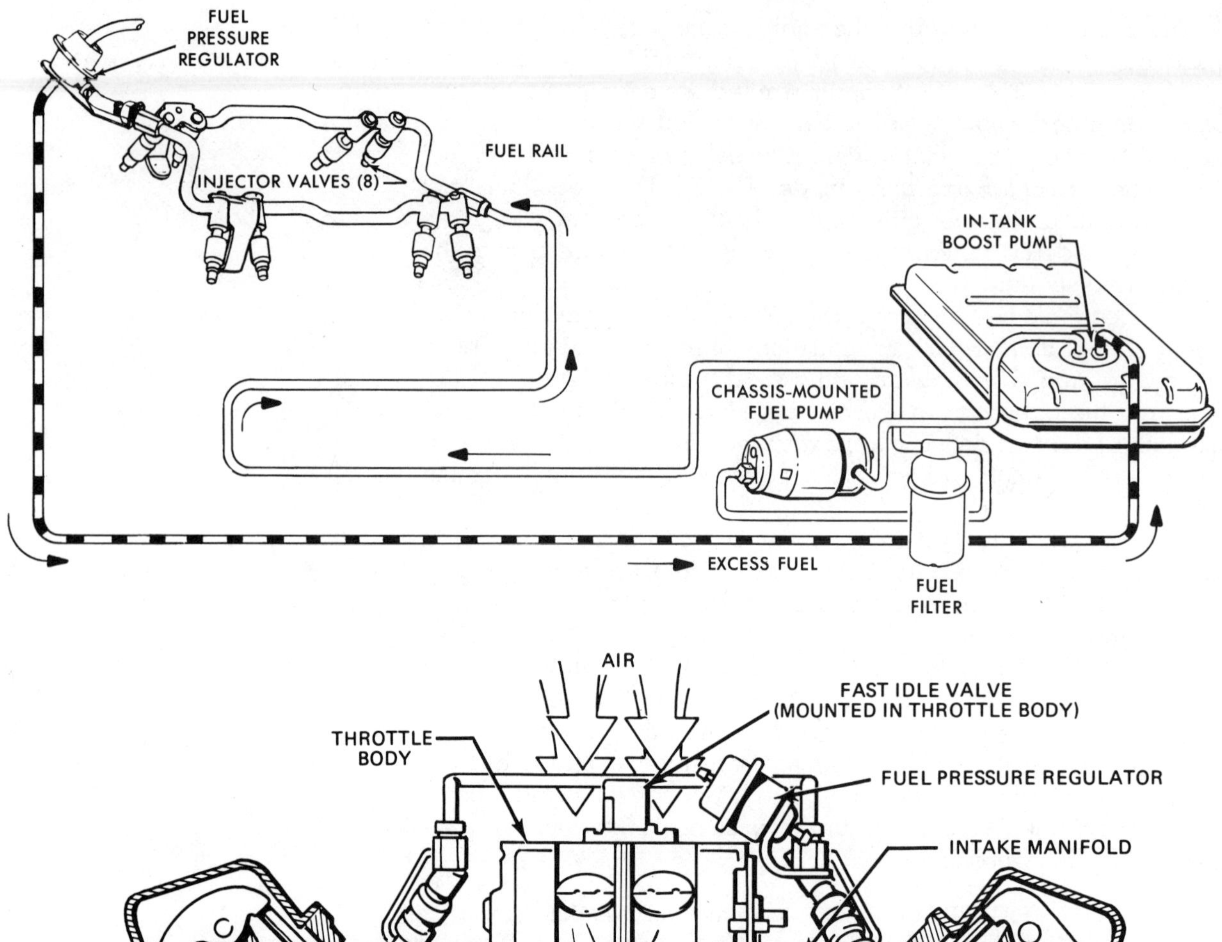

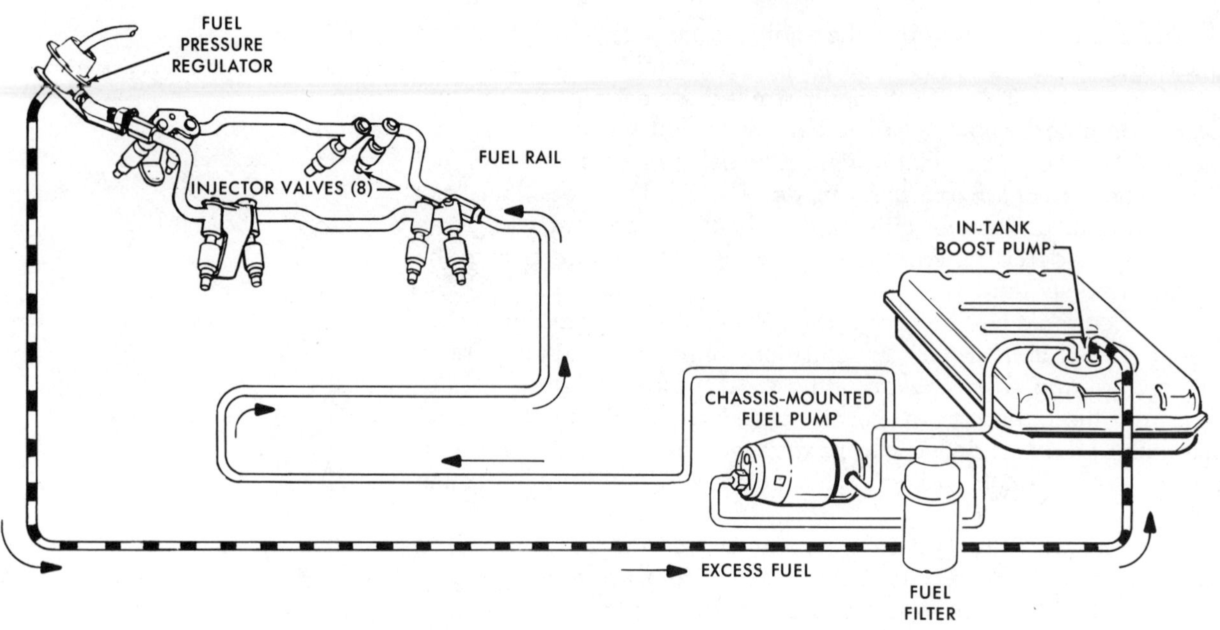

FIGURE 11-7 Fuel delivery and air induction system. (Courtesy Cadillac Motor Car Division, General Motors Corp.)

The electronic control unit ECU is a programmed analog computer. Different calibrated units are used on the different model engines. The ECU is connected to and receives power from the vehicle battery. The electronic fuel injector control components are connected to the ECU by means of a wiring harness.

Information is received relative to the following: electronic fuel injector sensors, engine coolant temperature, intake manifold air temperature, intake manifold absolute pressure, engine speed and firing position, as well as throttle position and change of position. The ECU transmits commands to bring about the activation of the following units: electric fuel pump, fast idle valve, injection valve, EGR solenoid, and the vacuum retard solenoid.

The desired air-fuel ratio for various driving and atmospheric conditions is designed into the ECU. As signals are received from the sensors, the ECU processes the signals and computes the engine fuel requirements. The ECU issues commands to the injector valves to open for a specific time duration (dwell). The duration of the command pulses varies as the operating conditions change.

A closed loop electronic fuel injection system is incorporated in a number of engines. The closed loop system is designed to sense the air-fuel ratio and make corrections through a feedback signal to bring about an ideal ratio. An exhaust oxygen sensor located in the exhaust manifold sends a signal to the ECU, which in turn sends a signal to adjust the pulse width of the injector spray.

When problems occur and it is suspected to be in the closed loop system, road test the vehicle. It is important to eliminate the possibility of electrical or mechanical problems other than the closed loop system. Make a visual inspection of all wires and connections to be sure all connections are clean and tight.

The closed loop system can be checked by inserting a test lamp having a two-candlepower bulb or less between the pigtail at the ECM and a positive battery connection. Start the engine and run for at least 2.5 minutes. If the light remains off, the system is satisfactory. If the light comes on during this period, disconnect the oxygen sensor and check the resistance between the harness center terminal and ground with an ohmmeter. The ohmmeter should read greater than one megaohm. If less, the wiring harness is shorted and needs to be replaced. A special analyzer is available to simplify the testing procedure. Figure 11-8 shows the tester connections for checking the ECU which controls the air-fuel delivery system. Manufacturer's instructions and specifications must be followed when using the tester.

Connect the ohmmeter between the harness center terminal and pin "J" of the ECU red connector. The meter should read less than 10 ohms. If more, the harness is shorted and needs to be repaired or replaced.

The oxygen sensor cable shield should be connected to pin "E" of the blue connector. There should be a complete circuit. If not, the shield must be repaired.

After repairs, connect the sensor and recheck. If the light remains off, the system is satisfactory. If the light comes on, replace the sensor.

To check out the total electronic fuel injection system a special analyzer must be used. Follow the instructions prescribed by the manufacturer of the analyzer for making the specific tests. Check against manufacturer's specifications and make the needed repairs and/or parts replacement.

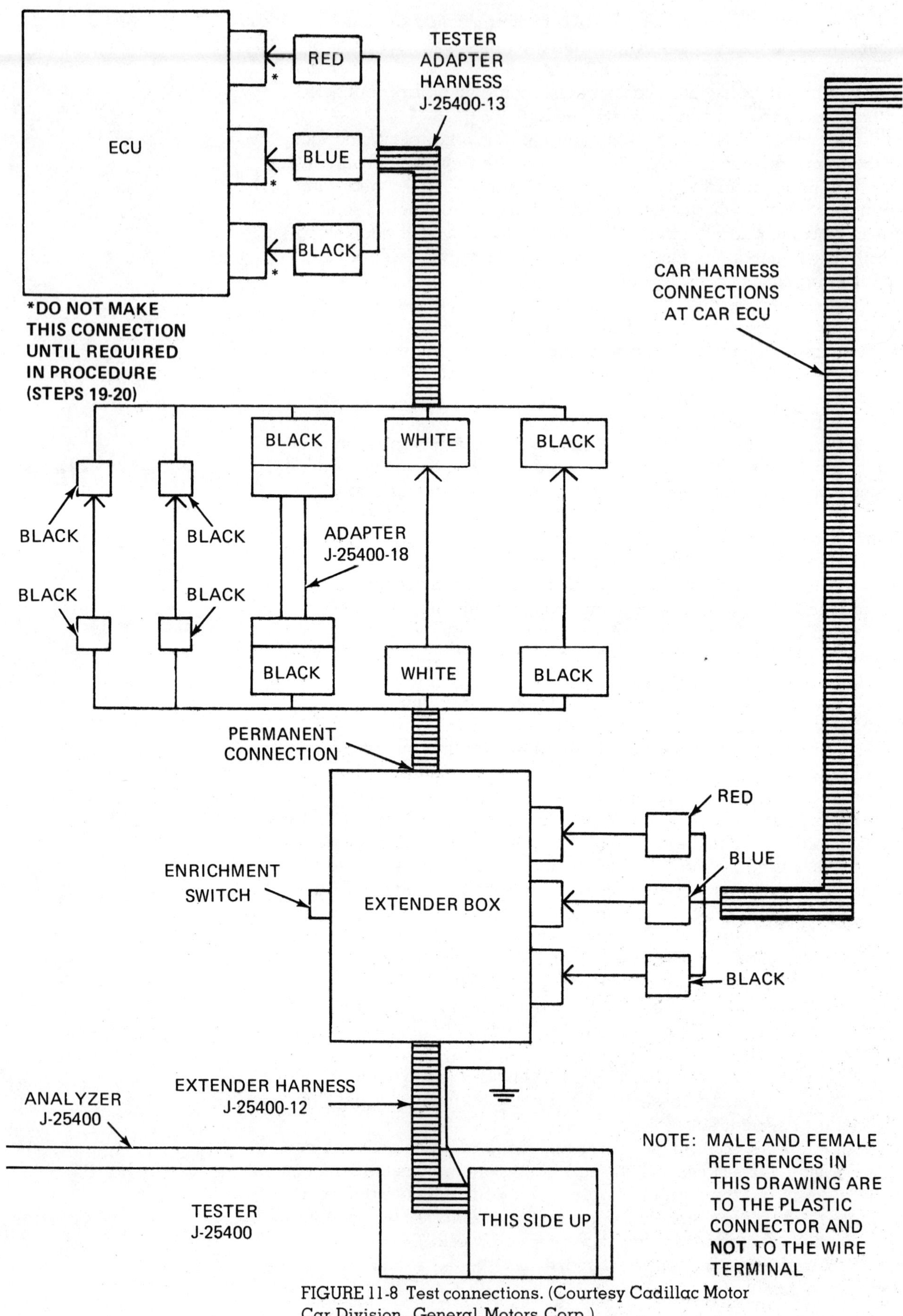

FIGURE 11-8 Test connections. (Courtesy Cadillac Motor Car Division, General Motors Corp.)

When operational problems occur which are not readily identified, a regular troubleshooting operation should be performed, the same as for a vehicle not equipped with a computer. As the system, for the most part, is electrically operated, always make a careful inspection of all wires and connections which are included in the system. All connections must be clean and tight. Any broken or frayed wire must be replaced. Vacuum may be used to actuate some components. Make sure all hoses are properly connected and there are no leaks. Always make sure fuel is getting to the injector system from the fuel tank.

GENERAL MOTORS DIGITAL ELECTRONIC FUEL INJECTION SYSTEM

Some General Motors products are equipped with a digital electronic fuel injection system that provides a means of fuel distribution for controlling exhaust emissions. This is done by establishing a program for a digital electronic control module (ECM) which will provide the correct quantity of fuel for a wide range of engine operating modes. Figure 11-9 shows the different components included in the digital electronic fuel injection system.

Sensors are used to determine existing operating conditions. This information is then sent to the ECM which in turn signals the injectors to provide the exact amount of fuel needed to satisfy the particular operating mode.

The digital electronic fuel injection system consists of electrically actuated fuel metering valves. When these are actuated, they spray a metered quantity of fuel into the engine intake manifold. Two injector

FIGURE 11-9 Digital electronic fuel injection system. (Courtesy Cadillac Motor Car Division, General Motors Corp.)

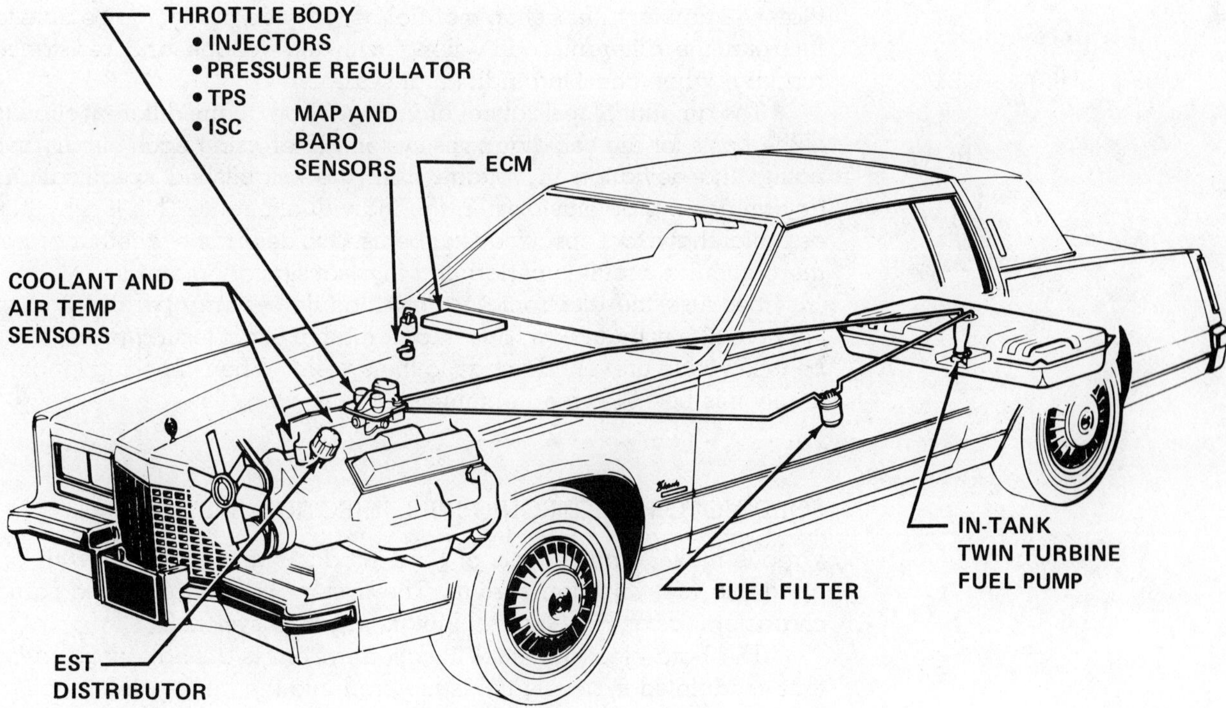

valves are mounted in the throttle body above the throttle plates with the metering tips directed into the throttle barrels. The injectors normally are actuated alternately.

The subsystem which makes up the digital electronic fuel injection system is basically the same as the electronic throttle body injection system. The system consists of a fuel supply system, air induction system, sensors, electronic control module ECM, electronic spark timing, idle speed control system, exhaust gas recirculation control, and a system diagnostic (check) light. Some differences exist between the fuel metering components for the digital electronic fuel injection system and the throttle body injection system, but both perform in basically the same manner.

The computer command control system, CCC, used on General Motors products monitors the various engine/vehicle operating modes and uses this information to signal different components in the electrical, fuel, and ignition system to provide a better operating vehicle with fewer emissions.

The basic operation of the system relative to the components which feed information to the ECM, and the units which are changed by signals from the ECM, are much the same for all engines, whether equipped with a carburetor or a fuel injection system.

From a service standpoint, most vehicles equipped with the CCC system utilize a check engine light with a self-diagnosis system. The electronic fuel injection system using an individual injector for each cylinder that is mounted on a rail does not use a self-diagnosis system; instead a special analyzer is necessary to locate troubles. All other systems utilize a trouble code system in conjunction with the self-diagnosis system to indicate the trouble areas.

As the number of components included in the computer system varies with the different makes and models of engines and vehicles, plus changes which are constantly being made, no universal code system for the self-diagnostic checks is used. Therefore, it is important that the manufacturer's shop manual be followed in order to be able to interpret the different codes along with the voltage and resistance reading, when checking individual systems.

The amount of resistance, or voltage drop, in the different circuits is the basis for the self-diagnosis system. Energizing each circuit and noting the deviation in voltage from the established specifications determines if problems exist in the individual circuit. This is why it is essential that exact specifications be used to determine whether or not the particular circuit is performing in a satisfactory manner.

Because the electronic control module system operates with a very small electrical flow, it is important that exact testing procedures be followed to prevent damage to the system. When checking for continuity it is best to use an ohmmeter.

FORD MOTOR ELECTRONIC FUEL INJECTION SYSTEM

Various makes and models of Ford products are equipped with an electronic fuel injection system. The system has many of the same characteristics as the General Motors injection system.

The Ford electronic fuel injection system is a single-point pulse time modulated system. Fuel is metered into the intake air stream, to meet the specific operating demands, by two solenoid operated injector valves. The injector valve nozzles are mounted on the throttle body above the throttle plates. The throttle body is mounted on the intake manifold in place of the regular carburetor. Figure 11-10 shows a three-quarter front view of a Ford Electronic fuel injection fuel charging assembly.

Fuel is supplied by an electric fuel pump located in the fuel tank. The fuel is filtered and delivered to the fuel charging assembly, where a regulator keeps the pressure at a constant 39 psi. Two injector nozzles, one in each barrel, are mounted in the body of the fuel charging assembly above the throttle plates. Fuel is supplied to the injectors by the pressure regulator. Excess fuel not needed by the engine is returned to the tank through a fuel return line.

The fuel charging assembly is made up of six different components which perform the fuel and air metering function. These include the air control, fuel injector nozzles, fuel pressure regulator, fuel pressure diagnostic valve, cold engine speed control, and throttle position sensor.

Airflow to the engine is controlled by two butterfly valves, the same as the throttle valves on a V8 engine with a conventional carburetor. The valves are operated by the accelerator pedal and linkage, the same as with a regular carburetor.

The injector nozzles which meter and atomize the fuel charge are located above the throttle plate. An electric control signal from the EECII electronic processor activates the injector solenoid, which raises the pintle off its seat, allowing fuel to flow into the air stream. The injector flow orifice is fixed and the fuel pressure is constant; therefore

FIGURE 11-10 Electronic fuel injection charging assembly. (Courtesy Ford Parts & Service Division, Ford Motor Co.)

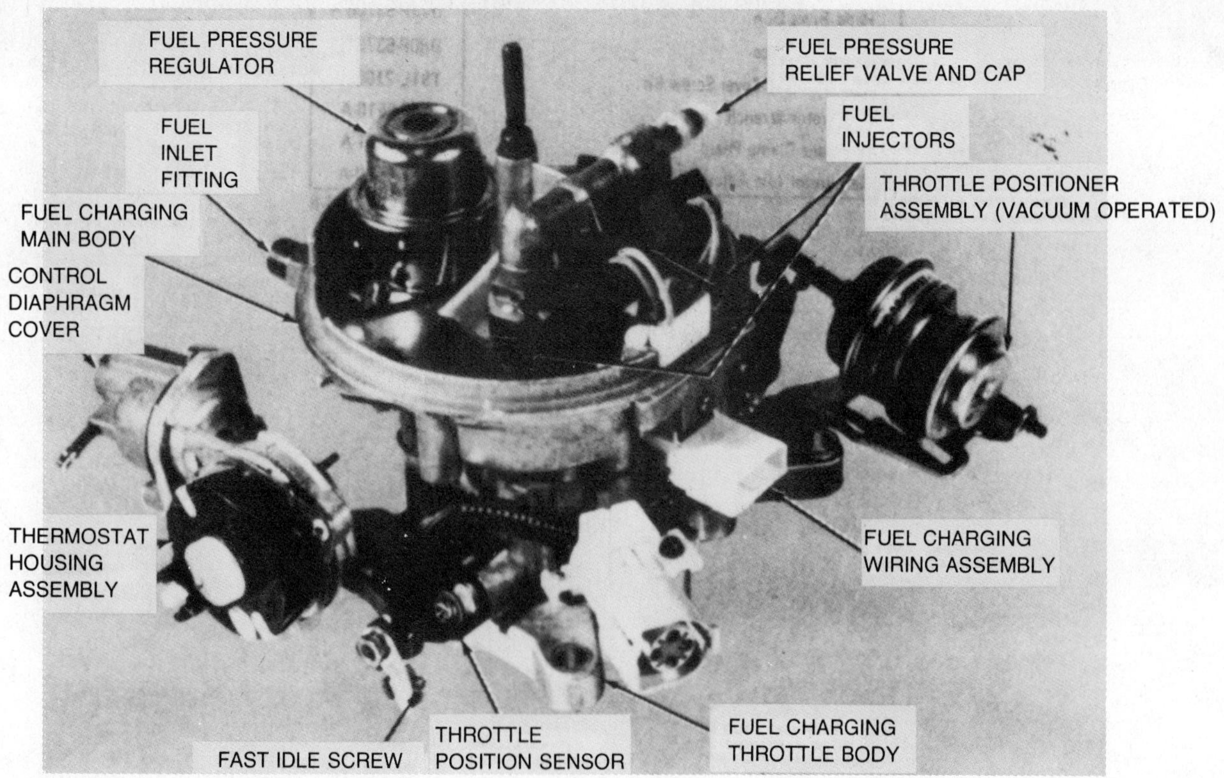

the fuel flow to the engine is controlled by the length of time the solenoid is energized. Figure 11-11 is an electronic fuel injector system injector unit which is mounted above the throttle plates and sprays fuel into the airstream.

The pressure regulator located in the fuel charging assembly maintains a constant pressure on the fuel to the injectors. It nullifies any effect of supply line pressure drop. The regulator also acts as a check valve, making fuel available for immediate restart after engine shutdown. This eliminates vapor formation.

A fuel pressure diagnostic valve (Schrader tire valve type) is located in the metering body. This permits easy metering of fuel pressure as well as a means of bleeding down the pressure if service must be performed to the system. A pressure gauge can be attached to the valve to determine line pressure. This will determine if the pump is functioning properly.

The cold engine speed control is a means of speeding up the engine when it is cold. A fast idle cam is used in the same manner as on a conventional carburetor. The cam is positioned by a bimetal spring and an electric positive temperature heating element. The power for the heating element is supplied by the generator stator when the engine is running. The heating element provides a better warmup profile and permits the throttle to return to idle speed in a gradual manner. There is an automatic kickdown from the high cam (fast idle) to an intermediate speed, controlled by the computer.

The EECII (computer) directs vacuum to the automatic kickdown

FIGURE 11-11 Fuel injector nozzle assembly. (Courtesy Ford Parts & Service Division, Ford Motor Co.)

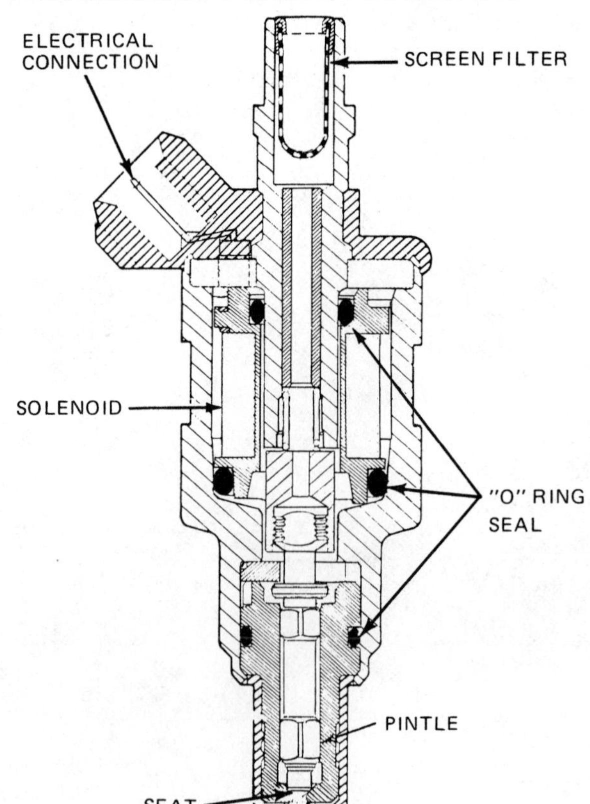

motor which moves the high speed cam to a lower speed according to a predetermined time after the engine starts.

The throttle position sensor is mounted on the throttle shaft and is used to supply a voltage output proportional to the change in throttle position. The sensor is used by the electronic engine control unit to determine the operating mode for selecting the correct fuel mixture, spark, and EGR position.

The fuel pump pressure is controlled by two relays, one governed by a vacuum switch and the other controlled by the EEC module that provides power for the pump under various operating conditions.

With the ignition switch off, the vacuum controlled relay is closed and the EEC controlled relay is opened. When the ignition switch is first turned on, both relays are closed, providing power to the pump to pressurize the fuel system. If the engine is not cranked, the EEC module will open the relay after approximately one second. When the engine starts, manifold vacuum increases, causing the vacuum switch to close and the vacuum controlled relay to open. This reduces voltage to the pump. Under heavy engine load, vacuum will dump, causing the vacuum switch to open and permits the vacuum relay to close, providing full voltage to the pump. The EEC senses engine speed and shuts off the pump by opening the EEC controlled relay when the engine stops or is below 120 RPM.

Any malfunction in the electric fuel pump system will result in loss or reduction of fuel flow to the engine. To determine if the pump is functioning properly, check the fuel tank for adequate fuel supply, check for leakage at all fittings and lines. Check all electrical connections. To check for electrical flow, connect a voltmeter to the wiring harness connector at the fuel charging assembly. Turn the ignition switch to "on" while watching the voltmeter. The voltage should rise to battery voltage and return to zero voltage after about one second. If this does not occur, check the electrical system.

The fuel pump is operating properly if the fuel pressure reaches 30 psi. The fuel flow should amount to 10 ounces, one-third quart, in ten seconds, and the pressure remains at 30 psi immediately after de-energization.

The EECII diagnosis for the electronic fuel injection system is included in the test procedure when testing the EEC system. This includes the quick test and the pinpoint test.

CHRYSLER ELECTRONIC FUEL INJECTION SYSTEM

The Chrysler electronic fuel injection system is a continuous flow, electronically controlled fuel injection system. A single system monitors the ratio of air/fuel electronically, compares it to an ideal ratio and makes adjustments according to the operating mode. The system is divided into two major subdivisions, the fuel supply subdivision and the fuel control subsystem.

The fuel supply subdivision supplies fuel to the fuel control subdivision. An in-tank electric fuel pump delivers fuel through a pair of filters to the control pump housing in the fuel control subsystem. Fuel is delivered under pressure, and since only a small portion of the fuel is used, a fuel return line is included in the system to return the unused fuel to the tank. Although the control pump housing is part of the fuel control subsystem, it serves as a reservoir for the control pump inlet to keep the pump primed with fuel. A control pump housing check valve prevents the fuel in the housing from draining back into the tank. Figure 11-12 shows the fuel flow circuits of a continuous-flow type electronic fuel injection system.

The fuel control subsystem is located between the fuel subsystem and the point where fuel is injected into the airstream. The fuel control subsystem is mounted on the hydraulic support plate assembly on top of the throttle body, which is mounted on the intake manifold. The control subsystem consists of a control pump which gives precise control to fuel metering in keeping with changing engine conditions. A fuel flow meter is incorporated to monitor the rate of fuel flow, and a temperature sensor checks fuel temperature. Both the flow and fuel temperature sensors are connected to the combustion control computer to provide information relative to the operating speed of the control pump motor.

A fuel pressure switch is located between the fuel flow meter and the fuel injectors. The switch is normally open when there is sufficient metering pressure in the circuit to start or run the engine. The switch is closed when there is insufficient metering pressure in the circuit. When closed with the ignition switch in the start position, the fuel pressure switch completes a bypass circuit that drives the control pump at full speed. This causes the pump to flush, prime, and pressurize the fuel control circuit for prompt engine starting.

Metered fuel entering the fuel injector assembly is directed to two pressure regulating valves. Each valve feeds its own fuel injection bar located over the throttle body assembly. The light load regulator valve

FIGURE 11-12 Fuel flow delivery and return circuits. (Courtesy Chrysler Corporation)

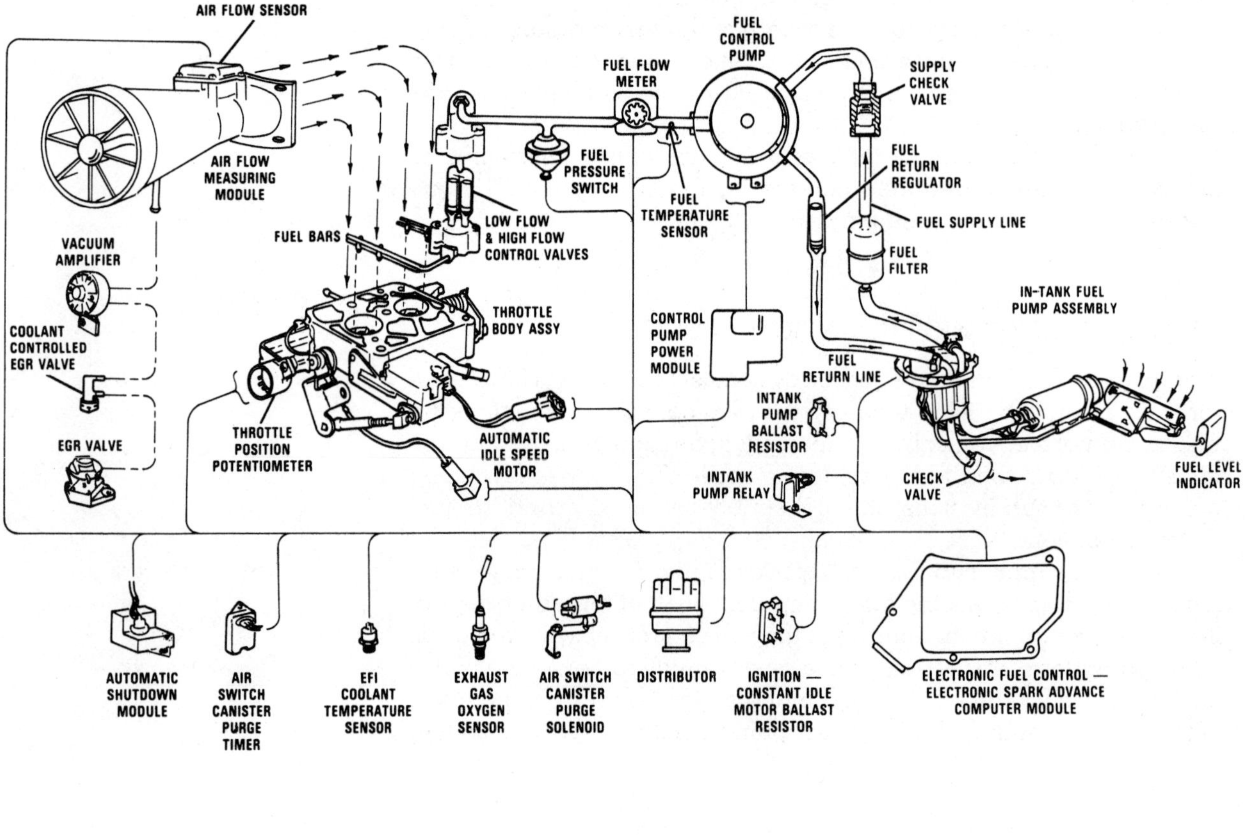

AIR FLOW SENSOR
FUEL CONTROL PUMP
FUEL FLOW METER
SUPPLY CHECK VALVE
AIR FLOW MEASURING MODULE
FUEL PRESSURE SWITCH
FUEL RETURN REGULATOR
FUEL TEMPERATURE SENSOR
FUEL SUPPLY LINE
VACUUM AMPLIFIER
FUEL BARS
LOW FLOW & HIGH FLOW CONTROL VALVES
FUEL FILTER
IN-TANK FUEL PUMP ASSEMBLY
COOLANT CONTROLLED EGR VALVE
THROTTLE BODY ASSY
CONTROL PUMP POWER MODULE
FUEL RETURN LINE
INTANK PUMP BALLAST RESISTOR
EGR VALVE
THROTTLE POSITION POTENTIOMETER
AUTOMATIC IDLE SPEED MOTOR
INTANK PUMP RELAY
CHECK VALVE
FUEL LEVEL INDICATOR
AUTOMATIC SHUTDOWN MODULE
AIR SWITCH CANISTER PURGE TIMER
EFI COOLANT TEMPERATURE SENSOR
EXHAUST GAS OXYGEN SENSOR
AIR SWITCH CANISTER PURGE SOLENOID
DISTRIBUTOR
IGNITION — CONSTANT IDLE MOTOR BALLAST RESISTOR
ELECTRONIC FUEL CONTROL — ELECTRONIC SPARK ADVANCE COMPUTER MODULE

opens when metered pressure reaches or exceeds 21 psi and delivers fuel to the light load injector bar. The light load circuit supplies all of the engine fuel requirements when metering pressure is between 21 and 34 psi.

When metered fuel pressures reach or exceed 34 psi, as in the case of a heavy load or when starting, the power regulator valve opens. This spray pattern is added to the air-fuel mixing process.

Residual fuel vapor is always present in any fuel system before engine startup. In the electronic fuel injection system fuel control circuit, the presence of fuel vapor is especially critical. The vapors tend to block the control pump so it pumps less fuel, and the vapor also tends to "confuse" the fuel flowmeter so that it reads more fuel than is actually passing through. To prevent this, a special priming bypass circuit is activated to drive the control pump at full speed when the ignition key is turned to start position. This will flush out the vapor, and prime and pressurize the system so injection can begin. The bypass circuit is activated only while the fuel pressure switch is in the closed low fuel pressure position. When the circuit becomes adequately pressurized, the fuel pressure switch opens and the bypass circuit is deactivated. This whole process starts and stops within the time it takes for the engine to revolve once.

The air induction system includes all units that are in physical contact with the intake air. The air induction system is divided into two major subdivisions the air supply subsystem and the air control subsystem. The system also contains a number of sensors and an actuator.

The electronic fuel induction system draws in outside air and delivers it through the air supply subsystem, to the hydraulic support plate, where it interfaces with the air control subsystem. En route, the air passes through the airflow sensor and air cleaner assemblies.

The airflow sensor measures engine induction airflow volume. This information is electronically compared with the fuel flowmeter information so as to insure precise air-fuel mixture control.

The functions of the electronic fuel injection air control subsystem take place within the throttle body assembly. Air-fuel mixing occurs, and the amount of mixture reaching the intake manifold is controlled. Major parts include the throttle plate and blade assembly, two sensors, a throttle position potentiometer, and a closed throttle switch, plus an actuator-automatic idle speed motor. Figure 11-13 shows the airflow through the air supply subsystem, air control subsystem and into the intake manifold.

The throttle body contains butterfly-type throttle blades which have a crescent-shaped segment ridge toward which the injector spray is directed. The ridges help to disperse the fuel spray for more uniform air-fuel mixing.

A throttle position sensor (potentiometer) sends signals to the combustion control computer relative to throttle position. This permits the computer to adjust the air/fuel ratio to meet the particular operating mode.

A closed throttle switch lcoated at the idle stop actuates the automatic idle speed circuit and returns the ignition timing to retard when the accelerator pedal is released. Depressing the accelerator causes the switch to open and reintroduces a preset amount of ignition timing advance.

As with a conventional fuel system, the driver turns the fuel sup-

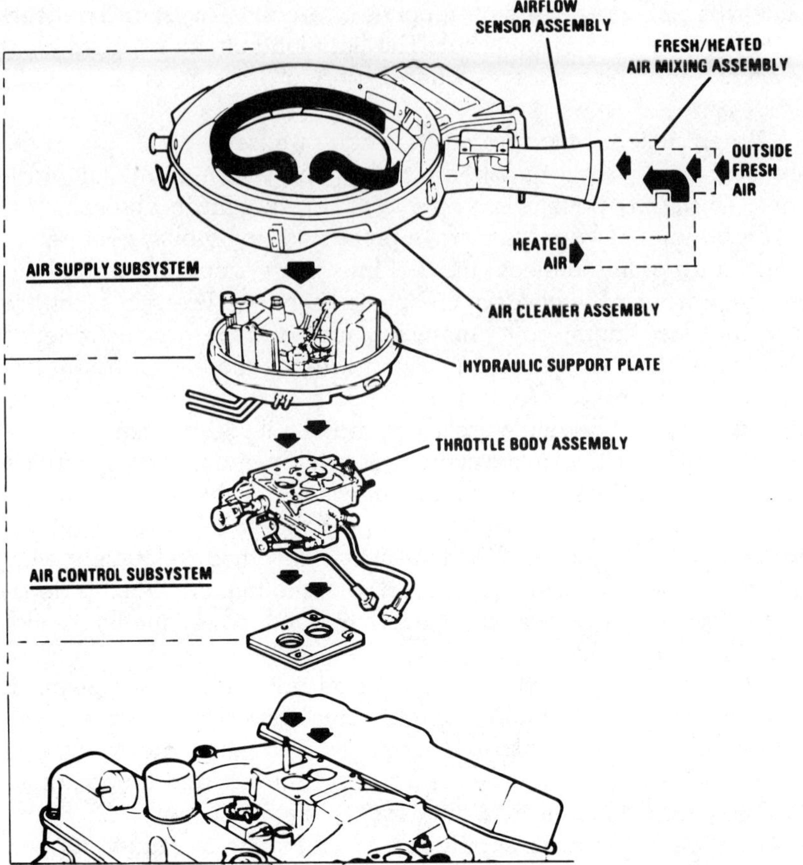

FIGURE 11-13 Electronic fuel injection air induction system. (Courtesy Chrysler Corporation)

ply and ignition off with the ignition key. When the engine is operating, the driver can vary the rate of flow by the use of the accelerator.

The electronic fuel injection system command functions also include automatic fuel flow metering to provide optimum air/fuel mixture for all operating modes; automatic ignition timing advance and retard; automatic throttle opening adjustment to provide optimum idle speed for all idle conditions, and an automatic fuel flow shutoff if certain ignition, engine speed or time requirements are not satisfied.

On an engine equipped with an electronic fuel injection system, all automatic control signals originate at the combustion control computer, with assistance from two other electronic modules: the power module and the automatic shutdown module. The combustion control computer is made aware of a wide variety of ambient and engine operating conditions through the use of numerous sensors. Such conditions are evaluated and commands are issued by the computer to the fuel, ignition, and air induction systems.

The sensors utilized on many models will include airflow, air temperature, fuel flowmeter, fuel temperature, fuel pressure switch, throttle position, closed throttle, closed throttle switch backup switch, engine speed, engine load, ignition, air conditioning "on," and time sensing.

Basically, the combustion control computer is the common functional center for four separate electronic circuits. These circuits include, (1) the electronic fuel injection circuit that controls air/fuel by initiating speed changes of the control pump, (2) an automatic calibration circuit that fine-tunes the electronic fuel injection unit for more precise control of the air/fuel ratio by monitoring the oxygen content of the exhaust gases leaving the combustion chamber, (3) the electronic spark advance circuit that initiates ignition power and controls timing by advancing or retarding spark impulses and, (4) the automatic idle speed circuit that adjusts engine idling to the desired RPM when the accelerator is closed.

When operational problems occur, perform the usual service operations and diagnostic procedures which would be done to a vehicle not equipped with a computer controlled fuel injection system. Make a visual inspection for loose connections, frayed insulation, loose hose clamps, and leaks in the vacuum or fuel lines. Check all of the connections inside the air cleaner. Outside of the air cleaner, make sure all sensor connections are clean and tight, and the wiring harness connections are fully plugged in and fit tightly.

Use extreme care to prevent grounding when breaking and reconnecting connectors during electrical tests and inspections. Shorting or energizing any terminal that may be connected to the combustion control computer may damage the CCC, or introduce another fault into the system. If it is necessary to crank the engine with the high tension lead disconnected from the distributor cap, the lead must be grounded or the CCC will be irreversibly damaged.

The electronic fuel injection system replaces the conventional fuel system; therefore fuel filters must be replaced when plugged or dirty, all connections must be tight, and there must be no leaks. Checking fuel flow, for the most part, is a visual inspection.

When normal testing procedures fail to locate the problem, or it has been established that troubles exist within units included in the combustion control computer system, the system must be checked in order to isolate the faulty unit.

To accurately check the combustion control computer system, a special electronic fuel injector tester and accessories are required to facilitate diagnosing EFI problems without endangering the test equipment or the EFI system.

The manufacturer's instructions for using the test equipment, the sequence of tests, and the manufacturer's specifications must be carefully followed for the tests to be meaningful. When the trouble is located, it is usually a matter of removing and replacing the component.

12 Troubleshooting Electrical—Electronic Problems and Engine Performance

Following a regular preventive maintenance schedule, as recommended by the manufacturer, will help reduce the chances of troubles occurring. When troubles do occur, locating the problem is generally the most difficult job in troubleshooting.

For an engine to function properly it must have good compression, proper air/fuel mixture and the necessary spark delivered at exactly the correct time. All of these basic factors must be taken into consideration in order to have an efficiently performing engine. Usually, excessive emissions, as well as excessive fuel consumption, are the result of engine malfunctions.

The terms diagnosis, troubleshooting and analysis are many times used interchangeably. Diagnosis is defined as an investigation or analysis of the cause or nature of a situation or problem, or a conclusion concerning the nature or cause of some particular condition. Analysis is the separating of the whole into its component parts and determining the relationship. In many instances diagnosis and analysis are used interchangeably. In both instances, it is a case of locating the particular unit that is causing the malfunction.

Troubleshooting may be defined as locating the trouble and then eliminating and correcting the cause of the problem. Troubleshooting goes a step further than diagnosis and analysis, by locating the trouble and making the needed repairs and/or adjustments to bring the vehicle back to its normal operating condition.

General Troubleshooting

When troubleshooting, always make the simple and most obvious checks first. Check for loose and/or corroded electrical connections, determine if there are fouled spark plugs, faulty secondary wires, or electronic ignition system troubles. Look for loose, cracked, damaged or improperly connected vacuum hoses. In troubleshooting, you should eliminate as soon as possible all components which are not involved in the problem, and definitely establish the trouble as being in a particular unit or system.

By using a few simple pieces of equipment such as a voltmeter, ohmmeter, test lamp and test leads, it should be possible to locate most problems.

In most cases where an engine fails to start or starts and then stops, there are some definite, simple procedures to follow that require very little in the way of equipment.

To check overall performance, pinpoint specific problems and make precise adjustments, rather sophisticated equipment is needed. Equipment such as a dwell meter, tachometer, timing advance light, battery tester, generator tester, vacuum gauge, compression gauge, oscilloscope, and an infrared emission tester are necessary. In addition, some service establishments will have a chassis dynamometer to simulate driving conditions.

Before attempting to locate problems of an electrical-electronic nature, it might be well to review some of the fundamentals of electrical circuits, basic testing, and circuit protection.

In order for an electrical apparatus to operate, there must be a complete electrical circuit. Electricity must be able to flow from the source of power (battery) to the operating component and return to the battery, usually through a ground—the metal parts of the engine and/or vehicle.

In addition, there is usually some means of turning the flow of electricity on and off to control the operation of the particular component. This will generally be some type of switching device such as a solenoid; a transistorized control unit; a sensor operated by temperature, pressure or vacuum; a vacuum control unit or a manually operated switch.

To prevent an electrical overload (short) circuit from damaging wires, switches or operating mechanism, most circuits will be protected by a fuse, circuit breaker or fusible link. When an electrical overload occurs, the fuse or fusible link, which is a strip of alloy metal with a low melting point, will melt and break the continuity of the electrical circuit, thus preventing an excessive current flow which might damage the wiring, instruments or electrical units. A circuit breaker may be used in some circuits to protect the wiring and electrical units. Most circuit breakers are of the thermal type, that will open, breaking the circuit when an overload occurs. It is most important to find and correct the cause of an electrical overload (short) that blows a fuse, fusible link or causes the circuit breaker to open the circuit.

Diagnostic connectors have been used on a number of vehicles for a period of time. The advent of the electronic computer control system with a self-diagnostic feature eliminated some of the need for a diagnostic connector. The diagnostic connector provides a convenient method of testing certain components which make up the ignition, charging, and starting systems. A special tester can be plugged into the connector for quick checking, or a voltmeter can be used on some vehicles without disturbing the unit being tested.

Copper wire, covered with an insulating material, is used in the

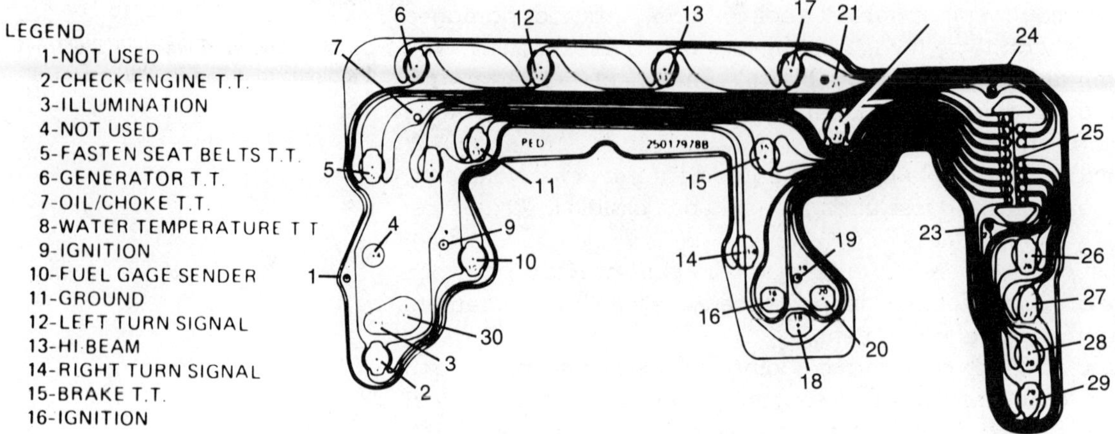

FIGURE 12-1 Instrument panel printed circuit. (Courtesy Chevrolet Motor Division, General Motors Corp.)

majority of cases to carry electricity from a power source to the operating unit. The size (gauge) of the wire is determined by the amount of electricity the circuit is designed to carry. Plug-in connectors are generally used at terminals to attach the wire to an operating unit or junction block. In some instances, screws may be used to attach the wires. Always make sure the connections are clean and tight.

Many manufacturers will use printed circuits to transmit electricity, particularly where the amperage draw is not too high and where space is a factor, such as in replacing the many wiring circuits on the back of the instrument panel. The printed circuit is a circuit made by applying a conductive material to an insulated panel in a pattern that provides an electrical circuit between the various components mounted on or connected to the panel. Care must be exercised when working around or on the panel, to not damage the various circuits. Figure 12-1 shows a typical instrument panel printed circuit. Individual circuits can be checked visually for breaks if a problem occurs in a circuit.

Chassis and Body Electrical Wiring Circuit Diagrams

The different automobile manufacturers have available basic chassis and body electrical wiring diagrams which show how each circuit gets its power, what the current paths are to the different components, and where the components are grounded. The wires are color coded to make tracing the circuit simpler.

Most circuits are enclosed in a harnness for protection and convenience. This makes visual inspection of an individual wire virtually impossible. Many of the wires attached to the different components located in the instrument panel will be enclosed in one harness, while another harness may contain the wires for the lighting circuit.

On most installations, the wires for a particular circuit will go to a connector block, sometimes called a bulkhead connector, where the wires plug into a receptacle. When the wires go into the engine compartment, a connector block (bulkhead connector) will generally be attached to the firewall. This permits connecting and disconnecting wires between the engine compartment and under the cowl inside the vehicle. Connectors may also be used at the various junctions where the circuit branches off to different locations and components.

When connectors are used, checking, servicing and/or replacement is easier. When trouble is suspected in a particular component or circuit, the wiring harness can be separated at the connector for testing purposes. A voltmeter or test lamp can be used to check for an open or short circuit. Figure 12-2 shows the various switches and sensors used in an electronic emission control system, along with the numerous connectors used, which permit disconnecting the different circuits for testing purposes.

FIGURE 12-2 Commonly used switches, sensors, and connectors. (Courtesy Chrysler Corporation)

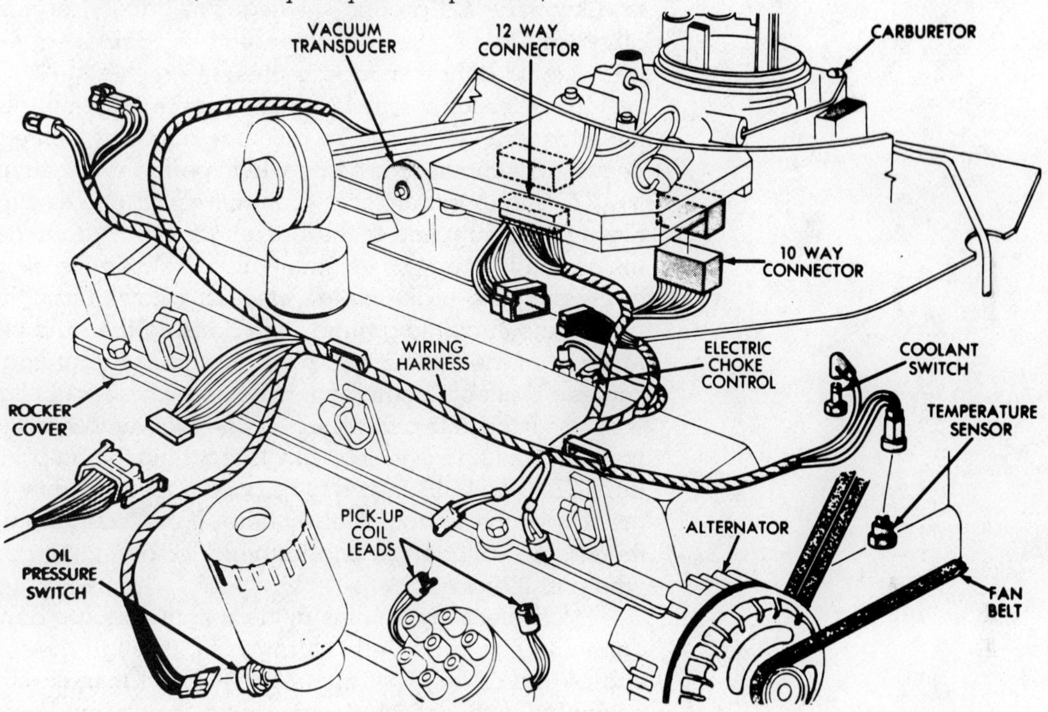

Electrical Circuit Testing

Failure in a circuit is usually the result of a short or open circuit. Open circuits are the result of a break in the line, poor connections or malfunctions in the components to be operated. Short circuits are usually caused by bare wires touching one another or grounding to a metal part of the vehicle. If the major portion of a circuit becomes inoperative simultaneously, the failure may be due to improper connections at a junction in the wiring harness, or a burned out fusible link. If only one circuit is inoperative, the problem may be due to an open circuit or short in the affected area. It is usually the result of a blown fuse, or bulb, if there is a light used in the circuit.

Only a few simple tools are required for electrical troubleshooting. These include a test light made with a 12 volt bulb, and two test leads which can be used to check available voltage and short circuits. A self-powered test lamp, consisting of a light bulb in a socket, a battery, and a set of test leads wired in series, is a valuable test tool.

When connected to two points of a continuous circuit, the light comes on. It is used for a continuity check, as well as for a ground check. A jumper wire, which is a length of wire with clips on each end, is used for bypassing a switch or open circuit.

A DC voltmeter is needed to measure circuit voltage. Connect the negative (minus) lead to ground and the positive lead to the voltage measuring point. An ohmmeter is used to measure resistance between connected points. The ohmmeter should only be used on de-energized circuits. Figure 12-3 shows the proper hookup for checking resistance at a connector in a circuit. This will determine if there is a resistance, short, or open circuit.

To make a voltage check, connect one lead of the 12 volt test light to a known good ground, or negative battery terminal. Connect the other test lead to the connector lead or component terminal. The test bulb should light if voltage is present.

In order for electricity to flow, there must be a complete circuit. Included in a circuit will be a source of power, some type of switch to activate the circuit, and a unit which performs some type of operation.

A simple example of a circuit could be the brakelight system. Electricity is supplied to the brakelight switch from the battery. When the switch is open, no electricity flows. When the switch is closed, by depressing the brake pedal, electricity flows through the bulb, completing the circuit to ground, and causing the bulb to light. Any malfunction in the system will result in the bulb not lighting. It now becomes a matter of finding out why the bulb does not light. The quickest way is to substitute a new bulb, if one is available, or use a test lamp or voltmeter to find out if electricity is reaching the bulb when the switch is turned on. If a bulb known to be good does not light when inserted into the socket, the trouble is elsewhere. If the test lamp does not light, or there is no voltage reading to the bulb socket, a problem exists elsewhere in the circuit.

Most electrical circuits in the automobile use only one feed wire, depending on a ground return circuit through the metal parts of the engine and/or vehicle frame. Always check to make sure the unit, such as the bulb, sensor, or electric motor, has a good ground to its metal mounting. If the switch is readily accessible, it is easy to connect a

FIGURE 12-3 Checking resistance in various circuits with an ohmmeter. (Courtesy Chrysler Corporation)

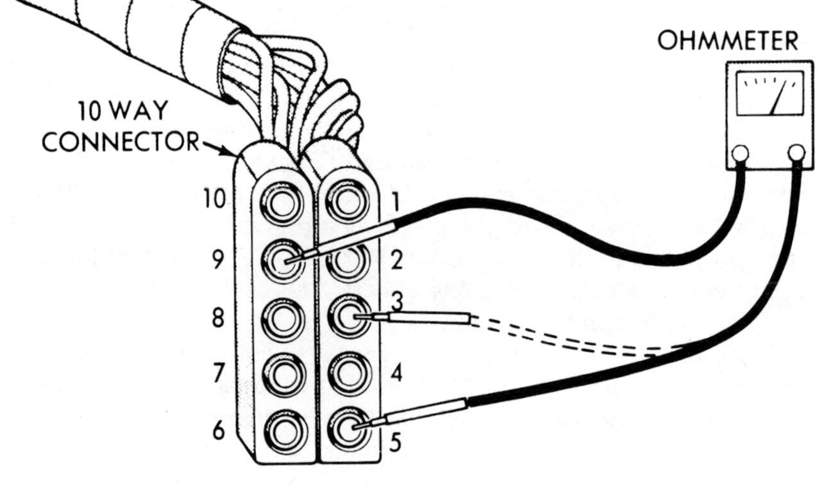

jumper wire to bypass the switch. If the bulb or working unit now lights or operates, the fault is in the switch. If the bulb does not light or the unit does not work, current is not getting to the switch, indicating there is a broken wire or faulty connection from the battery. All circuits are checked in much the same way.

Because most sensors (a form of switch), as well as the electrical control module, operate with a small current flow, it is generally best to use an ohmmeter to check for current flow. The ohmmeter can be used in place of a test lamp or voltmeter to check a circuit.

In order for the necessary current to flow in a circuit, resistance must be kept within specific minimums. This is necessary for any electrical or electronic component to function effectively.

Dirty and/or loose connections, and broken strands of wire will increase resistance to current flow in a circuit, resulting in a voltage drop. Visual inspection of wires and connections will, in many cases, locate bad connections. On the other hand, to make sure excessive resistance is not present, when there is any question relative to resistance, make a voltage drop test. A high resistance in any part of the circuit results in low voltage in other portions of the circuit.

FIGURE 12-4 Charging circuit resistance test. (Courtesy Chrysler Corporation)

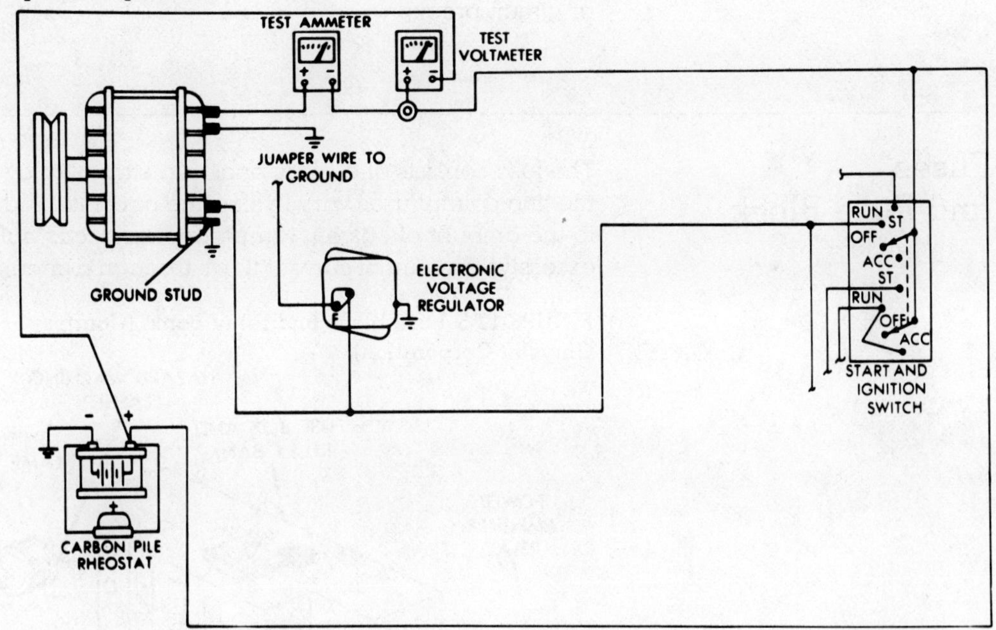

A voltage drop which exceeds 0.2 volts between the battery post and battery terminal, or other connections in the battery-starter circuit, indicates excessive resistance.

To make a voltage drop test, use a low range (expanded) scale 0 to 2.5-volt voltmeter. When making a voltage drop test at a connection, the prods on the voltmeter leads are tightly pressed against the metal part of the connector. When checking resistance, current must be flowing in the circuit while the test is being made. Figure 12-4 shows a voltmeter hookup to test the circuit resistance (voltage drop) between the generator output terminal and the battery.

A reading which exceeds 0.1 volt per connection indicates excessive resistance, except in the case of battery-starter connections where up to 0.2 volts is acceptable. A clean and tight connection will show no voltage reading when current is flowing in the circuit.

To check for a good ground in a light bulb socket, touch one prod of the voltmeter to the socket and the other prod to the socket housing. A voltmeter reading of over 0.1 volt indicates a poor ground connection. This also applies to any component which is grounded through the case.

Circuit Protection

Some means must be provided to prevent insulation from being burned off the wires or damaging the switch and/or operating units should an overload occur in the circuit. The overload will generally be the result of a short (ground) occurring in the circuit. When this happens, a larger than normal flow of electricity takes place. Because the circuit is designed to handle a specific amount of current, when a larger than normal flow occurs, the increase will dissipate itself in the form of heat, because of the circuit resistance to this surge of electricity. To prevent this, some type of protective device is incorporated in the circuit. This protective device may be in the form of a fuse, fusible link, or circuit breaker.

Fuses and Fuse Block

The fuse consists of a glass-enclosed strip of alloy metal having a low melting point. Fuses vary in size and capacity and are rated according to the amount of current (amperage) they can safely carry. When an excessive amount of current flows through a circuit, the overload heats

FIGURE 12-5 Fuse block and relay bank. (Courtesy Chrysler Corporation)

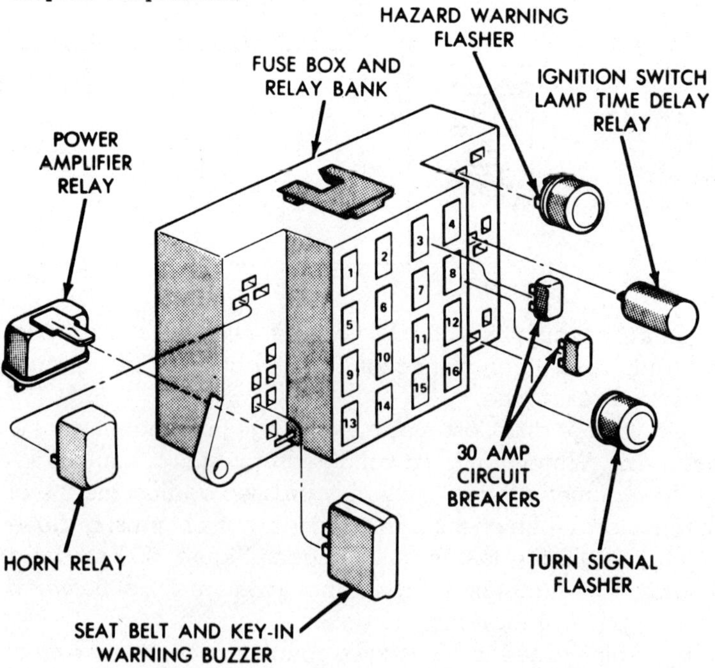

the fuse, causing the alloy metal strip to melt, breaking the continuity of the electrical circuit and stopping the flow of current. The fuse is removable and must be replaced in order to complete the circuit after the trouble in the circuit has been corrected.

Fuses are generally mounted in a fuse block (panel) that holds all, or nearly all, of the fuses used in the vehicle. The fuse panel is generally mounted near the underside of the instrument panel. Included on the fuse panel may be the turn signal flasher, the hazard flasher, warning buzzer, and in some cases, the circuit breakers, if used. The fuse panel is usually labeled relative to the fuse circuit and fuse amperage. Figure 12-5 is a line drawing of a fuse box and relay bank which contain the horn relay, warning buzzer, turn signal flasher, ignition switch lamp time delay relay, power amplifier relay, circuit breakers, and fuses.

To check or replace a fuse, pull it straight out of the holder or cavity. If the link (wire) in the fuse is broken, it must be replaced. A volt-ohmmeter or test lamp can be used to check for fuse continuity if there is a question as to whether or not the fuse is blown.

Fusible Link

A fusible link is a special wire placed in the wiring harness. It is generally covered by a special nonflammable insulation which will blister or bubble when the link is overloaded.

Some wiring harnesses incorporate fusible links to protect the circuit. Links may be used, rather than a fuse, in wiring circuits not normally fused, such as the ignition circuits and/or the engine compartment wiring harness.

When a fusible link is blown, it will usually kill an entire circuit. In some cases, the fusible links are color coded to match the circuit in

FIGURE 12-6 Fusible link. (Courtesy Chevrolet Motor Division, General Motors Corp.)

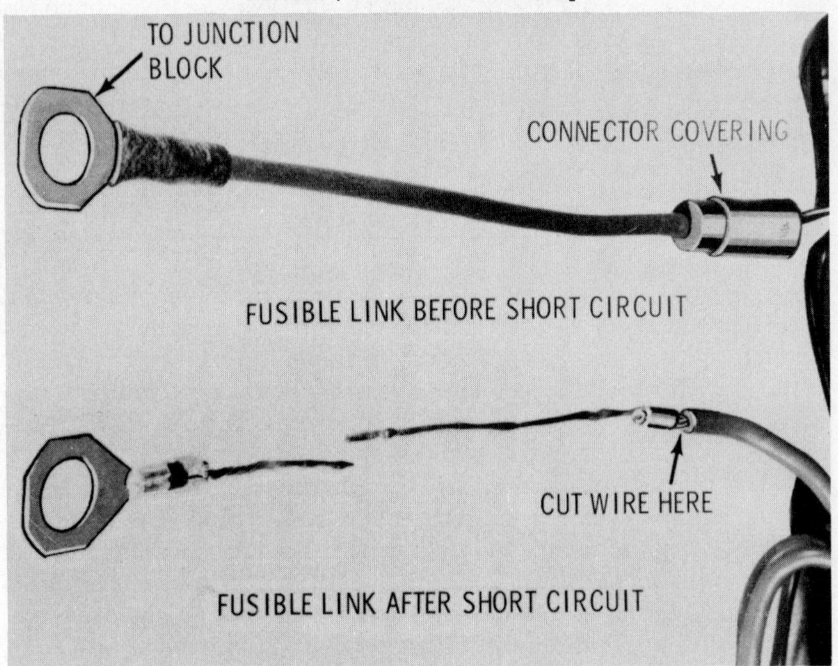

which they are used. It is important that the link be two or three sizes smaller than the original wire. The size of the link may also be marked on the insulation covering the link. Other installations may have a flag symbol molded into the insulation where the link is inserted.

A new fusible link can be installed after the short circuit in the system has been located and corrected. To replace the fusible link, disconnect the battery ground cable. Cut open the wiring harness insulation in the area of the damaged fusible link. Cut the fusible link out of the circuit. Remove one inch of insulation from both the new fusible link and the end of the wire in the circuit. Position the connector clip, if included with the link, around the new link and harness wire. Crimp the clip so all wires are securely fastened. Solder the connections with rosin core solder. If clips are not included with the link, weave the ends of the bare wires together and solder. Wrap the splice with a minimum of three layers of electrical tape. Tape the repaired wire into the wiring harness. Connect the battery ground cable. Figure 12-6 shows a typical fusible link before a short circuit and after a short has occurred that caused the wire to melt.

Circuit Breakers

Circuit breakers may be used in some circuits which carry more of a load than a single bulb or radio, etc. They may be used in circuits such as headlights, power locks, and windows. The circuit breaker is usually located on the fuse block.

The circuit breaker is a protective device that will open the circuit to prevent circuit damage when an overload occurs due to excessive current flow. When the current flow is too high, the circuit breaker contacts open to break the circuit, either by means of a bimetal blade that opens circuit contact points because of the heat created by excessive current flow, or a magnetic coil that moves an armature to open contact points when the current flow is too great. The advantage of the circuit breaker is that it keeps resetting itself. However, it continues to break the circuit until the overload is found and corrected.

The circuit breaker can be pulled out of its holder in the same manner as a fuse. Use a continuity test lamp or ohmmeter to determine if current flows through the circuit breaker. If not, replace the unit.

Engine Electrical Diagnostic Connector

An engine electrical diagnostic connector may be found on a number of vehicles. Since 1977, many full size General Motors vehicles, except Cadillac, have been equipped with a diagnostic connector. Also, a number of Chrysler Corporation products are equipped with a diagnostic connector. Ford Motor Co. did not use a connector for this purpose.

The purpose of the engine electrical diagnostic connector is to simplify engine electrical component and system diagnosis. The connector is a terminal panel for wires, which provides access to several test points within the starting, charging, and ignition system. It is useful in troubleshooting such problems as poor cranking, engine miss, engine not starting, and an unsatisfactory charging system.

A few General Motors vehicles equipped with automatic climate control air conditioning systems use an additional diagnostic connector to make checking of the automatic temperature control electrical system more convenient. Manufacturer's instructions and specifications must be carefully followed to perform meaningful checking of the systems.

The connector installed on Chrysler products is intended to be used only with the Chrysler Electronic Engine Performance Analyzer. It is possible to damage the generator, starting motor and/or neutral-start switch if wrong connections are made. A voltmeter should not be used on these vehicles to probe the connections for test purposes. When the special analyzer is used, carefully follow the manufacturer's recommendations relative to its use.

The widespread use of the computer-controlled emission control system with the self-diagnostic feature has reduced the use of this device on many present vehicles.

General Motors and Chrysler make available special test equipment which can be plugged into the diagnostic connector for a quick, accurate, and convenient checking sequence. On General Motors products, a voltmeter can be used at the diagnostic connector to check circuits for malfunctions if a special tester is not available.

By following the particular manufacturer's instructions relative to utilizing the diagnostic connector, either through the use of a special tester that plugs into the diagnostic connector, or, if not available (only General Motors products), by using a voltmeter, it is possible to check out the operation of a number of electrical components at the diagnostic connector without disturbing the particular unit.

The following information applies only to General Motors products. The common General Motors electrical diagnostic connector has ten terminals. There are three terminals in a group, followed by a space, and then seven additional terminals.

Figure 12-7 shows the location of the diagnostic connector in the engine compartment of a General Motors product. The cover on the connector must be removed to expose the terminals.

FIGURE 12-7 Diagnostic connector location. (Courtesy Oldsmobile Division, General Motors Corp.)

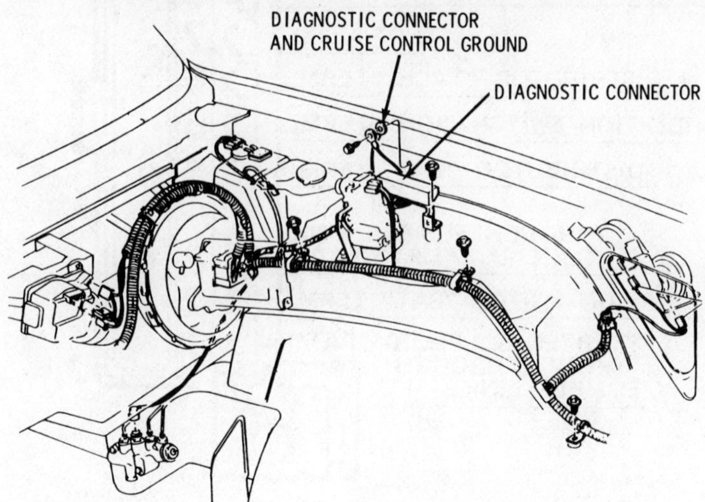

Whether an adapter and tester, or a voltmeter are used, in order for the tests to be meaningful, it is essential to be familiar with the location of the different connections. The terminals on the connector are arranged as 1, 2, 3, space, 4, 5, 6, 7, 8, 9, G. The G terminal is the ground connection. Some of the diagnostic connector terminal wires are spliced into the feed wire, instead of going directly to the connection on the unit. The resistance in the splice can be checked by making a voltage drop test.

The check point terminals are as follows:

1. Starter solenoid "Bat" terminal (through fusible link)
2. Ignition switch "Bat" terminal
3. Through fusible link to headlight switch
   Space
4. Distributor "Bat" terminal
5. Ignition switch "Ign" terminal
6. Distributor "Tach" terminal
7. Not used—no function
8. Starter solenoid "S" terminal
9. Ignition switch "Sol" terminal

G. Ground

Figure 12-8 shows the diagnostic connector terminals with the numbers as well as the name of the terminal. This applies to General Motors products using a diagnostic connector.

FIGURE 12-8 Engine electrical diagnostic connector terminals. (Courtesy Oldsmobile Division, General Motors Corp.)

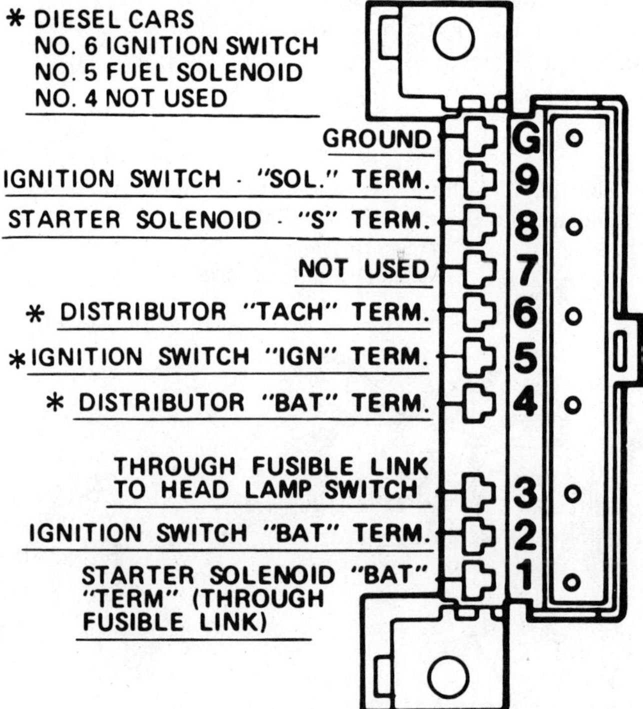

Poor Cranking—Solenoid Clicks or Chatters

Always check the obvious reasons for not cranking, such as a discharged battery or poor connections. If there is any question about the condition of the battery, substitute a battery known to be good, or charge the battery.

Connect the negative voltmeter lead to the G terminal of the diagnostic connector, and the positive voltmeter lead to the number 1 terminal of the connector. Turn the ignition key to the start position. If the voltmeter shows over 9 volts, disconnect the negative voltmeter lead from G and connect it to a good ground on the engine. If the voltage is still over 9 volts, replace or repair the starter motor. If a reading under 9 volts occurs, clean and tighten, or repair the battery cable. If the engine still does not crank, make a battery load test. Replace the battery if necessary.

Make a voltage drop test by connecting the negative voltmeter lead to the number 1 diagnostic connector, and the positive voltmeter lead to the positive battery post. Crank the engine. If the reading is over 0.7 volts, check for a corroded or loose ground cable at the battery, or the fusible link serving the starting motor may have blown.

Engine Does Not Crank—Solenoid Makes No Sound

Check the condition of the battery and for loose or corroded battery cables and/or a poor ground cable. Check the specific gravity of the battery, or the eye of the freedom battery. Check the charging rate and correct if necessary.

If the engine does not crank with a good battery and satisfactory connections, attach the positive lead of the voltmeter to the number 8 terminal of the diagnostic connector, and the negative lead to "G" ground. Turn the ignition switch to start. If the meter reads over 7 volts, repair or replace the starter solenoid. If under 7 volts, connect the positive voltmeter lead to the number 1 diagnostic terminal and turn the switch to start. If over 9 volts, connect the positive voltmeter lead to the number 9 diagnostic connector and turn the ignition switch to start. If over 7 volts, check for a loose or corroded bulkhead connector terminal, a bad starter safety switch, or switch adjustment. If under 7 volts, connect the positive lead of the voltmeter to the number 2 diagnostic terminal. If over 7 volts, replace the ignition switch. If under 7 volts, repair the loose or corroded red wire at the bulkhead connector. This is the wire that connects the battery lead to the ignition switch. If under 9 volts, connect the voltmeter to the battery and make a load test. If the battery is good, repair or replace the starter motor.

If the battery voltage is over 9.6 volts, make a voltage drop test by connecting the negative voltmeter lead to the number 1 diagnostic connector, and the positive lead to the positive battery terminal. Turn the ignition switch to start. If the meter reads over 0.7 volts, check for a corroded or loose positive cable or blown fusible link. Connect the positive voltmeter lead to number 1 terminal, and connect the negative voltmeter lead to the negative battery terminal. Turn the ignition key to start. If over 0.7 volts, check for a corroded or loose ground cable.

Engine Misses, Idles Rough or Cranks But Does Not Start

Check the secondary output on at least two spark plug wires, using a calibrated spark gap or output meter. Check for faulty spark plugs or wires, cracked or dirty distributor cap or rotor.

Connect a test lamp between the 4 and 6 terminals of the diagnostic connector. Run the engine at curb idle speed and observe the manner in which the light glows. The test light will indicate one of three possibilities. If one flash is brighter than the others, the cause of the misfire or rough idle is in the electrical system. A vacuum leak can also result in a rough idle. To check the electrical system, attach the voltmeter negative lead to the "G" terminal of the diagnostic connector and the positive voltmeter lead to the number 6 terminal of the connector. Let the engine idle, or crank the engine if it will not run. A voltmeter reading of over 9.6 volts with the engine idling, or over 7 volts with the engine cranking, indicates a malfunction in the HEI (high energy ignition) system. A meter reading of less than 9.6 volts at idle, or less than 7 volts with the engine being cranked, indicates further testing is necessary.

Move the positive voltmeter lead to the number 4 terminal of the connector. Let the engine idle, or operate the starting motor if the engine will not start. If the meter reading is over 9.6 volts with the engine at idle, or over 7 volts with the engine cranking, the number 6 wire from the connector to the distributor may be grounded. Check the wire before doing any further testing. The problem is usually in the distributor.

If the voltmeter reads less than 9.6 volts at idle, less than 7 volts while cranking, connect the positive voltmeter lead to the number 5 terminal of the connector. If the meter now reads over 9.6 volts at idle, or over 7 volts at cranking, check the bulkhead connector terminals for corrosion or loose connections. If the meter reads less than 9.6 volts at idle, or less than 7 at cranking, replace the ignition switch.

Frequent Battery Discharge—Low Battery, Generator —Indicator Light Functions OK

Before making any tests, be sure the generator drive belt is properly tightened so as not to slip and the battery is fully charged. Run the engine at approximately 1,500 RPMs for one minute. Turn the headlights on high beam, turn on the radio, air conditioner, or heater blower motor to high speed, and the rear window defogger blower, if so equipped. Keep the engine running. Connect the negative voltmeter test lead to the "G" terminal of the diagnostic connector, and the positive voltmeter lead to the number 1 terminal of the connector. If there is a reading of less than 12.5 volts, the charging system (generator-regulator) is malfunctioning. If the reading is more than 12.5 volts, turn off the engine and all accessories. Make sure all doors are closed, the under hood light and trunk light are off. All electrical components must be off before testing for a short that may be draining the battery. Disconnect the negative battery cable. Connect a 12-volt test light between the cable terminal and the battery post. If the lamp glows, a short exists that is draining the battery. Check the various circuits. If the light does not glow, frequent starting along with short trips may be the reason for a discharged battery. A faulty battery also may be the reason for the battery being discharged.

Battery Uses Too Much Water

Connect the voltmeter negative lead to the "G" terminal of the diagnostic connector, and the positive voltmeter lead to the number 1 terminal of the connector. Run the engine for one minute at 1,500 RPMs with all lights and accessories off. If the voltmeter reads over 15.5 volts, there is a problem in the generator-regulator assembly.

If the voltmeter reads under 15.5 volts, check for extended driving conditions in hot weather, which may cause the battery water to evaporate.

The number 3 terminal on the diagnostic connector can be used to determine if a complete headlight failure is the result of a burned out fusible link, a simultaneous lamp burn out, or a headlight switch malfunction. Connect a test light between the "G" terminal and the number 3 terminal of the diagnostic connector. Turn on the headlights. If the test light does not light, check the headlight wire to the battery for an open fusible link. If the test light works, look for a bad switch or burned out bulbs.

There are other ways to use the diagnostic connector to make troubleshooting easier. Instead of connecting the tachometer lead to the distributor, it is more convenient to connect to the number 6 connector. For burglar protection, connecting a jumper wire between ter-

FIGURE 12-9 Engine compartment electrical components. (Courtesy Chrysler Corporation)

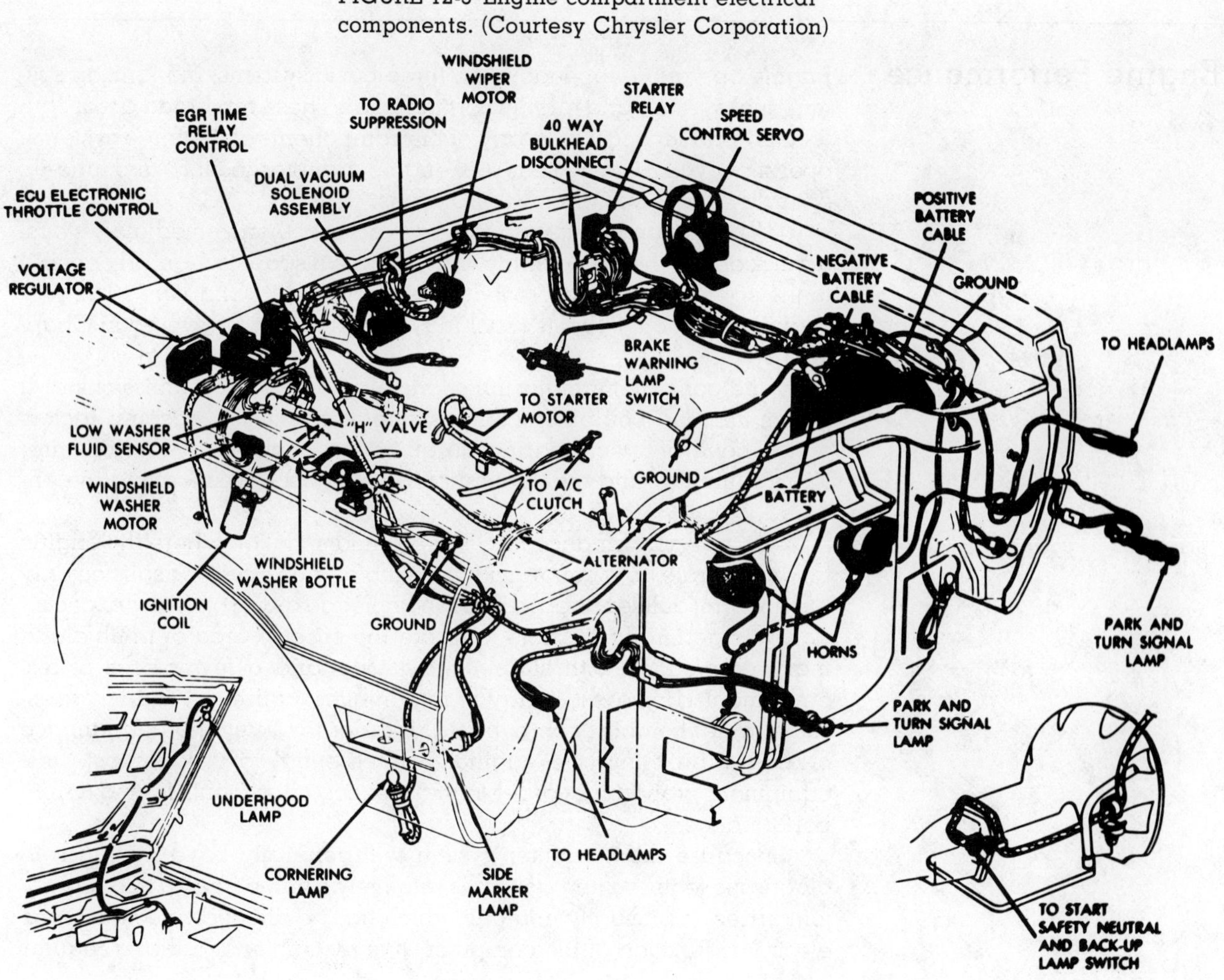

minals "G" and number 6 will prevent the engine from starting. To crank the engine without starting, connect a jumper wire between terminals 1 and 8. The engine will crank without starting. To bypass a faulty ignition switch, connect a jumper wire between the number 2 and 5 terminals. Use another wire to jump 2 and 8 terminals momentarily, to crank the engine. The engine will continue to run after removing the 2 and 8 jumper wire.

The special testers which may be used on General Motors products and Chrysler products are designed to plug into the diagnostic connector. It becomes a matter of turning the selector switch or plugging in test leads and checking the readings according to manufacturer's instructions and specifications for the particular circuit.

Many Chrysler products are equipped with a bulkhead disconnect which is fastened to the fire wall. There may be as many as 40 wire terminals in the bulkhead disconnect. Each terminal will be numbered. A master wiring diagram found in the manufacturer's shop manual describes the function of each wire number. This is helpful in tracing circuits for continuity and/or shorts. Figure 12-9 shows the wiring in the engine compartment, with the different connectors located on the bulkhead (fire wall) that permits disconnecting for test purposes and service.

Engine Performance

Engine operation depends upon three basic systems; the ignition system, fuel system, and engine compression. These are broad areas, but when a problem occurs in any of the components of the three systems, operation will be affected. All engine troubleshooting and tune-up operations revolve around these areas.

When an engine fails to run, or starts and then immediately stops, a quick check should be made to determine if spark is regularly getting to the spark plugs. This procedure is discussed in Chapter 7. The procedure to find out if fuel is reaching the carburetor is covered in Chapter 1.

The computer's major function is to keep engine emissions at a minimum. The computer controls and/or takes into account factors which have a direct bearing on all areas, such as air-fuel mixture, ignition timing, and the content of the exhaust gases leaving the engine.

Engine performance may vary from a situation where the engine fails to operate, to a condition where the engine operates satisfactorily but does not deliver as good gasoline mileage as the operator expects.

It is generally possible to locate the specific area of trouble and make corrections with simple hand tools and a few pieces of test equipment. However, today's automobiles utilize, in many cases, some rather complex components. In order to obtain the performance originally built into the engine, it is essential to use accurate test equipment properly, in order to make exact adjustments for maximum performance.

Because the computer system will generally have built-in self-diagnostic features, the system is relatively trouble free. When a problem arises, it is usually in a unit which has no direct connection to the electronic function of the computer. It is recommended that a regular tune-up and troubleshooting procedure be followed before checking the circuitry and components of the computer system. In most cases, this will clear up the performance problems.

Engine Tuneup

When operational problems occur, the engine is not performing as efficiently and as economically as it was designed to perform, and/or there are increased amounts of exhaust emissions being released into the atmosphere, manufacturers recommend a complete engine tuneup.

If there are no distinct operating problems, automobile manufacturers recommend a complete tune-up at approximately every 30,000 miles. Gradual wear and deterioration occur, and often are unnoticed by the driver. Replacing spark plugs, checking and resetting ignition timing, replacing the PCV valve, setting idle speed, etc., will make a noticeable improvement in performance and economy. When a problem occurs that is not readily identified and easily corrected, particularly in the case of an engine that has not been serviced in 25,000 to 30,000 miles, a complete tune-up is recommended as a starting point to correct the problem. This is a logical step to take.

Most modern engines will maintain the necessary compression for a great many miles if not abused. No engine will operate in a satisfactory manner if compression is uneven or low. Therefore, if a performance problem exists and the cause is not obvious, the logical place to start would be to check compression. No amount of adjusting or replacing components will make an engine operate efficiently if compression is not normal.

Manufacturers recommend a specific procedure for engine tune-up relating to a particular engine. The components to check and adjust are generally much the same for all vehicles, but specifications for the different components will vary according to the make and model of vehicle. For this reason, always check the manufacturer's specifications for the vehicle being serviced. Usually there is a decal in the engine compartment that lists the more common settings.

In general, the more common units to be checked, replaced or serviced include: spark plugs, drive belts, ignition timing, high tension wires, vacuum hoses, air cleaner, fuel filters, curb idle setting, fast idle setting, choke operation, PCV valve, EGR valve, ignition coil, distributor cap, distributor rotor, distributor advance and retard, battery condition and terminals, and generator charging rate.

A certain amount of test equipment is necessary to accurately perform a satisfactory tune-up operation. This should include a voltmeter with two scales or two meters, one having a 0 to 3-volt scale to measure voltage drop and another with a 0 to 20-volt scale to check line voltage and generator output voltage; an ammeter with scales 0 to 100 and 0 to 600 amperes to check generator output and for starter and battery testing; a carbon pile rheostat resistance unit is used for load testing a battery and checking starting motor amperage draw. These meters are available in a portable unit labeled as a volt-ampere tester. The unit includes fixed resistance units as well as a carbon pile variable resistance, in addition to a multi-scale voltmeter and ammeter. The unit can be used to check battery capacity, starting motor draw,

FIGURE 12-10 Starting/charging systems tester. (Courtesy Sun Electric Corporation)

charging system output, voltage regulator test, diode-stator test, and voltage drop test. Figure 12-10 is a typical starting and charging systems tester.

An ohmmeter is used to test for resistance in a circuit or component, as well as to check the secondary wires.

A dwellmeter is needed for older vehicles to check ignition contact point gap setting. It is used to check certain computer circuit operations on some vehicles. A tachometer is necessary to check and adjust engine RPMs. A vacuum gauge to check for the amount of manifold vacuum available, as well as for checking and setting carburetor idle adjustment (mixture), is necessary. A compression gauge is needed for checking the compression of individual cylinders to determine if there is cylinder leakage. A cylinder balance wiring harness, along with a tachometer, are used to locate individual cylinder problems. A power timing light is necessary to check ignition timing. A timing light incorporating a timing advance feature, can be used to determine and set initial timing, as well as checking the amount of advance at different RPMs. An infrared exhaust emission tester measures the amount of hydrocarbons and carbon monoxide being emitted from the engine exhaust system.

All of the equipment is available as separate units and can be used as such. However, service establishments doing any volume of automotive electrical and ignition service will be equipped with an engine tester (analyzer), consisting of most of the individual units such as a tachometer, vacuum gauge, dwell meter, combustion tester, cylinder leakage tester, timing advance meter, ammeter, voltmeter with a variable and fixed resistance unit, and infrared exhaust emission analyzer, along with an oscilloscope. The units are arranged to systematically test and evaluate problems in the compression, ignition, fuel, starting, charging, and emission systems. An interrogator diagnostic computer is shown in Figure 12-11. The analyzer can be preprogrammed with specifications for a specific vehicle. A digital display eliminates the interpretation and pinpoints the exact problem.

The latest test equipment of this type is computer controlled and may be capable of delivering a printout of engine operating conditions.

One of the most important testing and diagnosing tools is the oscilloscope analyzer, which provides a means for quick and accurate

FIGURE 12-11 Interrogator diagnostic computer. (Courtesy Sun Electric Corporation)

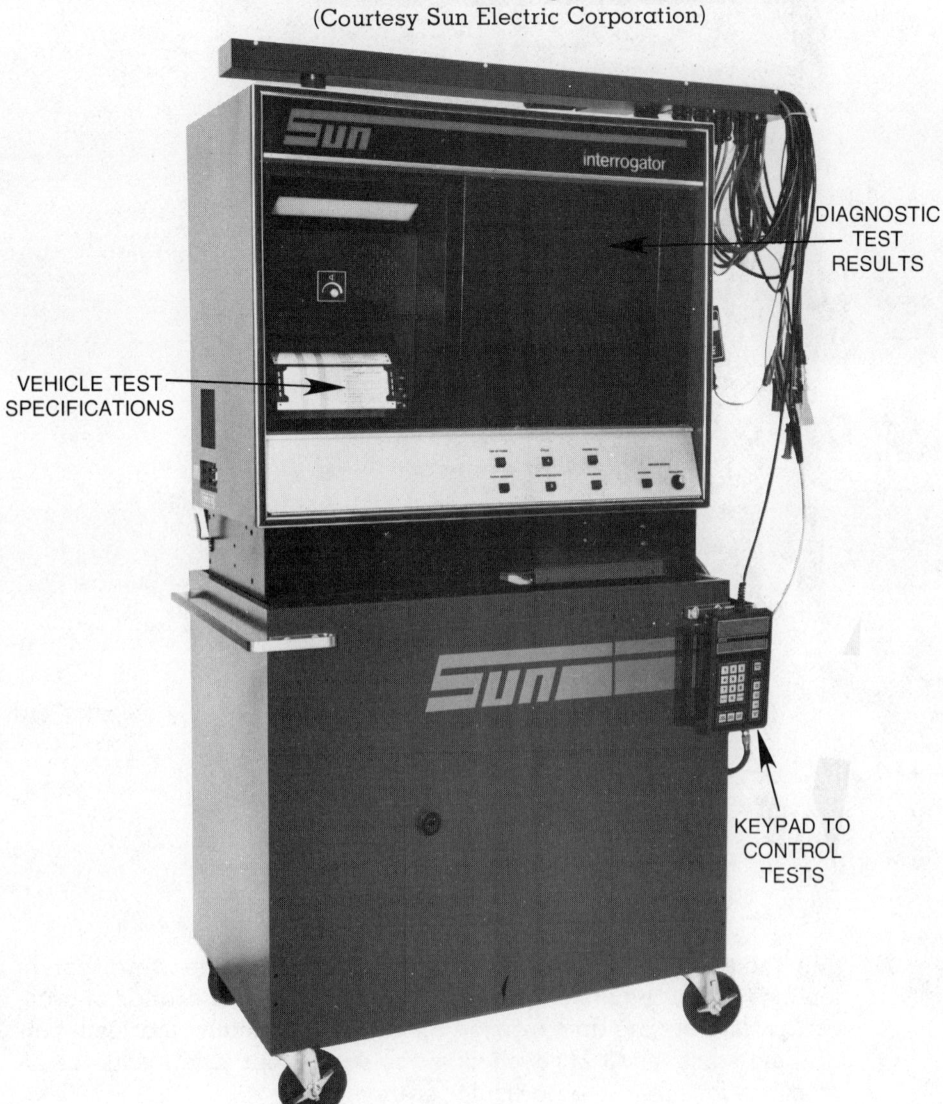

diagnosis of ignition system performance problems. This is included in most engine testers (analyzers). All phases of the ignition cycle can be displayed on an oscilloscope (cathode ray tube) television-type screen, exactly as they occur during engine operation. The scope is designed to show the operation of all cylinders or individual cylinders. Both the operating pattern of the primary circuit as well as the second is shown: A normal display of all cylinders will indicate an abnormal condition. Figure 12-12 shows a performance analyzer that uses a digital display to present information. The analyzer diagnoses problems in the conventional and electronic ignition system and charging system.

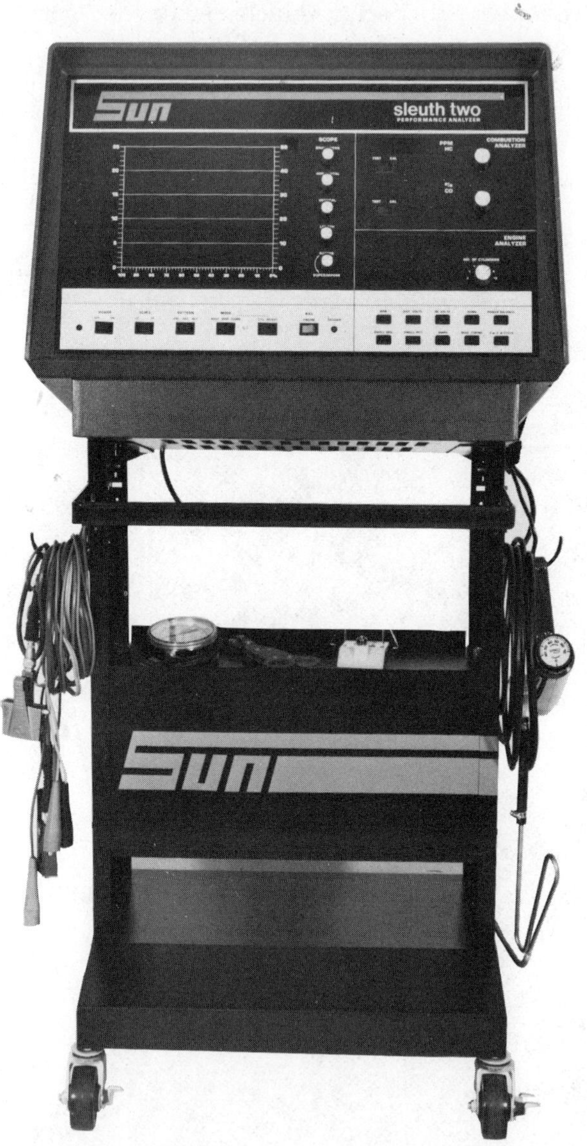

FIGURE 12-12 Complete engine analyzer with oscilloscope and combustion analyzer. (Courtesy Sun Electric Corporation)

The scope is invaluable for quickly determining the overall condition of ignition circuit components. There are several brands of oscilloscope and engine analyzers on the market. Basically, most will perform the same tests. Always follow the equipment manufacturer's instructions for use of the particular equipment.

Engine Troubles

Following are some of the more common engine performance complaints that occur, together with a definition of the symptoms and the most common causes of the problem.

Dieseling

Dieseling is when the engine continues to run after the ignition switch is turned off. The engine runs unevenly and knocks severely.

The throttle linkage, fast idle cam, or choke valve may be sticking. Check and reset the ignition timing, and check and reset, if necessary, the curb idle speed setting. If there is a carbon buildup, due to idling and slow driving, use a top engine cleaner to remove any carbon accumulation in the cylinders. If the problem still exists, try a different brand of gasoline. Sometimes, driving the vehicle at a high rate of speed for a short period of time will burn the carbon, loosen it, and blow it out the exhaust. To avoid violating speed laws, operate the vehicle with the transmission selector lever in "LO" range for a few miles.

Detonation (Ping or Spark Knock)

Detonation is a mild to severe ping, usually more pronounced during acceleration. It is a sharp metallic knock that changes with throttle opening.

When detonation is a problem check for engine overheating. Check and correct ignition timing and timing advance. If excessive combustion deposits are suspected, use a top engine cleaner to remove the carbon. The octane rating of the fuel being used may be too low. The EGR valve may not be functioning properly, this could cause the engine to detonate. Air leaking into the intake manifold can also cause detonation.

Rough Idling or Stalling

Rough idle or stalling is when the engine runs unevenly at idle. It may even cause the vehicle to shake and the engine to quit running.

In the case of a rough-running engine, or one that stalls, misses, hesitates, or has general overall poor performance, a cylinder balance check is helpful in locating the cylinder which may be malfunctioning. An oscilloscope can pinpoint which cylinder or cylinders are not performing as well as the others.

A rough-running engine at idle, and/or stalling out, may be due to: incorrect idle mixture adjustments; incorrect curb idle speed adjustment; incorrectly adjusted ignition timing; vacuum leaks in hoses or the carburetor; faulty PCV valve; faulty EGR valve operation; low compression readings; fouled, or improperly gapped spark plugs; improper operation of the carburetor feedback system; wrong fast idle setting; spark plug wires leaking; cracked distributor cap or rotor; dirty carburetor; improper choke adjustment; air leak in the intake manifold; restricted air cleaner, or the air cleaner vacuum motor or valve may not be functioning properly.

Engine Misfires

An engine miss is a steady pulsation, or jerking, that follows engine speed. It is usually more pronounced as engine load increases. It may not be as noticeable above 30 mph. The exhaust has a steady spitting sound at low speed or idle.

An engine miss may be due to leaking vacuum hoses, air leaks at the carburetor, faulty secondary wiring, faulty spark plugs, cracked distributor cap or rotor, compression leak in one or more cylinders, improper carburetor feedback system operation, leaking cylinder head gasket, improper carburetor adjustment, air leak in the intake manifold or the primary ignition circuit shorting intermittently.

Hesitates

Hesitation is the momentary lack of response when the accelerator is depressed. It may occur at any speed but is usually more severe when first starting to move after a stop.

Hesitation may result from an improperly operating choke, cracked secondary ignition wires, and/or poor connections, air cleaner heat valve not operating correctly, curb idle speed too low, ignition timing incorrect, poor compression, improper carburetor feedback operation (starved engine), faulty ignition coil, or leaking valves.

Surges

Surging is engine power variation under steady throttle or cruise. The vehicle seems to speed up and slow down with no change in throttle position.

Surging may be the result of low fuel level in the float bowl, low fuel pump pressure or volume, improper PCV valve airflow, restricted carburetor jets, restricted air cleaner filter, restricted fuel filter, EGR valve not functioning, improper feedback system operation, air leak in the carburetor, or the distributor advance system is not functioning properly.

Sluggish or Spongy

The engine delivers limited power under high speed or load. It does not accelerate as rapidly as it should and has limited top speed.

A sluggish engine may be the result of incorrect ignition timing, faulty fuel pump operation (engine starved for fuel), improper choke action, spark plugs improperly gapped or burned electrodes, and/or carbon deposits on the plugs; carburetor float level low, EGR valve malfunctioning, faulty carburetor accelerator pump action, improper carburetor feedback operation, weak ignition coil, clogged air cleaner, clogged muffler, clogged fuel filter, cracked distributor cap or rotor, distributor advance unit not functioning correctly, and a possible vacuum leak in some of the hoses or connections.

Engine Cuts Out

The engine has a significant or total loss of power at irregular intervals. It may occur repeatedly or intermittently and is usually worse under heavy acceleration.

Check for loose wires in the ignition system. Bare or shorted wires may also result in this condition. Check the volume of fuel from the fuel pump. Heavy deposits on the spark plugs, or faulty plugs, may cause the engine to cut out. Check the fuel lines for leaks. Foreign matter in the carburetor may cause the engine to cut out. Check the fuel filter. Check the fuel lines for leaks. Check for a clogged muffler which may cause the engine to stop running. A worn distributor shaft also may cause engine failure.

Poor Gasoline Mileage

Poor gasoline mileage may result from numerous conditions, including driving habits such as racing the engine, using the brakes too much, jack rabbit starts, etc. It is generally advisable, when the complaint is excessive fuel consumption, to start with a complete tune-up if the engine has not been tuned for some time. Numerous conditions can all contribute to excessive fuel consumption.

Excessive fuel consumption may be the result of a clogged air cleaner, or the damper door in the air cleaner snorkel not working properly. Spark plugs not properly gapped or glazed, dirty or burned will result in excess fuel consumption. Leaking secondary wires and/or leaking vacuum hoses cause additional fuel usage. Ignition timing and the ignition timing advance system operation affect fuel economy. If the carburetor float level is too high, and there is carburetor fuel leakage, or if the choke hangs up, more fuel than normal will be used.

Hard Starting

Hard starting, either hot or cold, may be the result of the driver not using the proper procedure for starting, such as "pumping" the accelerator too much, or not opening the accelerator enough on a cold engine. A general deterioration may result in the engine being hard to start. A complete tune-up will often correct the problem.

Check the fuel system to make sure fuel is present if the engine has not been run for a period of time. In the case of the hot engine, the fuel may have evaporated from the carburetor bowl. Check the ignition system, including the condition of the spark plugs, as well as the ignition timing and the condition of both the primary and secondary wires. Make sure the engine is cranked at the proper speed and the battery is fully charged. Vacuum leaks, as well as poor and/or uneven compression, result in hard starting. Improper choke setting and operation has a bearing on starting.

It can readily be seen that a relationship exists between the various performance troubles. There are many common components that may have a bearing on the problem, such as spark plugs, carburetor adjustments, fuel filter, air cleaner, EGR valve, PCV valve, timing, etc. If the trouble is pinpointed before servicing, you will know where to look to be sure the problem is corrected.

It is always a good idea to drive the vehicle before servicing, so as to identify the trouble yourself, rather than depending upon a complaint described by someone else. It also aids in determining whether the problem has been satisfactorily corrected after servicing.

Lighting Systems and Electrical–Electronic Accessories

In addition to the different lighting systems, numerous electrical-electronic accessories are used throughout the automobile. Some are essential for operation of the vehicle, such as lights, horn, windshield wipers, etc., while others such as cruise control, radio, air conditioning, power windows, power locks, power seat adjusters, are nice, but not classified as necessary for the safe operation of the vehicle.

As with other electrical components, accessories for the most part depend on electricity for their operation. Although there is a difference in the operating performance of the various units, many similarities exist. There must be a complete electrical circuit in order for the electrical units to operate. There must be some type of switching device to control the unit. Many of the operating units include some type of electric motor which drives a mechanical linkage. Examples could include the windshield wiper motor, the various air movers in the air conditioning and/or heating system, power windows, power seats, and rear window defogger. Some accessories will rely on vacuum for their operation, while others may use a combination of vacuum and electricity. Vacuum is treated, to some extent, like electricity, in that there must be a closed circuit without loss of vacuum within the system.

For troubleshooting and service, the various components may be categorized by manufacturers into different areas, such as lamps and lighting, instrument panel and gauges, and accessories. No attempt will be made to cover the specifics of the different electrical units. Instead, general information relative to operation and testing will be discussed.

Included in the lamp and lighting system may be the headlights, parking lights, side marker lights, tail lights, license plate light, instrument panel lights, interior lights, stop lights, cornering lights, hazard warning flasher, backup lights, glove box light, trunk light, brake system warning light, as well as other warning lights.

Instrument panel indicators commonly used on many vehicles may include the fuel level indicating system, temperature indicating system, oil pressure warning lamp, and generator indicating system.

Some vehicles are equipped with an electronic instrument cluster, including a tone generator as a warning chime. The electronic instrument cluster replaces the conventional mechanically and/or electrically operated gauges and indicators with an electronic display, plus additional informational units relative to fuel economy, elapsed time, distance yet to travel, etc.

Electrically operated accessories may include the motors and magnetic clutch for the air conditioning and heating system, cruise control unit, cigar lighter, horns, power mirror, electric locks, electric trunk opener, power windows, power seats, windshield wipers and washer, radio, concealed head lamp doors, seat belt buzzer, heated rear glass, clock, sun roof, plus additional accessories found on the different makes and models of vehicles.

There are many common factors involved in the various electrical systems. In every case, for electricity to flow, resulting in the component operating, there must be a complete circuit. Means must be provided for control so the operator can turn the unit "on" and "off," therefore some type of switch must be provided for in the circuit. As a safety factor to prevent component and/or circuit damage, a fuse, fusible link, or circuit breaker is usually inserted in the circuit.

A single-wire system is normally used for each of the operating units; therefore a good ground is essential. Usually, the metal case or base of the operating unit is attached to a metal component, or the engine or vehicle body. To make sure there is a good ground connection, a voltage drop test should be made between the suspected bad ground (case) and the mounting frame. Any voltage reading over 0.1 volts means the ground is bad.

A good ground is mandatory for proper light bulb operation. This is usually provided through the lamp socket-to housing-to vehicle. When plastic parts are used, an added ground wire is necessary. When changing bulbs, always check for corrosion around the base, and clean if necessary.

If a circuit switch is suspected to be malfunctioning, check the particular switch. In an inoperative circuit that uses a switch in series with the load, jump the terminals of the switch. If jumping the terminals powers the circuit, the switch is bad. This test also indicates if there is an open circuit.

In checking for circuit malfunctions, always start with the simple and work toward the more complex. Basically it is an elimination process. If the circuit is open, always check for a blown fuse.

Because of the wide variety of electrical accessories in general use, no attempt will be made to cover specific units. General information is presented which should enable a person to isolate the problem and perform the necessary service to correct the malfunction. Other than circuit repair, it is usually a matter of component replacement.

General information relative to the lighting system, cruise (speed) control system, turn signals, windshield wipers, electric motors, solenoids, radio, and other electrical-electronic units, follows.

Lighting Systems

The lighting system is made up of the various light bulbs and circuits used on the vehicle, with the exception of the indicating lights. In general, the headlight circuit is the main circuit and carries the greatest electrical load.

The headlights are controlled by the light switch generally located on the instrument panel. The switch also controls the parking lights, side marker lights, instrument lights, license plate light, tail light and interior (courtesy) lights. The interior lights are controlled by door switches that turn on when the doors are opened.

The license plate light, tail lights, parking lights and side marker lights operate when the light switch is pulled out to the first detent. Pulling the switch knob all the way out turns on the headlights. The instrument panel lights can be turned on when the switch is in either position. The intensity can be varied by rotating the knob. On most vehicles, the interior lights can be turned on by rotating the knob fully counterclockwise.

The directional signal lights are combined with the parking lights in front and with the stop and tail lights in the rear. The ignition switch must be on for the directional signal lights to operate. A flasher unit used in the circuit controls the operation of the directional signals. The flasher unit is usually located on the fuse panel.

Some vehicles are equipped with cornering lights which operate when the headlights or parking lights are on to provide additional light when turning. They are operated by the directional signal control.

A hazard warning flasher is included in the directional signal circuit. Pushing the hazard warning flasher control switch on will disconnect the directional signal flasher and energize the hazard warning flasher system, regardless of the position of the ignition switch or directional signal control.

Backup lights operate when the ignition switch is on. The backup lights are energized through the neutral-start switch, or a switch on the transmission. Placing the shift lever in reverse turns on the backup lights when the ignition switch is on.

Battery voltage is applied to the headlight switch at all times. The switch may include a self-resetting circuit breaker that opens the circuit if the current draw is too great. When the switch is in headlight position, pulled out as far as it will go, the dimmer switch directs current to either the "LO" beam bulbs or the "HI" beam. Current from the "HI" beam also flows to the high beam indicator. Figure 13-1 shows a typical front light wiring harness. The makeup of the various wiring harnesses will differ with the makes and models of vehicles, depending upon the equipment used and its location.

The headlights are of the sealed beam type; the bulb, lens, and reflector are all one unit. When necessary to replace a bulb assembly, remove the trim ring or bezel from around the lamp assembly. The retaining screws are now accessible. Do not turn or remove the screws that move the headlight assembly. These are used to control the aim of the light. Properly aiming the headlights requires special equipment. Figure 13-2 shows the location of both the horizontal and vertical aiming screws after the bezels have been removed. The bezel does not need to be removed, in most cases, in order to aim the headlamps. This installation is typical for most vehicles.

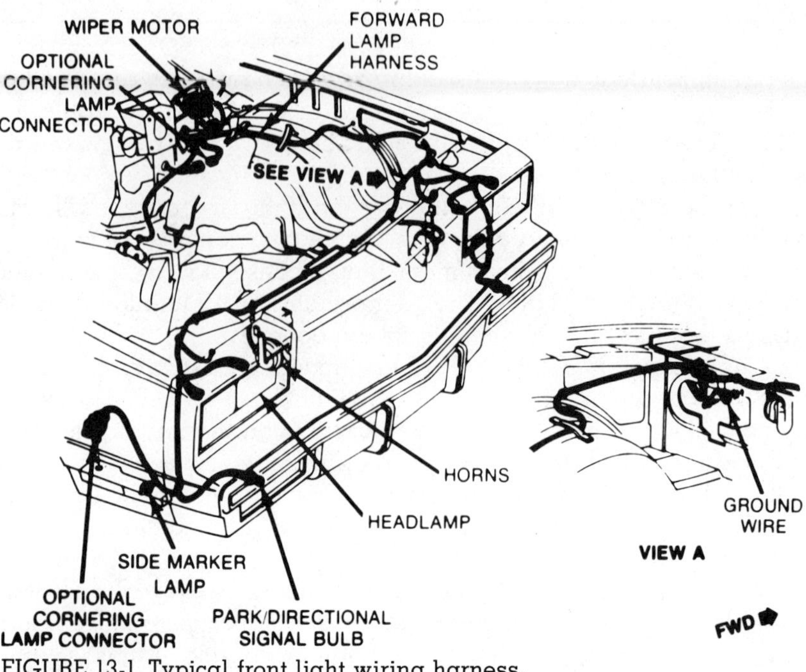

FIGURE 13-1 Typical front light wiring harness. (Courtesy Chevrolet Motor Division, General Motors Corp.)

FIGURE 13-2 Headlamp aiming screws. (Courtesy Oldsmobile Division, General Motors Corp.)

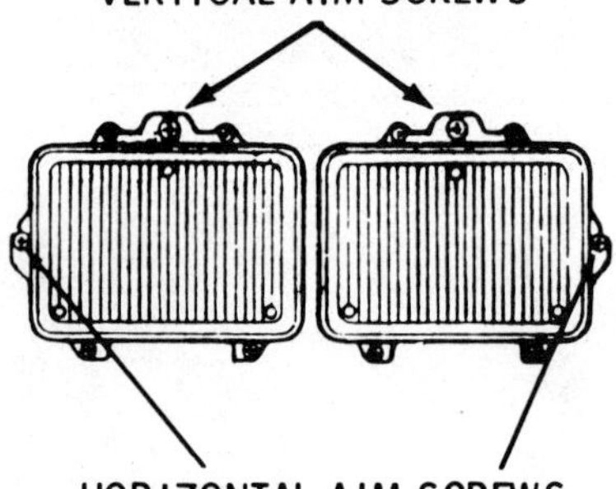

Some vehicles will use a dual headlight system, consisting of four sealed beam lights. The two outboard or upper lights are of the two-filament type for high and low beams. These lights are identified by a number (2) molded into the lens. The two inboard or lower bulbs are marked with a number (1). The bulbs cannot be installed improperly because the mounting lugs for numers (1) and (2) are offset at different angles.

Troubleshooting the Lighting System

Trouble in the lighting circuits may be caused by blown fuses, loose connections, open or shorted wires, burned out bulbs, switch failure, or inadequate ground. In each case, diagnosis requires tracing through the circuit until the source of trouble is located. Figure 13-3 is a wiring diagram of a headlight circuit, including the switch. The wires are color coded, which makes tracing the various circuits much simpler.

If the headlights flash on and off with the switch in the headlight position, it indicates a short circuit. Isolate the circuit by operating the dimmer switch. This will show which circuit is causing the trouble. If both headlights fail to operate in either "HI" or "LO," replace the dimmer switch.

Always check the fuse if one is used in the circuit. When a fuse is blown, check the circuit to determine why it was blown. If a particular bulb does not light, replace it if a good bulb is available, or check to make sure current is reaching the socket by testing the circuit with a voltmeter or 12-volt test lamp. The ground circuit can be checked by making a voltage drop test, or connecting a jumper wire between the light socket and a good ground. If the light now comes on, the ground is bad.

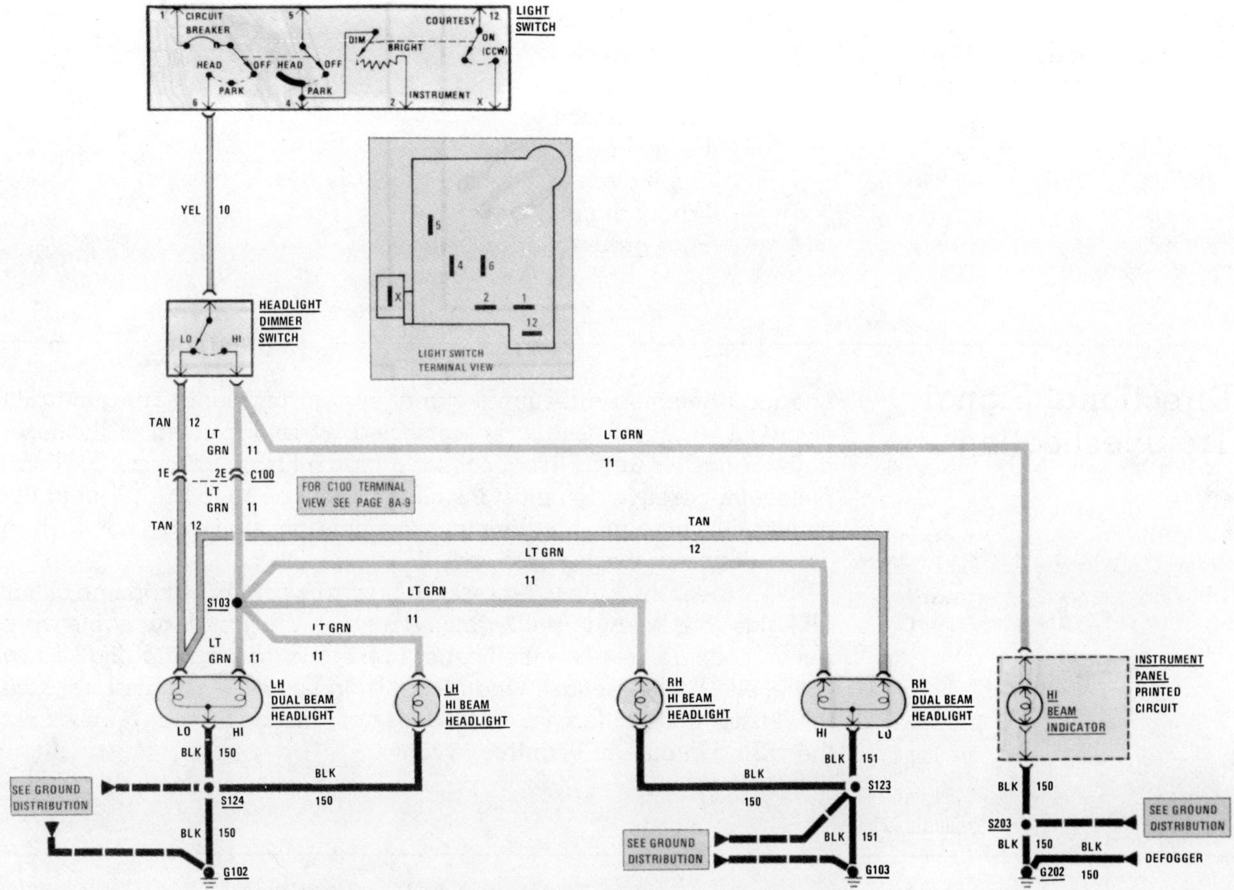

FIGURE 13-3 Headlight wiring diagram. (Courtesy Chevrolet Motor Division, General Motors Corp.)

With the exception of headlights, most bulbs can be replaced by removing the socket from the back of the light housing. When installing new bulbs, always replace with the same number bulb as was removed. Make sure the light socket is clean and free from corrosion.

Following is a list of reasons why the headlights may not function satisfactorily:

Headlights Dim—Engine Off or Idling
- Discharged battery
- Faulty battery
- High resistance in circuit
- Corroded or loose battery terminals
- Burned out bulb or bulbs

Headlights Dim—Engine Running Above Idle
- Faulty bulb or bulbs
- High resistance in circuit
- Faulty voltage regulator

Lights Flicker
- Momentary short circuit
- Loose connections or damaged wires

Light Bulbs Burn Out Frequently
- Loose connection in circuit
- Voltage regulator setting too high

Lights Will Not Come On
- Discharged battery
- Loose connections
- Faulty switch
- Burned out light bulb
- Open circuit
- Faulty dimmer switch
- Poor ground connections

Directional Signal Troubleshooting

The most common directional signal system problems are generally electrical and can usually be corrected by replacement of the fuse, bulb, or flasher unit. First check for a blown fuse if the system is completely inoperative. On most installations, if one bulb burns out in the circuit, the remaining bulbs may not come on, they may not flash at all, or they may flash improperly.

To check the bulbs, depress the hazard warning button and check all lights. Replace the bulb which does not function. If all lights work but do not flash, replace the flasher in the hazard warning. If all bulbs are good but do not flash when the turn indicator is actuated, replace the flasher unit. If the system still does not function correctly, check out the wiring circuit and control switch.

Park-Neutral Switch, Backup Light Switch

All vehicles are equipped with a park-neutral switch or mechanical no-start lockout which prevents the vehicle from being cranked if the transmission is in gear. Many installations will combine the park-neutral switch with a backup light switch. The switches may be mounted on the steering column or on the transmission, and can be adjusted to complete the ignition circuit when the transmission is in park-neutral and to energize the backup light circuit when shifted into reverse. Current is applied through a fuse to the backup lights. When the gear selector lever is shifted to reverse, the switch closes and current flows to the backup lights.

Lamp Monitors

Some vehicles are equipped with a light monitoring system that enables the driver to visually check the operation of the external lights from inside the vehicle. Some monitoring systems do not depend upon electricity for operation. A light conductor, in the form of a fiber optic, transmits light from the individual lights to the responsive monitors. The monitors are usually mounted on the front fenders. Should an individual light fail the monitor will not show light. Figure 13-4 shows a lamp monitor system for park, turn and headlamps. Light travels through the fiber optic from the lamp to the indicator housing on the front fender.

If the monitor fails to indicate a light with the light functioning, check the wiring harness for a disconnected or damaged fiber optic

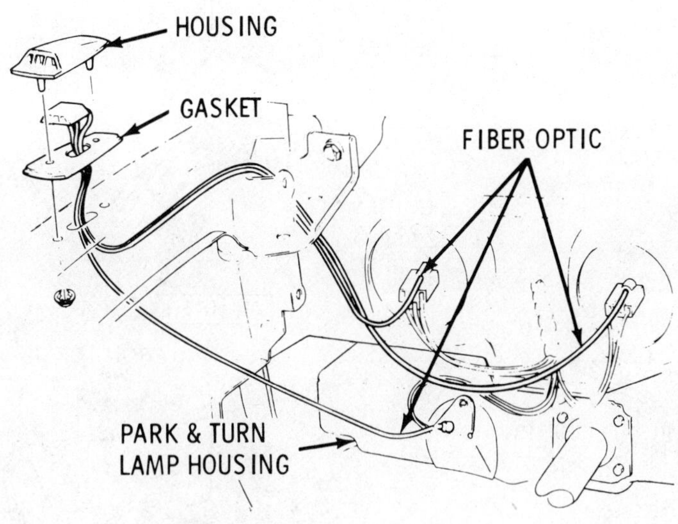

FIGURE 13-4 Fiber optic lamp monitoring system. (Courtesy Oldsmobile Division, General Motors Corp.)

between the monitor and the light. The system monitors the headlights, brake lights, tail lights, parking lights and turn signals.

An electrical lamp-out warning system is used on some vehicles. The system monitors the "LO" beam headlights, tail lights and brake lights. A transistor diode bridge amplifier is inserted in the wiring harness. A resistance wire is used, which senses a change in voltage drop across a special section of the wiring harness should a bulb fail to light. This provides a signal to the external message center, which flashes an outage message to the indicator on the instrument panel when the particular light circuit is turned on.

Optional Lighting Equipment

Included in the different lighting systems may be such equipment as automatic headlight dimmers to provide the operator with automatic switching of the vehicle headlight beams in response to light from an approaching vehicle's headlights. Some vehicles may be equipped with an automatic time delay switch, which results in the lights remaining on for a predetermined period of time after the light switch and ignition switch have been turned off. Another lighting accessory is in the form of a twilight switch to turn the headlights on when darkness occurs and turn them off when it is daylight. Various trade names are used by the different manufacturers.

The major components of the automatic headlight dimmer system include a sensor-amplifier unit, a power relay, a dimmer switch, a driver sensitivity control, and the interconnecting wiring harness. The sensor-amplifier unit combines a light-sensing photocell with a transistorized DC amplifier. This provides power to operate the relay for switching headlight beams.

Because the photocell controls the switching of the headlight beams, the mounting location of the unit is very important. There must be an unobstructed view of approaching vehicle headlights. The same unobstructed view must be present on a vehicle equipped with the twilight sentinel system.

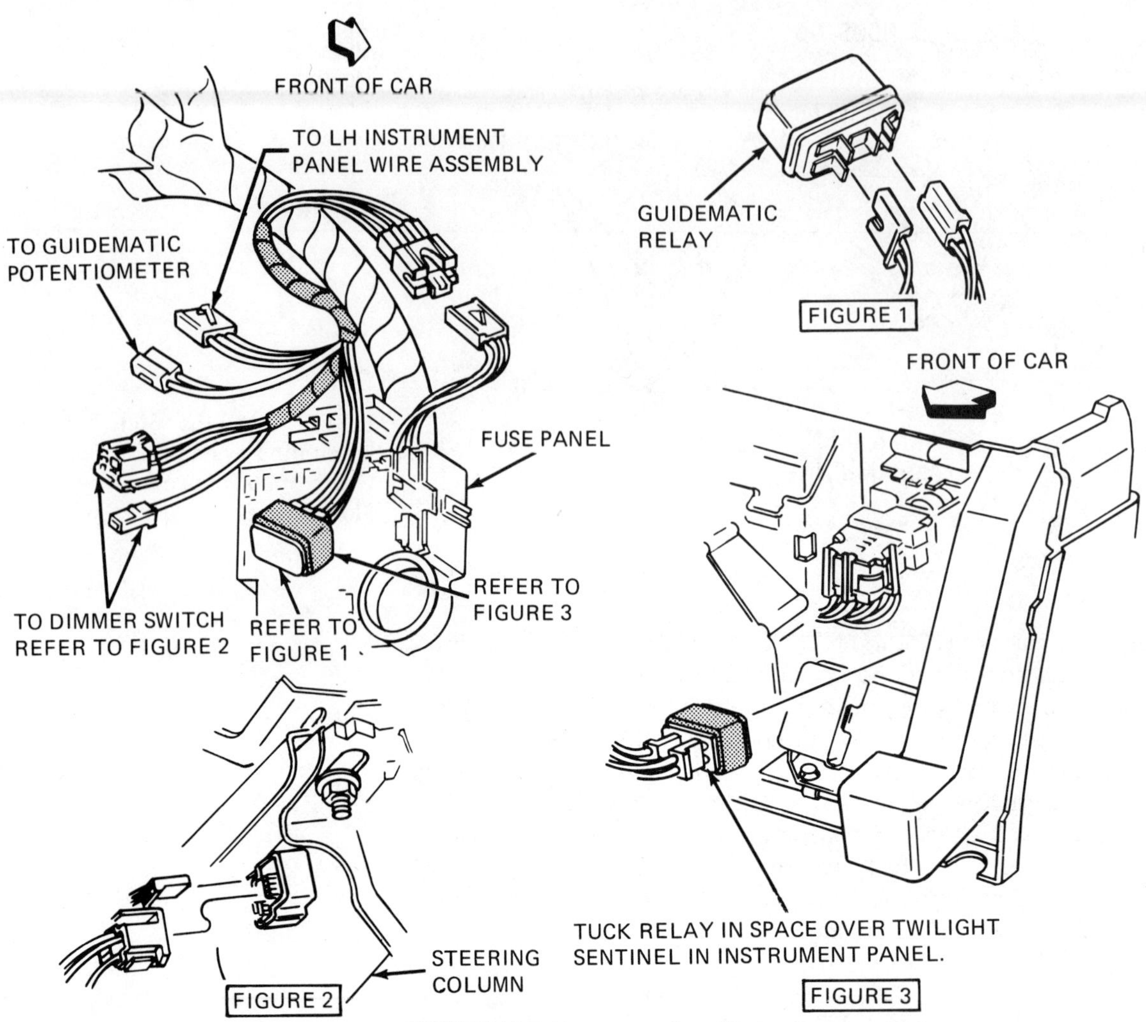

FIGURE 13-5 Automatic headlight dimmer system. (Courtesy Cadillac Motor Car Division, General Motors Corp.)

The sensitivity of either system is adjustable. A driver sensitivity control in the form of a potentiometer is incorporated in the light switch, permitting the driver to control the distance at which dimming will occur. The same applies to the twilight sentinal system. The driver can control the degree of sensitivity needed to switch the lights on or off. Both systems can be switched off and the lighting system operated in a regular manner. The photo-amplifier is a sealed unit and cannot be serviced. Through a process of elimination, if it is found that a problem exists in the photo-amplifier, the complete unit must be removed and replaced. When problems occur in the lighting system, a check of the circuit, including the fuses, light switch, and dimmer switch should be made in the same manner as with a regular lighting system. Figure 13-5 shows the components which make up the (Guide-Matic) headlight dimmer system. This system is available on some General Motors products.

Cruise (Speed) Control System

A number of vehicles are equipped with a cruise (speed) control system. The purpose of the cruise control system is to allow the operator to maintain a constant highway speed without continually applying foot pressure to the accelerator pedal. The system is designed to operate only at speeds above approximately 30 mph (50 km/h).

The cruise (speed) control unit is a system which employs engine manifold vacuum to control a throttle power unit. The power unit moves the throttle when speed adjustment is necessary, by receiving a varying amount of controlled manifold vacuum.

To engage the system the cruise control switch must be in the "on" position and the vehicle speed above 30 mph. On some vehicles, an off-on switch is located on the instrument panel and engagement switch is located at the end of the turn signal lever. Other vehicles will have all of the controls in the turn signal lever located on the steering column.

To engage the system, when the desired speed has been obtained, depress the set button located in the end of the control lever and release the button.

To disengage, normal brake application or a tap on the brake pedal will disengage the unit without erasing the set speed memory. Moving the switch to the "off" position, or turning the ignition switch to "off," will also disengage the system and in addition, erase the speed memory. To return to "cruise" after braking, momentarily move the slide switch toward "resume." The vehicle speed will then return to the preset speed.

To increase the speed setting, depress the accelerator pedal to the desired speed and momentarily push in and release the set button. On some installations, slide the resume button down until the desired increase in speed is obtained, then release the button.

The cruise (speed) control system most commonly used is composed of the operator's controls, a servo (throttle actuator) assembly, a speed sensor (transducer), a vacuum dump valve, and an amplifier assembly, along with the necessary electrical wires and vacuum hoses. Figure 13-6 is an illustration which shows the components which make up a typical electronic cruise control system.

Terminology may vary with the different makes of vehicles, but generally, the same basic units are used. The vacuum dump valve provides an additional safety feature. When the brake pedal is de-

FIGURE 13-6 Electronic cruise control system. (Courtesy American Motors Corporation)

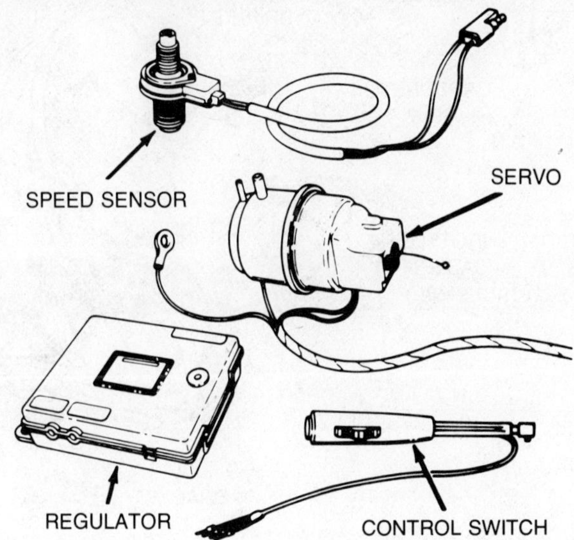

pressed, an electrical signal from the stop light circuit to the amplifier will turn off the system. In addition, the vacuum dump valve will mechanically release the vacuum in the servo unit when the brake pedal is depressed. This releases the throttle independently of the amplifier control. The servo assembly, or power unit, as it is labeled in some cases, may include the transducer (sensor) device in the assembly. It is mounted in the engine compartment and connected to the throttle linkage with an actuator cable or bead chain. The servo assembly moves the throttle linkage according to the amount of engine vacuum applied to the servo assembly diaphragm.

All cruise control systems basically operate on the same principle, the major difference being in the manner in which vehicle speed information is transmitted to the control unit. Some vehicles use an electronic cruise control system, while other vehicles depend upon the speedometer cable from the transmission to drive the transducer, and an additional cable from the transducer to drive the instrument panel speedometer.

In the case of the electro-mechanical operated cruise control system, vehicle speed information is transmitted to the servo (transducer) assembly by means of a mechanically driven cable from the transmission. The throttle is actuated according to the amount of vacuum applied to the diaphragm in the servo assembly. A solenoid in the servo unit controls the amount of vacuum applied to the diaphragm. The position of the shuttle-type solenoid valve which regulates vacuum depends upon the information received from the control on the control lever and the speed at which the cable is revolving. Figure 13-7 shows an electro-mechanical speed (cruise) control system. The speedometer

FIGURE 13-7 Electro-mechanical speed (cruise) control system. (Courtesy Chrysler Corporation)

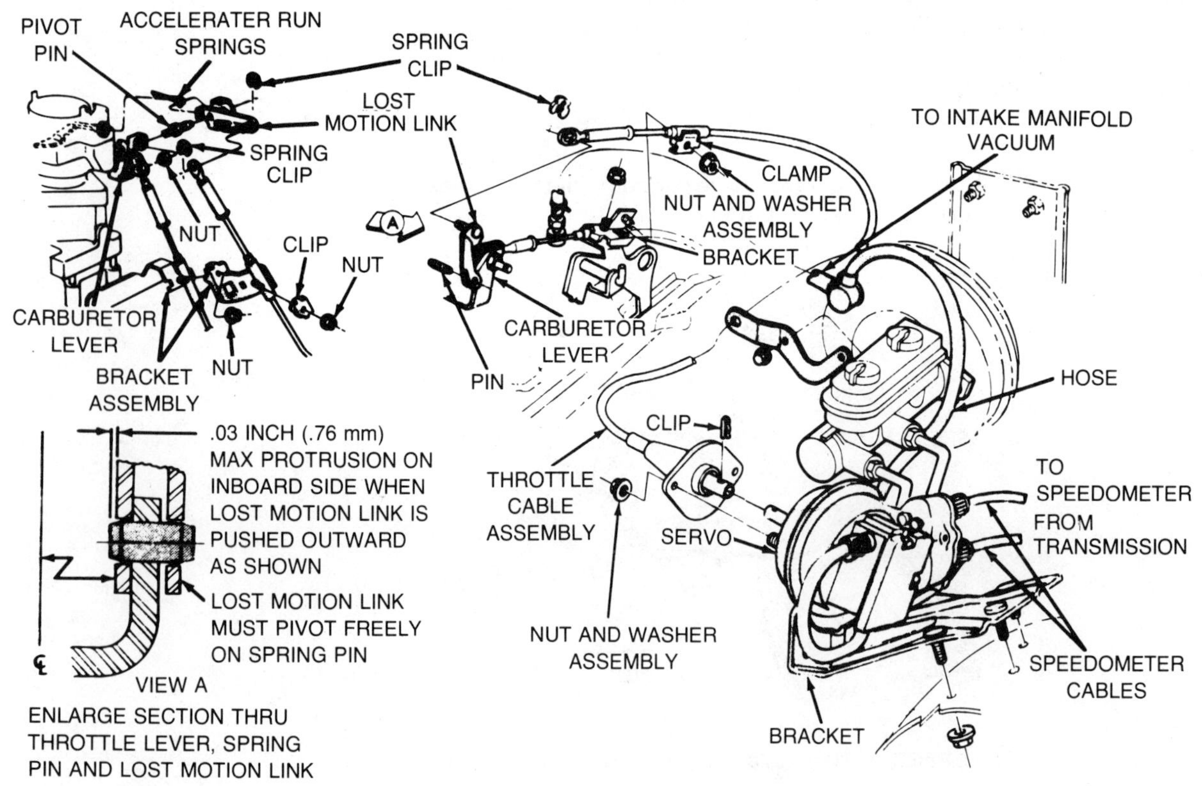

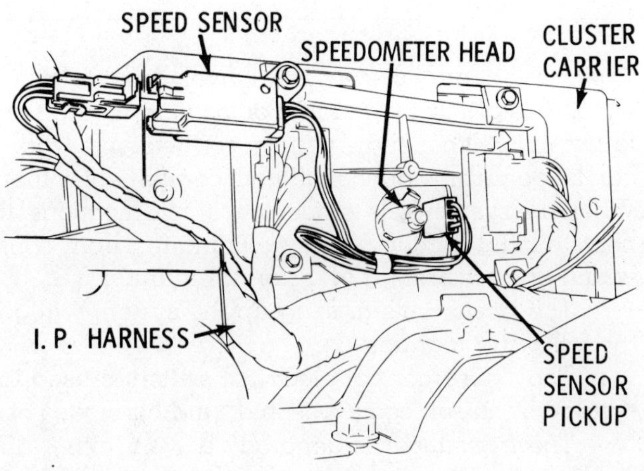

FIGURE 13-8 Speed sensor. (Courtesy Oldsmobile Division, General Motors Corp.)

cable transmits vehicle speed to the servo unit of the speed control.

Some vehicles with a cruise control system are equipped with an electronic instrument cluster and depend upon a speed signal generated by an electronic speedometer assembly. The speed signal current is applied as an input signal to the speed control amplifier which acts as the control signal to regulate the servo unit. This takes the place of the two-piece speedometer cable. Figure 13-8 shows the speed sensor located by the speedometer head. The speed sensor is a generator driven by the speedometer cable. The electricity produced by the sensor, which varies with vehicle speed, is used as a control signal to regulate the cruise control servo unit.

Another electronic cruise control system utilizes a speed sensor, consisting of a light-emitting diode and photo transistor. The photo transistor generates an electrical signal for the electronic controller when exposed to light from the light-emitting diode. Power is supplied to the diode when the cruise control system is on. Signals representative of vehicle speed are sensed by the photo transistor, which is activated by reflected light from each passing bar on the rotating speedometer speed cup drive magnet. The surface of the drive magnet is highly reflective to enhance the reflection of light to the photo transistor. Both the light-emitting diode and photo transistor are enclosed as one unit that attaches to the back of the speedometer cluster adjacent to the speedometer cable. The unit cannot be serviced. A wiring harness connects the speed sensor to the electronic controller. Input signals received from the sensor by the electronic controller are used to control the power unit solenoid valve which regulates the amount of vacuum supplied to the power unit in order to control the speed of the vehicle.

In addition to the two electronic cruise control systems just described, another system uses a speed sensor, driven by the speedometer cable, which is basically a tach-generator that functions as the source of current for the vehicle speed analog voltage. This voltage is applied to the amplifier when the system is in operation.

There are some "add-on" cruise control systems which use a speed sensor in the form of magnets fastened to the propeller shaft with a pickup coil attached to the underside of the vehicle body, close to the magnets. This supplies an electric current to the amplifier, according to vehicle speed. The amplified current is sent to the servo unit, which regulates the vehicle speed.

Troubleshooting the Cruise Control

The cruise control system is relatively trouble-free. When failure does occur, it is primarily a matter of locating the trouble and replacing the faulty unit. Other than wiring, connections, and hoses, little service can be performed on the different components other than replacement. When the system fails to operate, or malfunctions, the different components should be checked by eliminating from consideration the units which are performing in a normal manner.

The basic units making up the system will generally function in the following manner:

The cruise control electrical switch is used to control the cruise system in the set, coast, resume, and off modes of operation.

The transducer is generally driven, either directly or indirectly, by the speedometer cable. It is the speed sensing device and control unit. It senses vehicle speed and positions the servo unit to maintain the selected speed. It also performs the resume function in conjunction with the external resume control unit. The servo unit opens and closes the throttle as dictated by the transducer. The transducer and servo unit, on many installations, are incorporated into one unit.

The brake release switch disengages the system electrically when the brake pedal is depressed. In addition, the vacuum cruise brake release valve disengages the system pneumatically when the brake pedal is depressed.

Always make a visual inspection for such things as a blown fuse, bare, broken or disconnected wires, and damaged, disconnected or leaking vacuum hoses.

Because the speedometer cable transmits vehicle speed to the servo-transducer unit or speedometer head, it is important that the speedometer cable be routed properly, with no kinks or sharp bends. The system will not function with a broken speedometer cable unless it is an "add-on" system using magnets attached to the propeller shaft. If the speedometer speed indicator is erratic or varies, it indicates a problem with the speedometer cable.

The throttle linkage must operate freely and the actuator cable, or bead chain, must have minimum slack.

If the speed control does not operate, check the fuse, electrical, and vacuum connections. Depress the brake pedal to check brake light operation. If the brake lights do not come on, service the circuit. Check the actuator cable or chain adjustment to make sure there is no slack or tension on the linkage. Check to determine if vacuum is reaching the servo unit.

If the speed changes up and down, check the actuator cable, or bead chain, for adjustment. Check the speedometer cable for free operation. Any cable binding will show as erratic speedometer operation.

If the speed control does not resume, check the resume switch and circuit. Check servo operation and the amplifier circuit.

If the speed control does not disengage when the brakes are applied, check the stop light circuit, the vacuum dump valve, the servo action, and the amplifier circuit.

If the speed does not set, check the actuator cable for action. There should be tension on the cable, but no slack.

If the speed gradually increases or decreases, check the accelerator linkage for binding or excessive free play. Check the actuator linkage for adjustment.

PRELIMINARY CHECKS

1. Check Servo Chainor rod adjustment. Must have minimum slack.
2. Check vacuum hoses. Must be in good condition - no restrictions or leaks.
3. Check drive cable routings. No kinks or sharp bends.
4. Check throttle linkage or cable for binding.
5. Check adjustment of brake release switch and vacuum release valve.
6. Check engagement switch operation.
7. If steps 1 through 6 do not solve the problem, continue with diagnosis.

1. Check*gages fuse. If blown check wiring for short circuit and repair. A shorted resume solenoid diode could also cause blown fuse.
2. If fuse and preliminary checks ok, resume solenoid must be checked. Start engine and check source vacuum at resume solenoid (refer to picture at right). Disconnect two wire connector at resume solenoid. Use jumper wire to ground terminal which had black wire connected to it. Apply 12 volts to terminal which had gry/blk wire connected to it. Disconnect outlet vacuum hose (going to B fitting on transducer). Vacuum should be present. If not, replace resume solenoid. Applying voltage incorrectly to resume solenoid could damage diode. If above checks ok stop engine and reconnect electrical and vacuum connections.
3. To make test below turn ignition to run position and off/on/resume switch to on. Disconnect 2 wire connector at transducer (Engage-Hold Terminals).
4. Connect 12 volt test light to ground and to engage wire in connector. Push engage/coast button in all the way and slowly release.
5. Repeat test on hold wire in connector.

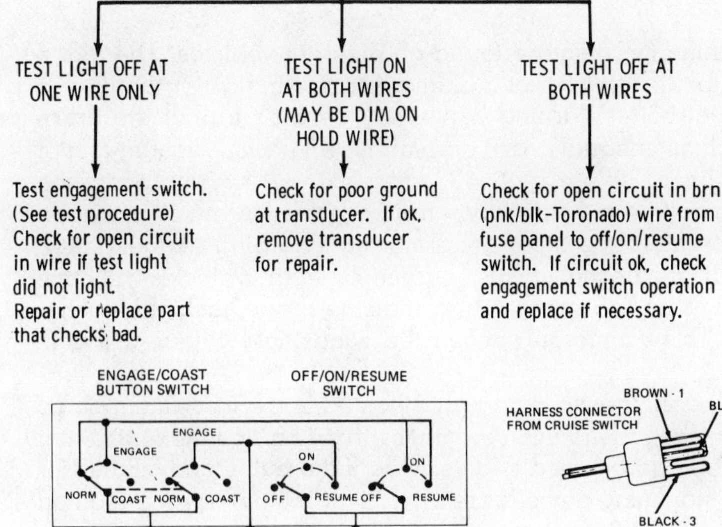

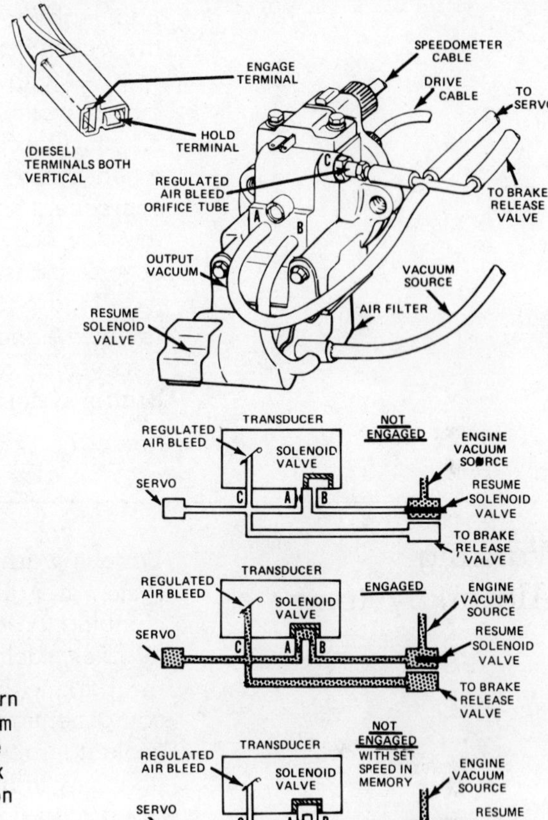

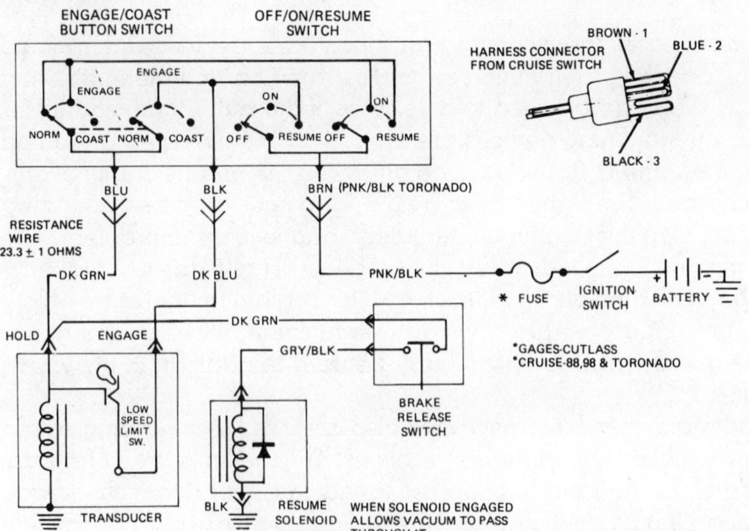

ENGAGEMENT SWITCH TEST PROCEDURE

USE AS SELF-POWERED TEST LIGHT. LIGHT WILL BE ON FOR EACH TEST IF SWITCH IS GOOD. CONNECTOR TERMINALS AND COLOR 1 – BROWN, 2 – BLUE, 3 – BLACK.

SWITCH POSITIONS		TERMINALS		
ENGAGE BUTTON	RESUME SWITCH	1 to 2	1 to 3	2 to 3
Released	on	closed	open	open
Fully Depressed	on	open	open	closed
Partially Released	on	closed	closed	closed
Released	resume	closed	closed	closed
Released	off	open	open	open

Figure 13-9 Electronic cruise control system diagnosis. (Courtesy Oldsmobile Division, General Motors Corp.)

If the vehicle surges, check speedometer cable operation, making sure there is no binding. Be sure the throttle and/or throttle linkage is not binding.

If there is excessive speed downhill, a weak throttle return spring may be the cause of the problem. A plugged transducer filter also can cause this problem if the vehicle is thus equipped.

If the vehicle cruises under or over the set speed, check for vacuum leaks in the system. Adjust the orifice tube, if so equipped, or set the lock-in screw to obtain a steady operating speed.

As with any electrical system, always check for a complete circuit. A voltmeter or test light can be used to check for a complete circuit. Check to make sure the switches are completing the circuit when turned on. This can be done by bypassing the switch. Each component has a specific resistance and/or voltage value. These readings are easy to obtain, but must be checked against manufacturer's specifications.

Figure 13-9 is a cruise control diagnosis diagram. This specifically refers to General Motors vehicles relative to wire colors, etc. However, it serves as a guide for troubleshooting almost any electronic cruise control system.

Warning (Alarm) Systems

Various warning systems are found on different vehicles. The alarm system may be in the form of a chime, buzzer, indicating light, or a combination of both. Warning lights may be used to indicate brake troubles, such as unequal brake pressure; low booster vacuum and/or the parking brake being applied. Malfunctions in engine operating components may be indicated by warning lights for low oil pressure, coolant temperature too high, generator not charging. A fuel gauge light may indicate the fuel tank is near empty. Some vehicles will have a warning light which comes on to indicate the windshield washer fluid is low. This occurs only when the windshield wipers are activated.

In most cases the warning lights located in the instrument panel will come on when the ignition switch is turned on and the engine not operating. This can be used to determine if the bulbs and circuits for the different indicating devices are operational. If the lights are all on before the engine is started and go out when the engine starts, everything is normal. If a light fails to go out, or comes on when operating the engine, stop the engine immediately, and locate the problem. The trouble may be in the indicating circuit, but is usually due to a malfunction in the unit being checked, such as high coolant temperature or low oil pressure. Figure 13-10 shows a three-function chime warning system. The audio warning system may be used in addition to the warning light.

Audio alarm warning systems also are used to a varying extent on different makes and models of vehicles. The system may include an audio alarm in the form of a buzzer to indicate that either the headlights or parking lights are on and the ignition switch is off. The current is generally supplied through the courtesy fuse; therefore check the fuse if the system fails to operate. Some vehicles may use a warning chime that sounds when opening the driver's door with the headlights on. The chime continues to operate until the door is closed or the lights are turned off.

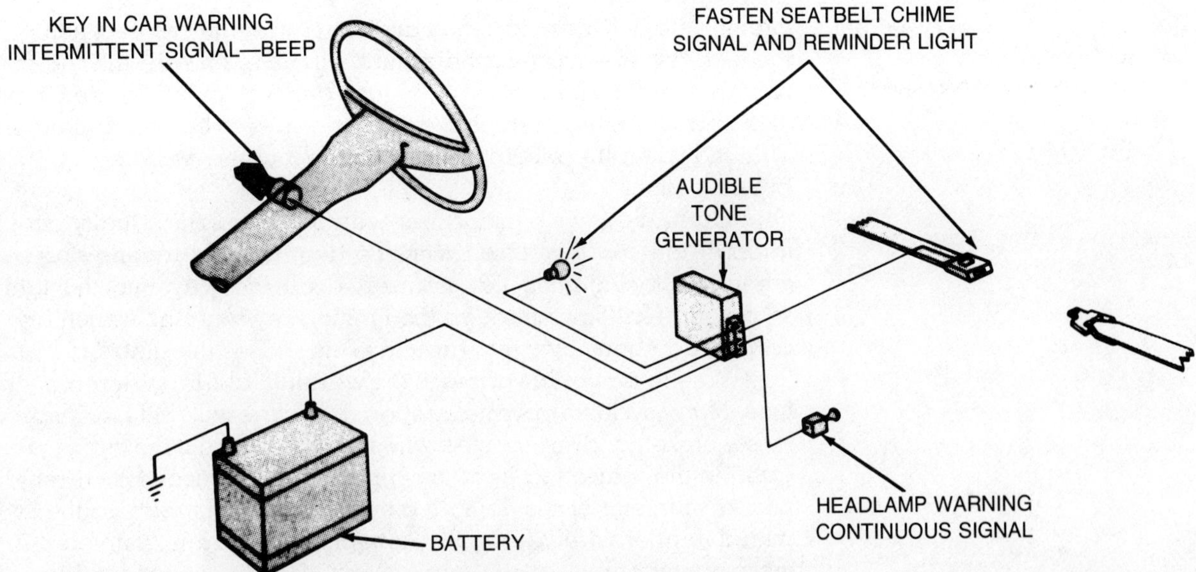

FIGURE 13-10 Three-function chime warning system. (Courtesy Chrysler Corporation)

A seat belt timer warning buzzer and "fasten belts" indicator light are standard equipment on most vehicles. When the driver's seat belt is not buckled, current flows through the audio alarm assembly and seat belt switch to ground, and through the "fasten belts" indicator light, to ground. Included in the circuit is a timing device which opens the

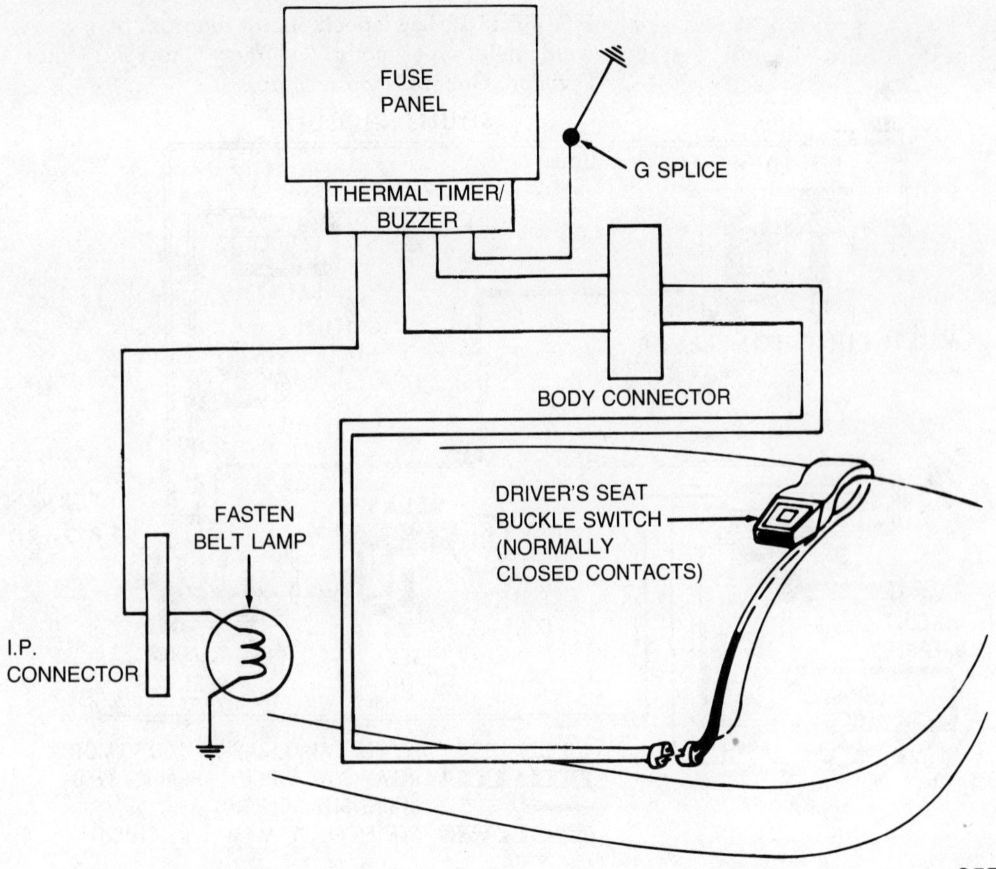

FIGURE 13-11 Seat belt warning system. (Courtesy American Motors Corporation)

circuit if the belt is not fastened after approximately six seconds. When the seat belt is engaged, the ground circuit is broken and the buzzer shuts off, and the light goes out. A tone generator may be used in place of a buzzer. Figure 13-11 is a drawing of a seat belt warning system. This indicates the electrical flow to the buzzer, warning lamp and buckle switch.

Current for the ignition key warning buzzer is usually supplied through the courtesy fuse. With the door on the driver's side open, whenever the ignition key is inserted all the way into the ignition switch, current flows through the ignition key warning switch and the driver's door jam switch to ground. This causes the alarm to sound.

Whenever trouble arises in the warning (alarm) system, check the fuse. Many systems operate through the courtesy light fuse. Inspect for loose, broken or disconnected wires. To determine if the circuit is energized to the indicating light, try a new bulb or check for current flow with a voltmeter or test light. If a switch is suspect, bypass the switch with a jumper wire. Generally, few problems are encountered in the warning system.

Windshield Wipers

Windshield wipers are electrically operated and are usually of the two-speed type. However, some vehicles may use a three-speed type and/or have an intermittent function for use during conditions of very light precipitation. With most installations, the electric washer system is used in conjunction with the wiper system.

Basically, the windshield wiper system consists of an electric

FIGURE 13-12 Low-speed circuit diagram of a windshield wiper motor. (Courtesy Chevrolet Motor Division, General Motors Corp.)

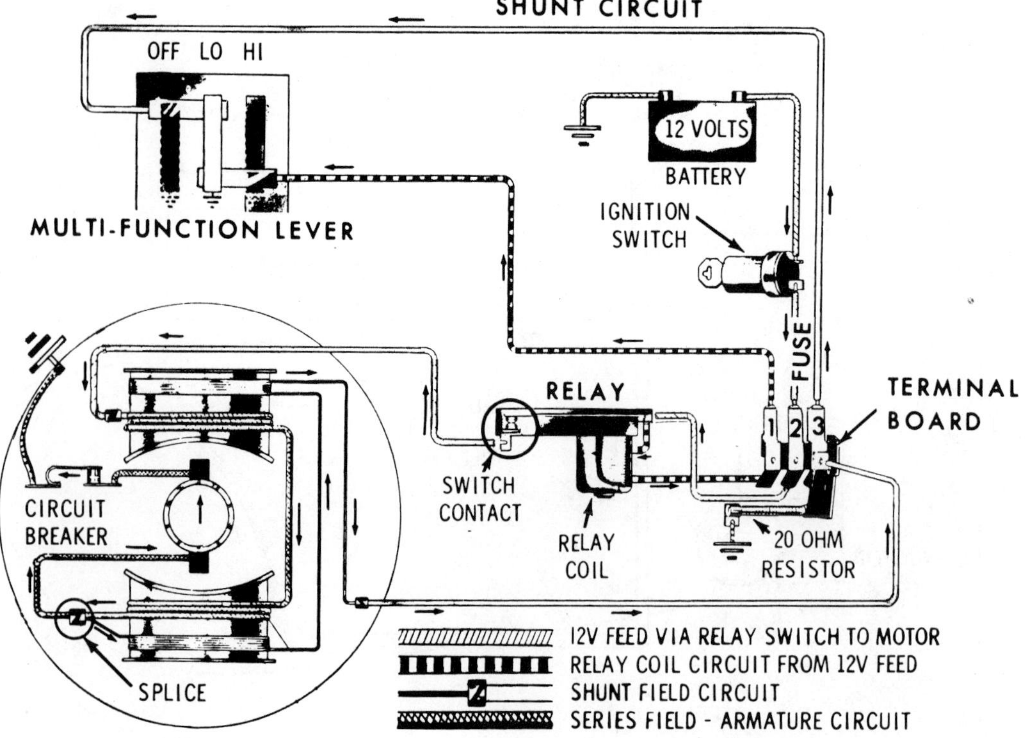

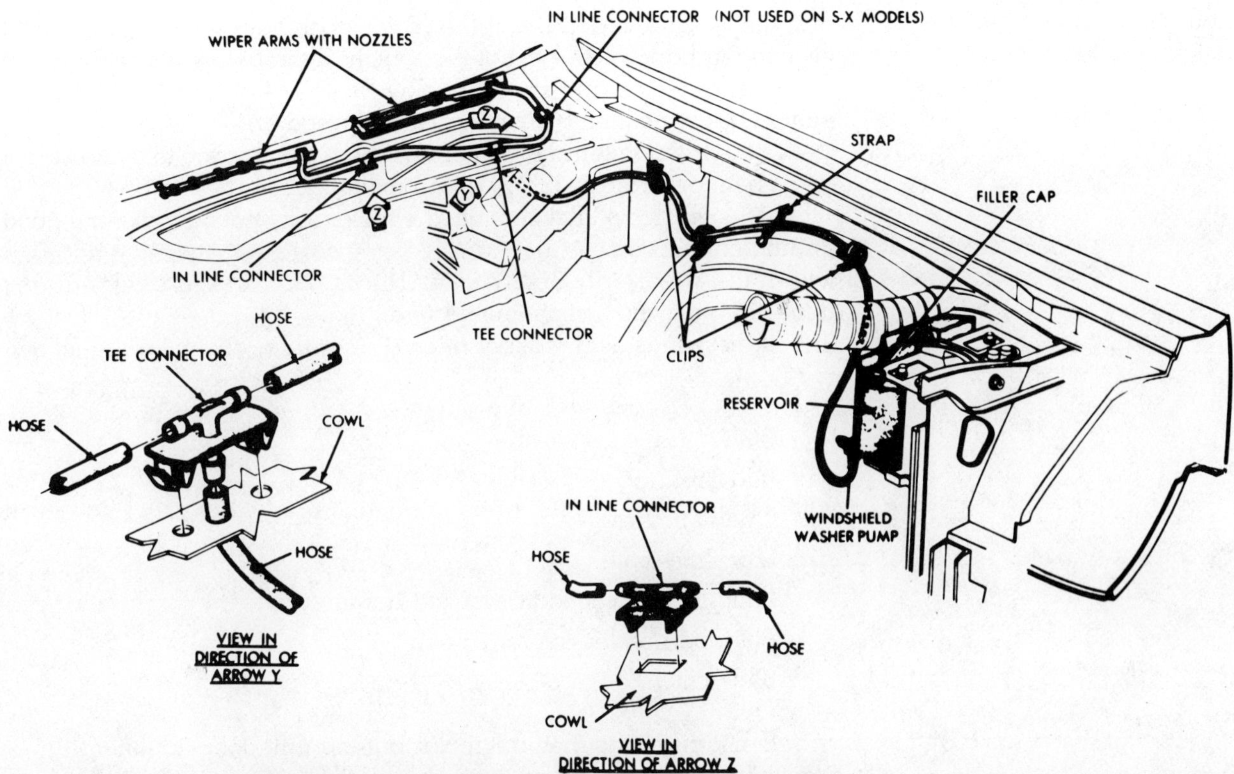

FIGURE 13-13 Windshield washer system. (Courtesy Chrysler Corporation)

motor which drives a reduction gear box. A control switch turns the wiper motor on and off and controls the wiper speed. Included in the control circuit is a park switch which returns wiper arms to a predetermined park position when the wiper motor is turned off. The speed of the wiper motor is determined by current flow to the appropriate set of brushes. The wipers can only be operated when the ignition switch is in accessory or ignition position. Figure 13-12 is a wiring diagram for a windshield wiper motor and controls. Because the switch is in low speed, a resistor is included in the circuit.

The windshield washer unit consists of a motor, separate from the wiper motor, and a pump assembly. The unit is usually located in the bottom of the washer solution jar. A multifunction switch turns both the washer and wiper motor on when the washer switch is activated. Figure 13-13 shows a windshield washer system. On this particular installation, the washer reservoir is part of the battery heat shield, with the washer pump located in the bottom of the reservoir.

When the windshield wipers fail to operate, check for a blown fuse or a damaged circuit breaker if used in place of a fuse. Check the circuit for loose or disconnected wires. Before condemning the wiper or washer motor, always check to make sure electricity is reaching the motors. This can be done by inserting a voltmeter or a 12-volt test light across the circuit at each motor. If the switch is suspected of being faulty, bypass the switch with a jumper wire. A voltage drop test can be made to determine if the motors are properly grounded. If a motor or switch fails to operate, it is best to replace the unit.

The motor ground can be checked by attaching a jumper wire from the motor ground wire to a known good ground. If the motor now operates, repair the ground circuit. If current is present to the motor and the ground is good, but the motor does not operate, listen for a click in the park relay (part of the switch assembly) when the ignition switch is turned on and off. If the relay clicks, the trouble is in the wiper motor. The windshield wipers must be turned on.

If the motor attempts to operate, check the linkage to make sure it is not bent or damaged. The gear box could also be worn.

If the wiper will not shut off, the motor may not be making a good ground connection.

If the wiper only operates in "HI" or "LO," or the blades do not return to park, the switch is defective.

If the windshield washer does not operate, check for the following:

Blown fuse
Bad ground
Open circuit
Low fluid level
Split, loose, pinched or kinked hoses
Plugged nozzles and/or screen
Bad switch

If electricity reaches the motor but the unit does not operate, replace the motor and pump assembly. If the motor operates the pump but the pump does not develop pressure, replace the pump and motor assembly.

Electric Motors

Numerous electric motors are used throughout the various makes and models of vehicles. The motors are commonly used to power concealed headlight doors, operate the sun roof, operate power seats, power door locks, power windows, power antenna, power tail gate lock, and blower motors for the heating, cooling and defogging systems.

The 12-volt permanent magnet type of reversible motor is most commonly used to power the various accessories. An internal circuit breaker is usually used to protect the circuit, together with a relay assembly to control motor operation. The direction of motor rotation is controlled by a switch and relay which reverses the current flow to change direction of rotation.

The switch, motor and relay assembly normally cannot be repaired. They must be replaced when a malfunction occurs. Figure 13-14 shows a motor used to operate concealed headlights. One motor operates both headlights. It is a reversible type motor.

When a unit fails to operate, always start by checking the fuse and then the circuit. A test light or voltmeter can be used to determine if current is reaching the motor and/or switch. If the switch is suspected of not functioning, use a jumper wire to apply electricity directly from the battery to the motor. If the motor now works, the switch needs to be replaced. Always check to make sure the motor has a good ground. This can be done by connecting a jumper wire between a known good ground and the motor case, or ground wire.

Make sure the mechanical aspects of the system are functioning

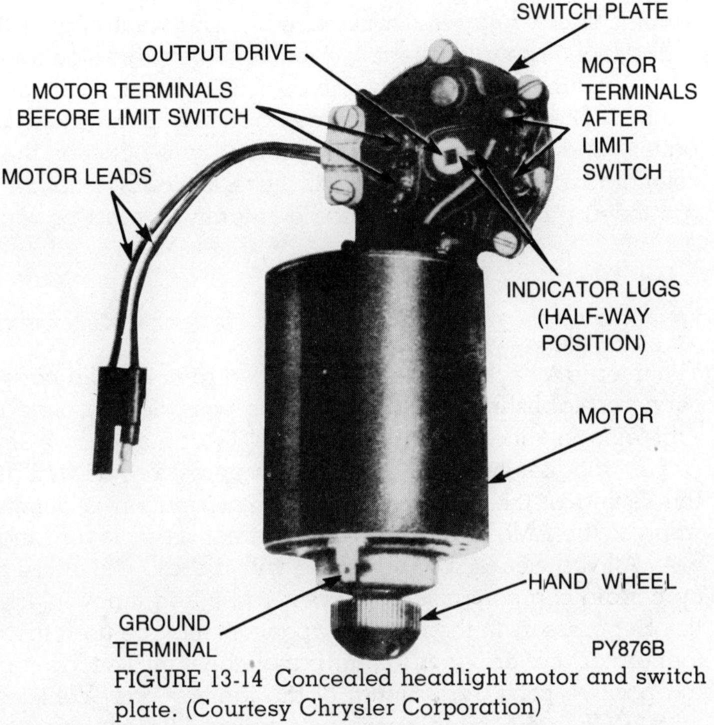

FIGURE 13-14 Concealed headlight motor and switch plate. (Courtesy Chrysler Corporation)

properly; that the glass is not binding in its track, the gear mechanism is functional, or, in the case of power seats, the seat tracks are free and clear so the seat can move freely.

Solenoids

Some vehicles having power locks and/or a power deck lid release, will use solenoids to lock and unlock the door, and in the case of a power deck lid, to release the deck lid latch. Here again, if a malfunction occurs, always check the current flow to the switch and solenoid. Figure 13-15 shows a solenoid used to operate electric door locks and

FIGURE 13-15 Solenoid used in the electric door lock mechanism. (Courtesy Chrysler Corporation)

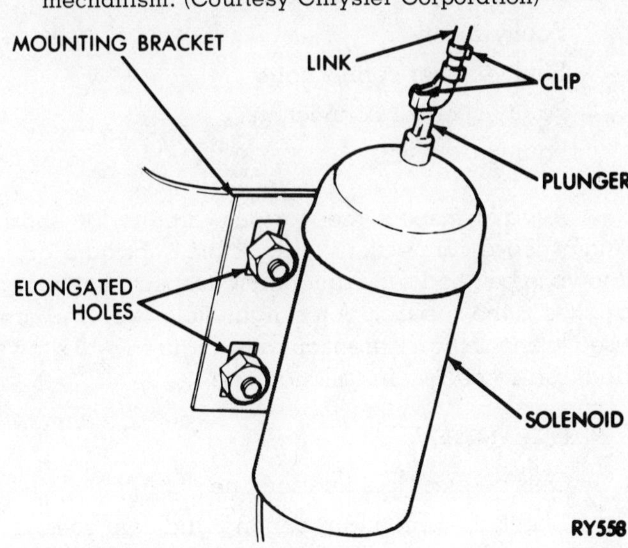

trunk locks. A relay is usually used in conjunction with the solenoid and switch. The alignment is adjustable through elongated holes.

A voltmeter or test light can be used to check if voltage is reaching the unit. The switch can be bypassed with a jumper wire between the battery and solenoid. Connect a jumper wire between the case of the solenoid and a good ground if there is doubt whether the unit is grounded properly. If the solenoid is faulty, it must be replaced.

Radios

The internal checking and servicing of a radio should be left to a radio service establishment. However, it is possible to isolate operational problems in different areas, such as the antenna system, radio receiver, speaker system, radio noise suppression, as well as to change the setting of the push buttons. The information is general and will apply to the AM/FM radio, AM/FM stereo, tape player, and CB radio.

All vehicles factory equipped with a radio will utilize suppressors on certain components to suppress radio frequency interference (static). Suppressors in the form of capacitors may be used in the charging (generator) system, instrument panel constant voltage regulator and the positive primary terminal of the ignition coil. Vehicles equipped with a CB radio may incorporate an additional capacitor in series between the windshield wiper motor and the wiring harness. On vehicles using a 100-ampere generator, a filter choke may be installed in series with the radio power lead. Ground straps are frequently used on the outside of the radio case and antenna to provide for a good ground to the vehicle and between the engine and body. All capacitors and ground straps must be mounted securely on a clean ground surface in order to function properly. All vehicles are equipped with radio resistance type spark plug wires to aid in the suppression of interference from the ignition system.

Following are some simple checks that can be made to isolate problems which might occur in the radio system:

RADIO INOPERATIVE:

Blown fuse
Antenna open or shorted
Faulty receiver
Faulty power connections
Faulty speaker connections
Faulty speaker

Always inspect the various circuits for shorts, broken wires, and/or loose connections. If possible substitute an antenna which is known to be good if the antenna is suspected of being faulty. The same applies to the speaker. A test light, voltmeter and/or ohmmeter can be used to check the different circuits. Figure 13-16 shows a schematic of a dual radio speaker installation.

RADIO NOISE:

Outside electrical interference
Check the antenna mounting and connections

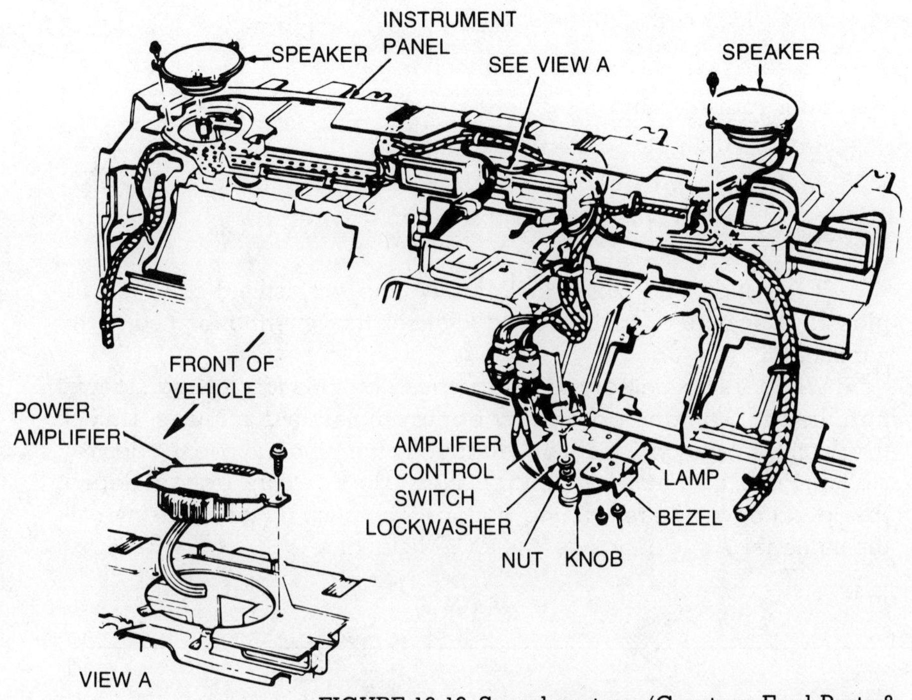

FIGURE 13-16 Sound system. (Courtesy Ford Parts & Service Division, Ford Motor Co.)

NOISE DOES NOT VARY WITH ENGINE SPEED:

Check electric motors, solenoids and switches as a source of noise

NOISE VARIES WITH ENGINE SPEED:

Insufficient or faulty engine ignition and radio frequency suppression devices

Disconnect the generator to find out if this is the cause of the noise.

Make sure the antenna is secure and the connections are clean and tight.

RADIO RECEPTION WEAK:

Shorted antenna leadin

Faulty radio

Antenna trimmer misadjusted

All radios are trimmed at the factory and should not require further adjustment. However, when a radio is reinstalled after repair, or if everything else checks out, adjust the trimmer in the following manner. The trimmer screw is located on the right side of most radio cases, near the antenna terminal. Manually tune the radio to a weak signal between 1400 and 1600 AM. Increase the volume and set the tone control to treble. Adjust the trimmer by carefully turning the screw back and forth until a point is found that produces the greatest volume and best reception.

RADIO RECEPTION DISTORTED:

Faulty speaker

Faulty radio

INTERMITTENT RECEPTION:

Loose power or antenna connection
Poor radio ground
Broken or shorted antenna leadin wire
Faulty speaker
Faulty radio

If a windshield antenna is faulty, the windshield must be replaced. A special tester is needed to check the antenna located in the windshield.

When it is necessary to set the push buttons for desired stations turn the radio on and operate for approximately five minutes. Unlock the push button by pulling it out. Manually tune the radio to the desired station. Push the button back into position to lock onto the station. Repeat the operation for the remaining stations. The push button adjustment is the same for AM stations as it is for FM stations.

Power Mirrors

Some vehicles may be equipped with outside power mirrors. The mirrors are operated by servo motors which both rotate and tilt the mirrors. The control switch is located in the driver's door arm rest. The motors, two for each mirror are part of the mirror head assembly and cannot be serviced. If problems occur always check the control circuit to make sure electricity is reaching the mirror motors. Figure 13-17 is the circuitry for power remote mirrors, including switches and motors.

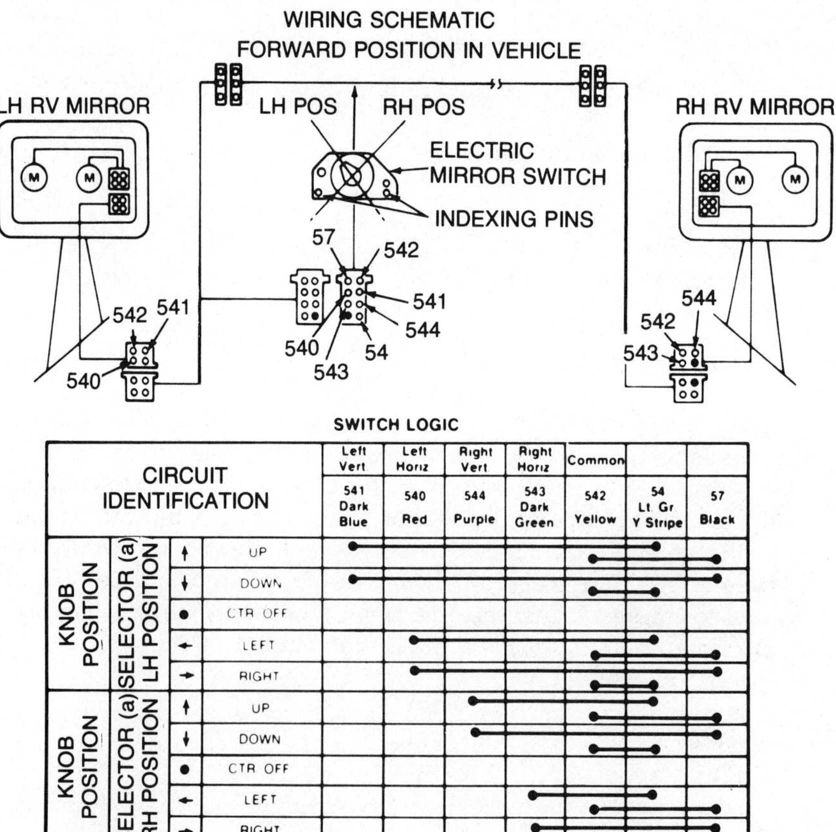

FIGURE 13-17 Power remote mirrors. (Courtesy Ford Parts & Service Division, Ford Motor Co.)

Electronic Instrument Cluster

The electronic instrument cluster is used as standard equipment in place of the conventional electro-mechanical gauge system on some vehicles, and is available on certain other vehicles. There is variation in the specific information presented by the different systems, but the information will generally relate to fuel consumption, travel distance and elapsed time, plus a warning system for vehicle components such as low oil pressure, high engine coolant temperature, and low brake pressure. The audio warning system arrangement may include an electronic tone generator.

The electronic instrument cluster permits the driver to monitor vehicle functions and obtain useful travel information at the touch of a button. The system is designed to operate without operator supplied information. A message center keyboard permits the operator to call upon the system for information that is helpful relative to time, speed and economy. A check out system gives the driver information relative to present operating conditions.

From nine to twelve push buttons may be used, depending on the particular design, to call up information from the microprocessor. Additional buttons may be used to set the clock and change the date. On some systems it is possible to convert from the standard U.S. reading to the metric system and vice versa by simply pressing a button. Figure 13-18 pictures an electronic instrument panel. Push buttons are used to call up certain types of information which is computed by the system.

FIGURE 13-18 Electronic instrument panel. (Courtesy Chrysler Corporation)

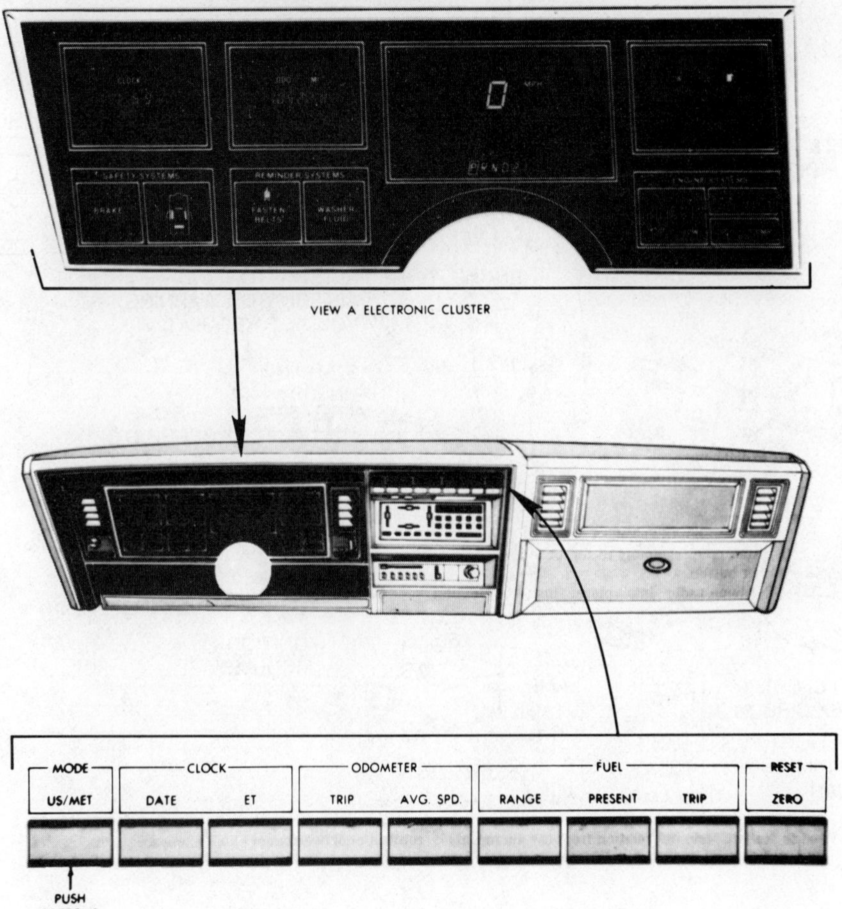

The system used on some vehicles includes a digital readout electronic speedometer, a bar graph readout electronic fuel gauge, together with a digital electronic message center.

The information to be displayed is selected from a push button on the center keyboard and is shown on the instrument panel. The display is updated every 45 seconds. Figure 13-19 shows the components and wiring circuits of an electronic instrument cluster.

Most of the electronic fuel gauges show the remaining fuel on a bar graph. The gauge processes the signal from the fuel level sensor through a microprocessor which counts, scales, digitally filters, and displays the result. The microprocessor also provides a buffered signal to actuate a low-fuel warning light.

The message center displays the time of day when the ignition switch is on.

FIGURE 13-19 Electronic instrument cluster system. (Courtesy Ford Parts & Service Division, Ford Motor Co.)

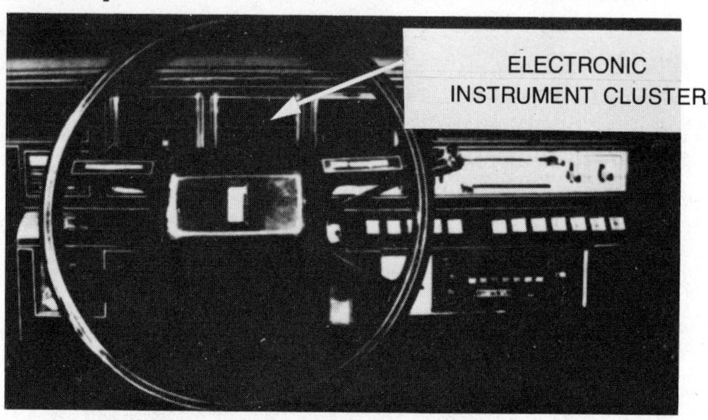

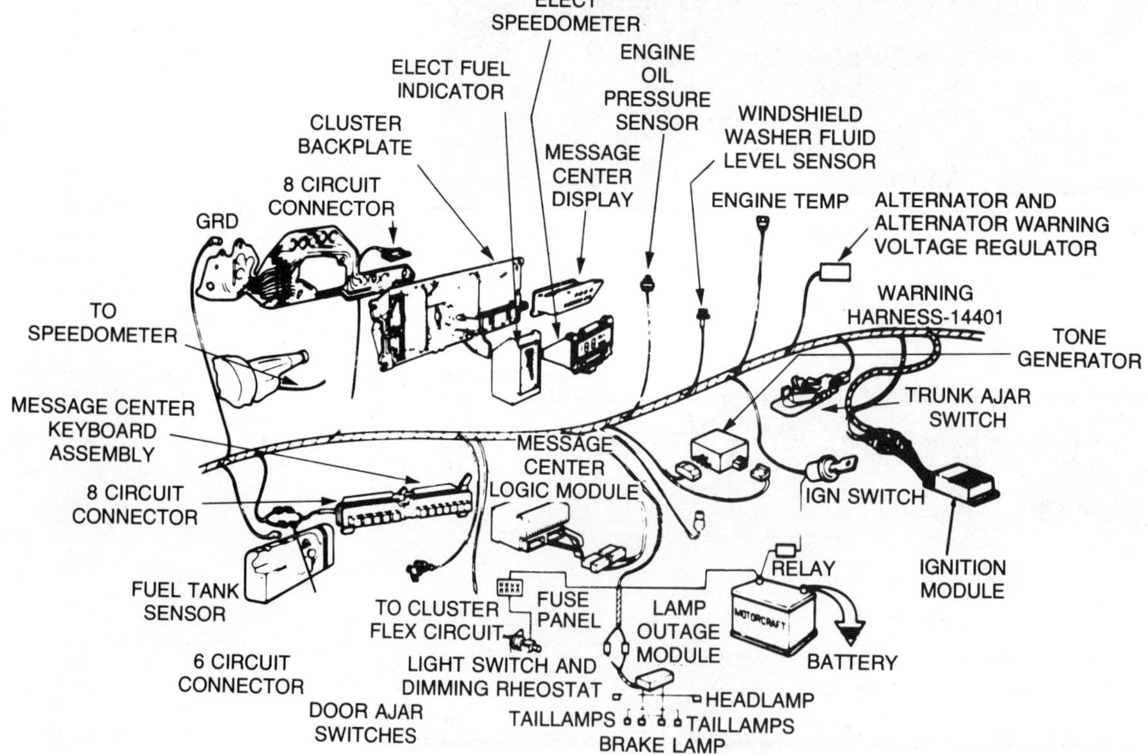

A system monitor in the message center, on some vehicles, functions when a message is required as determined by the different sensors used throughout the vehicle. The system checkout is activated when the engine is running, the headlights are on, and the brake pedal is depressed with the "checkout" button depressed. If no signal is received, the system is assumed to be in operating condition.

The warning messages may include brake pressure low, washer fluid low, trunk ajar, headlight out, tail light out, brake light out, charging system not functioning, oil pressure low, engine temperature too high, and less than 50 miles to empty.

The electronic system depends upon a microprocessor (message center logic module), together with various sensors for its operation. A system checkout and self-diagnostic feature is included in the different installations.

When malfunctions occur in the system, make a careful circuit check for damaged and/or disconnected wires and poor connections. Check to make sure there is a complete circuit between the message center and the various sensors. If the trouble cannot be located by visual inspection and simple circuit tests, it is essential that the manufacturer's diagnosing and troubleshooting procedures contained in the specific shop manuals be carefully followed.

In the case of Ford Motor products, the testing is basically an expanded electronic control module test using the same test equipment for the quick function test and pinpoint test as used with the Ford electronic engine control (EECII) system tests.

The Chrysler product system is designed for a self-diagnostic test. The instrument cluster has a self-test circuit activated by a switch. The switch is located under the electronic module. In order to get at the switch, the lower left bezel must be removed. There is a red control button which is pushed in to activate the test sequence.

To test, the vehicle battery must be connected, and the door, time delay (ignition key lamp or seat occupant switch inputs, but not the ignition or headlights) is on, and the test switch activated.

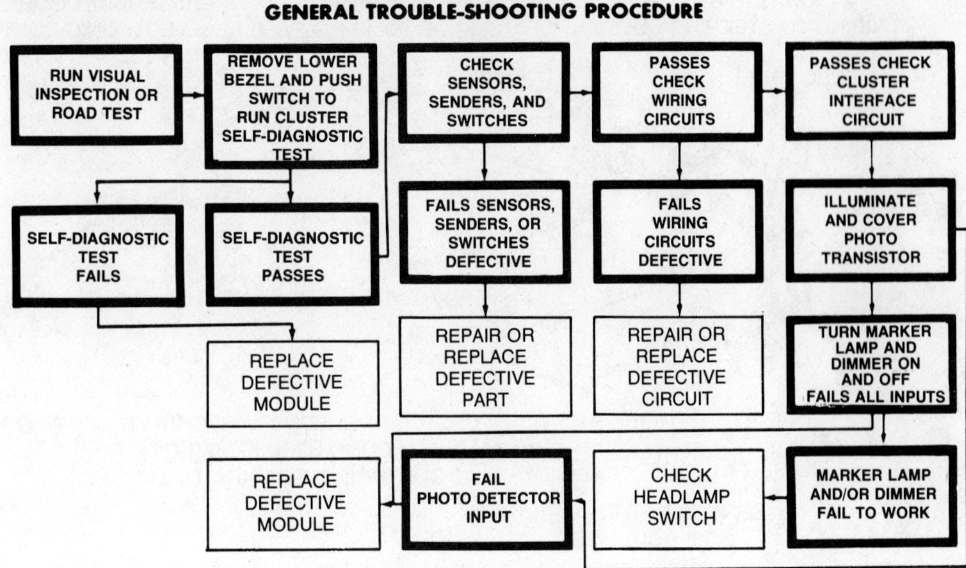

FIGURE 13-20 Electronic instrument cluster general troubleshooting procedure. (Courtesy Chrysler Corporation)

The test sequence takes 25 seconds. The cluster will simultaneously activate one common segment in each character for two seconds. The lighted segments will be changed in the characters in a logical manner. All segments will be activated by the microprocessor in this fashion. The detection of drive circuit troubles requires a visual inspection for broken or shorted segments and a good ground. Figure 13-20 shows the electronic instrument cluster general troubleshooting procedure that is activated by a special switch under the electronic module.

The cluster will proceed to conduct internal checks of the microprocessor system. If there are any detected problems, the odometer display will call out a failure ("fail 2" or "fail 3") and stop the test. If there are no detected troubles a message indicating test passing will be displayed on the odometer as ("pass 1" or "pass 2"). If there have been no detected failures all display segments will be turned on to indicate operative ones. The cluster will remain in this state until the ignition is turned on, at which time it will return to normal operating mode.

Keyless Door Entry System

A keyless door locking system is available on some vehicles. The system consists of two main components, a five-button coded keyboard on the outside panel of the driver's door, and an electronic microprocessor/relay module inside the cowl assembly.

The keyless system is programmed to unlock the driver's door and turn on the interior lights in response to an input code which has been established at the factory. The system is also programmed to unlock the trunk lid in response to an input code, and to lock all doors automatically when the driver's seat is occupied with the doors closed, the ignition switch turned on, and the transmission selector lever has passed through the "R" position.

FIGURE 13-21 Keyless entry system using a five-button keyboard. (Courtesy Ford Parts & Service Division, Ford Motor Co.)

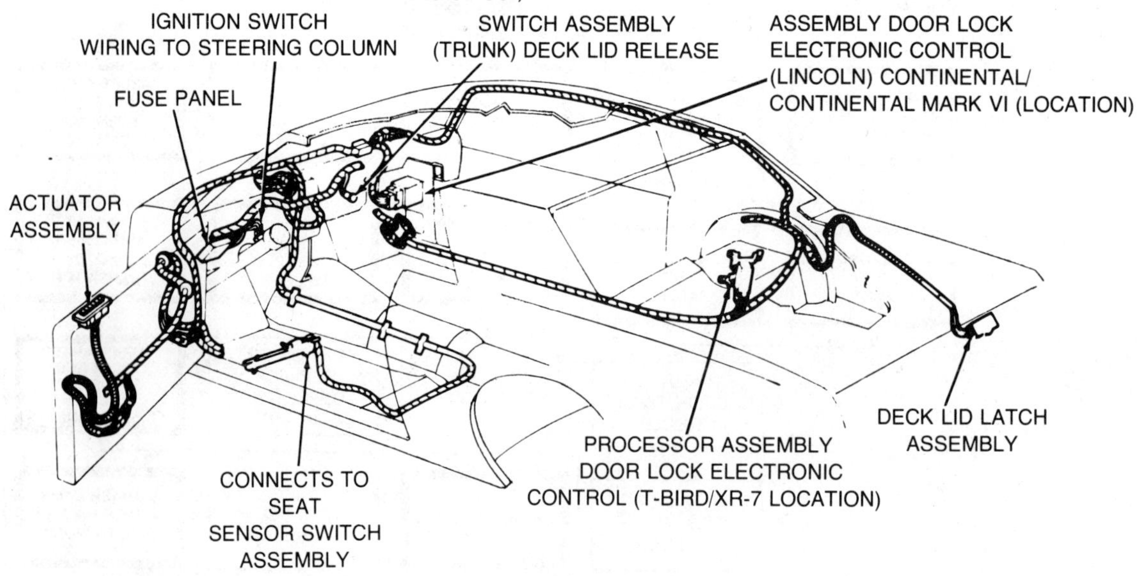

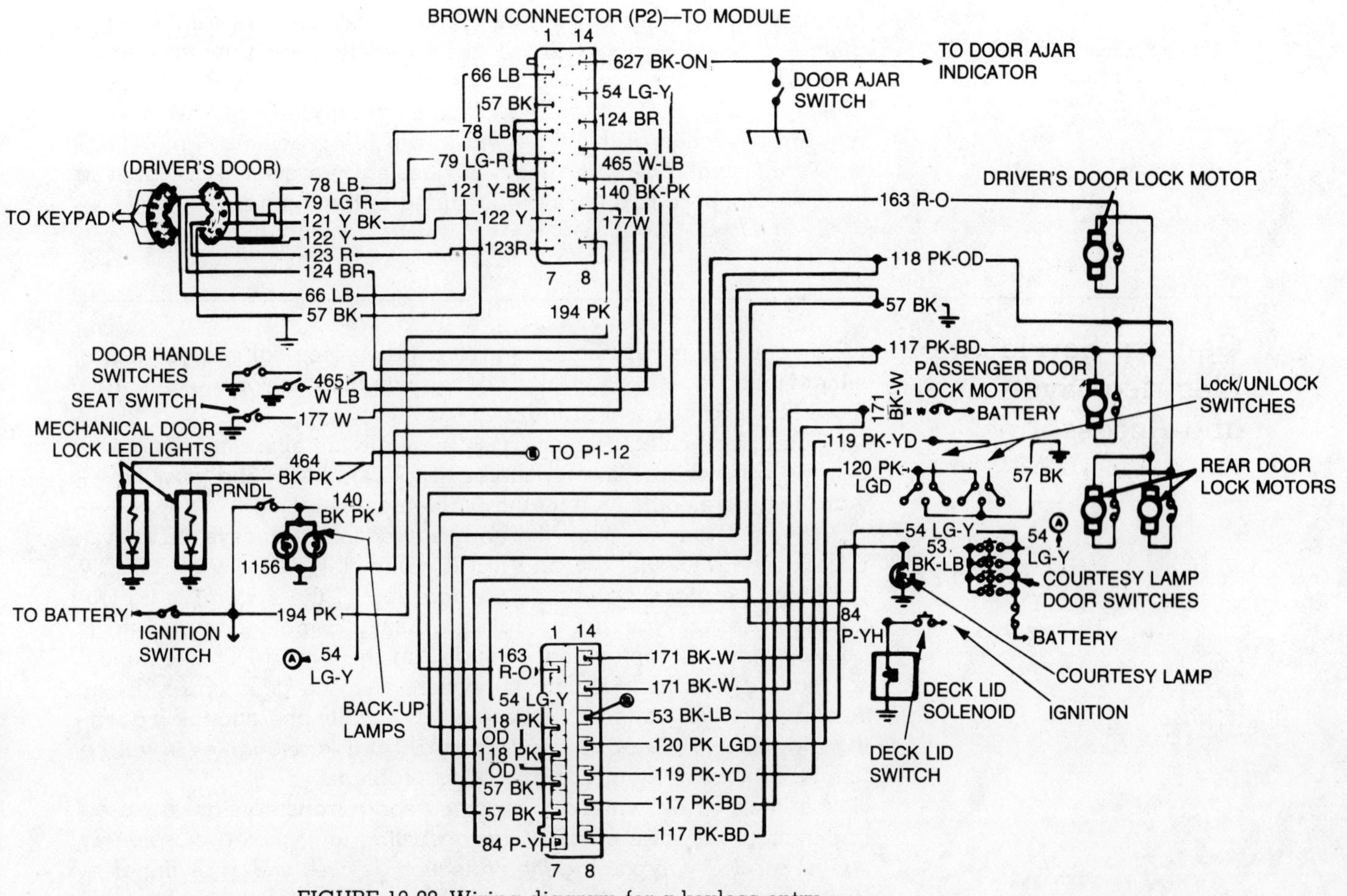

FIGURE 13-22 Wiring diagram for a keyless entry system. (Courtesy Ford Parts & Service Division, Ford Motor Co.)

The coded keyboard consists of five push button switches. Input to the keyless entry module is received from the door handles, driver's seat sensor, transmission backup light switch, ignition switch, electric door lock/unlock switches, and the code key pad buttons. The keyless entry module output signals the key pad lights, door locks, door actuating solenoids, trunk release solenoid, and the interior courtesy lights. Figure 13-21 is a schematic of a keyless door entry system, showing the keyboard and the electronic microprocessor/relay module.

When trouble occurs in the system, before proceeding with an electrical diagnosis, always make a mechanical check of the different components. Make sure all door locks operate freely without binding and make sure the battery is fully charged.

The electronic control for the keyless entry system includes a microprocessor-relay module which is tested in the same manner as the microprocessor control used with the electronically controlled emission system. A very specific procedure, using either a special tester or a digital volt-ohmmeter and jumper wires must be followed, involving the quick test and the pinpoint test. The manufacturer's test procedure sequence and specifications as outlined in the specific shop manual must be carefully followed.

Before attempting the complete test sequence, make a careful examination of all circuits for disconnected, broken, shorted, or pinched wires. Make certain all connections are clean and tight. If there is a question about a switch, bypass the switch with a jumper wire. The different solenoids can be checked by applying electricity directly to the unit. Make certain all units are properly grounded. Usually an inspection of this type will locate the problem. Figure 13-22 shows the wiring diagram for a keyless entry system. A number of other electrical components are included in the diagram.

General Servicing of Electrical Systems and Accessories

All automobile manufacturers have certain electrical accessories as either standard or optional units which will differ to some extent from those installed by other manufacturers.

Troubleshooting in most cases is usually an elimination process, starting with what is known and/or simple to check, and working toward the more complex until the problem is found.

First, determine what the normal function of the system is supposed to be and check to find if it is completely inoperative or only partially operating. Determine the makeup of the system; is it electrically operated, vacuum operated, or is it a combination of both? Is an electronic microprocessor included in the system? If mechanical components are included in the system such as gear boxes, locks, catches, etc., determine if they are mechanically operational. If a wiring diagram or manufacturer's shop manual is available, it will be helpful in tracing circuits and locating problems.

In most cases, when a microprocessor or transistors are not used in the circuit, a quick check of the operating unit, motor, or solenoid can be made by bypassing the protection devices and applying electricity directly to the operating units. If the unit does not operate at this point, it is faulty, assuming there is a good ground. In most cases when a unit is faulty it should be removed and replaced.

When electricity is the source of power, it must reach the unit which is to operate. Therefore, after a visual inspection, start with a circuit check. A test light and jumper wire are about all the equipment necessary. The battery must be fully charged if it is to operate the electrical components properly. Check to find out if electricity is reaching the fuse block. Check the fuse. Almost all circuits will operate through a fuse, fusible link, or circuit breaker. Make certain these units are not blown. Check to make certain current is reaching the switch. If there is a question about the switch, bypass it with a jumper wire.

Any electrical operating unit must have a good ground, either through the housing (case) or ground wire. This is easy to check out by using a jumper wire attached to a good ground on the vehicle body or engine.

Index

W

Z